ENEMY OF THE TRUTH

Enemy of the Truth: Myths, Forensics, and the Kennedy Assassination

by Sherry P. Fiester

JFK Lancer Productions & Publications, Inc.
401 North Carroll Avenue, #204
Southlake, Texas, 76092
www.jfklancer.com

Printed in the United States of America

ISBN: 978-0-9883050-0-7

1. The main category of the book—History, Twentieth Century, 1960s.
2. True Crime
3. Political History

First Edition, Second Printing, February 2013

ENEMY OF THE TRUTH

MYTHS, FORENSICS, AND THE KENNEDY ASSASSINATION

The great enemy of truth is very often not the lie
– deliberate, contrived, and dishonest –
but the myth, persistent, persuasive, and unrealistic.

John F. Kennedy, 1962

SHERRY P. FIESTER

JFK Lancer Productions & Publications, Inc.
Southlake, Texas

*With love and appreciation for my
faithful supporters, my husband Paul
and my sister, Debra.
In memory of my mother, Shirley.*

CONTENTS

TABLE OF FIGURES

BY JIM MARRS

FOREWORD

For entirely too long, supposition, theory and a yielding to authority have been the basis for beliefs concerning the assassination of President John F. Kennedy. Many accredited and credible experts have applied their expertise to the assassination case, yet no clear consensus has been produced. Just as one advances his or her analysis of an assassination topic, along comes another with conflicting views.

Sherry Fiester, a longtime student of forensic science, who separates scientific fact from informed speculation and uninformed theories, is now sharing her expertise. She undertakes to break out JFK assassination myths from demonstrable forensic fact, not an easy task considering the obfuscation and deceit long documented in the JFK case. Right off the bat, Fiester lays to rest the myth that the Dallas Police Department exercised all due diligence in following accepted protocols in the acquisition, handling and securing of assassination evidence. They did not.

By examining national standards for the investigation of a crime scene in place in 1963, she demonstrates numerous deficiencies at both local and national levels in the JFK assassination case. Critical evidence was tossed about, changed for photographic purposes, and even pocketed by persons at the scene. Some evidence, such as a third bullet casing and a length of wood reportedly from the Texas School Book Depository window, suddenly turned up days later.

Anyone undertaking a study of the JFK assassination must come with the understanding, as clearly pointed out by Fiester, that there exists no documented uninterrupted chain of custody for the collected evidence. Such malfeasance leads to questions over the authenticity of the evidence which can taint the entire case.

Fiester makes a cogent case that blood spatter seen in the Zapruder film has not been altered. In a conclusion sure to raise many researchers' eyebrows, Fiester provides a trajectory analysis of the fatal headshot that differs from both the Warren Commission and the House Select Committee.

While no single witness testimony can be relied upon, it should be noted that witnesses nearest the Texas School Book Depository thought shots came from that building, while witnesses on or near the Grassy Knoll thought shots came from there. But most interesting are the few witnesses in between these locations who said shots came from both directions. Of course, this would mean multiple shooters which was a consideration unacceptable to both the Warren Commission and the House Selection Committee on Assassinations.

There has never been a classic cover-up, meaning a lack of evidence and facts. Quite the contrary, in this case there have been too many facts, too much evidence, some of which contradicts the other, false leads, straw men, red herrings, and a multitude of theories. So it is helpful to follow Fiester's lead as she takes the reader down the tortuous path of winding one's way through the complexities of forensic science in relation to the Kennedy assassination. She explodes one myth after another including the idea that ear witness testimony can be considered reliable.

All of this goes to prove one essential fact: Due to the confusion and obfuscation created at the highest levels of the Federal Government, fifty years after the fact, there is still no clear consensus on what actually happened to President John F. Kennedy in Dallas' Dealey Plaza. Allow Sherry Fiester to help build your understanding of the assassination by presenting a foundation in the forensic sciences.

Jim Marrs is internationally recognized as a leading expert on the Kennedy assassination, a prolific author and frequent speaker on television and radio.

BY WILLIAM LEBLANC

PREFACE

Sherry Fiester is a retired Certified Senior Crime Scene Analyst with over 30 years of experience, a Law Enforcement Instructor, and is court certified as an expert in Crime Scene Investigation, Crime Scene Reconstruction and Bloodstain Pattern Analysis in Louisiana, Mississippi, and Florida. Author of many articles in professional publications, *Enemy of the Truth: Myths, Forensics, and the Kennedy Assassination* is Fiester's second book with a forensic focus.

I have known Sherry Fiester for over 16 years, investigated homicide cases with her, and observed her ability to teach others some of the forensic disciplines she addresses in her book. Having observed her investigative techniques, and impressive ability in reconstructing crime scenes, I expected *Enemy of the Truth* to reflect the same precise attention to detail I observed when Fiester was investigating homicides in the field. I was not disappointed.

The ballistics, blood spatter pattern interpretation, and trajectory reconstruction procedures used by Fiester are spot on. Her conclusions are accurate, and what should be expected, especially when considering the crime scene investigation procedures used on and after that fateful day. It is regrettable such a poor job was done by the first responders in securing the scene, the detectives in their investigation of the scene, and the medical examination of the wounds received by President Kennedy and Governor Connelly. Any Crime Scene Reconstructionist would have a difficult time accurately interpreting the information collected in this case. Fiester did a masterful job of painstakingly interpreting and using the available information to educate the reader so they can form their own opinion as to the number of shooters, how many shots were fired, and in determining the origin of the gunshots.

Fiester states her objective was to filter long held, but questionable beliefs in the Kennedy assassination through contemporary, reliable, established scientific disciplines. To meet that objective she selected eight commonly held theories and provided forensic information that would allow the reader to determine if the questioned concept was forensically sound. The abundant references reflect current research and supporting examples of her findings. The results of her work, presented in eight stand-alone chapters, should be of importance to anyone with an interest in the Kennedy assassination.

Forensics can be a complicated subject, yet Fiester provides the reader with easily understood, accurate, information. *Enemy of the Truth: Myths, Forensics and the Kennedy Assassination* is so comprehensive in its approach, this work should be used in the instruction of all new crime scene investigators nationwide.

William (Billy) LeBlanc is a Law Enforcement Officer with 37 years of experience and a member of the Board of Directors for the International Crime Scene Investigators Association. LeBlanc is a Certified Forensic Crime Scene Investigator, a certified FBI instructor, and an Instructor at The Criminal Justice Institute. A Court qualified Latent Print Examiner, Crime Scene Reconstructionist, Footwear and Tire Track Examiner, and Blood Stain Analyst, LeBlanc currently instructs crime scene related courses to Law Enforcement agencies nationally and abroad.

THE MAGIC OF THE MYTH

On an unusually warm November day in Dallas, John Fitzgerald Kennedy was assassinated while the presidential motorcade made its route through Dealey Plaza and before the last pocket of ebullient onlookers. Film and photography would capture the shooting death of the 35th President of the United States would aide in the investigations of two formal government inquiries. In the wake of the tragedy, Science and Forensics would find a new and fast growing ideology, the Myth.

> John F. Kennedy said, *The great enemy of truth is very often not the lie—deliberate, contrived, and dishonest—but the myth, persistent, persuasive, and unrealistic.*

After almost fifty years, the Kennedy assassination still has a sense of urgency in the minds of people around the world. The most studied murder investigation of the 21st Century remains plagued by questions and a variety of theories. The limousine stopped, and two simultaneous gunshots to Kennedy's head are unproven assertions that continue to dominate the research community. Regardless of how tenacious and believable an enduring claim may be, if lacking historical or scientific sustenance it is a myth.

Philosophies, knowledge, and experiential bias all shape the truth. Consequently, truth is often a matter of perspective—not irrefutable fact. Depending too heavily on life experiences can color the truth. Wrong conclusions extrapolated from faulty and outdated information distorts truth. The cognitive ability to integrate new information and reconcile conflicting data gives a sense of clarity and results in a more accurate discernment of what is truthful. We must continually re-examine what we perceive to be true and hold it accountable to new information, research, and technological advances. Filtering long held beliefs in the Kennedy assassination through contemporary, reliable, established scientific facts will help to dispel myths; the very thing Kennedy described as the great enemy of truth.

The majority of the unusual conclusions concerning the death of President Kennedy are anecdotal, unrealistic, and incorrect statements kept alive by those who would prefer fabrications that promote sensationalism as opposed to the quiet reality of fact. Unsubstantiated allegations continue to rear their head, summoning the naive to join forces in a "truth is stranger than fiction" campaign. Although imaginative and sometimes thought provoking, these theories occasionally rely upon the suspension of common sense. They also divert focus. While these intriguing, but unverifiable suppositions gather attention, they detract from the quality of information essential to explain this mysterious homicide. Myths are superficial, have no investigative depth, and ask the reader to take a leap of faith that having supporting scientific evidence does not require.

No matter how credible unsubstantiated claims may appear at first glance, unless proven correct, they are still myths, and myths will never be facts. Myths do not withstand scientific scrutiny. There is no place for biased and unverified information in the narration of our country. Hope for a factual record requires assertions be periodically reanalyzed to assure the perception of truth has not been scientifically proven obsolete. The insidious deceptiveness of prevailing myths concerning the Kennedy assassination must cease.

The skill of a magician is in controlling the focused attention of the audience. The success of a magician lies in the ability to create illusions that have the appearance of reality. Like magic, sensationalism relies on distraction. While mysterious and convoluted claims concerning the Kennedy assassination may capture attention, the need for authentication cannot be allowed to fall by the wayside. Otherwise, the melodramatic and exaggerated message of the myth becomes the focus rather than forensically proven truths. It is incumbent upon us to focus on scientific disciplines for an explanation and validation of concepts surrounding President Kennedy's death as only then will the magic of the myth be exposed as an illusion.

CHAPTER 1

DALLAS PD FOLLOWED PROTOCOL

I f the goal of the Dallas Police Department was to provide a quality, comprehensive and impartial investigation of the Texas School Book Depository in order to provide irrefutable evidence in the murder of President Kennedy, they failed.

The basic processes for preserving, photographing, and collecting physical evidence were flawed. Inferior techniques were used to develop latent fingerprint evidence; potential evidence was not properly documented, protected, or collected in a timely manner; and evidence that could have identified a potential accomplice or exonerated Oswald may have been inadvertently disregarded. Additionally, an unsupervised and inexperienced officer was left to process the crime scene in one of the most important cases in the department's history.

There are people who believe the Dallas Police Department did exemplary work with the crime scene investigation at the Texas School Book Depository. Those supporters stress the crime scene investigative standards of today should not be used to judge work competed in 1963. However, the Dallas Police Department, and especially the supervisors are accountable for not complying with the well-published and generally accepted national standards of 1963. Certainly, they are responsible for adhering to the self-proclaimed procedures of their own department. Unfortunately, it appears the crime scene investigation performed in the Texas School Depository Building is resolutely established to be severely deficient. Especially in light of the standards they set for themselves in their own department protocols.

NATIONAL INVESTIGATIVE STANDARDS 1963

The television series *CSI: Crime Scene Investigation* and other similar programs portray the modern crime scene investigators as highly trained, college-educated technicians who have received extensive specialized training in all disciplines of crime investigation.

In the 1960s, crime scene investigators rarely had special training in the collection of physical or trace evidence. They relied on the "tag-it and bag-it" method. This meant they just collected the evidence, placed it in a bag with an evidence tag describing the evidence and establishing a chain of custody. Some evidence would be sent to a crime lab for analysis, and the remainder would be given to an evidence custodian for safekeeping and later use in court. The emphasis for solving crimes, for most agencies, was placed on detectives catching the perpetrator by utilizing people skills; putting little or no emphasis on crime scene investigation. For most agencies, the physical evidence was only a minor part of the investigation, often used to confirm what detectives had already determined.

Although there were no certifications to ensure proficiency, and no specific experience or training requirements at the time of the assassination, there were generally accepted national standards for processing a crime scene. Paul L. Kirk in *Crime Investigation* (1953) documented the criteria for these standards.

1. Secure the scene to protect potential evidence, prevent witnesses from leaving the scene, and apprehend suspects
2. Perform an organized and thorough search
3. Photograph all potential evidence
4. Indicate on a sketch the location of all potential evidence

5. Complete a detailed description of the location and condition of potential evidence
6. Develop and collect fingerprints
7. Collect evidence (Kirk, 1953)

The investigation of crime scenes and the evidence collected and analyzed may prove the innocence or guilt of a defendant. That level of responsibility demands professional ethics and integrity. Education, training, experience and technical skills all influence crime scene investigation. Law enforcement agencies have an obligation to seek the truth impartially and tenaciously. Investigators should never be biased for or against a suspect; they should conduct a thorough, competent, and complete investigation; and should never exaggerate or understate their findings.

Crime scene investigators should be diligent in the proper search, collection, and preservation of evidence and follow prescribed protocol to preserve the chain of custody and prevent cross-contamination or degradation of physical evidence. Justice depends on police agencies treating every victim equally, and investigating every crime scene with uniform precision. Only meticulous adherence to nationally accepted guidelines can ensure justice for victims without discrimination. However, occasionally, a crime scene investigation is deprived of appropriate attention. Apparently, this is what happened on November 22, 1963, when the President of the United States was assassinated.

Dallas PD and National Standards

There are those who believe the Dallas Police conducted a detailed crime scene investigation inside the Texas School Book Depository during the investigation of President Kennedy's assassination. Others are not convinced. Every agency involved in this investigation was under tremendous pressure to solve the case. One might expect that type of scrutiny would have motivated the investigators to perform a meticulous search for clues and utilize the latest forensic techniques. However, crime scene forensics was not a significant aspect of criminal investigations at the time of the assassination. Good police work relied more on having accomplished interrogators who could elicit confessions from suspects and less on gathering physical evidence. Successful convictions in the 1960s rarely depended exclusively on physical evidence.

Once an arrest was made, getting a confession became the investigative focus and Dallas Police Department had Oswald in custody.

The Dallas Police Department in the 1960s was comprised of men who possessed few investigative skills beyond the basic police training received on the job as a rookie, and only a few may have had opportunities to enhance their investigative abilities outside on the job training. Officers who commanded supervisory roles, especially detectives, were the exception; they often had years of experience and multiple opportunities for training in the latest police techniques. Those individuals in supervisory positions directed the investigation of President Kennedy. Subsequently, any failure of the Dallas Police Department to follow their own standards of investigation resides with those individual supervisors. This begs the question, why did the supervisors allow the investigation to become compromised? They apparently investigated the Kennedy assassination as any other homicide, relying upon established investigative habits for a successful outcome. For the Dallas Police Department investigators, was it business as usual, resulting in an investigation that was well below nationally accepted standards? Perhaps the events and the resulting media frenzy overwhelmed the Dallas Police Department. Likely, it was a combination of a multitude of issues. Examining the standards that should have governed the investigation, and comparing them to the actions taken by the Dallas Police Department, answers the question, "Did Dallas Police Department follow protocol?"

The crime scene investigative unit, called the crime lab, was a part of the Identification Bureau of the 1963 Dallas Police Department. The 1963 crime scene investigative procedures for the unit are not of record. However, reference to those procedures are contained within statements and testimony provided by Dallas Police personnel regarding the crime scene investigation of the Kennedy assassination.

As supervisor of the Dallas Police Department's Crime Lab, Lieutenant Carl Day's testimony concerning his investigative expertise is of particular interest. During his testimony before the Warren Commission, Day mentioned four important criteria when processing crime scenes: (1) take photographs; (2) complete a scale drawing of the scene; (3) fingerprint the area and collect developed prints; and (4) collect all other evidence (4H250).

Day failed to mention three additional procedures that should have been a part of the agency protocol as dictated by nationally recognized standards: (1) secure the scene to protect potential evidence and prevent witnesses and suspects from fleeing; (2) conduct an organized and thorough search; and (3) complete a detailed narrative concerning all activities undertaken while processing the crime scene (Kirk, 1953).

Day was the supervisor for the Dallas Police Department unit that investigated homicide crime scenes in a city ranked 14th in size in the nation and in a state leading the nation in recorded murders from 1960 through 1963. Therefore, it is reasonable to believe a fifteen-year veteran of that unit would have had experience in investigating homicide scenes. It is also reasonable to expect Day was exposed to multiple opportunities to training referencing national standards for investigating crime scenes. Published works describing in detail the generally recognized national standards for investigating crime scenes have been readily available since the early 1950s. Media coverage of trials such as the Samuel Sheppard trial in 1956 was extensive, detailed, and captured the attention of the nation. The Sheppard trial focused exclusively on the crime scene investigation, and subsequent reporting familiarized the public with nationally accepted investigative standards. Investigative procedures presented in the Sheppard trial were still in effect in 1963. Following, is a look at those standards and the subsequent evidence that demonstrates the Dallas Police Department either complied with or ignored. The Dallas Police Department, and specifically Day as the supervisor, should have been familiar with the well-published and generally accepted crime scene investigation standards of 1963. At minimum, Day and other officers on the crime scene should have complied with the self-proclaimed procedures of their own department. Unfortunately, the official assassination records documenting their actions indicates they did not (U. S. Census Bureau, 1963).

SECURING THE SCENE

The first priority upon arrival at a crime scene is to ensure the safety of officers and the public by determining the perpetrator is not present. Once officers are confident the perpetrator is not present, they are to detain potential witnesses, or others found at the location. Comprehensive questioning of witnesses may assist with (a) identifying the perpetrator, (b) providing a description of the perpetrator for dissemination, and (c) indicating items within the scene the perpetrator may have touched or taken (Heffron, 1958).

National protocols indicate the secondary responsibility of officers present is to protect the scene from contamination. This means restricting entry to unauthorized personnel by placing officers at strategic locations and all points of entry. Dallas officers should have been posted immediately at each point of entry, permitting only those individuals with a specific purpose to enter the scene (Kirk, 1953).

By the early 1950s, nationally accepted standards of protecting the scene from contamination and securing potential witnesses and suspects were well established. Personnel with access to the scene were to utilize caution to prevent alteration of the scene, contamination of or destruction of potential evidence. Investigators were to wear cotton gloves to prevent depositing their own fingerprints on items of evidence. Evidentiary items were not to be touched prior to their documentation with photography and placement in a sketch. Officers were not to discard items such as matches, cigarettes, disposable food containers, or trash within the crime scene. Officers were to be cognizant of small items of evidence that could be stepped on, or bloodstains that could be smeared. Transient evidence that may degrade or disappear quickly, such as smoke or a particular odor, was to be immediately documented in written form. In essence, until all evidence was collected, the crime scene investigation complete, and the scene ready to be released, the scene was to be carefully preserved (Kirk, 1953).

DALLAS POLICE DEPARTMENT: SECURING THE SCENE

Some members of the Dallas Police Department believed the shooter had fired from within the Texas School Book Depository. Their initial response to that supposition, rushing into the building to apprehend the perpetrator, was appropriate. The safety and well-being of the public was paramount, therefore, the removal of potential threats to the police and others must take precedence over evidence that may be present within the crime scene. However, once it was determined the shooter was no longer in the building, the next action should have been to secure the scene.

Securing the scene should not have required an order from a supervisor; it is the most basic element in police work and the initial responsibility of the first officer on the scene. Every point of entry or exit available to the public should have been protected from unauthorized entry. The fact that the scene was chaotic does not mean basic police work can be ignored. However, a Warren Commission timeline focusing on securing the scene indicates it was ignored.

1. At 12:30 p.m., Central Standard Time, the shooting of President John F. Kennedy occurred.
2. At approximately 12:30 p.m. to 12:32 p.m., Dallas Police Department Officer Marrion L. Baker entered the Texas School Book Depository Building searching for an unknown shooter.
3. At approximately 12:37 p.m. to 12:40 p.m., Dallas Police Department Inspector J. Herbert Sawyer ordered the building sealed.
4. At approximately 12:50 p.m., Secret Service Agent Forrest V. Sorrels entered an unsecured door at the rear of the Texas School Book Depository Building (7H 348).

Secret Service Agent Sorrels entering an unsecured door suggests the building was not secure until at least 13 minutes after Inspector Sawyer ordered the building sealed (CE3131). Unfortunately, it did not stop there. Day stated in his FBI interview:

There were many people there on the afternoon of November 22, 1963, who he assumed were newsmen, whose identity he did not know (26H805).

Obviously, police procedures for directing patrol officers and criminal investigators to protect crime scenes were in place within the department, as evidenced by Inspector Sawyer's order to seal the building, but it appears there was no compliance to that order until Dallas Police Department Homicide and Robbery Captain Fritz arrived. Fritz testified he arrived at the hospital at 12:45 and at the Texas School Book Depository Building at 12:58. When asked if there were guards on the building doors he replied,

"I am not sure, but I don't—there has been some question about that, but the reason I don't think that—this may differ with someone else, but I am going to tell you what I know. After I arrived, one of the officers asked me if I would like to have the building sealed and I told him I would" (4H204, 205).

Assigning an officer to guard every point of entry at the Texas School Book Depository may have been problematic in the initial confusion following the assassination. However, one has to wonder why Captain Will Fritz, head of the homicide unit, or Lieutenant Day, head of the crime lab, failed to enforce their responsibilities of protecting the crime scene once the suspected perpetrator was in custody. For that matter, no one with the Dallas Police Department took steps to protect the crime scene from contamination.

Day, Fritz, and other supervisors present on the sixth floor of the Texas School Book Depository were ultimately responsible for the assassination investigation and the possibility of their investigation being compromised should have motivated them to take the necessary steps to ensure the scene was protected. More importantly, the police should not have allowed anyone other than law enforcement to remain on the sixth floor while they searched for evidence.

NEWS MEDIA

The curious nature of news media is what makes them good at their job. Unfortunately, curiosity, when allowed to run unrestrained, can be destructive to potential evidence, resulting in an investigation with distorted conclusions. The official record contains several examples of reporters having access to the crime scene while the scene was still being processed for physical evidence. FBI Special Agents Vincent Drain and James Bookhout interviewed Day concerning persons other than police officers, who were present on the sixth floor on the afternoon of the shooting. Their report stated:

On Saturday, November 23, 1963, many persons unknown to him had apparently been on the sixth floor of the Texas School Book Depository building, and had taken a lot of photographs, in view of the fact that he noticed many empty film pack cartons where the boxes were

located, and the boxes had been rearranged, apparently for the purpose
of taking photographs (CE3131, 26H805).

FBI Special Agent Vincent Drain interviewed Crime Scene Investigator
Robert Lee Studebaker on September 9, 1964 concerning his activities on the
sixth floor of the Texas School Book Depository. Studebaker told the agents,
"There were literally dozens of news media representatives from radio and
television stations, newspapers and magazines on the sixth floor." There were
"no restrictions on newsmen and law enforcement officers from moving freely
about the building. Any of these individuals may have possibly handled the
four cardboard boxes that were sent to the FBI Laboratory for examination."
Studebaker also confirmed that on Saturday, November 23, newsmen were all
over the building, particularly on the sixth floor. He indicated the reporters
were "generally looking for and examining anything that might have been
related to the shooting of President Kennedy and Governor John B. Connally"
(CE 3131, 26H807).

Day and Studebaker's statements to the FBI concerning the press having
unrestricted and unsupervised access to the sixth floor was corroborated by
the Warren Commission testimony of Ira Beers, a 1963 photographer for the
Dallas Morning News. Regrettably, Beers was not asked who had allowed the
unauthorized persons to enter a crime scene while it was still being processed.

> *GRIFFIN: Can you give us an estimate of what time that would have
> been when you were up there taking the pictures on the sixth floor?*

> *BEERS: This would be strictly a guess, an estimate. It would be
> sometime around the vicinity of 4 o'clock. It was quite late in the
> afternoon. Probably later.*

> *GRIFFIN: Now in your pictures that you took, were any of the objects
> that were allegedly found up there on the sixth floor photographed, such
> as the position of the rifle and the placement of the boxes and other
> materials in the window from which the assassin is believed to have
> shot?*

> *BEERS: Yes. Prior to admitting us to the building, I made pictures of a sack, very long narrow sack type of affair that was brought down from there, and a pop bottle and some pieces of chicken, and I also made a picture of the rifle which I believe it was Lieutenant Carl Day from the Dallas police crime lab brought that. And upon going in the building, I photographed the area where the rifle was found. I photographed the area around the window from which the assassin was supposedly seated, and I moved into that area and made a picture from the window, supposedly the window from which the bullets were fired, that showed a little corner of the boxes which possibly the rifle rested on. It shows the street down below where the automobile was traveling when the President was killed (13H105).*

With such a high profile case, there must have been an inordinate amount of pressure on the Dallas Police Department to provide accurate and timely information to the public. Normally, limited information is released to the media until a full understanding of the event has been developed and evidence has been secured. Access to a crime scene via media should be denied to prevent contamination or alteration of the scene and interference with investigative procedures. If it is deemed necessary for the press to enter a crime scene before its release, they should be escorted and their movements carefully monitored. Allowing the media on the sixth floor while evidence was still being discovered and processed was inexcusable and reflected the lack of importance the Dallas Police Department placed on securing the scene.

EVIDENCE CONTAMINATION

The most important aspect of crime scene investigation is securing the crime scene, and that means protecting the evidence from contamination. Unless you can show evidence is uncontaminated, its use in court may be rejected. Changing the condition of an item of evidence or altering it in any way from its original condition is called *contamination*. Lieutenant Carl Day, supervisor of the crime scene division, testified after the rifle was discovered at approximately 1:22 p.m., it was photographed, and he personally took it to the police department for additional processing. At about 3 p.m. that same day, Day said he returned to the depository and remained there until about 6 p.m. No questions were asked of Day concerning whether the scene had been secured while he was gone or under whose supervision Studebaker was working.

> DAY: *I went back to the School Book Depository and stayed there. It was around three that I got back, and I was in that building until about 6, directing the other officers as to what we needed in the way of photographs and some drawing, and so forth.*

> BELIN: *What did you do when you got back, what photographs did you take?*

> DAY: *We went, made the outside photographs of the street, we made more photographs inside, and did further checking for prints by using dust on the boxes around the window (4H264).*

Day's testimony indicates the boxes around the window were processed for fingerprints after his 3 p.m. arrival. There are no assurances the cartons were processed before the press was allowed on the sixth floor of the school book depository.

Crime Scene Detective Bobby Brown stated while assisting with sketching on November 24, he handled the cardboard boxes, stacked by the window ,allegedly used by Oswald as a rest for his rifle. These were the same four boxes to which the media had access, and that were left unprotected several days before being collected. Moreover, we do not really know if those are the same boxes originally located in the window. Studebaker testified he moved the cartons and then later replaced them in an effort to re-create the scene so he could take photographs. Brown also indicated the measurements used to complete the sketch of the sixth floor were taken after the crime scene was left unsecured and occupied by unidentified media and possibly members of the public. So it is possible, multiple items were moved (CE 3131, 26H808; 7H137).

One might anticipate someone other than law enforcement touching or moving evidence due to lack of training and lacking the understanding not all evidence is easily identified. The inquisitiveness and inexperience of a rookie may inadvertently lead to inappropriately handled evidence. A detective consciously compromising evidence is untenable.

CHAIN OF CUSTODY

Chain of custody is a legal term referring to the ability to guarantee the identity and integrity of items collected as evidence on a crime scene. For purposes of litigation, it is necessary to have a written record that documents the possession, handling, and location of evidence from the moment it is collected until used in court. A well-maintained chain of custody assures contamination and evidence alteration has not taken place, and establishes proof the item selected at the crime scene is the same evidence presented in a court of law. Based on Day's testimony, it appears the chain of custody for the casings is questionable. The envelope was unsealed. The names of persons possessing physical evidence with a notation of the date and times they possessed the evidence was not documented. Apparently, from the time of collection at approximately until 10 p. m. that evening, the person possessing the casings is unknown.

> BELIN: *Had the shells been out of your possession then?*
>
> DAY: *Mr. Sims had the shells from the time they were moved from the building or he took them from me at that time, and the shells I did not see again until around 10 o'clock.*
>
> BELIN: *Who gave them to you at 10 o'clock?*
>
> DAY: *They were in this group of evidence being collected to turn over to the FBI. I don't know who brought them back.*
>
> BELIN: *Was the envelope sealed?*
>
> DAY: *No, sir.*
>
> BELIN: *Had it been sealed when you gave it to Mr. Sims?*

DAY: No, sir; no.

BELIN: Was the envelope sealed?

DAY: No, sir.

DAY: No, sir; no (4H254).

In direct conflict with Day's testimony, Dallas Police Crime Scene Detective Richard M. Sims testified he did not retain possession of the casings when they were collected.

SIMS: I picked them up from the floor and he had an envelope there and he held the envelope open.

BALL: You didn't take them in your possession, did you?

SIMS: No, sir; I don't believe I did (7H163).

SOUVENIRS

Some of the evidence collected by the Dallas Police Department during its investigation of President Kennedy's murder was kept as souvenirs by some members of the department, as evidenced in Gary Savage's book, *JFK: First Day Evidence* (1993). Savage describes how his uncle, Rusty Livingston, a detective assigned to the Dallas Police Crime Lab at the time of the assassination, admitted he kept five original photographs showing fingerprints located on the trigger housing of the rifle allegedly used by Lee Oswald. An original fingerprint card taken from Oswald in the morgue was also retained by Livingston. Savage claims Livingston kept five 8 x 10 photographs that were never forwarded to the Warren Commission as personal mementos. This action was clearly a breach of the chain of custody for evidence in the criminal investigation of Kennedy's death (Savage, 1993).

It is rumored DPD Sergeant Gerald Hill provided evidentiary photographs to author Judy Bonner for her book, *Investigation of a Homicide: The Murder of John F. Kennedy* (1969). Detective Studebaker, who took many of the crime scene photographs inside the book depository, told the House Select

Committee on Assassinations (HSCA) he had made numerous copies of evidence photos for fellow officers (McAdams, 2011). The HSCA received "first-generation photographs" meaning they were made directly from the original negatives from such individuals as the widow of Dallas Police Officer Roscoe White, the widow of George de Mohrenschildt, and Dallas Detective Richard Stovall (HSCA 6:141).

Police are ethically obligated to preserve the integrity of the investigation and their agency's reputation. It is important to prevent even the appearance of impropriety and unbiased investigation on the part of those whose duty it was to conduct a fair investigation. The actual taking of items related to the assassination investigation was illegal and unprincipled.

SEARCHING THE SCENE

After ensuring the crime scene is secure, the next step is to perform an organized and legal search to locate physical evidence. During the search of a crime scene it may be difficult to identify potential evidence. Not every object found at the crime scene is related to the crime under investigation. To determine what might be evidence, investigators search for items appearing to be related to the crime, such as blood spatter, a weapon, or a broken window. Investigators should look for items appearing to be out of place in the environment. For example, a pair of work gloves in a bedroom, a rope in a bathroom, or a shovel in a kitchen would normally not be in these locations and might hold potential clues.

Officers have one opportunity to search a crime scene properly. In 1963, national standards for crime scene searches were well-established; the search was to begin with a preliminary walk-through by investigators to evaluate items as potential evidence. This walk-through provided information for planning the search and recognizing special problem areas. Officers were to be particularly aware of fragile and transient evidence and the need for immediate documentation and protection. Personnel were then assembled outside the search area and provided information gathered on the preliminary walk-through. The subsequent search of visible and concealed areas should be thorough to avoid evidence loss or contamination. Searchers were cautioned not to alter or destroy evidence. The searchers were then divided into groups and personnel designated specific responsibilities of which the most common were photography, written descriptive documentation of evidence, sketching, and the collection of evidence (Kirk, 1953).

The search for evidence was commonly documented through photography with simultaneously written descriptive notes. Comprehensive descriptions of potential items of evidence discovered during the search were to be recorded in written form for later inclusion in an investigators report or in the legend of the final crime scene sketch. In reviewing reports from that era, it appears the majority of agencies utilized the detective's narrative report to describe crime scenes. Other agencies recorded comprehensive descriptions on evidence packaging in evidence collection logs and in the crime scene investigators' narrative report (Kirk, 1953).

The best method of systematically searching the scene is determined based upon the preliminary walk-through. A line search utilizes people standing adjacent to each other, slowly moving forward as they scan for potential evidence. A spiral search begins in the center of a crime scene circling slowly as you continually move toward the scene perimeter. A grid search is similar to a line search, but utilizes a second line search perpendicular to the first. A grid search ensures an area is examined for evidence from more than one viewpoint and is believed to be the most effective for locating potential evidence. A sectional search divides a large crime scene into smaller areas and then utilizes one of the previously described search methods. Regardless of what search method is used, items relocated or repositioned to facilitate the search should be photographed prior to being moved (Kirk, 1953).

The importance of physical evidence is that it can establish a crime was committed and identify the specific crime. Evidence can help establish when the offense was committed, help identify who committed the crime, explain how the crime was committed, and suggest why it was committed. Logic and experience assist investigators in determining the value of physical evidence. A successful crime scene search locates, identifies, and preserves all items with evidentiary value.

DALLAS POLICE DEPARTMENT: SEARCHING THE SCENE

Although national standards for crime scene searches indicated the search was to begin with a preliminary walk-through, under the circumstances this was not completed as the safety of the officers and the public was thought to be in jeopardy. Once it was determined no perpetrator was present, personnel should have been assembled outside the search area to determine the type of search to be used and designated specific responsibilities. The most common duties to be completed during a search were photography, written descriptive documentation of evidence, sketching, and the collection of evidence; all responsibilities commonly assigned to crime scene investigators (Kirk, 1953)

During the initial search of the book depository, officers from the Dallas Police Department and the Dallas Sheriff's office were inside the depository looking for evidence. In addition, the *Dallas Morning News* crew consisting of photographer Jack Beers, chief photographer Tom Dillard, and reporter-cameraman Tom Alyea, followed officers throughout the sixth floor as they searched for clues. There is no record of who was in charge of the search or what type of search method was used. In addition, there is no information indicating who was responsible for documenting when, where or what items were found. A successful crime scene search is orderly and systematically covers the entire crime scene. This one was not.

WHO WAS IN CHARGE?

Crime scene investigation is a coordinated effort to recognize, protect, develop, collect, and secure physical evidence to be used in court. While scene investigation is a team undertaking, a supervisor is designated to be responsible for overseeing the process. A forty-year veteran of the department, Dallas Police Captain J. W. Fritz was the most senior officer on the scene. Fritz testified immediately after the rifle was located he left the building, clearly indicating he was not the scene supervisor. Following the discovery of the rifle at 1:22 p.m., Day testified he took the rifle to the police department, returning to the TSBD at approximately 3 p.m. So who was in charge?

Evidently, for over an hour Studebaker had no supervision or direction concerning:

1.   What was to be considered evidence

2. What evidence required fingerprint processing
3. What method was used to develop fingerprints
4. What investigative steps were used in order to comply with national or departmental standards

Any homicide, especially one as importance as the murder of the President of the United States, should have required the need for an experienced crime scene investigator. It was a poor decision for Day to leave Studebaker unsupervised to process the crime scene when he had been assigned to the crime lab for less than two months (7H137).

MISSED EVIDENCE

One of the primary goals of a crime scene investigation is to identify and collect evidence that may prove a fact or reconstruct the events in a crime. The Dallas Police Department failed to complete a preliminary walk-through by investigators to evaluate items as potential evidence. Disorganized and unsystematic searches can result in missed evidence, especially when the scene encompasses a large area. Searchers included untrained personnel who may not have understood what should be considered evidence or how to prevent evidence contamination. The very foundation for processing a crime scene is based upon the crime scene search, which actually locates evidence. Regrettably, the Dallas Police Department performed their search of the sixth floor of the Texas School Book Depository in a haphazard manner, and as a result neglected to locate all items of evidence.

Evidence of the failure of the Dallas Police Department to conduct a methodical and organized search of the Texas School Book Depository was reflected in the discoveries of Frankie Kaiser. On December 2, 1963, Kaiser, a Texas School Book Depository employee, discovered Oswald's blue jacket and a clipboard purportedly used by Oswald. Kaiser testified, "It was just laying there in the plain open—and just the plain open boxes—you see, we've got a pretty good space back there and I just noticed it laying over there." The clipboard was recovered on the TSBD sixth floor only a few feet from where the rifle was recovered, undoubtedly demonstrating the search conducted on the day of the assassination was not as thorough as it should have been (6H342-343).

PHOTOGRAPHING THE SCENE

National standards at the time of the assassination suggest the next step in processing a crime scene was to take photographs. Existing standards dictated nothing was to be touched, picked up, or moved until it was photographed. Photographs should be an accurate representation of the location and condition of the crime scene and provide a permanent visual record of the scene for later use. The photographic documentation of the evidence will also serve as a basis for comparison, should any suspicions of tampering arise (Kirk, 1953).

Photography also provides information concerning the overall condition of the scene, identification of general items within the scene, the location, and condition of items prior to collection. When items within a crime scene have been moved, investigators are directed not to attempt reconstruction of the scene prior to taking photographs; protocol dictated photographing the scene exactly as discovered. If during a search, anything is moved before photos are taken, investigators are to document the alteration information in the report narrative (Kirk, 1953).

Photographs should be relevant to understanding what transpired during the commission of the crime; for example, photographing door locks may indicate forced entry or the lack of forced entry. Crime scene photographs should record the scene as it was initially found. Photographs should be free from distortion representative of the crime scene. Photographs taken at various distances provide overall, general, and specific photographic views of the crime scene. Overall photographs with overlapping viewpoints ensure no item of interest is inadvertently omitted. General photographs taken at midrange show items of evidence and indicate the relationship to other items within the scene. Specific photographs of items of evidence should be taken with the inclusion of a ruler to assist with size reference (Kirk, 1953).

Crime scene photography requires an established chain of custody to be offered as an item of evidence in court. Photographers need to be able to testify they took the photograph, be able to identify the subject of the photograph, know when and where the photograph was taken, and confirm the photograph is a fair and accurate representative of the scene.

Dallas Police Department: Photographing the Scene

Photographing a crime scene requires specific procedures be followed to ensure the photographs present the scene and evidence in an accurate manner. Studebaker had less than two months of crime scene training. His lack of experience may explain why crime scene photographs were not taken of some evidence and other items were moved then replaced before photographs were taken. Any homicide, especially one with the importance of the murder of the President of the United States, should have suggested the need for an experienced crime scene investigator. It was an irresponsible decision for Day to leave Studebaker unsupervised to complete photographs and process the crime scene (7H137).

Day described Dallas Police Department protocol as requiring photographs of evidence in its original location and condition, and prior to collection. Therefore, indications that evidence was collected and processed without being photographed, or evidence was repositioned in an attempt to re-create a scene, would be in direct conflict with both local and national protocols. Rusty Livingston, assigned to the Dallas Police Department's crime scene investigative unit, wrote in *JFK: First Day Evidence* (1993), "We had a heck of a time with some officers picking up things at a crime scene before we had photographs" (Savage, 1993, p. 156).

The Piece of Wood

Included in the November 30, 1963 report prepared by FBI Special Agent Robert P. Gemberling was a statement completed by special agent Vincent Drain concerning an item collected from the sixth floor Texas School Book Depository. Drain reported a piece of wood, approximately 40 inches long and 3/4 inches in width, was received from Dallas Police Department Captain George Doughty on November 30, 1963. The report indicates Doughty stated he collected the wood from the window ledge believed to be the window used by the shooter. Drain indicated the article was delivered to the FBI laboratory on November 30, 1963 (Drain, 1963).

The Dallas Police Department indicates this piece of wood was released to Drain with other items on November 28, 1963 at 10 PM. The item was described as one piece of wood 1" x 1" x 30" from the window where shots were thought to be fired. There are no photographs of the piece of wood and no mention of the piece of wood in Doughty's Warren Commission testimony. Warren Commission Document 899, FBI letterhead memorandum dated April 27, 1964 states Day was interviewed April 23, 1964 concerning the strip of wood. Day advised he removed a small strip of wood for the purpose of latent fingerprint examination from the sill of the window allegedly used in the shooting death of President Kennedy. Day indicated he gave the item to Doughty who later released it to the FBI (Westbrook, 1963).

THE BOXES

The area allegedly used by the shooter was located on the sixth floor of the Texas School Book Depository. Cartons of books were apparently used by the shooter to conceal his location, perhaps as seating while shooting through the window and probably to support the rifle while firing the weapon. These cartons could easily have contained hair, fiber, fingerprints, or shoe prints deposited by the shooter. In fact, that particular area had the potential of yielding a great deal of evidence and should have been protected from contamination or alteration. Dallas Sheriff's Deputy Luke Mooney first discovered that area, commonly referred to as the sniper's nest. When Mooney examined a photograph of the boxes within the sniper's nest, he testified they appeared to have been moved (3H285).

When Day testified, it became obvious boxes were moved prior to being photographed and then replaced in an effort to reconstruct the scene. Tom C. Dillard captured an image of the Texas School Book Depository sixth floor window a few seconds after the last shot was fired, which was later introduced as Commission Exhibit 482. When Day testified before the Warren Commission, he was asked to look at Dillard's photographs of the exterior of the Texas School Book Depository. Day testified the position of the boxes in the window in the photographs taken by Dillard did not coincide with the photographs he took. Comparing the two photographs proved the boxes in the window had been moved prior to Day's arrival.

> DAY: I just don't know. I can't explain that box there depicted from the outside as related to the pictures that I took inside.

BELIN: In other words, what you are saying is that on the sixth floor window the westernmost box on Exhibit 482, you cannot then relate to any of the boxes shown on Exhibits 715 or 716?

DAY: That is correct.

DAY: Yes, that is just not the same box. It is not the same box. This is the first time I have seen No. 482.

DAY: I still don't quite understand that one in relation to pictures here unless something was moved after this was taken, before I got there (4H252-253).

The third source validating evidence had been moved prior to being photographed comes from Tom Alyea, a newsreel photographer for Dallas television station, WFAA. Alyea was present while officers searched for clues at the Texas School Book Depository sixth floor.

Det. Studebaker was alone at this site until after Lt. Day left the building with the rifle. We in the search team went to the sniper's site. The barricade had been completely dismantled and the boxes from the West side of the barricade had been removed and placed in various locations around the site. We did not realize at the time that Studebaker had not recorded on film the original placement of the boxes in the barricade. He also had removed the shooting support boxes on the window ledge and stacked them one on top of the other on the floor inside. He took a picture of this reconstructed arrangement. This is the view researchers have of the shooting support boxes that were originally on the brick window ledge. The corner of the outside box was positioned over the lower window channel that tilted the box at an angle.

Capt. Fritz had seen the photographs and had directed the crime lab to correct the shots of the window boxes and the casings on the floor. He had seen the original placement and ordered the crime lab to correct it. Neither Lt. Day nor Det. Studebaker had seen the original placement, so they procured my film from the TV station to get it right.

The high angle shot (shots) were made to show the original placement. Their reconstruction was close, but not exact. However, they did not bring the casings with them so they did not make the correction of the original placement of the shell casings (Alyea, n. d.).

Based upon testimony of officers present on the sixth floor, and the statements of Tom Alyea, it appears critical evidence was moved and then repositioned before being photographed. Day could not reconcile the differences in the photographs he took of the book cartons in the window from inside the building with the photograph Dillard took of the book cartons in the window from outside the building immediately after the shooting. Furthermore, he could not explain the discrepancy. The only conceivable explanation is they had been moved prior to Day taking his photographs.

THE LARGE PAPER BAG

Dallas Detectives Marvin Johnson and L. D. Montgomery were ordered by Fritz to protect the area around the "sniper's nest." Detective Johnson testified before the Commission he saw a brown paper sack made out of heavy wrapping paper in that area. Later in Johnson's testimony, he said L. D. Montgomery, his partner, picked the bag up off the floor and unfolded it (7H103).

When Detective Studebaker testified about the folded paper bag in the sniper's nest, he said he picked it up and fingerprinted it but neglected to photograph it. In fact, the sack does not show in any photographs (7H144).

THE SHELL CASINGS

Luke Mooney was a plainclothes deputy sheriff who assisted in the search of the sixth floor of the Texas School Book Depository. Mooney watched the motorcade from the front of the Dallas Criminal Courts Building. Upon hearing the shots, Mooney ran toward the Grassy Knoll and jumped the fence into the railroad yard. A few moments later, Mooney was directed to the book depository where he entered the building and joined other officers in a search for the suspect. Mooney is credited with being the first to discover the sniper's nest on the sixth floor. Mooney testified he witnessed Captain Fritz pick up the spent shell casings inside the sniper's nest before they were photographed. He also testified the casings were not in the same position in the photographs as he observed them the day of the assassination. Mooney was asked if the spent casings were given to Captain Fritz. His reply indicated Fritz collected the casings. He also indicated the locations of the casings in the photographs were not as he remembered them on the sixth floor of the TSBD (3H286).

> *MOONEY: Yes, sir; he was the first officer that picked them up, as far as I know, because I stood there and watched him go over and pick them up and look at them. As far as I could tell, I couldn't even tell what caliber they were, because I didn't get down that close to them. They were brass cartridges, brass shells.*

> *BALL: Is this the position of the cartridges as shown on 510, as you saw them?*

> *MOONEY: Yes, sir. That is just about the way they were laying, to the best of my knowledge. I do know there was—one was further away, and these other two were relatively close together—on this particular area. But these cartridges—this one and this one looks like they are further apart than they actually was.*

> *BALL: You think that the cartridges are in the same position as when you saw them in this picture 510?*

> *MOONEY: As far as my knowledge, they are; pretty close to right (3H286).*

Detective Marvin Johnson also testified the photographs of the casings were not as he remembered them on the day of the assassination. When asked about the location of the spent casings, Johnson testified, "All I can say, at the time these hulls were mentioned, I went over there and looked. I don't remember them being that far out." He added, "Well, of course, I couldn't remember exactly how far. It was my impression that they were all three next to the wall. I could have been wrong. I thought they were all three closer to the wall" (7H102).

Perhaps the most extraordinary account of evidence being collected and then being replaced to re-create the scene for photography purposes comes from Tom Alyea, a local television news photographer. Alyea entered the

Texas School Book Depository with police officers during the initial search and filmed various aspects of the search and the discovery of evidence. An interview with Alyea conducted by Connie Kritzberg, author of *Secrets from the Sixth Floor Window,* was posted online. Alyea provided additional information as an addendum.

> *The barricade on the sixth floor ran parallel to the windows, extending in an "L" shape that ended against the front wall between the first and second twin windows. The height of the stack of boxes was a minimum of 5 ft. [corrected to 4.5 feet]. I looked over the barricade and saw three shell casings laying on the floor in front of the second window in the two window casement. They were scattered in an area that could be covered by a bushel basket. They were located about half way between the inside of the barricade. I set my lens focus at the estimated distance from the camera to the floor, held the camera over the top of the barricade, and filmed them before anybody went into the enclosure. I could not position my eye to the camera's viewfinder to get the shot. After filming the casings with my wide-angle lens, from a height of 5 ft. [Corrected to 4.5 feet], I asked Captain Fritz, who was standing at my side, if I could go behind the barricade and get a close-up shot of the casings. He told me that it would be better if I got my shots from outside the barricade. He then rounded the pile of boxes and entered the enclosure. This was the first time anybody walked between the barricade and the windows.*
>
> *Fritz then walked to the casings, picked them up, and held them in his hand over the top of the boxes for me to get a close-up shot of the evidence. I filmed about eight seconds of a close-up shot of the shell casings in Captain Fritz's hand. I stopped filming, and thanked him. I do not recall if he placed them in his pocket or returned them back to the floor, because I was preoccupied with recording other views of the crime scene. I have been asked many times if I thought it was peculiar that the Captain of Homicide picked up evidence with his hands. Actually, that was the first thought that came to me when he did it, but I rationalized that he was the homicide expert and no prints could be taken from spent shell casings. Therefore, any photograph of shell casings taken after this, is staged and not correct.*

*After Capt. Fritz held the casing over the barricade for me to film,
he turned to examine the shooting support boxes on the windowsill.
I couldn't see the captain put the casings in his coat pocket because
his coat pocket was below the top of the barricade. He did not return
them to the floor and he did not have them in his hand when he was
examining the shooting support boxes. Over thirty minutes later, after
the rifle was discovered and the crime lab arrived, Capt. Fritz reached
into his pocket and handed the casings to Det. Studebaker to include
in the photographs he would take of the sniper's nest crime scene. We
stayed at the rifle site to watch Lt. Day dust the rifle. You have seen
my footage of this. Studebaker never saw the original placement of the
casings so he tossed them on the floor and photographed them.*

*Capt. Fritz had seen the photographs and had directed the crime lab
to correct the shots of the window boxes and the casings on the floor. He
had seen the original placement and ordered the crime lab to correct it.
Neither Lt. Day nor Det. Studebaker had seen the original placement,
so they procured my film from the TV station to get it right. The high
angle shot (shots) were made to show the original placement. Their
reconstruction was close, but not exact. However, they did not bring the
casings with them so they did not make the correction of the original
placement of the shell casings (Tom Alyea, n. d.).*

Both Mooney and Johnson testified the photographs shown to them were
not representative of the casings as they saw them on the sixth floor the day
of the assassination. Moody discovered the sniper's nest and therefore saw the
casings in their original position. Moody and Alyea both stated they observed
Fritz pick up the casings. Alyea says Fritz handed the casings to Studebaker
who just threw the casings down in front of the window and photographed
them. Studebaker's random placement of the casings is likely the position
detective Johnson remembers. According to Alyea, when Fritz saw the
photographs taken by Studebaker he realized they were incorrect. Fritz wanted
the photographs redone to depict them more accurately. The film taken over
the barricade by Alyea showing the unaltered sniper's nest was obtained to
assist Studebaker in placement of boxes in the window for reconstructive
photographs. Alyea theorized, because the casings were released to the FBI
and unavailable, reconstruction photography of the casings was not possible.

In light of that information, the subsequent testimony of Fritz concerning the cartridges is particularly disturbing. Fritz, and other officers, testified repeatedly nothing had been moved prior to photographs. Fritz testified, "I told them not to move the cartridges, not to touch anything until we could get the crime lab to take pictures of them just as they were lying there." The duplicity of Fritz providing testimony that would later be proven false is inexcusable (4H205).

On more than one occasion during his testimony, Studebaker stated he was on the sixth floor when the casings were found and that nothing had been discovered prior to his arrival. Studebaker also specifically testified he was present when the casings were discovered and he immediately went over and took photographs of the casings.

> STUDEBAKER: No; they hadn't found anything when we got there.
>
> BALL: After you were there a little while, did somebody find something?
>
> STUDEBAKER: They. They found the empty hulls in the southeast corner of the building—they found three empty hulls and we went over there and took photographs of that.
>
> STUDEBAKER: Now, I took two of the photographs and Lieutenant Day took two. We took double shots on each one. These are the ones I took myself—these pictures. There's [sic] the two pictures that I took. This one was right before anything was moved. There is a hull here, a hull here, and a hull over here (7H139).

Day's testimony contradicts Studebaker.

> BELIN: What did you do when you got to the sixth floor?
>
> DAY: I had to go up the stairs. The elevator—we couldn't figure out how to run it. When I got to the head of the stairs, I believe it was the patrolman standing there, I am not sure, stated they had found some

hulls over in the northeast corner of the building, and I proceeded to
that area- excuse me- southeast corner of the building (4H249).

Studebaker's testimony is disturbing because he indicates the casings were located after his arrival and that they were immediately photographed. If that were true, officer testimony concerning the casings would have been consistent. Unfortunately, Dallas Police Department officers repeatedly provided inconsistent testimony, and in the process raised questions concerning the reliability of collected evidence and the professionalism of the department. Testimony and photographic evidence support the suggestion that the crime scene may have been re-created, photographed, and the photographs submitted under the guise of an unaltered scene.

SKETCHING THE SCENE

National standards for processing crime scenes in 1963 dictated that a detailed sketch should be completed. Maurice Dienstein, in *Technics for the Crime Investigator* (1952), addressed sketching the scene by writing, "Nothing is to be touched, picked up, or moved until it has been located on a sketch" (Dienstein, 1952, p. 20).

One advantage in having a sketch of the scene is it can be used by the investigator when interviewing and interrogating subjects. Sketches can also ensure accuracy when preparing written investigative reports. A crime scene sketch establishes a permanent record of an article of evidence and its location within the crime scene. Specific information such as distances and relationships between various pieces of evidence can be clarified with a sketch. Occasionally, photography processes will fail or the photograph is deemed too graphic to present in court. When this happens a detailed sketch can help judges, juries, witnesses, and others to visualize the crime scene (Dienstein, 1952).

A sketch presents an overhead and simplistic view of the crime scene. While not drawn to scale, sketches are proportional and representative of the scene. The sketch should include measurements and sufficient details for a scaled diagram, if necessary. The sketch is a rough drawing indicating the general location of walls, doors, windows, furniture or any item of evidence. Then accurate measurements are taken along the perimeter walls, indicating the precise location of doors and windows. The measurements are proportionally reduced on the rough sketch, and objects are drawn in. Significant items within the room, including potential evidence, is to be included within the sketch. Measurements showing the location of items within the scene can be completed by triangulation or rectangular coordinates such as from two walls or permanently established points (Kirk, 1953).

Usually a rough sketch is completed while at the scene and retained in the event it is needed later. Based upon the information from the rough sketch, a final sketch is prepared for inclusion in a report. The final sketch should be based upon a specific scale of reference; for example, the reference scale may indicate 1/8 inch equals 1 foot. Each sketch should display a legend that includes the location of the crime scene, a case number, scene location, compass direction, the reference scale, the name of the officers taking measurements and completing the sketch, the date and time the rough drawing was completed and the date and time the final sketch was completed.

DALLAS POLICE DEPARTMENT: SKETCHING THE SCENE

National standards for processing crime scenes in 1963, dictated evidence was not to be handled, moved, or collected until photographed, as well as located on a sketch, and meticulously described for later reference (Dienstein, 1952). As such, completing a crime scene sketch was apparently a procedure routinely observed by Dallas crime scene investigators. Dallas crime scene officer Rusty Livingston is quoted in *JFK: First Day Evidence as* saying:

> On a murder scene, we'd usually make a scaled drawing of the scene. No matter what shift it was on, it had to be ready the next morning when the Chief arrived (Savage, 1993, p. 82).

Two finished sketches were completed, one of the sixth floor of the Texas School Book Depository and a second depicting a 14 foot square area near the window purportedly used by the shooter. The hand drawn, finished sketch demonstrates the arrangement of the boxed book cartons in a 14' x 14' area, located in the southeast corner of the sixth floor of the Texas School Book Depository. The sketch of that 14' x 14' area, prepared on November 25, 1963 at 10 a.m. by detectives B. G. Brown and R. L. Studebaker, does not indicate the location of the casings, the large paper bag, or the cartons in the window. The only evidence located within the sketch is the box containing the developed palm print. The rough sketch depicting the arrangement of the boxes contained no date, or indication of who compiled the information (Brown, 1963; Unknown, 1963).

A finished sketch was also completed by R. L. Studebaker on November 22, 1963. This sketch was of the entire sixth floor of the Texas School Book Depository and indicated the location of the 9 ½" square wooden posts supporting the structure, windows, the service elevators, the stairs, the location from which the rifle was recovered, and a shaded area representing the alleged location of the shooter (Studebaker, 1963).

The accuracy of the placement of the boxes in the finished sketch of the 14' x 14' area is debatable based upon testimony indicating boxes were moved and then replaced to reconstruct the crime scene. This is compounded by testimony documenting an unknown number of unauthorized people having unsupervised access to the sixth floor before either sketch was completed.

DESCRIBING THE SCENE

Recording detailed descriptions of the crime scene in a written report was an integral part of the generally accepted national standards for crime scene investigation in 1963. According to Dienstein, the evidence was to be "minutely described as to location, condition, and any other pertinent observation" (p. 20). The investigative report should contain a narrative that provides a comprehensive description of the scene and investigated procedures completed. Report narratives are the foundation of criminal investigations (Dienstein, 1952, p. 20).

The length of the descriptive narrative increases with case complexity, increased items of evidence, and larger scenes to describe. The amount of information described in the narrative should be dictated by the amount of relevant information available, and all information that could reasonably relate to the crime should be included. The narrative should include information concerning items that appear to be out of place, and items that appear to be missing should also be included. Situational circumstances such as open doors, particular odors, or rain should also be documented in the narrative. The initial phase of any investigation is critical, and the written narrative documentation of basic factual observations of the crime scene and evidence collected assist in determining the success or failure of an investigation.

The narrative in an investigative report should encompass a comprehensive description of the crime scene, the crime scene search, and the discovery of possible articles of evidence. Rough notes should be taken from the time the investigator is advised to respond to a crime scene until the crime scene is released. That information should be finalized as an investigative report as soon as possible in order to ensure the most detailed, comprehensive, and accurate report possible.

THE DALLAS POLICE DEPARTMENT: DESCRIBING THE SCENE

The most informative report provided was submitted by Day in letter form dated January 8, 1964, addressed to G. L. Lumpkin, Deputy of the Police Service Division. The report was included as an attachment in a letter from the FBI to the Warren Commission dated September 18, 1964 and marked as Commission Exhibit 3145. Day's report contains the following information:

1. At 1:12 p.m. on November 22, 1963, Lt. J. C. Day and Detective R. L. Studebaker arrived at 411 Elm Street, commonly known as the Texas School Book Depository.
2. Detectives J. B. Hicks and H. R. Williams arrived about 3 p.m.
3. Upon arrival, Day and Studebaker were directed to the sixth floor of the Texas School Book Depository, where three spent rifle shell casings had been located in the southeast corner of the building immediately adjacent to a window. The casings were unsuccessfully processed for fingerprints, marked for identification, and released to Detective Sims.
4. About 1:25 p.m., a rifle was located near the stairs in the northwest portion of the sixth floor. The weapon was unloaded, unsuccessfully processed for fingerprints, marked for identification, and released to Capt. Fritz. The rifle was taken by Lt. Day to the Identification Bureau about 2 p.m.
5. Lt. Day returned to 411 Elm St. about 2:45 p.m.

6. About 50 photographs were taken and a scaled drawing was made of the sixth floor by detectives J. B. Hicks and R. L. Studebaker. [This sketch was actually completed by Brown and Studebaker] (Brown, 1963).

7. Cartons were dusted for fingerprints found in the area where the rifle was found and near the window where the spent shells were found. A palm print was developed on the top northwest corner of the carton appearing to have been used by the assassin to sit on while aiming the rifle. The carton used to sit on, and three cartons stacked by the window apparently used to steady the rifle were collected as evidence.

8. Lt. Day returned to the identification Bureau, about 7 p.m. and successfully developed fingerprints from the rifle. Two fingerprints were found on the side of the rifle near the trigger and magazine housing and a palm print was found on the underside of a gun barrel near the end of the stock. The rifle was released to the FBI.

9. Paraffin casts were made of Oswald's hands and the right side of his face about 9 p.m. by Sgt. W. E. Barnes and Detective J. B. Hicks.

10. All other collected evidence was released November 22 at 11:45 p.m. to FBI Agent Vince Drain (CE 3145, 26H829).

The crime scene investigation report for the homicide of President John F. Kennedy is less than 700 words. As an example of Day's unusual brevity, compare the information concerning only the palm print collected from the rifle from Day's report to the description provided in the accompanying interview completed by the FBI. The following is the comparison of how the palm print was addressed.

DAY: A palm print was found on the underside of a gun barrel near the end of the stock. It appeared to be from the right palm and fingers of Lee Harvey Oswald (CE3145, 26H 830).

FBI REPORT: Day advised he took the wooden part of the rifle off by loosening three or four screws that uncovered what he considered to be an old, dried print with a loop formation underneath the barrel. He stated it appeared to him to be the right palm print of some individual. This print was found on the underside of the barrel which was completely covered by the wooden stock of the gun and not visible until he had removed the wooden portion of the gun. Lt. Day estimated this print was within 3 inches of the front end of the wooden stock. Lt. Day advised he dusted this print with black powder and made one lift. Later in the report, the FBI continued, Lt. Day related that after he made the lift of the palm print on the underside of the barrel, he could still see this palm print on the underside of the barrel of the gun and would have photographed the same had he not been ordered to cease his examination (CE3145, 26H831-832).

The volume of information defined in the narrative should be reflective of the relevant information available, and all information that could reasonably relate to the crime should be included. The report submitted by Day is obviously lacking documentation of the Dallas Police Department crime scene investigation unit's activities.

Information omitted within in the crime scene report includes:

1. Documentation of steps taken to secure the scene
2. Methods used to prevent unauthorized access
   a. Methods used to prevent contamination of the scene
   b. How possession of the scene was maintained
   c. The date and time the scene was officially released
3. Documentation of the search
   a. Methods used to prevent contamination of the scene
   b. How possession of the scene was maintained
   c. The date and time the scene was officially released
4. Documentation of the search
   a. Who participated in the search
   b. What method of search was utilized
   c. Known contamination of the scene
5. Who directed the investigation of the crime scene
   a. A description of investigative steps completed
   b. Investigator responsible for crime scene processing
   c. Known investigative errors
6. Completion of a descriptive narrative
   a. A comprehensive depiction of the crime scene
   b. A list of all collected items of evidence

c. A detailed description of each item collected and its condition
d. A record of whether the evidence was photographed and sketched
e. Location, time and date of collection of physical evidence
f. Who collected physical evidence
g. Date and time of any subsequent evidence processing and the results
h. Chain of possession for all evidence insuring its integrity (Kirk, 1953).

Crime scene investigative report narratives are the foundation of criminal investigations, providing leads to identify potential perpetrators and their actions on a crime scene. They are routinely utilized by the judicial system to help determine what happened, positively identify who may have been involved, and document the integrity of collected physical evidence to support those findings. Unfortunately, Day's crime scene investigative report had to be heavily augmented by FBI interviews and Warren Commission testimony due to his deficiency in documenting the crime scene investigation of President Kennedy's homicide.

FINGERPRINTING THE SCENE

Fingerprints are unique to each individual and have been used for over a century for identification and crime-solving purposes. Skin on the hands is unique because it does not have hair follicles or oil glands, and because it is composed of ridges that increase friction assisting with gripping objects. These friction ridges are composed of rows of sweat pores, or eccrine glands which constantly secrete perspiration. Oil transferred from other parts of the body adheres to the ridges on the fingertips. That oil and other contaminates transfers with the perspiration to other surfaces upon contact (Hawthorne, 2009).

There are three basic forms of fingerprint evidence found at crime scenes: patent prints, plastic prints, and latent prints. Patent prints are fingerprints that can be easily visualized without enhancement. An example would be bloody fingerprints left on a doorknob. Plastic prints are those left in soft surfaces such as a fingerprint in chewing gum pressed under a table. Latent prints are invisible or less visible and require enhancement so they can be easily seen. The majority of fingerprint evidence collected at most crime scenes is from developed or lifted latent fingerprints (Hawthorne, 2009).

DEVELOPING LATENT FINGERPRINTS WITH POWDERS

Identifying the absorbent characteristics of a surface is paramount to the selection of the correct developing technique. Latent fingerprints on porous surfaces such as paper, cardboard, and wood should be developed chemically; latent fingerprints on nonporous surfaces such as glass, metal, and plastics should be developed with powders. The most common method for developing latent fingerprints is by a technique known as powder dusting. Fingerprint powders are created from volcanic ash and come in various colors to insure contrast with the surface containing the latent print. The fingerprint powder adheres to the moisture and oils transferred from the skin to the surface upon contact. The powder is applied to a surface using a fiber brush and, as the particles attach to the moisture of the impression, the print becomes visible. Once the print has been fully developed, it should be photographed in place. Then the print is removed from the surface with adhesive tape and transferred to a clean lift card (Scott, 1951).

Developed in 1950, magnetic powder is useful on textured, non-metallic surfaces, including some paper. This powder is comprised of regular fingerprint powder mixed with magnetized iron particles. In place of a fiber brush, a magnetic applicator is used to apply the powder. When placing the end of the applicator into the magnetic powder, a ball of magnetic powder will form, making a brush-like appearance at the base. The latent print is developed by gently moving the ball of magnetic powder over the surface to be processed. Like regular fingerprint powder, magnetic powder particles attach to moisture transferred from friction ridges to a surface upon contact (Hawthorne, 2009).

DEVELOPING LATENT FINGERPRINTS WITH CHEMICALS

At the time of the assassination, chemical development of latent fingerprints on paper or other porous surfaces commonly included the use of silver nitrate, ninhydrin, or iodine. Each chemical reacted to a different component of latent fingerprints, and could be used consecutively on paper products.

Silver nitrate, the most common method used in 1963 was dependent upon a chemical reaction with silver chloride present in fingerprint deposits. Silver nitrate has been in use since 1891 to develop latent fingerprints on paper or untreated wood.

Ninhydrin has been known to develop fifty-year-old prints from paper products. Ninhydrin solutions were introduced in the mid-1950s as a method for developing latent prints and applied by spraying, swabbing, or dipping. Ninhydrin reacts with amino acids in fingerprint secretion residue. Slightly less common was the use of iodine crystals. When iodine crystals are warmed, they produce a vapor that is absorbed by the fats in fingerprint secretion residue, developing a yellowish brown latent print (Yamashita, 2011).

Dallas Police Department: Fingerprinting the Scene

There were several techniques available to the Dallas Police Department to assist with developing latent fingerprints. Using the correct methods of developing prints from a variety of surfaces increases the investigators' chance of success. The absorbent characteristics of an item's surface help determine the appropriate technique to use when developing latent fingerprints. Latent fingerprints on porous surfaces such as paper, cardboard, and wood should be developed chemically; latent fingerprints on nonporous surfaces such as glass, metal, and plastics should be developed with powders. Magnetic powders can be used on a wider variety of surfaces with the exception of metals and some varnishes.

Fingerprint Training

Silver nitrate has been used since 1891 to develop latent fingerprints on paper products. Reacting with silver chloride, the developing prints turn black on exposure to light. However, because the background can also stain, it is not the chemical of choice when developing prints on paper. Ninhydrin, in use since 1910, is the most productive means of latent print development on porous items such as paper and cardboard. Because amino acids are always present in human perspiration, and do not migrate with age on paper products, distinct fingerprints can be developed after long periods using ninhydrin. The long-term use of chemicals in developing latent prints on paper products is well established; therefore, it is reasonable to accept that methods of developing prints with silver nitrate and ninhydrin would have been a part of the curriculum of any fingerprinting school or conference embracing that subject (Gaensslen, 2001).

The training and experience in fingerprinting evidence an investigator possesses has a direct effect upon the success in developing latent fingerprints at a crime scene. Based on Day's testimony, it appears he attended an advanced latent print school conducted by the FBI, which, combined with his 15 years of experience and other training, strongly suggests he should have been familiar with the available chemical latent fingerprint development techniques. Day had sufficient training and experience to determine paper products were best processed with chemicals as opposed to fingerprint powders. Powders are not the best choice for developing prints on paper products, yet it appears that was the only process used on the sixth floor of the Texas School Book Depository. Rusty Livingston, assigned to the Dallas Police Department crime lab, stated in his book *JFK: First Day Evidence,* the Dallas Police Department identification unit "commonly used silver nitrate to process paper products for latent prints" (4H250; Savage, 1993, p. 181).

Fritz, and particularly Day, should have made certain that a chemical development technique was utilized on the cardboard boxes discovered adjacent to the window believed to be used by the shooter. However, it appears only powders were used to develop latent prints.

> *BELIN: Let me ask you this in an effort, perhaps, to save time. In all of your processing of prints, did you use anything other than this black powder at the scene that day?*

> *DAY: No, sir (4H259).*

Dallas Police Department's success in processing the cardboard boxes was limited to one latent print and one palm print developed with black powder. Using the silver nitrate method, the FBI developed 27 identifiable latent prints from the four cardboard boxes and collected them all as evidence (R566).

It is obvious the Dallas Police Department considered developing fingerprint evidence an integral part of crime scene investigation. In fact, Day testified developing and collecting fingerprint evidence was a part of the Dallas

Police Department's crime scene investigative responsibilities. Therefore, the decision to limit processing of the cardboard boxes to magnetic powder is mystifying (4H250).

STUDEBAKER'S FINGERPRINT TRAINING

It appears from Day's own testimony he disregarded his training regarding the use of chemicals on paper products, as powder was the least desirable method to use to develop fingerprints. The same cannot be said of Detective Studebaker, who had neither the training nor experience to know the difference. Studebaker's Warren Commission testimony concerning his training and length of time assigned to the identification unit indicates just how deficient he was: "It's just on-the-job training—you go out with old officers and learn how to dust for prints and take pictures and fingerprints" (7H137-138).

Unbelievably, an unsupervised person with no formal crime scene investigative training and with only seven weeks of crime scene experience was delegated to develop latent fingerprints, and collect and photograph evidence in the homicide investigation of the President of the United States.

THE CONTAMINATION OF FINGERPRINT EVIDENCE

Acceptable national standards for protecting the crime scene include prohibiting alteration of the crime scene by depositing evidence from investigators. The use of gloves to prevent officers from depositing their fingerprints on potential evidence was specifically mentioned by Kirk (1953). Two experts gave testimony concerning latent fingerprints developed on evidence removed from the Texas School Book Depository. FBI Special Agents Sebastian Latona and Arthur Mandella testified fourteen of nineteen identifiable latent fingerprints and four of six identifiable latent palm prints were those of Studebaker; indicating he was not wearing gloves and therefore not following acceptable national standards for protecting the crime scene (WCR566).

It is logical to conclude that this contamination could have been prevented. When asked about his crime scene investigative training and experience Studebaker stated he had seven weeks of on-the-job training. Since testimony shows both Fritz and Day left the crime scene shortly after the rifle was discovered, it appears Studebaker was left unsupervised to decide how potential evidence should be processed for latent prints, and determine what techniques he should utilize to develop latent prints on those items. Studebaker, who possessed just seven weeks of experience and no formal training, was left with the responsibility of processing evidence likely touched by the perpetrator of President Kennedy's murder. While the decision to relinquish that authority to Studebaker did not break any rules, it certainly displayed in both Fritz and Day a lack of supervisory skills and poor judgment.

COLLECTING EVIDENCE

An agency's ability to solve crimes in the early 1960s was often dependent upon the experienced investigator's aptitude to question witnesses and suspects, and familiarity with the people and location where crimes occurred. Subsequently, physical evidence held minimal impact on cases solved by confessions or witnesses' statements; as a result, few items of evidence were normally collected under those circumstances. National standards for processing crime scenes in 1963 indicated that the last step in processing a crime scene should be to collect evidence. Of course, what items were collected was dependent upon what was perceived as physical evidence.

Forensic identification limitations at the time of the assassination often presented a bias as to what would be collected as evidence and what items would be deemed insignificant and, therefore, not collected. Today, if an unknown latent print is developed it can be submitted to the Automated Fingerprint Identification System (AFIS) to possibly identify the individual who deposited the print. Prior to AFIS, law enforcement had to rely on developing a suspect, and then obtaining inked fingerprint impressions for comparison. If there was no suspect, latent fingerprints were considered useless, and therefore seldom developed and collected.

There is no specific order for collection of the evidence, but some types of evidence, by their nature, should be given priority over other types of evidence. Fragile evidence such as evaporating liquids, shoe prints in dust, or gunpowder residue should be photographed, recorded in a sketch, documented in narrative form, and collected as soon as possible. Transient evidence, such as changes in lighting conditions or furniture moved by responding personnel, should be photographed and documented in narrative form as soon as possible to assure proper recall of events. Trace evidence, such as hair and fibers, should be described in the narrative and collected prior to larger and more stable types of evidence (Kirk, 1953).

It is difficult to generalize about the collection of physical evidence, but each item collected should be packaged separately to prevent cross-contamination. Once an item is collected as evidence, it should be placed in a paper bag, sealed at the crime scene, and identified with a full description. In addition, the location of recovery, the name of the officer collecting the item, the date and time of collection, and an agency evidence number should all be included (Kirk, 1953).

INTEGRITY OF EVIDENCE

Evidence admissibility in court is centered upon an uninterrupted chain of custody. It is important to demonstrate that the evidence introduced at trial is the same evidence collected at the crime scene, and that access was controlled and documented. Preserving evidence begins with the appropriate packaging in a sealed, tamper-proof container. Each package is to be identified with a detailed description of the enclosed item, where and when it was collected, and the signature of the person who collected the item. If the evidence is examined for analysis, the package should be opened from a different access point, such as the side or bottom of the container, leaving the initial seal unbroken. The date, time, and reason for examining the item should be documented on the packaging, along with the signature of the examiner. Correct and consistent information recorded on evidence labels and consistent procedural documentation is essential for preserving the integrity of collected evidence (Kirk, 1953).

Collected evidence is to be accompanied by a chain of possession, identifying each person who had control over the item. This running log of persons having access to the evidence is normally placed on the evidence packaging or on a tag attached to the evidence. Some agencies utilized a separate evidence collection sheet detailing all items of evidence, with a place for signatures indicating who may have checked out, or had access to, particular items of evidence (Kirk, 1953).

Physical evidence is to be protected from contamination, degradation, alteration, or destruction. The protection of physical evidence is accomplished primarily by collecting the item in a timely manner, in the proper container, storing it under the correct temperature guidelines, and limiting the number of persons with access to the evidence. Collected evidence is normally maintained in a locked location and access to the evidence for testing is carefully documented to ensure a chain of custody to preserve the integrity of the evidence. Preserving the integrity of physical evidence is vital to the use of collected evidence in solving crimes. If the integrity of an item of evidence is uncertain, the use of items in legal proceedings could be jeopardized.

DALLAS POLICE DEPARTMENT: COLLECTING EVIDENCE

Basic crime scene investigation centers on the premise physical evidence can identify victims and perpetrators in addition to suggesting activities undertaken in the commission of a crime. Due to the limitations of forensic analysis at the time of the assassination, there may have been a bias as to what should have been collected as evidence and what items may have been deemed insignificant and therefore not collected.

There is no documentation indicating who determined what evidence should be collected, a detailed list of evidence collected, nor any documentation of who collected the evidence. Some of those issues are answered in fragmented testimony provided to the Warren Commission and addressed by the FBI in various interviews. However, even the official crime scene investigation report completed by Day does not completely address the issues in question.

THE RIFLE

FBI Special Agent Albert Sayers interviewed Dallas County Deputy Constable Seymour Weitzman in the presence of detective C. W. Brown on November 23, 1963. The FBI Gemberling Report of November 30, 1963 indicates Weitzman provided specific observations of the weapon prior to Fritz taking it from him.

> *FBI REPORT: Mr. Weitzman described a rifle, which was found as a 7.65 caliber Mauser bolt action rifle, which loads from a five shot clip, which is locked on the underside of the receiver forward of the trigger guard. The metal parts of this rifle were of a gunmetal color, gray or*

blue, in the rear portion of the bolt and were visibly worn. The wooden portion of this rifle was dark brown in color, and with rough wood, apparently having been used or damaged to considerable extent. This rifle was equipped with a four power 18 scope of apparent Japanese manufacture. It was also equipped with a thick brown-black leather bandolier type sling. After he had observed this rifle to the extent described above, Capt. Fritz appeared and took the rifle from him (R124-125; Sayers, 1963).

Weitzman described the rifle with specific details, including the clip was locked on the underside of the receiver and the rear portion of the bolt was worn. Normally, once the last round of ammunition is chambered, the clip falls from a weapon. To describe the malfunctioning clip and other details of the rifle without actually handling it would be unlikely. Weitzman's contemporaneous statements directly conflict with later accounts of the rifle being collected by Day.

THE CASINGS

When a bullet is fired from a weapon, it travels down the barrel that contains small ridges and grooves that can be used as a means of matching the bullet to the particular weapon. Casings that hold the bullet also contain identifying marks. The examination of ballistic evidence can link bullets and casings to a single source or weapon. Additionally, fingerprints, hair fiber, and blood may be discovered on ballistic evidence. Three casings were collected on the sixth floor of the Texas School Book Depository adjacent to the window from which it is believed the shooter fired.

To demonstrate positive identification of the casings found at the crime scene, the casings were inscribed by Day. However, when they were marked by Day is disturbingly ambiguous. Day testified the initials GD were inscribed on one of the casings. He postulated they were the initials of Captain George Doughty; however, when the casings were collected, Doughty was not on the scene.

BELIN: Is there any other testimony you have with regard to the chain of possession of this shell from the time it was first found until the time it got back to your office?

DAY: No, sir; I told you in our conversation in Dallas that I marked those at the scene. After reviewing my records, I didn't think I was on all three of those hulls that you have, indicating I did not mark them at the scene, then I remembered putting them in the envelope, and Sims taking them. It was further confirmed today when I noticed that the third hull, which I did not give you, or come to me through you, does not have my mark on it.

BELIN: Your testimony now is that you did not mark any of the hulls at the scene?

DAY: Those three; no, sir.

DAY: That is a hull that does not have my marking on it.

Each shell casing should have been placed in an individual container preventing it from damage, and sealed to protect it from contamination or alteration. Instead, all three casings were placed in a single, unsealed envelope creating questions concerning the chain of custody.

DAY: At that time they were placed in an envelope.

BELIN: Was the envelope sealed?

DAY: No, sir.

BELIN: Had it been sealed when you gave it to Mr. Sims?

DAY: No, sir; no.

DAY: That is a hull that does not have my marking on it.

BELIN: Do you know whether or not this was one of the hulls that was found at the school book depository building?

DAY: I think it is.

BELIN: What makes you think it is?

DAY: It has the initials "G. D." on it, which is George Doughty, the captain that I worked under.

BELIN: Was he there at the scene?

DAY: No, sir; this hull came up; this hull that is not marked came up, later. I didn't send that.

BELIN: This was—

DAY: That was retained. That is the hull that was retained by homicide division when the other two were originally sent in with the gun.

BELIN: You are referring now to Commission Exhibit 543 as being the one that was retained in your possession for a while?

DAY: It is the one that I did not see again.

BELIN: It appears to be flattened out here. Do you know or have you any independent recollection as to whether or not it was flattened out at the small end when you saw it?

DAY: No, sir; I don't (4H253-255).

The exact location of each individual casing that was recovered should have been noted on the container. Because this was not done, there is no information indicating where these shell casings were located prior to collection.

DAY: The only writing on it was, "Lieut. J. C. Day." Down here at the bottom. "Dallas Police Department and the date."

DAY: "R. M. S." stands for R. M. Sims, the detective whom I turned it over to. That is the date and the time that he took it from me.

BELIN: What date and time does it show?

DAY: November 22, 1963, 1:23 p.m. (4H253, 256).

Warren Commission testimony provided by Day indicates the three spent shells (Commission Exhibits 543, 544, and 545) were picked up by detective Sims and placed in an envelope held by Day.

> *DAY: .... Mr. Sims picked them up by the ends and handed them to me. I processed each of the three; did not find fingerprints (4H253).*

Deputy Mooney's testimony contradicted that account by stating Fritz actually collected the casings.

> *MOONEY: Yes, sir; he was the first officer that picked them up, as far as I know, because I stood there and watched him go over and pick them up and look at them. As far as I could tell, I couldn't even tell what caliber they were, because I didn't get down that close to them. They were brass cartridges; brass shells (3H286).*

> *MOONEY: Well, I stayed up there not over 15 or 20 minutes longer— after Captain Will Fritz and his officers came over there, Captain Fritz picked up the cartridges, began to examine them, of course I left that particular area. By that time, there was a number of officers up there. The floor was covered with officers. And we were searching, trying to find the weapon at that time (3H289).*

Standards require a chain of custody immediately be established to form a continuous record documenting who collected and retained possession of the casings. However, that was not done, so there is confusion concerning who collected the casings. There is also incongruent testimony from Sims and Day concerning who took possession of the casings. Sims stated he did not take possession of the casings, however, Day testified he did. Day also testified the unsealed envelope containing only two of the casings was placed on his desk at an unknown time by an unknown person.

> *SIMS: I picked them up from the floor and he had an envelope there and he held the envelope open.*

BALL: You didn't take them in your possession, did you?

SIMS: No, sir; I don't believe I did (7H163).

DAY: At that time, they were placed in an envelope and the envelope marked. The three hulls were not marked at that time. Mr. Sims took possession of them.

BELIN: Had the shells been out of your possession then?

DAY: Mr. Sims had the shells from the time they were moved from the building or he took them from me at that time, and the shells I did not see again until around 10 o'clock.

BELIN: Who gave them to you at 10 o'clock?

DAY: They were in this group of evidence being collected to turn over to the FBI. I don't know who brought them back.

DAY: About 10 o'clock in the evening, this envelope came back to me with two hulls in it. I say it came to me, it was in a group of stuff, a group of evidence, we were getting ready to release to the FBI. I don't know who brought them back. Vince Drain, FBI, was present with the stuff, the first I noticed it. At that time, there were two hulls inside. I was advised the homicide division was retaining the third for their use. At that time, I marked the two hulls inside of this, still inside this envelope (4H253- 254).

When Day testified to the Warren Commission in April, he stated he could not recall who returned the spent casings to him. On May 7, 1964, Day provided an affidavit to the Warren Commission stating it was Captain C. N. Dhority. However, there is no documentation indicating when or why the hulls were relinquished by Sims to Dhority.

DAY: Since returning to Dallas, Detective C. N. Dhority has called my attention to the fact he brought the three hulls in the envelope to me and asked me to check them again for fingerprints even though I had checked them when they were picked up on the sixth floor of the Texas School Book Depository about 1:20 p.m. November 22, 1963 by Detective R. M. Sims and myself and placed in a manila envelope. Since talking to Dhority, I remember now that he was the one who returned the shells to me about 10:00 p.m. and stated that his office wanted to retain one. He left me two shells and the envelope that Detective Sims and I had previously marked. It was then that I scratched my name on the two shells that were released at 11:45 p.m. (7H401-402).

In a June 23, 1964 affidavit, Day amended his testimony stating his initials were on all three casings and Dhority's initials were on two of the casings. Day also changed the date the casings were initialed for identification, but not based upon his individual recall. "Both Detective R. L. Studebaker and Detective R. M. Sims, who were present at the window when the hulls were picked up, state I marked them as they were found under the window" (7H402).

Based on the testimony of Moody, Day, and Sims, it cannot be established by whom, when, or where the casings were initially recovered from the Texas School Book Depository. Since the chain of custody for the casings is also suspect, we cannot positively state the casings entered into evidence are the same casings collected from the sixth floor.

THE LARGE PAPER BAG

The question of how Oswald may have brought the Mannlicher Carcano into the Texas School Book Depository was supposedly answered by the discovery of a homemade paper bag. Studebaker stated he collected a homemade paper bag from the floor adjacent to the box located in front of the window from which the shooter allegedly fired. Day testified he noted on the bag it might have been used to carry the rifle. The paper bag would definitely be a key piece of evidence; however, Studebaker failed to photograph the bag prior to collection.

DAY: This is the sack found on the sixth floor in the southeast corner of the building on November 22, 1963.

BELIN: Do you have any identification on that to so indicate?

DAY: It has my name on it, and it also has other writing that I put on there for the information of the FBI.

BELIN: Could you read what you wrote on there?

DAY: Found next to the sixth floor window gun fired from. May have been used to carry gun. Lieutenant J. C. Day.

BELIN: When did you write that?

DAY: I wrote that at the time the sack was found before it left our possession (4H267).

Studebaker testified to collecting the paper bag as evidence prior to completing the photography. The paper bag was also processed for latent fingerprints by Studebaker; however, he indicated he was unfamiliar with the dimensions of the bag.

STUDEBAKER: It was doubled—it was a piece of paper about this long and it was doubled over.

BALL: How long was it, approximately?

STUDEBAKER: I don't know—I picked it up and dusted it and they took it down there and sent it to Washington and that's the last I have seen of it, and I don't know (7H144).

When asked a second time about the size of the paper bag, Studebaker was able to give an approximation of measurements.

BALL: Now how big was this paper that you saw—you saw the wrapper—tell me about how big a paper bag was—how long was it?

STUDEBAKER: It was about, I would say, 3 and a half to 4 feet long.

BALL: The paper bag?

STUDEBAKER: Yes.

BALL: And how wide was it?

STUDEBAKER: Approximately 8 inches (7H144).

There is also conflicting testimony concerning who collected the paper bag as evidence. Detective Johnson testified Detective Montgomery collected the paper bag, while Montgomery testified Studebaker collected the evidence.

JOHNSON: Yes, sir. We found this brown paper sack or case. It was made out of heavy wrapping paper. Actually, it looked similar to the paper that those books was wrapped in. It was just a long narrow paper bag.

BELIN: Do you know who found it?

JOHNSON: I know that the first I saw of it, L. D. Montgomery, my partner, picked it up off the floor, and it was folded up, and he unfolded it.

JOHNSON: I would say that the sack was folded up here and it was east of the pipes in the corner. To the best of my memory, that is where my partner picked it up. I was standing there when he picked it up (7H103-104).

BALL: You picked it up?

MONTGOMERY: Wait just a minute no; I didn't pick it up. I believe Mr. Studebaker did. We left it laying right there so they could check it for prints (7H98).

According to sworn statements given to the FBI, the Dallas Police Department witness list, and testimony given to the Warren Commission, the large paper bag was collected by Studebaker, Day, and Montgomery. Obviously, more than one person is grossly mistaken and perjury may have resulted. Moreover, the question of where the large paper bag was located is in question. Unfortunately, because the standard concerning crime scene searches was not adhered to, we have no way of ever knowing the truth.

COMPROMISED EVIDENCE

Integrity of evidence is compromised when it is not properly documented, collected, and preserved. All evidence should be photographed and placed on a sketch. It should be collected in a timely manner and placed in a sealed container labeled with the appropriate identifying information. All evidence should be accompanied by a chain of custody, notations of which documents were obtained, and who had access to the evidence from the moment it was collected. Not all evidence collected from the Texas School Book Depository was photographed. Evidence collected was not placed on a sketch. There are questions concerning who collected the evidence and who had access to it, because there is no chain of custody accompanying the evidence. Available information suggests the original location for the three casings, the large paper bag, and the boxes in the window allegedly used by the sniper, may all have been moved from their original location. Additionally, the boxes and the casings appear to have been photographed after they were moved and then replaced within the crime scene in an effort to restore the crime scene to its original state. Based on those criteria, the integrity of the casings, the boxes, and the large paper bag supposedly used to transport the rifle are all suspect.

Protecting the integrity of evidence begins with the first officers on the scene and continues until the case is adjudicated and the court orders a release or destruction of the evidence. A comprehensive description of a collected item, accompanied by careful documentation of its location and condition, helps to establish the reliability of evidence. Careful handling and appropriate storage must be undertaken to ensure the evidence is not altered or contaminated. Documentation of the discovery of evidence detailing its location and condition, accompanied by a meticulous description, helps to protect the fidelity of evidence. Careful handling must be undertaken to ensure the evidence is not altered or contaminated. Evidence needs to be photographed in place and measurements taken to facilitate completion of a sketch. A chain of custody, indicating every person having access to the item of evidence, must be maintained diligently.

DPD INVESTIGATION CONCLUSIONS

Warren Commission testimony indicates the homicide investigation of President Kennedy by the Dallas Police Department is unacceptable. The basic processes for preserving, photographing, and collecting physical evidence inside the Texas School Book Depository were flawed. That could have been avoided by adhering to the protocols Day testified were standard for the department. Experienced investigators knowingly used inferior techniques to develop latent fingerprint evidence. Officers neglected to document, protect, and collect all potential evidence in a timely manner. Evidence was disregarded that could have identified an accomplice or exonerated Oswald. Additionally, and most importantly, an unsupervised and inexperienced officer was left to process the crime scene in one of the most important cases in the history of our country.

The Dallas Police Department in the 1960s likely employed men who were doing the best job possible, while possessing few investigative skills beyond the basic police training and limited formal education. Officers who commanded supervisory roles were the exception; they often had years of experience and multiple opportunities for training in the latest police techniques. The investigation of President Kennedy was directed by those individuals in supervisory positions. Subsequently, any failure of the Dallas Police Department to follow their own standards of investigation resides with those individual supervisors. Which begs the question, why did the supervisors allow the investigation to become compromised?

MEMORIES AND HABITS

There is an old adage that states practice makes perfect. While one can perfect skills or techniques by repetitiveness, if you continuously practice a technique incorrectly, you are creating an inferior habit. When a behavior is performed many times the behavior becomes controlled by an automated process called *habit*. Without habits, we would either have to act spontaneously to daily reoccurring events, or deliberately consider and develop a plan for everything we do.

Explicit is defined as unconcealed, open, recognizable, and specific. Explicit memories are conscious memories of situations that can readily be recalled with specific details. When explicitly recalling an event, detailed memories, such as the context in which the event occurred, are easily verbalized: such as the time of day an event took place, the location, and the people that were present. When giving directions to a lost traveler, talking about our childhood, or recalling a favorite vacation, we rely on explicit memory (Eysenck, 2004).

Habits allow us to perform routine acts regularly and without conscious effort. Memories that provide access to skills and technical knowledge to aid in the performance of a task are implicit memories. Implicit means hidden, unspoken, embedded, or inherent. In a sense, habits are implicit memories because they reside in the unconscious mind. We do not deliberately recall how to do some things, such as brushing our teeth or driving, because they have become implicit memories, or habits (Aarts, 2000).

Implicit memory is a type of procedural memory in which previous experiences aid in the performance of a task without conscious awareness of recall. Riding a bike is an example of an implicit memory stored as a habit. Although the rider may not have ridden on a bike for many years, the ability to ride is easily recalled without consciously recalling a particular instance of actually riding a bike. Emotionally driven experiences often are stored as implicit memories (Eysenck, 2004).

Implicit memory also leads to the illusion-of-truth effect, which advocates subjects are more likely to perceive as true statements those they have already heard or that they are familiar with, regardless of their veracity. So the more often the false information is heard, the more real it becomes (Hasher, 1977).

Law enforcement officers are not exempt from using implicit memories; each day they successfully implement mentally linked behaviors to achieve objectives. Continually utilizing the same process, methodology, or techniques, creates a mental link between the repeated procedure and the objective. The more one engages in a task, the stronger the association becomes and the easier it is to complete the task without conscious effort. Law enforcement officers can develop implicit memories that become habits, if the behavior is routine and associated with a specific environment. The more frequently they engage in a particular behavior in similar circumstances or environments, the stronger the association becomes between the behavior and that situation. The more frequent the setting, the easier it is to produce the behavior. Subsequently, if a police officer repeatedly chooses a particular method to draw his weapon, it becomes more than just a technique; it becomes an instinctive behavior. Some people call this muscle memory. However, it is not the muscle remembering an action, but rather the officer's implicit memory. In simpler terms, the memory becomes a habit. A police officer's posture is an example of behavior directed habits. When standing and questioning an individual, police officers position their body and their hands in a particular position to facilitate a rapid response to possible physical attack. This becomes so ingrained they can find themselves unconsciously assuming that body posture even when speaking with family members (Thorn, 2010).

Explicit memory is a type of long-term memory requiring conscious thought and relates to time and place. For example, when you think of an occasion or item, such as an automobile, your memory can bring up a whole host of associated memories concerning an automobile. Explicit memory is also called autobiographical memory, because it consists of the recollection of singular events in the life of a person. It is the memory of life experiences centered on oneself. The more one references explicit memories, the easier they are to recall (Eysenck, 2004).

Explicit memory can become a cognitive habit when repetition of a thought decreases the biochemical resistance to that thought reoccurring. Imagine taking a walk through a dense forest. The first time you go through the forest, there is a lot of resistance to your passage. However, subsequent walks are less difficult. The first time an event requires a decision, the officer weighs many options and determines what decision is best applied. In subsequent events similar in nature, fewer options are considered. Ultimately, when in that circumstance, officers immediately make their decision without considering the options. When making a decision under a particular set of circumstances, cognitive resistance is reduced and the possibility of having that thought again increases. Cognitive habits are similar to remembered decisions. Cognitive habits for law enforcement officers include using consistent verbiage in report narratives and structuring a report in a particular manner (Thorn, 2010; Eysenck, 2004).

Although some people may confuse them, habits and conscious explicit memories are not the same. When remembering a procedure, you are aware that it is a memory and you understand on a cognitive level the relationship between actions and consequences of the actions. For example, if an officer had previously experienced a perpetrator turning his shirt inside out to conceal bloodstains, seeing seams and a tag exposed on another suspect's shirt may recall that earlier case. Habits are instinctive and persistent actions carried out regardless of integrated new information. This is especially evident under extreme stress (Yin, 2006).

STRESS AND HABITS

Law enforcement officers nationwide qualify with their weapons at the firing range on a regular basis. For many years, between shooting the prescribed number of rounds at targets placed at various distances, the officers were told to holster a safe and empty weapon. Firearm instruction was restructured to train police officers at the range to reload and holster only a fully loaded weapon in the 1980s. The shooting procedure changed due to the horrific consequence of stress induced habitual behavior. Shooting incidents during the 1980s revealed law enforcement officers were killed with empty weapons in their holsters. The officers in the midst of that firefight cognitively understood they needed to reload their weapon immediately and continue firing. Unfortunately, stress prompted habitual behavior led these officers to holster an empty weapon or recover empty brass casings before reloading their weapon. Because of a habitual response, police officers lost their lives (Grossman, 2004).

Stress and emotional distractions are counterproductive to intellectual responses to problems. Complex tasks utilize working memory, and affect the brain's ability to store and manage information. Under significant emotional stimulus, memory is restricted and the brain unconsciously relies upon habitual cognitive and behavioral responses. This means as an emotional situation increases in intensity, the ability to use logic for decision-making decreases. Under stress or when in a significantly emotional state, the brain takes everything already known about a situation and puts itself on an intellectual cruise control addressing the problem at hand with established habits. Unfortunately, if the established habits are poor, the outcome may be less than desirable or expected (Schwabe, 2009).

CONFIRMATION BIAS

Many law enforcement officers consider the majority of their cases as routine, even some death investigations. A seasoned detective may investigate a hundred or more self-inflicted shooting deaths. For investigators, crime scenes begin to take on a certain familiarity, and a quick assessment of any crime scene with a firearm found next to the victim may result in the investigator assuming the death is self-inflicted. The observations and actions of observers are influenced by their expectations. Before the actual investigation is initiated, the conclusion can be inappropriately established. When this happens, there is often an unconscious tendency to seek evidence that supports that pre-existing theory or opinion and a disregarding of evidence conflicting with the theory. Selectively focusing on evidence to support a conclusion, instead of integrating all evidence to form an impartial conclusion, is called *confirmation bias* (Turvey, 2009; Eysenck, 2004).

When confirmation bias is the basis for an investigation, officers may be tempted to cut corners in order to dedicate their efforts to cases they deem more important, more challenging, and even perhaps more worthy. With the majority of calls considered routine, officers may ignore proper procedure on a regular basis, thereby developing the mindset and behavioral habits of poorly structured investigative techniques. When an unusual or high profile crime occurs, that same officer feels enormous pressure to complete an accurate and thorough investigation in a timely manner. That pressure creates stress that in turn results in working memory loss. With hampered cognitive abilities, the officer may revert to habitual behaviors and habitual cognitive choices. Evidence suggests that the Dallas Police Department investigation was driven by confirmation bias stemming from the arrest of Lee Harvey Oswald. After all, the Dallas Police Department had their man; all they had to do was prove it (Turvey, 2009).

CONCLUSION

The Dallas Police Department's investigation of the Texas School Book Depository created doubt concerning their ability and truthfulness that is still being addressed today. Not all evidence was collected, the authenticity of the collected evidence is in question, and there is no documented and uninterrupted chain of custody for the collected evidence. Conflicting testimony is a strong indication of critical evidence being compromised and of crime scene staging for photography purposes. Overwhelming evidence suggests officers conducting the investigation inside the Texas School Book Depository were improperly supervised and failed to follow national or departmental protocols. The media had unrestricted access to the crime scene and evidence, compromising the integrity of the investigation. Officers improperly collected key evidence and then re-created the scene in an attempt to disguise that fact; and then these same officers testified under oath the crime scene had not been compromised.

The crime scene was processed by Studebaker, who was markedly inexperienced, poorly trained, and lacking the necessary skills for such an assignment without proper supervision. Items were collected without being photographed, and the shell casings and the boxes in the window were both moved and then incorrectly replaced before being photographed. Poor choices concerning photography, sketching, fingerprint processing, and the collection of evidence dominated the investigation of the Texas School Book Depository. It is apparent their investigation of the Texas School Book Depository was lacking and evidently Carl Day agreed.

> *DAY: The difference here was the national publicity and the confusion surrounding it, which limited our opportunity for doing our work exactly as it should have been done (Sneed, 1998, p. 237).*

There are several possible explanations as to why the Dallas Police Department failed to follow its own guidelines, and likely, it was a combination of several things. Belief Oswald was a single perpetrator and a desire to develop and utilize evidence to support that theory may have initiated confirmation bias, resulting in a narrow scope of evidence being pursued, processed, and collected. They may have inaccurately assessed the potential evidentiary value of items. The Dallas Police Department may have been seeking evidence that supported Oswald's guilt, while ignoring evidence that may have exonerated him or pointed to another perpetrator.

Maybe confirmation bias was the reason for such poor crime scene investigative work; maybe it was poor work habits. Regardless, a suspect was in custody and evidence was needed for trial. However, failing to follow the proper procedures concerning the processing of crime scenes can create reasonable doubt in the minds of the jury. There must be no suggestion of compromised evidence to ensure judgment is correctly and fairly administrative. If the goal of the Dallas Police Department was to provide a quality, comprehensive, and impartial investigation of the Texas School Book Depository in order to provide irrefutable evidence in the murder of President Kennedy, they failed. The basic processes for preserving, photographing, and collecting physical evidence used at the Texas School Book Depository were flawed. Inferior techniques to develop latent fingerprint evidence were utilized, potential evidence was not properly documented, protected, or collected in a timely manner, and evidence that could have identified an accomplice or exonerated Oswald may have been inadvertently disregarded.

There are people who believe the Dallas Police Department, under extreme circumstances, adequately performed their crime scene investigation in the Texas School Book Depository. Those supporters stress the investigative standards of today should not be used to judge work competed in 1963. However, the Dallas Police Department, and especially the supervisors, should be held accountable for not complying with the well-published and generally accepted national standards of 1963. Certainly, they are responsible for adhering to the self-proclaimed procedures of their own department. Unfortunately, it appears the investigation is resolutely established as severely deficient.

The Dallas Police Department likely wanted to provide a quality, complete and unbiased investigation of the Texas School Book Depository in order to provide undeniable evidence in the murder of President Kennedy, but they did not. Instead, the Dallas Police Department's crime scene investigative work is decisively inadequate; discounting forever the myth, they followed contemporaneous protocol and standards while processing the Texas School Book Depository in the shooting death of President Kennedy.

CHAPTER 2

EAR WITNESSES

T he cornerstone of the JFK assassination conspiracy controversy originated in witnesses' statements concerning gunshots originating from the Grassy Knoll. Every day we trust our proficiency to determine the location of the sounds. Is it possible, for some witnesses on that day in Dealey Plaza, that ability was faulty?

Witnesses reported the fatal headshot came from the Texas School Book Depository, behind the fence at the Grassy Knoll and from the triple overpass. Each witness firmly believed what they heard proved the location of the shooter. It seems improbable that persons in the same general location hearing gunshots would believe they came from various directions; however, that is exactly what happened.

SOUND AND HEARING

The auditory system is one of the human body's most intricate and mysterious of the sensory systems. Sound is pressure waves traveling outward from a vibrating source to the ears. Sounds have different characteristics like pitch, timbre, and intensity. The sound waves that arrive at the ears merge information from different sources to form a single complex pattern of vibrations that is conveyed through the stirrup, a bone in the ear, to the cochlea within the inner ear (Blauert, 1997).

Inside the cochlea are thousands of hair-like nerve endings called *cilia*. Vibrations of the cilia are transferred to the brain through the auditory nerve. The auditory perceptual system manages to sort out information about the different sounds from these complex conduits and identify individual sounds. This system is so complex that we can hear different types of sounds from different locations at the same time. Exactly how information is processed is not fully understood (Blauert, 1997).

There are two types of hearing: pattern hearing that is innate and localization, or spatial hearing, that is learned. We are born with the innate ability to perceive sound vibrations through the ear. Recognizing particular visual facial patterns help to identify specific individuals. In a similar manner, recognizing audio patterns allow us to identify sounds (Blauert, 1997).

Particular waves and frequencies develop characteristic patterns that the brain learns to distinguish as belonging to a certain sound. Pattern recognition identifies everything from words to bird songs. Localization hearing develops as we establish systems of pattern recognition in which the ears, eyes, and brain cooperate to perceive the accurate direction of a sound source. Localization identifies who is speaking and where the bird is located (Blauert, 1997).

SPATIAL HEARING OR LOCALIZATION

The ability to recognize the source or location of a particular sound is called *spatial hearing* or *localization*. With spatial hearing, we can determine the direction and distance of sounds. There are two major classes of information that the auditory system utilizes to localize sounds, direction, and distance. Direction is the variance in arrival time of sound waves between each ear. Distance is the perceived intensity of those sound waves. Direction perception is interpreted when receiving sound in one ear before the other. The sound of an approaching train indicates approach from a particular side when looking straight ahead. The intensity or volume of the sound indicates the distance from the train. The sound gets louder as the train approaches. If sound reaches both ears at the same time, up and down or front and back can be confused. That spatial uncertainty is referred to as the *Cone of Confusion* (Blauert, 1997).

Determining the direction or distance of sound is different from determining location or origin of sound. Defining the exact location of a sound employs the integration of the azimuth, zenith, and distance information. The azimuth, or horizontal angle coordinate, determines if a sound is located to the left or the right of a listener. The zenith, or elevation coordinate, distinguishes between sounds that are up or down, relative to the listener. Finally, the distance coordinate decides how far away a sound is from the receiver. It is by combining perceptions of horizontal angle, distance, and elevation that the brain determines the exact location of sound (Blauert, 1997).

There are times when localization is easily misinterpreted. The brain is capable of discriminating between very small differences in the arrival time of sounds when the distance travelled is short. For example, in an indoor setting, the walls of rooms are normally close enough that reflected sound waves provide accurate localization of sounds. However, sound waves that travel a great distance before reaching the ear can distort hearing and result in listeners inaccurately determining the origin of the sound. Hearing a distant siren outdoors and being unsure of its approaching direction is an illustration of the difficulty of distance sound localization. The clarity or quality of the sound is also a determining factor in localization. The origin of a sustained tone in a reverberant room is difficult to locate because the tone is diffused; but a sharp click can be precisely located (Blauert, 1997).

ORGANIZING SOUND

Spatial sound uses the brain's ability to determine where sound originates, and if that sound is important or insignificant. The ear, body, and brain work in harmony to decode correctly, a handful of simultaneous and possibly conflicting acoustical cues. The brain is constantly monitoring the surroundings for acoustical information used to navigate the environment. Spatial sound is critical in organizing acoustical environment. The brain separates sounds, then identifies and selects sounds of interest. When in a large room where people are speaking in conversations at different frequencies and intensities, spatial sound allows us to single out a particular voice. The ear hears the hum of the ventilation system, many conversations, chairs scraping the floor, and music playing. Spatial sound selects the particular sounds of interest and ignores non-essential sounds and voices allowing a conversation in a crowded room (Blauert, 1997).

The perception of the spatial aspects of sound is essential to safety and well-being. For instance, ascertaining the location of a growling dog, or crossing a busy city street both rely on localization. Alarms, horns and shouts all use localization. Spatial sound provides identification of a sound source within a few degrees of precision and in a fraction of a second (Blauert, 1997).

SURFACE DISTORTION

Sounds that travel directly from the source to the ear are direct sounds, and sounds that reflect off surfaces are indirect sounds. It is easier to interpret the location of direct sounds than indirect sounds. It is easier to interpret the location of indirect sounds in interior environments than indirect sounds in exterior environments. Echoes and reverberation outdoors result in difficulty determining sound localization because exterior environments present surfaces that vary in absorption and sound reflective characteristics. Locating a sound originating within a room with walls and ceiling of consistent reflective characteristics is easier than locating a sound originating in an open field (Goodridge, 1997).

Mixed acoustical surfaces result in poor determinations concerning direction because the sound waves are reflected in mixed time. The timing difference between when a sound is perceived by each ear assists in determining location origin from side to side; subsequently, variance in timing due to surface characteristics in reflected sound can affect correct localization or direction. Timing differences of only a few milliseconds can be distinguished, and at about 40 to 50 milliseconds, a distinct echo is heard. Although listeners may be aware of only the original or direct sound at delays of a few milliseconds, the brain processes the echoes and uses the variance in received sound to determine location. Therefore, reverberation, head position, orientation, and movement can distort the source signal and result in localization errors (Blauert, 1997).

Localization is possible when reflected sound waves from a single source reach the ears at different times. Localization interprets sound for both horizontal and vertical angles. When the delay between the first and second sounds is short, we normally perceive the sound origin as coming from the first sound perceived. Perceiving sound as coming from the source that reaches the ears first is the precedence effect. The intensity or loudness of the sound also influences decision-making in determining the source location. However, some reflected or indirect sounds may produce the same level of intensity as direct sounds, creating confusion in determining the sound source location (Goldstein, 2001).

DISTANCE DISTORTION

Increasing the distance the sound has to travel to the two ears results in an inability to determine which ear receives the sound first. When the source locations are far enough away, they create cones of confusion. That confusion can make correctly interpreting front and back, up and down and even some side angles impossible. Hearing a helicopter, but having to scan the sky to determine its location, demonstrates how distance inhibits the ability detect correct sound locations. A rifle fired from a distance creates that same phenomenon and hunters are often unable to determine the direction from which the shooter was firing (Popper, 2005).

Multiple surfaces with different reflective qualities create hearing cones of confusion. Distance or surfaces positioned at diverse vertical and horizontal angles also create hearing cones of confusion. Even when testing in an environment with less reflective characteristics, sound localization at increased distances was correctly detected only 81% of the time. Adding multiple surfaces with different reflective qualities at diverse vertical and horizontal angles would drop the percentage of determining the correct sound origin dramatically. Therefore, increased distance combined with disparity in elevation and a variety of reflective surfaces would significantly diminish the ability to determine correctly a sound's point of origin (Dorffner, 2001).

VISION AND LOCALIZATION

We tend to think of the five senses operating independently: we do not have to be able to touch in order to hear, we do not have to be able to taste in order to see. The five senses work together to bring clarity to perceptions. Hearing helps us to negotiate surroundings, holds strong emotional and communicative interest, and assists with the perception of distance and location. While we may think we hear only with our ears, vision plays an important role. A good example of vision assisting with hearing is easily demonstrated by having a conversation in a crowded room. A phenomenon commonly referred to as the cocktail party effect is known as the ability to focus listening attention on a single source amid a variety of conversations and background noise. Because we are looking at the person speaking, we are able to ignore the background noise and other conversations (Blauert, 1997).

The brain routinely integrates visual and audible information to ascertain the origin of sounds. Independent auditory localization is poor under typical conditions. Localization errors of 4° to 10° dominate the horizontal plane and increase dramatically when determining elevations. The detection area with fewer errors is forward on the horizontal plane. Errors in determining localization increase dramatically without visualization (Blauert, 1997).

Seeing a motorcycle identifies the source of the rumbling motor sound we hear. However, upon hearing the sound of the motor sound first, the driver will instinctively check the vehicle mirrors in order to visualize the location of the motorcycle and confirm the localization of the sound. Seeing the sound source always improves the accuracy of auditory localization. Typically, perception of localization is based upon audiovisual agreement. When we hear sound, we instinctively look in a particular direction to confirm the sound's origin. Recent findings show that while vision can complement auditory input, if the visual and auditory data is conflicting, the visual content will override the auditory content. Therefore, we are more likely to believe what we see than what we hear when analyzing data to determine localization (Ghazanfar, 2011).

The brain decides where a sound source is located largely based on visual cues. However, vision routinely overrides hearing. The role vision plays in auditory localization is so strong it overrides hearing in determining where a sound originated, even when the visual input is incorrect. When watching television the sound seems to come from the actors on the screen, although it may actually come from nearby speakers, which may be placed far from the television. An example of how visual perception can supersede the auditory input is demonstrated by the McGurk Effect.

THE MCGURK EFFECT

The *McGurk Effect* is the phenomena of visual cues overriding what the ears hear when defining localization. Researchers Harry McGurk and John McDonald conducted an unusual experiment in 1976. Experiments show when receiving conflicting visual and audio information, the visual signals consistently overrides audio signals. Subjects watched a videotape of a person pronouncing a syllable with open lip involvement and one with the lips closed. The audio track was altered and then synchronized with the picture. While the video subject actually said ga-ga, the listener heard ba-ba. When the research subjects watched the video they integrated the visual with the audio to conclude that a blended, third syllable, da-da had been spoken. To clarify, they did not identify the sound as the one that was actually spoken when the video was taped, nor did they choose the sound that was actually recorded. The research subjects were unaware they were given conflicting visual and audio information. The subjects consistently determined a blended third version was in the recording. Their response proved under conflict, vision always overrides hearing (McGurk, 1976).

There may have been an opportunity for witnesses of the assassination to experience the McGurk Effect. The ability of the mind to override what it hears when processing conflicting visual information may have affected persons in Dealey Plaza. Witnesses who saw smoke reported the shots originated from that location. The opportunity for the visual override of hearing localization increases when considering the surface and distance distortion experienced by assassination witnesses.

THE SOUND OF GUNSHOTS

Comprehending the acoustical characteristics of gunshots requires a basic understanding of how they are created. There are three distinct categories of sounds created when firing a weapon: mechanical action, muzzle blast, and supersonic shock wave. The shock wave and muzzle blast sounds, like other physical wave phenomena, are subject to reflection, dilution, absorption, diversion, focusing, and other wave modifications as they propagate (Maher, 2007).

ACOUSTICAL PROPERTIES
All surfaces have some acoustical properties in that they will absorb, reflect, or transmit sound striking them. Sound wave reflection, absorption, and diffusion alter gunshot sound localization (Maher, 2007).

When a sound wave strikes a flat surface, some energy is absorbed by the surface, reducing its intensity. The remainder of the wave reflects off the surface at a new angle. Soft, porous materials can absorb 80 % or more of the intensity of sound waves. Hard surfaces, such as asphalt or concrete, reflect most of the sound wave. When sound waves strike vegetation-covered ground, reflected waves are diffused in various directions. Multi-directional reflected sound also diminishes the perceived volume or intensity. The brain cannot distinguish arrival times or intensities of dense clusters of sound waves that have bounced off multiple surfaces. Secondary sound waves, created by reflection and diffusion, overlap and create interference with each other and the original waves, making the sound less clear and correct localization difficult (Kang, 2010; Schindler, 2007).

MECHANICAL ACTION
For some firearms, the sound of the mechanical action may be detectable. This includes the sound of the trigger and hammer mechanism, the ejection of spent cartridges, and the positioning of new ammunition by the gun's automatic or manual loading system. The mechanical action is generally considerably quieter than the muzzle blast and projectile shock wave. Mechanical action is normally detected by someone who is experienced with these sounds being located close enough to the firearm to hear them (Maher, 2007).

MUZZLE BLAST
When you pull the trigger of a gun, a spring mechanism hammers a metal firing pin into the back end of the cartridge, striking the primer. The primer compound ignites, sending a flame into the cartridge case. Gunpowder in the cartridge case starts to burn, causing it to change from a solid material to a gas. This change creates pressure within the cartridge, which in turn forces the bullet down the barrel of the gun. This pressure can be 3000 pounds per square inch or more. The rapidly expanding propellant gas produces noise known as the pressure wave. As the expanding gases exit the barrel of the weapon, they create a loud bang, because the gas is exceeding the speed of sound. The sound of the explosion is discharged from the gun in all directions, but the majority of the acoustic energy is expelled in the direction the gun barrel is pointing (Maher, 2007).

The explosive shock wave and sound energy emanating from the barrel is referred to as the muzzle blast. Muzzle blasts are extremely high intensity acoustic waves that are many times louder than a jet engine and last only a few milliseconds. The muzzle blast acoustic wave radiates outward in a spherical fashion, spreading through the air at the speed of sound while interacting with adjacent surfaces, obstacles, temperature, wind, and humidity (Maher, 2007).

SUPERSONIC SHOCK WAVE

In addition to the muzzle blast, if the bullet travels at supersonic speed, the supersonic projectile's passage through the air launches an acoustic shock wave propagating outward from the bullet's path. The shock wave expands in conic fashion behind the bullet, with the wave front spreading outward at the speed of sound. The direction of the shooter can be determined by the muzzle blast, but not by the shock wave (Beck, 2011).

DISTORTING GUNSHOT SOUNDS

Gunshots produce several distinct and separate noises of varying intensities. It is possible for a shooter to manipulate the resulting sound of gunshots through a variety of techniques. This can be accomplished by several methods, such as subsonic ammunition, suppressors, and muzzle flash protectors. Any of these techniques can influence the perception of a gunshot location source by changing the sound characteristics.

WEATHER DISTORTION

Wind, air temperature, and relative humidity all affect correct assessment of localization. Although wind speeds are an insignificant fraction of the speed of sound, wind alteration causes a direction-dependent change in sound speed. If the air itself is moving due to wind, the sound spreading through the air will be carried in the moving air. The wind effect can be viewed as a shift in the origin of the sound. In other words, the trajectory of the muzzle blast sound wave or supersonic sound wave is altered by the wind as it moves toward the listener; so by the time it arrives, the perceived location of the sound origin has been shifted (Maher, 2007).

The speed of sound in air increases with increasing temperature. Each degree Celsius rise in temperature increases the speed of sound by approximately 0.61 meters per second. The air temperature changes with elevation, resulting in inconsistencies in sound speed. In the daytime, the ground surface is often warmer than the upper air. Under these conditions, sound distribution is bent upwards slightly due to the temperature gradient. Conversely, when the temperature near the ground is likely to be lower than that of the upper air, sound waves are bent downwards. Bending sound waves distorts localization. The dissipation of sound waves also increases exponentially with increasing humidity. Localization at distances is difficult with increased relative humidity. The farther the listener is from the discharged firearm, the greater the opportunity for all atmospheric conditions to affect localization (Maher, 2007).

According to atmospheric records from Love Field at 11:55am, the wind was 13 knots, WSW (approximate bearing 248°). At 12:30pm, it was again 13 knots, this time due W (bearing 270°). At 1:00 pm, the wind had increased to 17 knots and was WNW (292°). Love Field is about 6 miles northwest of Dealey Plaza. The air temperature in Dealey Plaza at the time of the assassination was 65° Fahrenheit (HSCA 8H26).

Environmental Distortion

Snipers can effectively mask their location by positioning themselves so the bullet will travel adjacent to large hard objects. The surface will reflect the "crack" sound from the supersonic bullet much more effectively than the "bang" sound from a non-suppressed shot. As a result, it is impossible for an observer to tell from which direction the shot emanates; it will sound as if it is coming from every direction in a perfectly chosen environment.

Dealey Plaza has a variety of large, hard surfaces: three streets, adjacent multiple story buildings, a triple overpass with abutments and concrete pavilions, all with various elevations. There is a wide array of absorption, attenuation, and reflection properties of objects encountered by the acoustical waves in Dealey Plaza, as a result, sound reverberates in a confusing manner.

Suppressors Distortion

Echoes may have easily inflated the number of shots reported during the assassination and interfered with the calculation of the source. Hearing the shock wave from the bullet, combined with muzzle blast and an echo would create much uncertainty in the listener. Tests indicate a person located near the muzzle blast was more likely to report that as the origin of the shots. Similarly, a person near the Texas School Book Depository was more likely to report that location as the origin of the shots. A suppressed muzzle shock is created utilizing equipment or by firing from inside a building window. Without the sound of the muzzle blast, listeners would only have the shock wave and consequential reverberations on which to base their conclusions. It would have been to the shooter's advantage to distort the sound origin by use of a suppressor, firing alongside a hard surface or discharging the weapon from within a vehicle or building (Minnery, 1981).

Suppressors are occasionally described as silencers. This is inaccurate, as the sound is dampened but not eliminated by using a suppressor. People generally associate suppressors with handguns, as opposed to rifles. You cannot silence rifle bullets that travel at supersonic speeds creating a sonic boom. A suppressor screws on to the end of the barrel of the weapon to suppress the sound of the muzzle blast. The volume of the suppressor is normally twenty to thirty times greater than the volume of the barrel of the weapon. With the suppressor attached, once the weapon is fired, the pressurized gas behind the bullet has a larger space in which to expand. As a result, the pressure of the hot gas falls significantly, perhaps to as little as 100 pounds per inch. The pressure released is significantly lower when the bullet exits through the hole in the suppressor; as a result, the sound of the gun firing is quieter (Minnery, 1981).

With a high velocity weapon, it is very difficult to do more than suppress or distort the sound. Muzzle blasts can be muffled, however, the sound of the shock wave created by a high velocity bullet cannot be modified. Suppressors are appliances with simple baffles that muffle muzzle blasts, much like a muffler on a car. Gun suppressors work primarily by slowing the release of the propellant gases and converting some of the noise energy to heat. The suppressor contains specially designed chambers or baffles to slow the release of the propellant gases; the sound ultimately converts to heat in these chambers. Bursting a balloon demonstrates suppressor activity. If you prick a tightly inflated balloon with a pin, the resulting pop will make a loud noise. The resulting pop will make very little noise, if the balloon is only partially inflated (Minnery, 1981).

The greater the noise generated by firing a weapon, the larger the suppressor would need to be in order to restrict the intensity of the sound. Suppressors for rifles are bulky devices and difficult to conceal. However, despite the engineering difficulties in devising suppressors for rifles, the utility of silenced weapons has not been lost on the United States military (Minnery, 1981).

MILITARY USE OF SUPPRESSORS

In 1940, the M-1 .30 caliber carbine was developed in England for the United States military. It came equipped with a non-detachable suppressor developed by Bell Laboratory, integrated onto the barrel with a six-groove, right-hand twist. In 1947, under a special contract with the Remington Arms Company the silenced sniper version of a .30 caliber rifle was developed. The Springfield M190384 came equipped with a detachable Maxim silencer. The M1 had a range of 100 yards and the Springfield M190384 had a range of 300 yards, meaning either of these weapons had an effective range for use within Dealey Plaza. Neither of the weapons had a silenced shot. The M1 carbine sounded like a sharp handclap followed by a distinctive hissing sound. Subsequently, the weapons were not bulk manufactured; only 1000 trial weapons were ever produced. They were not truly silenced weapons, merely quieted. The silenced sniper version of the .30 caliber rifle was released to the CIA at an unknown date (US Department of Army, 1968).

It appears by 1963, the CIA did possess these suppressed sniper weapons. As of 1963, the best available suppressed rifles were still the modified M1 and the Springfield rifles. Suppressor technology remained at a virtual standstill into the 1960s. In 1968, the United States Army conducted a study, which concluded the best-suppressed rifles continued to be the M-1 .30 caliber carbine and the Springfield M1903A4 (US Department of Army, 1968).

1909 SUPPRESSOR EXPERIMENT

In 1909, Hiram Maxim conducted an experiment addressing the ability to determine where a rifle shot originated when the shooter was using a suppressor. The experiment was set up with a trench dug below ground that would contain the listeners. Riflemen fired from points north, south, east, and west of the trench. The listeners seated in the trench were to determine the direction from which the rifle had been fired (Maxim, 1909).

Experimental rifle shots were fired only 200 yards away from listeners, while standing directly out in the open. First, there was a loud crack, then the boom of the gun. The bullet reached listeners first traveling at a velocity of 2600 feet per second. The noise from the muzzle blast, traveling at about 1100 feet per second, was heard as a distinct second sound. Hearing two separate sounds enabled the listeners to locate with absolute accuracy from which direction the bullet had been fired (Maxim, 1909).

The next set of experimental shots was completed with a suppressor; the signal was given and the first crack was heard overhead. The listeners looked at each other in amazement; the second sound they expected to hear did not materialize. Without the second sound of the muzzle blast, the listeners were unable to determine from which direction the rifleman had fired. This confusion in determining the point of origin of the sound was magnified in cases where there were trees or hills in the landscape that formed reflective surfaces (Maxim, 1909).

In the Maxim experiment it was determined the sound from the rifle in an open field radiated outward 3 1/4 miles in a circular pattern. This suppressor created an oblong sound pattern approximately 3/8 of a mile behind the weapon, and extending out 3/8 of a mile on each side of the line of sight. This long zone of noise created confusion in determining the location of origin of the shot. Confusion concerning the origin of the sound was exaggerated when reflective surfaces such as buildings, hills, or trees were incorporated into the experiment (Maxim, 1909).

SHOCK WAVE AND MUZZLE BLAST CONFUSION

A rifle bullet travels at supersonic speeds, generating a shock wave that spreads acoustically in the shape of a cone, with the bullet as the tip. The muzzle blast is propagated at the speed of sound and spreads out spherically from the weapon. The shock wave and the muzzle blast are both very loud and can be confused. The time between the arrivals of the two sounds to a given listener can vary considerably depending on their position with respect to the location of the rifle and the path of the bullet. The relative intensity from the two sounds can also vary from one listener location to another. As the sounds arrive closer together, the ability to distinguish between the muzzle blast, indicating the source, and the shock wave created by the path of the bullet is greatly diminished (Green, 1979).

FRONT TO BACK REVERSAL

The sound of shock waves created by the projectile and the muzzle blast are very brief. Listeners would otherwise have an opportunity to execute head motion to tell if the source was in front or behind. Shock waves last approximately one millisecond and muzzle blast waves last approximately five milliseconds. Therefore, front to back reversal in determining the source is common. We are much less adept at localizing sound sources behind us than to the front. For a sound directly behind us, we receive almost no direct signal, but only diffracted and reflected signals, as sound waves move around the head and reflect off other surfaces (Green, 1979; Schindler, 2007).

When the muzzle blast is suppressed, listeners rely on the shock wave to determine localization. Sound localization based upon the shock wave yields incorrect localization of sound source. This means witnesses in Dealey Plaza that were close to the path of the bullet were very likely incorrect in their judgment on the source of the sound and the placement of the shooter (Green, 1979).

LOCALIZATION ERRORS

We routinely trust the ability to determine the location of the source of a sound utilizing spatial hearing; whether by looking in the direction of an approaching ambulance at an intersection or by determining whom in a group is speaking at a party. However, spatial hearing or localization can be degraded under a variety of circumstances.

1. Inexperience or lack of familiarity with a particular sound can hinder sound localization (Blauert, 1997).
2. When insecure as to the location of an unfamiliar sound, research shows the most reported direction is behind (Blauert, 1997).
3. Auditory temporal processing, utilized in sound localization, degenerates congruent with advancing age (Dobreva, 2011).
4. Very high frequency or very low frequency sound waves result in localization errors (Yost, 2004).
5. Reverberation or sound reflection increases the ability to determine the distance of a source but degrades localization (Santarelli, 1999).

6. If visual and auditory data is conflicting, the visual content will override the auditory content, which may result in erroneously perceived localization (Ghazanfar, 2011).
7. Wind, air temperature, and relative humidity in the air affect correct assessment of localization. Moreover, the farther the hearer is from the discharged firearm, the greater the opportunity for all atmospheric conditions to affect correct localization (Maher, 2007).

Because the sound waves created by a projectile last approximately 1 milliseconds and muzzle blast sound waves last approximately 5 milliseconds, listeners can develop "cones of confusion" resulting in front to back reversal in localization determinations (Green, 1979).

Over time, the brain learns to recognize specific wave forms and frequencies as characteristic patterns belonging to a certain sound, much as we recognize a particular person's face by a visual pattern. We also establish systems of pattern recognition in which the ear, eye, and brain collaborate to perceive the direction and location of the sound sources with some accuracy. Localization can be mistaken under certain circumstances that may have affected the witnesses in Dealey Plaza.

INTERFERING ECHOES OR REVERBERATION

The buildings around Dealey Plaza cause strong echoes or reverberations. Some echoes followed the initial sound by 0.5 to 1.5 seconds. Echoes of this magnitude may have easily inflated the number of shots reported during the assassination and interfered with the calculation of the source. Hearing the shock wave from the bullet, combined with muzzle blast and an echo would create much uncertainty in the listener (Green, 1979).

Tests indicate a person located near the muzzle blast was more likely to report that as the origin of the shots. Similarly, a person near the Texas School Book Depository was more likely to report that location as the origin of the shots. If a suppressed muzzle shock was created either mechanically or by firing from inside the Depository window, the listeners would only have the shock wave and consequential reverberations on which to base their conclusions (Green, 1979).

HSCA AND SOUND LOCALIZATION

The House Select Committee on Assassinations (HSCA) contracted D. M. Green of Bolt, Beranek, and Newman Incorporated to analyze the statements of Dealey Plaza witnesses concerning their perceived determination of where the gunshots' sound were originating. Green analyzed the statements of 178 persons in Dealey Plaza and published the results in a report titled "Analysis of Earwitness Reports Relating to the Assassination of President John F. Kennedy." The analysis report contained an examination of statements given by witnesses present in Dealey Plaza in 1963. The Green analysis report encompassed an examination of how sounds of gunfire in Dealey Plaza would be perceived by witnesses in different locations, and reports of trained listeners who were present during acoustical reconstruction in August 1978. The report stressed all witness statements must be studied with a clear understanding of acoustical characteristics of gunfire in a reverberating environment (Green, 1979).

The statements were obtained in interviews conducted by the Dallas Police Department and the FBI and from sworn testimony in the Warren Report. The House Select Committee on Assassinations report indicated, of the 100 witnesses who were able to determine where they believe the shots originated, only forty-nine indicated the Texas School Book Depository. Twenty-one believed the Grassy Knoll was the origin of a shot. Surprisingly, thirty witnesses perceived the shots as originating from an additional unspecified location (Green, 1979).

The House Select Committee on Assassinations also addressed shots that may have been recorded on the Dallas Police dictabelt, allegedly made from a patrol officer's microphone in Dealey Plaza at the time of the shooting. In May 1978, the Committee contracted with Bolt, Beranek, and Newman, Inc. to complete acoustical analysis. Scientist James Barger identified six impulses that could have been caused by a loud noise, such as a gunshot, a conclusion suggesting more than one shooter, and therefore a conspiracy. Seeking confirmation, the House Select Committee pursued an independent review of Barger's analysis by Queen's College, New York, Professor Mark Weiss and his research associate, Ernest Aschkenasy. Weiss and Aschkenasy determined Barger's analysis was valid, resulting in acoustical test performed in Dealey Plaza in August 1978 (HSCA 5:645-689).

Microphones were placed at thirty-six separate positions, and shots were fired from the sixth floor southeast corner of the Texas School Book Depository Building window and from the area behind the fence on the Grassy Knoll. Four hundred and thirty two shots were recorded. The acoustical characteristics of the shots were compared with the six impulses noted on the dictabelt recording, totaling of 2592 comparisons. Barger testified before House Select Committee on Assassinations that the studies indicated the 1963 recording contained four sounds attributed to probable gunshots. Three of the impulses coordinated with an origin point at the Texas School Book Depository sixth floor, and one impulse, the third in the sequence, corresponded with an origination point on the Grassy Knoll, with a probability of 50 percent. Unfortunately, the tests ignored other locations as possible origins of a shot (HSCA 5:645-689).

Weiss and Aschkenasy considered the impact of echo-generating sources around the vicinity of the knoll, thereby calculating what acoustical characteristics would have been created by a shot from the Grassy Knoll location. Each location of a microphone relative to a shooter's location by echoes generated off constant structures would produce a unique sound travel pattern that they referred to as a sound fingerprint. The experts considered numerous variables, including air temperature in 1963 and buildings structured after 1963, into consideration. Their conclusion that impulse number three was a shot fired from the Grassy Knoll was supported by a certainty factor of at least ninety-five percent (HSCA 5:555-624).

Regrettably, various and subsequent studies addressing the experiments have both refuted and confirmed the test methods and results. These conflicting conclusions are also hampered by ambiguity concerning the location of the motorcycle recording the sounds on the dictabelt, the accuracy of the methodology used to conduct the tests, and limiting considered gunfire origins to only two locations—leaving the nonprofessional in a quandary as what to believe.

Stewart Galanor, an assassination researcher, developed a database which allowed the correlations between witness locations and their perception of origin and number of shots (Galanor 2002).

DEALEY PLAZA LOCALIZATION

The ability to locate the origin of a sound is dependent upon several elements.

1. The direction the listener is facing
2. The distance the listener is from the sound
3. Elevation of the listener relative to the sound source
4. The acoustical characteristics of the environment
5. Atmospheric conditions (Blauert, 1997)

These variables affect the hearing perception of each of the listeners differently, resulting in conflicting interpretation of the sound. Subsequently, as shown by witness testimony, a correct understanding of the location of source of gunshots fired in Dealey Plaza was challenging at best and emphatically deemed unreliable (Blauert, 1997).

Some witnesses reported hearing more than one type of gunshot. This is significant, as research indicates ear witnesses seldom make a mistake when making a distinction between different weapon sounds fired in the same incident. They report hearing pops, bangs, or booms; but when a single ear witness reports a combination of sounds, it is a strong indication more than one weapon was fired. What makes a gun sound the way it does is determined by three key factors: (a) the caliber and amount of grain of the bullet, (b) the length of the barrel, (c) and the environment. A weapon of similar caliber with a shorter barrel has a louder sound and is higher in pitch. Longer barrels are lower in pitch and not as loud (Clark, 2011; Garrison, 2003).

The House Select Committee on Assassinations report indicated forty-nine witnesses (27.5 percent) believed the shots had come from the Texas School Book Depository. Twenty-one witnesses (11.8 percent) believed the shots had come from the Grassy Knoll. Thirty witnesses (16.9 percent) believed the shots had originated elsewhere. Seventy-eight witnesses (43.8 percent) were unable to tell from which direction the shots were fired. Only four individuals believed shots had originated from more than one location (Green, 1979).

One would anticipate witnesses in similar areas of the Plaza would have similar perceptions of the location of the origin of the shots. Surprisingly, witnesses located in the same general area did not consistently perceive the shots as coming from a single location. Witnesses to the shooting in Dealey Plaza also had differences of opinion concerning the number of shots. A sampling of witnesses positioned in similar locations within the Plaza provided diverse sound localization information, in addition to differences of opinion concerning the number of shots.

WITNESSES AND LOCALIZATION

Witnesses in different locations within Dealey Plaza perceived the gunshots as originating from varied locations. Additionally, witnesses in the same locations perceived the sounds as coming from different locations within the Plaza.

WITNESSES ON THE TRIPLE OVERPASS
Sound Origin: Texas School Book Depository
James Simmons, employee for Union Terminal Railroad, advised it was his opinion the shots came from the direction of the Texas School Book Depository (CE1416, 22H 833).

At the time of the assassination, Dallas Police Department Officer J. D. Foster was standing on top of the triple underpass. Concerning the source of the shots, he stated shots came from the back, in toward the corner of Elm and Houston Streets (6H251).

Sound Origin: Grassy Knoll
Sam M. Holland, signal supervisor for Union Terminal Railroad stated he looked over toward the arcade and trees and saw a puff of smoke come from the trees. He said he heard three more shots after the first shot, but observed only one puff of smoke (19H 480).

Sound Origin Identified As: Unknown
Ewell Cowsert, switchman for Union Terminal Railroad advised just as President Kennedy's car passed the Texas School Book Depository Building, he heard two or three shots ring out, and saw President Kennedy slump forward in his seat. Cowsert said he has no idea where the shots came from and as the area near the Texas School Book Depository Building was a scene of extreme confusion, he could not recall having noticed any one person (22H 836).

Walter Luke Winborn, Union Terminal Railroad switchman, heard three distinct shots ring out. He was not able to ascertain exactly where the shots were fired from and his attention remained on President Kennedy and the motorcycle escort. He stated, however, the shots sounded as if they all came from the same area (CE 1422, 22H 833).

WITNESSES NEAR THE INTERSECTION OF MAIN AND HOUSTON STREETS
Sound Origin: Unknown
Roger D. Craig, a Dallas County Sheriff's Deputy, testified it was hard to tell the source of the shots due to the echo. He felt there were actually two explosions with each shot (6H263).

Sound Origin: Grassy Knoll
Harold Elkins stated he immediately ran to the area between the railroads and the Texas School Book Depository, thinking that was where it sounded like the shots had been fired (19H540).

WITNESSES NEAR THE INTERSECTION OF ELM AND HOUSTON STREETS
Sound Origin: Unknown
Martha Reed, a Texas School Book Depository employee, stated she did not know where the shots came from (CE 1381, 22H669).

Carl Jones, a Texas School Book Depository employee, was located on the Depository front steps. He had no idea where the shots came from that killed President Kennedy (CE 1381, 22H657).

Sound Origin: Triple Overpass
Dolores Kounas, a Texas School Book Depository employee, was standing on the south side of Elm near the intersection of Houston. Kounas told the FBI she heard three shots. She also stated, "It sounded as though the shots were coming from the triple underpass" (CE 1436, 22H846).

Virgie Baker, a bookkeeper at the Texas School Book Depository, was located in front of the depository building. Baker indicated he heard three shots, stating, "It sounded as though these sounds were coming from the direction of the triple underpass" (7H510).

Ochus Campbell was Vice President of the Texas School Book Depository and stood in front of the book depository. Campbell stated he heard shots being fired from a point that he thought was near the railroad tracks located over the viaduct on Elm Street (CE 1381, 22H638).

Wesley Frazier was a Texas School Book Depository employee who was located on the depository front steps. In his March 11, 1964 Warren Commission testimony he indicated hearing three shots. Concerning the origin of the shots, Frazier stated, "Well to be frank with you, I thought it come from down there, you know, where that underpass is" (2H234).

Sound Origin: Grassy Knoll
Joe Marshall Smith, a Dallas Police Officer, stated, "I heard the shots and thought they were coming from bushes of the overpass" (CE 1358, 22H600).

WITNESSES IN THE TEXAS SCHOOL BOOK DEPOSITORY
Sound Origin: Texas School Book Depository
Bonnie Ray Williams, an employee of Texas School Book Depository, was looking out a window on the fifth floor. In his Dallas Police Department report, Williams stated he heard two shots, which sounded like they came right over his head (Volume 24H 229).

Sound Origin: Grassy Knoll
Victoria Adams, the office survey representative for Scott Foresman Company, was looking out the window on the fourth floor of the Texas School Book Depository. She testified before the Warren Commission stating, "And we heard a shot, and it was a pause, and then a second shot, and then a third shot. It sounded like a firecracker or cannon at a football game; it seemed as if it came from the right below, rather than from the left above" (6H388).

Dorothy Ann Gardner was a Texas School Book Depository employee located by a window on the fourth floor of the Texas School Book Depository. She recalled hearing three gunshots. Concerning the origin of the shots, she stated, "I thought at the time the shots were reported, they came from a point to the west of the building" (CE 1381, 22H648).

WITNESSES IN THE MOTORCADE
Sound Origin: Texas School Book Depository
Secret Service Agent George Hinckley, located in the follow-up car, described three gunshots. Concerning the origin of the shots, Hinckley said, "It appeared to come from the right and rear and seemed to me to be at ground level" (18H762).

United States Senator Ralph Yarborough was in the Vice President's limousine. He said, "I heard three shots and no more. All seem [*sic*] to come from my right rear" (7H440).

Sound Origin: Grassy Knoll
Secret Service Agent Forrest Sorrels, located in the lead car testified he heard three shots. Concerning the origin of the shots, he stated, "I looked towards the top of the terrace to my right, as the sound of the shots seemed to come from that direction" (7H345-346).

Sound Origin: Overpass
Dallas Police Department Motorcycle Officer Bobby Hargis recalled hearing two shots. Concerning the origin of the shots, he stated, "At that time there was something in my head that said that they probably could have been coming from the railroad overpass" (6H294).

Secret Service Agent Paul Landis was in the Secret Service follow-up car. Landis said, "my reaction at this time was that the shot came from somewhere towards the front, but I did not see anyone on the overpass and looked along the right-hand side of the road." Concerning the number of shots, Landis stated he did not recall hearing a third shot (18H759).

David Powers, a Presidential aide, was located in the Secret Service follow-up car. Powers said, "My first impression was that the shots came from the right and overhead, but I also had a fleeting impression that the noise appeared to come from the front, in the area of the triple overpass" (7H473).

Sound Origin: Unknown
B. J. Martin, Dallas Police Motorcycle Officer riding to the left rear of the limousine stated, "I couldn't tell from which direction it was coming—any of the shots" (6H289).

Secret Service Agent William McIntyre, located in the follow-up car, indicated he heard three shots. Concerning the source of the shots, he stated, "None of us could determine the origin of the shots" (18H747).

WITNESSES ON THE GRASSY KNOLL
Sound Origin: Grassy Knoll
Emmet Hudson, the groundskeeper for Dealey Plaza, was seated on the steps of the Grassy Knoll. During his Warren Commission testimony, he stated he heard three shots. "The shots that I heard definitely came from behind and above me" (7H560).

William Eugene Newman, a mechanical engineer, was standing on the north side of Elm Street. He thought the shot came from the garden directly behind him, was on an elevation from where he was, right on the curb (19H490).

Sound Origin: Texas School Book Depository
Charles Hester stated he heard two shots fired from what appeared to be a building located on the corner of Elm Street and Houston Street (CE 1429, 19H478).

Sound Origin: Unknown
When Abraham Zapruder, an owner of a garment company, was asked about the number of shots he heard, he responded, "I thought I heard two, it could be three, because to my estimation I thought he was hit on the second—I really don't know." A few moments later, he testified, "I never even heard a third shot." Zapruder, when asked if he formed an opinion at the time as to what direction the shots came from, responded, "No." He later elaborated by stating, "There was too much reverberation. There was an echo, which gave me a sound all over" (7H572).

WITNESSES IN THE MEDIAN BETWEEN ELM AND MAIN STREETS
Sound Origin: Grassy Knoll
Jean Hill was located on the south side of Elm Street near the limousine. In her March 24, 1964 deposition, she indicated hearing 4 to 6 shots (6H207). Concerning the source of the shots, she stated, "I frankly thought they were coming from the Knoll" (6H212).

Sound Origin: Unknown:
Mary Moorman indicated she could not determine where the shots came from (CE 1426, 22H838).

Based upon the sampling of witness testimony, there appears to be no consensus in audibly locating the origin of the gunshots within Dealey Plaza; nor does there appear to be consistency in determining the number of shots fired within Dealey Plaza. In fact, every generalized location within the Plaza had witnesses maintaining opposing conclusions concerning the origin of the gunshots.

HSCA FINDINGS

The House Select Committee on Assassinations determined there were three basic errors in judgment relating to the source, based on Green's report: confusion was between the shock wave and the muzzle blast, front to back reversal, and misjudgment due to interfering echoes. The buildings around Dealey Plaza caused strong reverberations or echoes, making localization difficult. A muzzle blast can be muffled mechanically with a suppressor or shooting from inside a building. Either process would have resulted in localization based primarily on the shock wave, creating extreme uncertainty and disagreement for the origin of the shots. As a result, no one witness can be assigned any more credibility than another can. However, despite the various causes for confusion, if there had been shots from more than one location, they should have been distinctive and different enough to result in a larger number of witnesses reporting multiple localization origins (Green, 1979).

Localization accuracy depends mainly on elements such as the symmetry of the auditory system of the listener, the type and behavior of the sound source, and the acoustic conditions of the surrounding space. It also depends on the familiarity of the listener with the sound being interpreted and on the visual cues available to the listener. Consequently, locating the source of gunshots within Dealey Plaza was complicated. Moreover, the resulting sounds were likely distorted by echo or reverberation from the various reflective surfaces, topography, and buildings in the Plaza. Sound waves reaching listeners, in unexpected and inconsistent manners, result in misleading interpretation of direction and distance (Green, 1979).

Audio studies within Dealey Plaza show the further the listeners stand from the muzzle blast, the more likely their localization conclusion will be incorrect. The closer the listener is to the path of the bullet, the more likely the localization of the sound will be incorrect. This incorrect conclusion occurs because the listener is standing near the shock wave. This means witnesses in Dealey Plaza close to the path of the bullet were very likely incorrect in their judgment on the source of the sound and the placement of the shooter.

Tests indicate a person located near the muzzle blast was more likely to interpret correctly the origin of the shots. However, if the muzzle blast is complicated by reverberation, a front to back confusion may occur. Moreover, if a shot had a suppressed muzzle blast, created either mechanically or by firing from inside the Depository window, the listeners would only have the shock wave and its consequential reverberations on which to base their conclusions (Green, 1979).

CONCLUSION

Every day we trust our ability to determine the location of the source of a sound by utilizing localization or spatial hearing. We instinctively use localization when determining who in a group is speaking or when hearing a siren at an intersection. Spatial hearing, or localization, can be degraded under a variety of circumstances. The most fundamental explanation for directionality in hearing is based on the difference in intensity and timing in which the two ears perceive sound. But perception can be distorted if the sound source is short in length, of unusually low or high frequency, of equal or almost equal distance from both ears of the listener, created under certain atmospheric conditions, perceived by a person in echoic environments, experienced in different sound source and listener elevations, or experienced by persons close to the source.

Visual input can control where the brain believes sound is originating, even when the audio cues indicate the sound is coming from a different location. Because vision plays such a strong role in localization, seeing something that correlates visually with the sound may mislead the hearer in determining the origin of the sound.

Dealey Plaza has a wide variety of vertical and horizontal surfaces with an extensive range of reflective and absorptive characteristics and elevations. The excessive number of echoes created within Dealey Plaza may have easily inflated the number of shots reported during the assassination and dramatically interfered with the calculation of the source. Hearing the shock wave from the bullet, combined with muzzle blast and multiple echo reverberations, would create considerable uncertainty in the listener. Witnesses' ability to determine the number and source of gunshots would depend upon their perception of the received sound wave's angle, elevation, distance and reflection or absorption. The most significant influence is distance, so the further away the hearer was from the shooter, the less likely he was to identify the shooter's correct location.

Visual cues, distance from the muzzle blast, distance and angle to the sonic wave, reverberation and echoes from the environment, elevation as related to the muzzle blast and sonic wave, and the intensity or loudness of a sound all influence the ability to locate correctly the origin of the sound. The witnesses in Dealey Plaza dealt with all of these factors. Witnesses were at different elevations, distances, and angles to muzzle blast and sonic waves traveling at different elevations. Subsequently, as shown by witness testimony, correct interpretation of the location of the source of gunshots fired in Dealey Plaza is problematic at best.

The basis of conspiracy originally centered on witness claims of hearing gunshots from the Grassy Knoll or the triple overpass. Locating the source of gunshots within Dealey Plaza was complex. The sounds were likely distorted by echo or reverberation from the various reflective surfaces. Sound waves reached listeners in unanticipated and erratic manners. As a result, basing the location of possible shooters in Dealey Plaza solely on the statements of ear witnesses is categorically unreliable.

CHAPTER 3

BLOOD IN ZAPRUDER IS FAKED

A stunned nation watched the shooting death of President Kennedy on television with startling clarity for the first time in 1975. For many viewers, the back and to the left movement of the President following the headshot established the legitimacy of a shot from the front. Conversely, advocates of a single shooter from behind the President believe the Zapruder film depicts exiting blood forcefully pushing the President backward. Soon, the blood became the focus of attention, and advocates of an altered film determined the blood in the Zapruder film was irrefutably faked.

ABRAHAM ZAPRUDER

Abraham Zapruder was born in Kovel, Ukraine in 1905. His Russian-Jewish family immigrated to the United States in 1920 in the wake of the Russian Civil War. Zapruder worked as a clothing pattern maker in Manhattan's garment district while studying English at night. Zapruder and his wife Lillian married in 1933, and in 1941 relocated to Dallas, Texas to work for *Nardis*, a local sportswear company. In 1954, he co-founded Jennifer Juniors, Inc., producing the Chalet and Jennifer Juniors brand of women's clothing, whose offices were established in the Dal Tex building located east of the Texas School Book Depository.

On November 22, 1963, as the President's motorcade traveled through Dealey Plaza, Zapruder unexpectedly captured the President's assassination on film. He used an 8 millimeter Bell & Howell Zoomatic Director Series Model 414 PD movie camera, a top-of-the-line model at that time. Steadied by his receptionist Marilyn Sitzman, Zapruder stood atop a four-foot concrete pedestal in Dealey Plaza. The elevated view from the pedestal was unobstructed by people lining the sidewalk on the North side of Elm Street. As the Presidential limousine traveled west on Elm Street, multiple shots rang out, yet Zapruder continued to film the assassination as it unfolded. Except for a few brief moments when the Presidential limousine traveled behind a large road sign, Zapruder's film captured the assassination from beginning to end.

When the shooting stopped, Zapruder and Sitzman began the walk back to their office when they encountered reporter Henry McCormick of the *Dallas Morning News*. Zapruder asked McCormick to locate Secret Service agent Forrest Sorrels of the Dallas office to report he had filmed the assassination. When McCormick and Sorrels arrived at the Dal Tex Building, Zapruder agreed to relinquish the film, under the condition it would be used only to investigate the shooting of President Kennedy.

THE FILM

Zapruder, McCormick, and Sorrels took the film to local television station, WFAA, to have the film developed. While there, Abraham Zapruder consented to a live television interview with program director, Jay Watson. During the interview Zapruder described what he saw as the President moved past his location.

> *WATSON (Station WFAA Dallas): ...would you tell us your story please, sir?*
>
> *ZAPRUDER: I got out in, uh, about a half-hour earlier to get a good spot to shoot some pictures. And I found a spot, one of these concrete blocks they have down near that park, near the underpass. And I got on top there, there was another girl from my office, she was right behind me. And as I was shooting, as the President was coming down from Houston Street making his turn, it was about a half-way down*

there, I heard a shot, and he slumped to the side, like this. Then I heard another shot or two, I couldn't say it was one or two, and I saw his head practically open up [places fingers of right hand to right side of head in a narrow cone, over his right ear], all blood and everything, and I kept on shooting. That's about all, I'm just sick, I can't...

WATSON: I think that pretty well expresses the entire feelings of the whole world.

ZAPRUDER: I must have been in the line of fire.

WATSON: ... today. Excuse me; go ahead, sir.

ZAPRUDER: I say I must have been in the line of fire where I seen [sic] that picture where it was. I was right on that, uh, concrete block, as I said. And as I explained before, is a sickening scene. At first I thought perhaps it's a, uh, it sounded like, uh, somebody make a joke, you hear a, a shot and somebody grabs their stomach (Zapruder, 1963).

The television studio was unable to develop Zapruder's film; subsequently Sorrels drove Zapruder and his assistant, Erwin Swartz, to Eastman Kodak's Dallas processing plant. The unique process used to develop Kodachrome movie film required one machine to process the film and a second machine to make copies. The local Kodak office was able to process the film, but did not have the equipment to copy the film. Zapruder and Sorrels allowed the Jamison Film Company to make three duplicates. Sorrels and Zapruder then took the original and the three undeveloped copies back to Kodak for processing. Zapruder kept the original and one copy. Sorrels sent the other two copies to Secret Service headquarters in Washington, D.C. by courier jet. Zapruder sold the print rights to *Life* magazine for $50,000 later that evening; on November 25 *Life* purchased all rights to the film for a total of $150,000 (Marrs, 2002).

In its November 29, 1963 issue *Life* magazine, published approximately 30 frames of the Zapruder film. The December 7, 1963 John F. Kennedy Memorial Edition and the October 2, 1964 publication also contained Zapruder Frames. *Life* magazine published approximately 30 frames from the

Zapruder film in the November 25, 1966 edition of the magazine in an article titled "A Matter of Reasonable Doubt."

For the public, the complete Zapruder film remained unviewed in motion picture format for six years. In 1969 New Orleans, Louisiana, District Attorney Jim Garrison brought Clay Shaw to trial on charges of conspiring to assassinate President John F. Kennedy. Garrison subpoenaed the Zapruder film and played it in open court. Soon, bootlegged copies of the Zapruder film were in the hands of assassination researchers nationwide (Marrs, 2002).

On March 6, 1975, the American Broadcasting Company network television show *Good Night America,* hosted by Geraldo Rivera, featured assassination researchers Robert Groden and Dick Gregory. Rivera televised the Zapruder film for the first time to the American public during his show. That showing led to the forming of the Hart-Schweiker Investigation, which led to the Church Committee Investigation on Intelligence Activities by the United States, which ultimately resulted in the House Select Committee on Assassinations Investigation. The movie *JFK* was released in 1991. The public's grass roots reaction of indignation and disbelief led to the passage of *The President John F. Kennedy Assassination Records Collection Act of 1992* (also known as the JFK Act) and the formation of the U.S. Assassination Records Review Board. Official investigative groups were not the only ones studying the soundless, color film; researchers were meticulously studying unauthorized copies across the nation (Marrs, 2002).

ZAPRUDER FILM AUTHENTICITY QUESTIONED

Perhaps no greater debate has raged in the history of the study of the death of JFK than has arisen over the authenticity of a 27-second home movie of the assassination, known as 'the Zapruder film'. Some students of the crime take it as the absolute foundation for understanding what actually transpired. Others are not so sure (Fetzer, 2003, ix).

As copies of the Zapruder film became available, researchers began to examine it in depth. Many began to question the authenticity of the homemade movie, focusing on individual anomalies and discrepancies such as people displaying unusually rapid movements or contradicting witness statements.

The Great Zapruder Film Hoax: Deceit and Deception in the Death of JFK, edited by James Fetzer (2003), published research conclusions addressing the authenticity of the Zapruder film. The webpage titled "JFK Assassination Film Hoax" (Costella, n. d.) later summarized the book. *The Great Zapruder Film Hoax: Deceit and Deception in the Death of JFK "Part II: How the Editing was Done"* focuses on purported mistakes made by forgers assembling the counterfeit Zapruder film. A frame-by-frame examination of the Zapruder film reveals a slight forward movement of the President's head preceded the familiar back and to the left movement. John Costella states this slight forward movement has only three possible explanations:

1. He was hit by two bullets at almost the same time (one from behind and then one from the front).
2. He was hit from behind, and a jet of brain matter exploding from the front caused his head to recoil backwards.
3. He was hit from behind and some sort of muscle reaction caused his head to fly backwards (Costella, n. d.).

John Costella then goes on to explain that in the 1990s researchers developed a fourth explanation—film alteration. *The Great Zapruder Film Hoax: Deceit and Deception in the Death of JFK* describes the blood as an example of blatant alteration and provides three points as proof for the reader to consider.

1. The blood appeared to be painted on, and then exposed to a genuine strip of film.
2. The blood disappears into thin air, when it should spread out in subsequent frames and land on people or objects in the car.
3. The blood disappears in three frames or 1/6 of a second, which is impossible (Costella, n. d.).

The Great Zapruder Film Hoax: Deceit and Deception in the Death of JFK, "Part II: How the Editing was Done" questions the legitimacy of the blood spray. David Healy, author of the first chapter, "Technical Aspects of Film Alteration" explains the film editing method used to add the fake blood to the individual frames of the film. The second chapter, "A Scientist's Verdict: The Film is a Fabrication," written by John Costella, PhD, explains why the blood spatter in the Zapruder film could not be authentic. Each point developed by Healy and Costella to prove fabrication of the blood requires confirmation or refutation to evaluate the veracity of their findings. The first claim advanced by Healy is the ability to achieve film alteration existed at the time of the assassination. Without the ability to add blood to the Zapruder film, alternation becomes a moot point (Fetzer, 2003).

FILM ALTERATION

Film expert David Healy asserts the blood in Frame 313 is a fabrication; an added special effect introduced to conceal the true cause of death. Healy, a specialist in video and film production and postproduction with more than thirty years in television and film production experience, authored the chapter entitled "Technical Aspects of Film Alteration." His experience is extensive in the field, including the design, engineering, and building of both television production studios and editing facilities. He is familiar with the film optical business in the early 1960s and video composing techniques used today. Healy discusses several aspects of film alteration and concludes glass painting was used to add the blood in the fabricated Zapruder film (Fetzer, 2003).

ALTERATION TECHNIQUES

Frame removal, frame size alteration, slowing or accelerating action, and composite framing are all methods of film editing. One of the simpler methods used to edit film is to use glass painting to add objects to film. Healy suggests film editors used the technique glass painting to alter the Zapruder film. The process includes projecting the original film through glass containing the content to be added to the film, and capturing the combined images on a new piece of film. Composite photographs are discussed, as is the revelation that successful film or photography editing was documented more than 100 years before the assassination. Healy offers an overview of optical printers and how they were routinely used with matte-insert technology for special effects in 1960s movies. Healy concludes by speculating the glass painting technique was used to produce the blood spray in Zapruder Frame 313 (Fetzer, 2003).

The Great Zapruder Film Hoax: Deceit and Deception in the Death of JFK advocates specialists with the skills necessary to manipulate the content of films were reluctant to disclose alteration techniques except to trade apprentices; therefore, alteration procedures represented in contemporaneous publications misrepresented the actual level of available expertise. The book suggests technical abilities of film editing at the time of the assassination was literally a black art, and various editing techniques were closely guarded secrets. Therefore, confirmation of the abilities of film alteration technicians would be difficult to confirm (Fetzer, 2003). That statement does not appear to be accurate.

In August 1935, readers of the American magazine *Popular Science* learned firsthand how to add special effects to movies. One of the things depicted in the article was how to add images to film with a technique called *glass painting*. The August edition contained an article titled "Camera Wizards of the Movies Bring Realism to the Screen" by John E. Lodge that not only describes the glass painting special technique, but also contained several drawings depicting movie makers employing the procedure. Lodge explained how moving clouds, chimney smoke, buildings and even a background countryside location could be added to a movie by painting the needed effect on a sheet of glass placed in front of the camera. The painted material is seamlessly added to form a composite image when the action behind the painted glass is filmed. Lodge asserted the results of the technique, referred to as glass shots in the article, are so realistic that the added portions of the final product are undetectable except by experts in the field (Lodge, 1935).

It appears the necessary level of expertise was available in 1963 to alter the Zapruder film, and articles in popular magazines and scientific journals support that ability. Regrettably, *The Great Zapruder Film Hoax: Deceit and Deception in the Death of JFK* neglected to address the equally essential availability of expertise in blood spatter analysis in the 1960s. The blood spatter pattern created in Zapruder Frame 313 is consistent with back spatter created by gunshot injuries. Film revisionists would need familiarity with the timing, distribution, and dissipation of forcefully expelled blood to re-create an accurate pattern. In particular, they would have to be able to distinguish the differences in forward spatter and back spatter patterns, and how spatter determines the direction the shot originated. The question is not one of whether the editing techniques were available, but rather, was the required knowledge of blood spatter available.

JUNK SCIENCE OR JUST SCIENCE

Blood stain pattern analysts recognize the blood obscuring the President's face in the Zapruder film as back spatter and realize the blood indicates the projectile struck the President from the front. Critics of the authenticity of the Zapruder film believe the blood in the film is faked, and subsequently reject any information founded upon bloodstain pattern analysis in the Zapruder film. Others believe the blood is genuine, but suggest analysis relying upon the Zapruder film is utilizing poor methodology with too much uncertainty to arrive at conclusions that are reliable. In order for bloodstain pattern analysis to be accepted as relevant in the Kennedy assassination, and in addition prove the blood is genuine, certain criteria must be met.

1. Bloodstain pattern analysis must be established as a trustworthy scientific field of study.
2. The attributes of the blood spatter pattern in the Zapruder film must coincide with known blood spatter pattern characteristics.
3. It is essential to prove knowledge of those patterns characteristics were unavailable to film experts in 1963.

Those benchmarks must be addressed successfully; otherwise, when analysts identify the blood in frame 313 as back spatter, they will have to succumb to the claims of detractors declaring bloodstain pattern analysis in the Kennedy assassination as "junk science."

A TRUSTWORTHY SCIENTIFIC FIELD OF STUDY

A bloodstain pattern is a distribution of bloodstains with identifiable characteristics that can be consistently reproduced and studied to form dependable determinations concerning the manner in which the pattern was produced. Bloodstain pattern analysis refers to the examination of the shape, location and distribution of blood stains for interpreting the events connected with bloodshed. This is based on the principle that bloodstain patterns have characteristics that are indicative of the forces that created them. Analysis incorporates information gathering, observation, documentation, analysis, assessment, conclusion, and technical review. Bloodstain pattern analysis is based on general principles of physics, chemistry, biology, and mathematics and is widely recognized as reliable and credible evidence in a court of law. Bloodstain pattern analysis is capable of testing for validity by other researchers working under the same conditions.

Many published studies support the acceptance of spatter analysis in the scientific community, as well as case law to support its validity. Studies and publications date its use back to the late 1800s, with routine use on crime scenes internationally since the 1970s. Scientific meetings hosted by professional organizations and government agencies in the United States and other countries offer the principles and procedures of analysis. Professional organizations that recognize bloodstain pattern analysis include the International Association of Bloodstain Pattern Analysts (IABPA), International Association for Identification (IAI) and Association for Crime Scene Reconstruction (ACSR).

The Federal Bureau of Investigation organizes and sponsors Scientific Working Groups to address issues arising within specific forensic disciplines. In the spring of 2002, the Scientific Working Group on Bloodstain Pattern Analysis (SWGSTAIN) was formed. SWGSTAIN members come from various fields, both nationally and internationally, including law enforcement; federal, state, and local laboratories; and the private sector and academia. SWGSTAIN provides a professional environment in which bloodstain pattern analysts can discuss and evaluate procedures, techniques, protocols, quality assurance, education, and research. SWGSTAIN's ultimate goal is to use these professional exchanges to address practical issues within the field of bloodstain pattern analysis and to build consensus-based best practice guidelines for the discipline (Federal Bureau of Investigation, 2009).

Analysts have successfully re-created patterns utilizing various mechanisms of force directed toward a multitude of target surfaces with consistent results. The ensuing patterns are documented with video, photographs, and written accounts. Patterns and individual stains are documented by noting stain distribution, shape, diameters, and directionality. When blood is impacted with sufficient force, blood droplets are dispersed with reproducible characteristics that assist with categorizing patterns into possible methods used to disperse the blood. Analysts can then differentiate between blood spatter patterns shed during a bludgeoning as opposed to a shooting.

Historically, the relationship between the velocity of the object striking the blood and the average size of the resulting individual stains classified impact spatter patterns. Patterns identified in this way were commonly referred to as low velocity impact spatter, medium velocity impact spatter and high velocity impact spatter. Patterns created by different mechanisms, such as blunt trauma injuries and shooting injuries, can appear similar; therefore, determining the correct category can be problematic.

In an effort to minimize incorrect characterization based upon velocity, in 2009 the Scientific Working Group on Bloodstain Pattern Analysis (SWGSTAIN) designated the specific mechanism used to create patterns containing minute stains as impacted and projected. Impact patterns are the result of an object forcefully striking liquid blood, such as bludgeoning or gunshot injuries (Federal Bureau of Investigations, 2009).

EARLY CONTRIBUTIONS

Although, for the public, this discipline is relatively new, the history of publications concerning Bloodstain Pattern Analysis dates to the late 1800s. While others were certainly contributors to the study of bloodstain pattern interpretation, no one preceded the significant study of bloodstain patterns completed in 1895 by Eduard Piotrowski. Demonstrating a good understanding of practical application of bloodstain pattern interpretation, Piotrowski interpreted results to draw meaningful conclusions. Much like today, he conducted experiments capturing spattered blood on targets for study, noting stain shape and directionality (MacDonell, 1992).

The first time geometric principles were used to determine angles of impact and convergence was in 1939. Victor Balthazard, a French scientist and professor in forensic medicine in Paris, France, with R. Piedelievre, Henri Desolille, and L. Derobert, conducted research and experimentation with trajectories and patterns. Their research, *Etude Des De Sang Projete,* which translated is *Study of Blood Project,* was presented at the Twenty Second Conference of Forensic Medicine (James, 2005).

MODERN CONTRIBUTIONS
Dr. Paul Kirk

Renowned criminologist and professor of criminalistics at the University of California-Berkley, Dr. Paul Leland Kirk (1902-1970), is credited with recognition of bloodstain pattern analysis as a forensic discipline. Kirk established criminology as an academic discipline, making advances to the university's program and conducting important research in the field. Under the direction of Kirk, criminalistics became an accepted academic discipline at the University of California at Berkeley. The discipline sought to incorporate the methods and technology of the scientific community with the investigative judicial community. In Kirk's groundbreaking publication *Crime Investigation,* he explained the benefits of blood spatter analysis in the chapter titled "Blood: Physical Investigation" (Kirk, 1952).

Neurosurgeon Dr. Samuel Sheppard was convicted of murdering his pregnant wife Marilyn Sheppard in their home in the early morning hours of July 4, 1954. Dr. Sheppard claimed his wife was killed by a bushy-haired man who also attacked him and knocked him unconscious. Sheppard was brought to trial in the autumn of 1954. At that time, the case was noted for its extensive publicity and what the U.S. Supreme Court later called a "carnival atmosphere." Many have compared it to the O.J. Simpson trial in terms of the lurid press coverage it generated (DeSario, 2003).

Sheppard's attorney, William Corrigan, argued Sheppard had severe injuries and the intruder inflicted those injuries. The defense further argued the crime scene was extremely bloody, and except for a small spot on his trousers, the only blood evidence on Dr. Sheppard's body were small bloodstains found on his wristwatch. Mary Cowan, the coroner's medical technologist, testified the blood was not from contact with a wound, but was blood spattered at the time of the bludgeoning. That had to mean Sheppard had to have been present and in proximity to the victim when she was beaten to death. Consequently, the jury found Sheppard guilty and he was sentenced to life in prison (DeSario, 2003).

Kirk challenged Cowan's opinion in the 1966 trial. Kirk concluded one blood spot from the crime scene was from someone other than Sam or Marilyn and the killer was left-handed. He offered expert opinion the blood on Sam's watch came from touching the body, presumably when he felt for a pulse.

Primarily as the result of Kirk's testimony, the second jury declared Samuel H. Sheppard not guilty. The trial was a significant landmark in the recognition of bloodstain evidence by the legal system, resulting in a rapidly increasing interest in blood spatter analysis (DeSario, 2003).

Herbert MacDonell

Blood spatter expert Herbert L. MacDonell shared Kirk's view that known procedures for interpreting bloodstains at crime scenes were sufficient to reconstruct what had occurred at the time of bloodshed. With the assistance of a Law Enforcement Assistance Administration Grant, MacDonell conducted research to re-create and duplicate bloodstain patterns commonly observed on crime scenes. In 1971, MacDonell documented his research in *Flight Characteristics and Stain Patterns of Human Blood,* published by the US Department of Justice. With an expanded and technical look at individual stains and patterns, MacDonell's work captured the attention of law enforcement and crime labs nationwide. MacDonell is widely recognized as the "father" of bloodstain pattern analysis in the Western hemisphere (James, 2005).

This author was a speaker candidate for the October 1995 conference hosted by the Coalition on Political Assassinations (COPA) in Washington, DC. The presentation focused on the blood captured in Zapruder Frame 313, identifying the blood as back spatter, thereby proving the fatal headshot came from the front. COPA scientific panel member Herbert MacDonell reviewed the submitted abstract for approval. MacDonell approved the presentation, stating the technique and conclusion were forensically sound, but commented the finding was "old news; everyone knows that blood in the Zapruder film represents back spatter" (MacDonell, 1995).

BLOOD SPATTER PATTERN CHARACTERISTICS

The technical aspects of blood spatter analysis have developed to include videography of patterns as they are created. Analysts' video provided forceful impact patterns as they are created by firing a weapon through targets containing human blood. Careful studies of the video allow an analyst to visualize the creation and dissipation of forward and back spatter. Subsequently, the characteristics of forward and back spatter resulting from gunshot wounds are well documented in books and scientific publications.

Bloodstain patterns consist of individual bloodstains with specific size, shape, and distribution. Recognition of specific characteristics that correlate with velocity enables the analyst to identify the pattern as having origin from forceful impact. Impact patterns can have stains ranging from 0.01 millimeter to 4.0 millimeter in diameter. There is considerable overlap in the size of stains in different impact patterns, so differentiating between shootings and bludgeonings, or even some mechanical injuries, may prove difficult. Spatter from a perforating shooting injury generates two distinct types of impact patterns: back spatter, which is associated with entry wounds, and forward spatter, which is associated with exit wounds. In order to understand how these patterns are created, the mechanics of gunshot injuries to the head must be examined (James, 2005).

GUNSHOT INJURIES TO THE HEAD

When a projectile strikes a human head, it begins the progression of specific events. The bullet enters the skull by forming a small entrance hole. The force of the bullet striking the skull creates fractures moving away from the impact site. The fractures take a straight line from the point of impact on the vault to the base of the skull, and are not deflected by the sutures. These defects, called *radiating fractures,* are completed before the bullet has exited the skull. When the bullet strikes the skull, the velocity is suddenly slowed, thereby transferring some kinetic energy to the target. This initial transfer of energy causes the target to move minutely into the force, and against the line of fire, prior to movement with the force of the moving bullet (Karger, 2008).

The higher a projectile's velocity upon hitting a target, and the faster the forward momentum is disrupted, the more energy is transferred into the target, thus causing more damage. Velocity and mass determine the bullet's kinetic energy, and the wounding potential relies on the efficient transfer of kinetic energy to tissues. Pressure builds, and as the projectile traverses the head, there are only the entrance wound and any consequent fractures for release of that pressure. Therefore, within 3 to 5 milliseconds, blood is expelled out the hole from which the bullet entered as back spatter (Karger, 2008).

It is suggested as a bullet traverses tissue, backward streaming of blood and other fluid or tissue particles may transpire. These particles flow along the sides of the bullet in the opposite direction to which it is traveling. Some of this material is then projected out of the entry wound. This phenomenon called *tail splashing* may be considered an early stage of temporary cavitation, as it occurs as soon as the bullet enters the target (Karger, 2008).

The bullet, which may expand, fragment or tumble, then passes through the brain, creating a permanent cavity by crushing tissue. If the bullet fractures, each fracture has the ability to create additional permanent cavities (Fackler, 1987).

Bullet design and its propensity for fragmentation, combined with tissue resistance, demonstrated in elasticity and density slows the projectile. This rapid deceleration transfers kinetic energy to the surrounding tissues, which dramatically move backward, forward, and sideward, thereby, producing a temporary cavity within the tissue. As energy from the slowing projectile is transmitted, a series of tissue pulsations moving at right angles to the bullet path is created. This movement is called *temporary cavity formation*. Over a period of five to ten milliseconds, the cavity enlarges then collapses repeatedly. Tissue elasticity perpetuates this process until all of the kinetic energy is expended. Consequently, tissues as far away as 40 times the diameter of the bullet are stretched, torn, and sheared. As the brain is incompressible, the increased internal pressure of the temporary cavity causes the tissues to seek an avenue to alleviate that pressure. As a result, blood is forcefully ejected from both entry and exit wounds (DiMaio, 1999; Karger, 2008).

The force of the temporary cavitation pushes against the fractured skull, resulting in additional fractures called *concentric fractures*. These fractures move in a circular or semicircular manner around the entry site, perpendicular to the radial fractures. This occurs as cavitation is in process and may actually stop further propagation of radial fractures. Since the brain is encased by the closed and inflexible structure of the skull, breaking the skull open is the only way temporary cavity pressure can be relieved. The fractured skull may, or may not, remain intact. If the scalp tears from the force of the temporary cavitation, bone fragments may be ejected from the skull. In this event, blood and tissue will forcefully exit from the opening created by the missing bone fragment. If a portion of the scalp adheres to the dislodged bone fragment, a bone avulsion is produced. Figure 1 illustrates Radial Fractures, Concentric Fractures, and Bone Avulsion. A temporary cavity produced in tissue damaged by a fragmented bullet causes a much larger permanent cavity. Thus, projectile fragmentation can turn the energy used in temporary cavitation into a truly destructive force, because it is focused on areas weakened by fragment paths, rather than being absorbed evenly by the tissue mass. Cavitation begins before the bullet has reached the point of exiting the skull (Fackler, 1987; Karger, 2008).

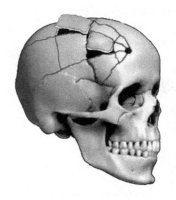

(FIGURE 1) Skull Fractures, Avulsions, and Dislodged Bone Fragments

If the bullet leaves the skull, it typically creates an irregularly shaped exit hole that is normally larger than the corresponding entry wound. Blood and brain matter will exit the skull from the exit hole in the same path of the bullet until the head bursts from the accumulated pressure, creating an even larger and more irregularly shaped exit wound. Brain matter ejects out all available openings as forward spatter, the largest of which is usually the expanded exit wound, with its final size depending on the force of the internal pressure (DiMaio, 1999).

FORWARD/BACK SPATTER PATTERNS

There are two categories of blood spatter generated by gunshot wounds: forward spatter and back spatter. Forward spatter is ejected from the exit wound and travels in the same direction as the bullet. Back spatter is ejected from the entrance wound and travels against the line of fire, and back towards the shooter. Although forward and back spatter patterns display some common features, there are also some dissimilarities. By studying forward and back spatter patterns, created during a singular incident, those differences are identified. Once the characteristics of the patterns are recognized, the distinction between forward and back spatter are defined. By differentiating between forward and back spatter in shooting incidents, the identification of the direction of the origin of force is possible (James, 2005).

The forward and back spatter in Figure 2 was taken during research by Terry Laber, Bart Epstein and Michael Taylor. The photograph is a video capture of

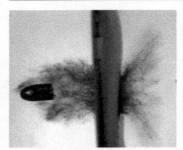

(FIGURE 2) Back Spatter and
Forward Spatter Pattern Shapes

a .44 caliber bullet striking a 1.5 inch thick bloody sponge wrapped in tape. The video is a part of the Bloodstain Pattern Analysis Video Collection completed by Midwest Forensics Resource Center (MFRC) and produced by U.S. Department of Energy by Iowa State University. Note the difference in the overall shape of the two patterns. A slight difference is back spatter patterns tend to move to the side quickly, forming a wide cone, while forward spatter has a more pronounced forward travel with the cone shape developing more slowly, due to the presence of increased velocity, larger stains and increased blood volume (James, 2005; MFRC, 2008).

The forward spatter and back spatter in all circumstances consistently produce patterns with specific characteristics, regardless of changing variables, such as expressed blood volume and projectile velocity. The lab studies, like the crime scene shootings, utilized a wide range of weapons and calibers, and at various distances. In every instance during the experimental shooting of bloody targets, regardless of projectile velocity or blood volume, blood was dispersed back toward the shooter and propelled forward in the continued direction of travel of the projectile (James, 2005).

The consistency of patterns produced in actual shootings and lab settings made practical comparisons of the two individual patterns created from a single incident possible. The forward and back spatter patterns produced in the field and the forward and back spatter patterns produced in the lab were identical in characteristics. Consequently, blood spatter is unquestionably determined to be reproducible, reliable and credible evidence (James, 2005).

SIMILAR CHARACTERISTICS
Some elements of forward and back spatter patterns are identical; those similarities include:

1. Shape of stains: On targets capturing expelled forward and back spatter patterns, the stains near the center of the pattern were circular

in shape, a result of the blood striking the target surface at or near a perpendicular angle. At the perimeters of both forward and back spatter patterns, the stains were more elliptically shaped, a result of the blood striking the target at an angle.

2. Stain distribution: The distribution of the droplets was more concentrated when the target surface was near the bloody target, with the distance between the droplets increasing as the droplets moved away from the bloody target.

3. Pattern shape: Both types of patterns leave the injury site and travel outward in a basic conical shape, moving in every possible direction. A slight difference is back spatter patterns tend to move to the side forming a wide cone, while forward spatter has a more forward travel with the cone shape developing more slowly, due to the presence of increased velocity, larger stains and increased blood volume (James, 2005).

DISSIMILAR CHARACTERISTICS

Forward and back spatter patterns also exhibit divergent characteristics:

1. Distance: Forward spatter consistently travels farther than back spatter created in the same incident. In some cases, forward spatter has been observed traveling well in excess of fifteen feet. Back spatter consistently travels a shorter distance than forward spatter created in the same incident. Back spatter is not observed traveling more than four feet.

2. Blood volume: Forward spatter patterns held a larger volume of blood, expressed as individual stains, when compared to back spatter created in the same incident.

3. Tissue dispersement: Tissue fragments frequently permeate forward spatter pattern. Fragments in the forward spatter varied in size and were occasionally large. When observed in head wounds, the fragments consisted of both soft tissue and bone fragments. Occasionally, tissue fragments were observed in back spatter, however they were found to be markedly smaller in size and fewer in quantity than tissue fragments in forward spatter.

4. Pattern dimensions: Increased blood volume resulted in increased pattern dimensions; therefore, back spatter patterns are smaller

than forward spatter patterns created in the same incident. Pattern dimensions for back spatter are approximately four feet; conversely, large exit wounds can result in forward spatter with sufficient projectile velocity traveling ten to twenty feet.

5.   Velocity of blood: The videotape used to capture patterns as they were created records 30 frames per second. The video utilized approximately 4-5 frames to capture the forceful impact pattern when a low velocity, large caliber projectiles with a high KE rate struck a large volume of blood. This means that particular pattern was created in its entirety in 1/6 of a second. Some patterns were created in less than 1/6 of a second. Back spatter dissipates faster than forward spatter, due to air resistance and gravity acting on the small stain volume.

6.   Stain size: Forward and back spatter targets displayed a multitude of minuscule blood droplets, some resembling an atomized spray or mist. No single stain size is exclusive to a particular range of impact velocity. However, forward spatter is likely to result in predominantly larger stains than back spatter (James, 2005).

VELOCITY

Blood spatter analysts have observed forward and back spatter in the Zapruder film. Forward spatter had a greater velocity than back spatter and moved away from the immediate area of the President much faster than back spatter. One easily identified portion of the forward spatter in the Zapruder film is the whitish object projected from the head, forward of the President. Because the angle the fragment was moving relative to Zapruder is unknown, the exact speed of the fragment cannot be determined; however, estimates are between 65 to 1120 feet per second. Canadian blood spatter analyst, Michael J. Sweet (1954-2006), published research regarding the velocity of blood projected from forceful impact. Utilizing human blood, Sweet's research documented blood leaving the point of the impact travelled 3.59 times faster than the velocity of the impacting object (Sweet, 1993).

Considering the projectile striking Kennedy likely left the barrel at over 2000 feet per second, the velocity of blood movement in the Zapruder film is reasonable. The blood considered bogus by *The Great Zapruder Film Hoax:*

Deceit and Deception in the Death of JFK in frame 313 is consistent with blood and tissue spatter ejected because of a gunshot wound to the head.

Examination of the high speed videos of blood dispersed as the result of gunshots allows the measurement of distance and time in impact spatter. The research revealed blood droplets projected from a shooting occurs within hundreds of thousands of a second, not tenths of a second. The research recordings were taken at 10,000 feet per second, meaning each frame represents 1/237000 a second. Figure 3, taken from a research video taken as a .44 caliber bullet strikes a bloody sponge, indicates back spatter is initiated 0.000400 seconds after the bullet strikes the target. The emerging forward spatter is observed at 0.000500 seconds. The video frame time stamped at 0.000700 indicates the forward spatter has already moved

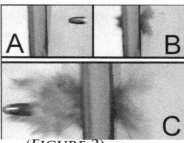

(**FIGURE 3**) Back Spatter created 0.000400 Seconds after Bullet Strikes Target, before Bullet Exits

twice the distance from the sponge as the back spatter created in the same shooting incident. This indicates the forward spatter moves at a greater velocity than the back spatter (MFRC, 2008).

Itek Corporation, located in Massachusetts, stemmed from a research group developing aerial surveillance cameras for the Pentagon at Boston University. In 1975, CBS News asked Itek to study the original Zapruder film using the most advanced techniques and equipment available. Over a period of several months, Itek studied the film, conducted precision measurements, and provided their conclusions in a 94-page report. Concerning the forward blood spatter, they reported the following:

> *It is hypothesized that in fact the several outlines shown are actually two or three major particles. They would appear as several particles here, if they were spinning as they moved, and, if one side was highly reflective. For example, a particle with a wet and a dry side would act as a specular reflector when the wet side reflected sunlight towards the camera.*

The distances between the President's head and the furthermost particles of each trajectory are such that calculations reveal they were traveling at velocities on the order of 80 mph. For a particle to hold together at such a velocity it would quite likely have to be composed of a cohesive substance, such as a bone fragment. The velocity calculations were made from the plane of the photograph and, therefore, represent minimum velocities.

The velocities of the particles were computed from measurements on the three furthermost particles visible in frame 313 which were associated with the three separate trajectories defined in Figure 3.3.15. The velocity of the median velocity particle was = to 87 mph. The particles which are evident in frame 314 are traveling at velocities slower than the upper particles (Itek, 1976, p. 59, 62).

BACK SPATTER RESEARCH

Experimental research directed towards the examination of back spatter was first published in 1982. *The Summary Report of the Bloodstain Pattern Analysis Research Group* was completed by Sanford Regional Crime Laboratory, Tampa Regional Crime Laboratory, Tallahassee Regional Crime Laboratory, Jacksonville Regional Crime Laboratory, and Pensacola Regional Crime Laboratory. The scientists utilized .22 caliber, .38 caliber, 30.06 caliber and 12 gauge #1, 16 pellet ammunition to shoot bloody sponges. Paper targets were placed alongside, behind and in front of the sponges to capture the static aftermath of the dispersed blood. Back spatter was observed to be conical in shape and the individual stain characteristics documented (Parker, 1982).

The *Journal of Forensic Sciences* published a 1983 article entitled "Back Spatters of Blood" by Forensic Pathologists and Chief Medical Examiner Dr. Boyd G. Stevens of the San Francisco Medical Examiner's Coroner's Office in California and Dr. Terrence B. Allen, a forensic pathology fellow. The authors recognized the occurrence of minute droplets of blood being expelled from gunshot entry wounds traveling back against the line of fire. They also conceded back spatter of blood from gunshot wounds was a complex phenomenon that was not completely understood. The authors acknowledged the occurrence of back spatter was not widely recognized, but was commonly seen in gunshot wounds to the head. To reproduce back spatter patterns, the researchers fired through a blood-soaked sponge encased in various materials, such as plastic, rubber and tape. They determined back spatter expelled from the bloody sponges was more common with large caliber hand guns. In conclusion, Stephens and Allen indicated, "back spatter of blood from gunshot wounds should not be considered an anomaly, but a common characteristic of gunshot wounds to the head" (Stephens, 1983, p. 439).

In a 1986 *Journal of Forensic Sciences* article, authors Peter Pizzola, Steven Roth and Peter DeForest refer to the new study of back spatter. They indicated precaution must be applied when making interpretations from bloodstain patterns at crime scenes, citing a number of complexities that must be recognized. They noted the existence of blood spattered backward from an entrance wound has been called into question, and called on the scientific community for additional research (Pizzola, 1986).

EVIDENCE WASHED AWAY
Some assassination researchers contend valuable spatter evidence on and within the limousine was altered or removed by the movements of Mrs. Kennedy and Clint Hill on the vehicle trunk, by passengers inside the vehicle, by medical personnel when removing the shooting victims, and apparent cleaning at Parkland Hospital. However, their conception of how blood spatter is utilized is inaccurate. Analysis of blood spatter is used to determine specific information, including:

1. The mechanism in which the blood spatter is produced
2. The possible location of the victim at the time of injury
3. The direction of force that imparted the injury
4. The sequence of multiple injuries
5. The validity of witness statements

The questions can all be definitively answered by autopsy, and examining the Zapruder film and other photographic evidence. Furthermore, not all blood spatter was removed or altered. There is obviously blood remaining within the limousine as evidenced in photographs taken after the assassination, and blood remained on the vehicle exterior, as evidenced by testimony. Had the vehicle remained in pristine condition, the resulting blood spatter from Connally's wounds may have assisted in positioning Connally's body at the time of his shooting injuries. However, no additional evidence could have been extrapolated concerning the fatal headshot of President Kennedy.

WITNESSES TO THE SPATTER

The Great Zapruder Film Hoax: Deceit and Deception in the Death of JFK preface contains the statement "Witnesses take precedence over photographs and films" (Fetzer, 2003, p. xvii). However, it appears that Fetzer's adherence to this edict is not steadfast. Witnesses described seeing blood similar to that depicted in the Zapruder film, yet Fetzer discounts that testimony. In direct conflict with the hypothesis of the blood proving film alteration, the Warren Commission testimony of several witnesses describes blood that appears consistent with that illustrated in the Zapruder film. If the testimony of these witnesses is truthful, the blood droplets dispersed is consistent with blood spatter.

> PHILLIP L. WILLIS: ... *my little daughter ran back and said, "Oh, Daddy, they have shot our President. His whole head blew up, and it looked like a red halo"... and she went back and told her mother the same thing. And her mother said, "Yes; I saw it" (7H496).*

> JAMES W. ALTGENS: *There was [sic] flesh particles that flew out of the side of his head in my direction from where I was standing (7H518).*

> HUGH W. BETZNER, JR.: *I saw a flash of pink ...I saw fragments going up in the air (19H467).*

> MRS. JACK FRENZEN: *...noticed blood appearing on the side of President Kennedy's head (24H 525).*

> DR. TONI GLOVER: *...his head exploded...it was a bunch of gray stuff. It glinted off the sun (JFK Lancer Dallas Conference, 2012)*

> BILL NEWMAN: *I remember seeing the blood in front of his face. It was like a red mist or a cloud of blood in front of his face, and then it just disappeared (Newman, 1995).*

TONI FOSTER: I remember [his head] looked like confetti, it was just blown off. It hit him back here [puts her hand on the right rear of her head] and it was just like confetti. The spray went behind him (Conway, 2000).

How the blood mist would appear to a witness is partly dependent on the location of the witness in relation to it. Phillip Willis reported his daughter described the blood as a red halo, and her mother acknowledged the description given by her daughter as something she also observed. A halo suggests the blood was surrounding the head in a circular manner. Blood moves away from the wound in a conical manner, radiating outward in every possible direction. Observers could perceive the blood as surrounding the head, so this comment by the Phillips child is appropriate, if she observed blood spatter resulting from a gunshot wound to the head. Altgens, Betzner, Franzen and Glover spoke of tissue fragments being ejected from the head wound; this too is representative of blood spatter. This author spoke with Newman in 1995. When asked to describe his observations concerning the blood, he stated he was standing about 15 feet from the President when he heard the gunshot and saw the blood suddenly appear in front of the President, and then, as suddenly, disappear. Newman described the blood spray as a mist, indicating the individual blood droplets were extremely small, like spray paint or cloud. The *Scientific Working Group on Bloodstain Pattern Analysis* published recommended terminology for use when teaching, discussing, writing or testifying on bloodstain pattern analysis. That recommended terminology included "*Mist Pattern:* a bloodstain pattern resulting from blood reduced to a spray of micro-drops as a result of the force applied" (Federal Bureau of Investigations, 2009).

Contemporaneous statements by witnesses of the assassination support visual conformation of blood spatter leaving the President's head. Scientific books and professional journals verify back spatter was not studied until the 1980s.

The characteristics of the blood spray in the Zapruder film are congruent with back spatter produced in scientific labs and documented in professional books and journals currently being published. All available evidence reinforces the legitimacy of the blood in the Zapruder film, proving blood spatter analysis in the assassination of President Kennedy is not junk science, but real science.

A Fabricated Film

John Costella, Ph.D. authored *The Great Zapruder Film Hoax: Deceit and Deception in the Death of JFK* chapter "A Scientist's Verdict: The Film is a Fabrication." Dr. Costella of Australia has a degree in both engineering and science. He has completed a Ph.D. in theoretical physics specializing in high energy physics, Einstein's theory of relativity, and classical electrodynamics. Costella describes key elements he believes prove the blood in Zapruder is altered in that chapter, but he also summarizes his findings online.

> *More recently, scientists have discovered that there is something else about the shot to JFK's head on the forged film that is fake—and can be proved to be fake: the spray of blood that appears at the moment he is shot. But what tells us that this "blood" is fake is the fact that it disappears into thin air! If it was real, the "blood" should spread out in the frames after Frame 313, and then land on people or objects in the car. But within a couple of frames, it disappears altogether.*

> *Scientists were able to test whether the blood really did disappear. They analyzed the film frames around the shot to JFK's head. Every color picture can be broken down into red, green, and blue light. (If you look closely at your TV, you can see the little red, green and blue lights!) The total red, green, and blue light in each of the frames was measured by computer, and put onto a graph. The graphs show that the "spray" disappears within three frames, or one-sixth of a second. This can't happen! Even if you dropped a lead weight from JFK's temple, it wouldn't drop into the car this fast!*

> *The scientists were also able to show that the "spray" could not have been moving so fast that it shot right out of view before Frame 314. But even if the blood could have, where would it have ended up? It would have gone all over the Connallys, and the windows and interior of the limousine. But a frame published only weeks after the assassination, in color, showed no blood at all (Fetzer, 2003).*

The Great Zapruder Film Hoax: Deceit and Deception in the Death of JFK chapter "A Scientist's Verdict: The Film is a Fabrication" expands upon the lead ball and blood droplet comparison. Costella indicates mathematical analysis has determined the rate of dissipation is faster than a lead weight in free fall, and therefore much too rapid to be authentic blood spatter. His calculations determine a lead ball originating from the center of the bloody spray would take half a dozen frames to drop out of view, but drops of blood should take longer (Fetzer, 2003).

DISAPPEARING BLOOD

The most apparent error in Costella's summation is the statement concerning the dissipation of blood and its being deposited on passengers in the vehicle. He argues the blood spray should have been deposited on Governor and Mrs. Connally, but was not. He also insists blood should have accumulated within the interior of the limousine, and refers to a color printing of a Zapruder Frame published only weeks after the assassination that showed no blood (Fetzer, 2003).

Nellie Connally, wife of Gov. Connally, seated to the left and in front of President Kennedy, stated she saw tiny bits of bloody matter falling on her person and all over the limousine (Rees, n. d.). Special Agent Roy H. Kellerman was located in the right front seat of the Presidential limousine, at the time of the assassination. Kellerman's Warren Commission testimony was that upon arrival at the hospital, he discovered body matter and flesh all over his coat (2H61). Secret Service Agent Clint Hill rode on the running board of the Secret Service car immediately behind the Presidential limousine. His Warren Commission testimony stated blood and bits of brain were all over the rear portion of the car (2H141).

Robert A. Frazier, Special Agent of the Federal Bureau of Investigation and Chief of the Firearms & Tools Marks in the Physics and Chemistry Section, examined the limousine following the assassination. Frazier described the blood he observed in the limousine when testifying in the Clay Shaw trial in Louisiana.

> *FRAZIER: We found blood and tissue all over the outside areas of the vehicle from the hood ornament, over the complete area of the*

hood, on the outside of the windshield, also on the inside surface of the windshield, and all over the entire exterior portion of the car, that is, the side rails down both sides of the car, and of course considerable quantities inside the car and on the trunk lid area (Frazier, 1969).

VISUALIZING BLOOD SPATTER

Visual acuity describes the ability to see detail or the sharpness of vision. Being able to see details depends on several factors, including:

- The ambient illumination and the contrast between the foreground and background
- The smallest item that the retina can resolve at a given viewing distance (Goldstein, 2010).

Visualization of impact spatter is therefore dependent upon the size of the stain and the distance the viewer is from the stain, and the color contrast between the stain and the background surface (Goldstein, 2010).

The human eyes work by allowing light to enter through the pupil. The lens of the eye is used to focus light rays onto the retina, which is the surface at the back of the eye, sensitive to light. The retina consists of two types of receptor cells known as rods and cones. Rods allow us to differentiate between shades of black and white, while cones allow us to see color. Most cones are concentrated in a particularly sensitive region of the retina called the *fovea*, which enables us to see the detail. The receptor cells use the optic nerve to transmit signals to the brain, which interprets the signals from both eyes to construct the image we see (Goldstein, 2010).

AMBIENT ILLUMINATION AND CONTRAST

Color vision is the ability to distinguish between differences in wavelengths of light. The principal attributes of color vision are hue, for example red or green saturation: the degree in which it is mixed with white, such as red compared to pink, and brightness, or how much light is reflected. Brightness, or illumination, is the amount of light reflected from a specific color; dark colors do not reflect as much light as lighter colors and therefore have less brightness. Brightness allows us to see differences in objects of similar hue, saturation and intensity, such as various shades of red. Contrast sensitivity is the ability to perceive the difference in brightness between a foreground color and a background color (Goldstein, 2010).

The relationship between the sizes of an object, the distance to that object, and the illumination, or brightness of the object to be observed, is easily demonstrated. Large dark dots placed on dark fields with similar reflective qualities result in poor color contrast; however, they can still be seen at a given distance. Small dark dots placed on dark fields, with similar reflective qualities, result in poor color contrast and often cannot be easily seen at that same distance. This indicates the relationship between distances, the degree of contrast required for detectability and the need for brightness are all influenced by the size of the object. Small objects require a shorter distance and a higher level of contrast, or increased brightness of either the object or the background field, in order to be detected. In other words, a small white dot on a black field is easily detected, as is a small black dot on a white field, unless distance overcomes the ability to focus on the object. However, at both close and distant distances a small black dot on a dark green field is much harder to see due to lack of contrast and lack of reflected light, or brightness of either color (Goldstein, 2010).

Dried blood is not the bright red you see as it leaves the body. When completely dried, it appears reddish-brown or dark brown. Color is defined by the amount of red, green and blue it contains. The red/green/blue component of an individual color has a specific RGB number that exclusively identifies it. The ability to determine the ease in which we can visualize adjacent colors can be measured using a contrast calculator. By utilizing a color contrast calculator the brightness difference and hue difference in colors can be compared to determine a contrast threshold. Provided the brightness difference is greater than 125, the colors have sufficient light to dark contrast to promote ease in visualization. The color difference must be greater than 500 to provide adequate hue contrast for ease in visualization. If the color difference is 500 or less, it means the hues are too similar to provide good visual acuity (Pearl, 2012).

The RGB number for the midnight blue paint on the Presidential limousine is unknown to the author, however R14, G22 and B85 is a dark blue color. RGB values of R96, G45 and B11 result in a reddish brown color that would represent dried blood. Entering the RGB numbers for the dark blue and reddish brown colors into a contrast calculator, provides a brightness difference of 29, and a 179 point difference for hue. Each reading is significantly below what is needed for visual acuity (Pearl, 2012).

SIZE AND VIEWING DISTANCE

Visual acuity tests are the most common tests used to evaluate eyesight by measuring the eye's ability to see details at near and far distances. The primary measurement tool is the letter chart, read at a specific distance. The smaller the letters become, the harder it is to recognize the letters. The top letter, usually the largest, is 3.49 inches or 88.7 millimeter high. The smallest line has letters that someone with normal vision should be able to read at 4 feet. The letters intended to be clear at 4 feet are 2 millimeter in height, much larger than blood spatter that ranges less than one millimeter in diameter. Which suggest seeing something half the size of the letters used in the eye chart may not be readily seen at 4 feet (Freidrichsen, 2005).

In figure 4, the small water droplets are not as noticeable in the smaller, inset photograph as in the larger duplicated photograph. This is a good example of how the size of items can be difficult to visualize at a distance.

Spatter produced as the result of gunshot wounds can result in mist like stains that are .1 millimeter or less in diameter; much smaller than the 0.5 millimeter diameter lead used in a fine point mechanical pencil. The majority of the stains will be near 1.00 millimeter in diameter, about the thickness of a dime. Forward spatter

(FIGURE 4) Small Objects are Difficult to Visualize at a Distance

may also contain stains that can also be as large as 4 millimeter in diameter, about the width of the head of a match from a standard matchbook. It is reasonable to believe an observer standing a few feet away from the limousine may not have detected blood spatter, due to poor color contrast and the size of the blood spatter stains (James, 2005).

The pedestal on which Zapruder stood was about 70 feet from Kennedy at the time of the fatal shot. It is reasonable to believe blood spatter the size of a match head or smaller could not have been captured by his camera at that distance. However, we know blood spatter was present within the vehicle from witness testimony.

Nellie Connally, wife of Gov. Connally, seated to the left and in front of President Kennedy, stated she saw "tiny bits of bloody matter" falling on her person and all over the limousine (Rees, n. d.).

Special Agent Roy H. Kellerman was located in the right front seat of the Presidential limousine at the time of the assassination.

> *KELLERMAN: Senator, between all the matter that was-between all the matter that was blown off from an injured person, this stuff all came over.*
>
> *COOPER: What was that?*
>
> *KELLERMAN: Body matter, flesh.*
>
> *SPECTER: When did you first notice the substance which you have described as body matter?*
>
> *KELLERMAN: When I got to the hospital, sir, it was all over my coat.*
>
> *SPECTER: Can you describe what it was in a little more detail, as it appeared to you at that time?*
>
> *KELLERMAN: This is a rather poor comparison, but let's says you take a little handful of matter-I am going to use sawdust for want of a better item and just throw it (2H78-79).*

Secret Service Agent Clint Hill rode on the running board of the Secret Service car immediately behind the Presidential limousine.

> HILL. *The right rear portion of his head was missing. It was lying in the rear seat of the car. His brain was exposed. There was blood and bits of brain all over the entire rear portion of the car (2H141).*

Color contrast from the blood spatter, against the surface it is deposited on, can also influence the ability to see the individual stains. Too little contrast makes it hard to distinguish an object from the background; therefore, from even a few feet a minute dried bloodstain on a dark surface is difficult to detect. We know the blood was deposited on the limousine interior and exterior. There is witness testimony that confirms that. Therefore, we are only left to surmise the reason the blood was not easily visualized in the limousine in the Zapruder Frame was the lack of color contrast and brightness in the color of the dried blood.

Unfortunately, photographs of the limousine subsequent to the Zapruder film are not taken at a distance conducive to visualizing minute particulates and blood stains of the size produced in a shooting incident. However, the lack of ability to observe these minute bloodstains should not be interpreted as film alteration.

IMPOSSIBLE VELOCITY

The Great Zapruder Film Hoax: Deceit and Deception in the Death of JFK questions the dissipation timing of the blood in the Zapruder film.

> *These results confirm that what is visible to the naked eye is not just an optical illusion. The spray that appears in frame 313 starts to disappear immediately, and far too rapidly, to represent physically real matter: it had essentially disappeared completely within six frames, which is, we recall, the time needed for a lead weight to drop out of sight (Fetzer, 2003)!*

John Costella, PhD, author of the chapter titled "A Scientist Verdict: The Film Is a Fabrication," indicates mathematical analysis has determined the rate of dissipation is much too rapid to be authentic blood spatter. His calculations determine a lead ball originating from the center of the bloody spray would take half a dozen frames to drop out of view, but drops of blood should take longer (Fetzer, 2003).

As objects fall through the atmosphere, they must contend with air resistance. Relationships between the weight and size of an object to air resistance result in objects falling at different speeds, and objects that are more massive fall faster than smaller objects. Logically, the blood droplets would fall from the Zapruder frames at a slower rate than a lead weight. However, the blood in the Zapruder film is not simply a group of blood droplets in free fall: it is blood forcefully dispersed as the result of a gunshot injury. Therefore, the velocity created in that type of event must be examined.

The Bell & Howell 414PD camera used by Zapruder has a shutter exposure time of 0.025 second (or 1/40th of a second) per frame. Abraham Zapruder's camera took about 18 frames per second: therefore, each frame represents about 55.6 milliseconds, and each frame exposure lasts 27 milliseconds. Consequently, each frame consists of an image that is approximately 27 milliseconds in length, with an unexposed time of approximately 28 milliseconds in length. Blood is easily observed in three frames. By using color analysis of the film, it could be argued the blood is present during six frames. Six frames of the Zapruder film represent 333.6 milliseconds or 0.3336 seconds. Costella contends 1/3 of a second is inconsistent with the time required for creating and disbursing back spatter resulting from a gunshot. Moreover, the white streak identified as a forward moving object observed in frames 314 and 315 is calculated to be moving at a speed of at least 135 feet per second or more, described as incredible in *The Great Zapruder Film Hoax: Deceit and Deception in the Death of JFK* (Fetzer, 2003).

IRREFUTABLE VELOCITY

The Midwest Forensics Resource Center (MFRC) is a National Institute of Justice sponsored facility at Iowa State University. The mission of the MFRC Research and Development Program is to provide research and technological advances in forensic science for the benefit of the forensic community. In 2007, the MFRC Research and Development Program began research that was published as *High-Speed Digital Video Analysis of Bloodstain Pattern Formation from Common Bloodletting Mechanisms*. This project systematically studied the formation of common bloodstain patterns by using a high-speed digital video (HSDV) camera to record the blood transfer as it occurs. The project, a collaborative effort between Terry Laber with the Forensic Science Laboratory, Minnesota Bureau of Criminal Apprehension; Bart Epstein a Forensic Consultant; and Dr. Michael Taylor of the Institute of Environmental Science and Research, published their findings in 2008 and made the videos available for viewing online (MFRC, 2008).

Examination of the high speed videos of blood dispersed as the result of gunshots allows the measurement of distance and time in impact spatter. The research revealed blood droplets projected as a result of a shooting are generated within hundreds of thousands of a second, not tenths of a second. The research recordings were taken at 10,000 frames per second, meaning each frame represents 1/237000 a second. The research video taken as a .44 caliber bullet strikes a bloody sponge indicates back spatter is immediately initiated. The adjacent graphic was captured 0.000600 of a second after the bullet struck the sponge.

1. Frame 4: The bullet strikes the sponge at frame 4 with a time stamp of 0.000400 seconds; back spatter is visibly being formed.
2. Frame 5: The bullet is captured within the sponge at a time stamp of 0.000500 seconds. The emerging forward spatter is observed at a distance equal from the sponge as the existing back spatter, even as the projectile has not exited.
3. Frame 6: With a time stamp of 0.000600 seconds, the projectile has completely exited the sponge. The forward spatter at this point already appears to be projecting away from the sponge at a greater distance than the back spatter.
4. Frame 7: The frame time stamped at 0.000700 indicates the forward spatter has already moved twice the distance from the sponge as the back spatter created in the same shooting incident. This indicates the forward spatter is moving at a greater velocity than the back spatter.
5. Frame 229: The last frame of the video is time stamped 0.022900 seconds, and shows very little blood being expelled from the sponge (MFRC, 2008).

Costella maintains 1/3 of a second is too short a time to generate and disperse impact spatter resulting from a gunshot wound. However, the pattern depicted in the research video is created and expended in 0.022500 of a second. The timing duration of the pattern increases with an increase in blood volume expelled. The MFRC research video associated with the Figure 5 indicates at 0.000600 seconds, the forward spatter velocity was already twice that of the back spatter back spatter. The research proved the time for the creation and dissipation of forceful impact patterns is consistently comparable to the Zapruder film (MFRC, 2008).

Zapruder's camera captured images at 18.3 frames per second. That speed would record the development of blood spatter in the same film frame as the target was struck by the fired shot, not several frames later. A high velocity force would generate blood droplets with a velocity greater than 150 feet per second. Once impacted, blood is forcefully projected from an injury site; air resistance and the downward force of gravity immediately and progressively slow the velocity of the projected blood drop. Smaller droplets of blood, such as those found in back spatter, are impacted by air resistance and gravity faster than larger drops of blood found in forward spatter. Consequently, due to the smaller size of blood

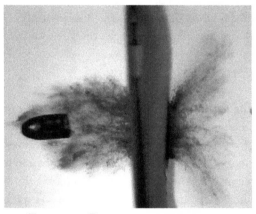

(**FIGURE 5**) Forward Spatter at twice the distance as Back Spatter at 0.000600 Seconds

droplets found in back spatter, that pattern does not travel as fast, or as far, as forward spatter before it begins to follow a parabolic arc and fall to the surrounding surfaces. Consequently, back spatter usually travels no farther than approximately three feet. Forward spatter commonly contains larger blood drops and tissue, and can result in a forward momentum of ten feet or more (HSCA 6:14, James, 2005).

Additional research regarding the velocity of blood projected by forceful impact was completed by Canadian blood spatter analyst Michael J. Sweet. Utilizing human blood, his research documented blood leaving the point of the impact travelled 3.59 times faster than the velocity of the impacting object. Utilizing the ratio determined in Sweet's research, blood impacted at approximately 100 feet per second would be initially projected from the impact site at approximately 359 feet per second. The Zapruder film was recorded at eighteen frames per second, thus projected blood would travel 19.9 feet in one frame. Forward and back spatter are created in gunshot injuries within milliseconds. Modern imaging technology allows researchers to conduct experiments for studying the development, distribution and dispersion of forceful impact blood spatter, and form reproducible conclusions. This technology was unavailable in the 1960s, yet the Zapruder film recorded blood dispersed at a velocity consistent with patterns created by a gunshot injury. Costella claims that the velocity and pattern timeframe of the blood depicted in the Zapruder film is impossible. Scientific research shows that allegation is scientifically proven false (Sweet, 1993).

CONCLUSION

The Zapruder film has been the foundation of many investigative aspects of the Kennedy Assassination. The timing of the film provides the timing reference of the assassination. The individual frames have been used to place the victims and vehicles in correct positions and location within Dealey Plaza for reconstruction of the event. Unfortunately, the authenticity of the Zapruder film is frequently used as a scapegoat to explain confusing irregularities of the Kennedy assassination.

One of those anomalies has been the blood that partially obscures Kennedy's face at Zapruder Frame 313. Advocates of a single shooter from behind Kennedy believe the blood in the Zapruder film is genuine. They contend the blood is escaping from the President's exit wound, violently propelling him rearward in a phenomenon called the *jet effect*. For many years, researchers who buttressed a frontal shot were at odds to explain the blood, unless they supported two simultaneous shots to the head, or film alteration. In 1982, the mystery surrounding the blood captured in the film was slowly being solved.

In 1982, there was a nationwide surge of interest in bloodstain pattern analysis. Professional organizations were organized, general terminology accepted, and standardized analysis procedures established. Experimental research began to focus on the blood expelled from gunshot entry wounds. Research specifically directed towards the examination of back spatter was first published in 1982. The mechanics of how back spatter is created were still a focus of study late as 1986, with forensic publications advising additional research was still needed.

Scientific journals, books, and research published since the early 1990s indicate the blood observed in the Zapruder film displays accurate characteristics of back spatter. The pattern creation and dissipation rate documented in the Zapruder at approximately 0.33 seconds parallels to back spatter research. The shape of the pattern and the distance it extends from the wound is consistent with back spatter. In fact, all available information concerning the blood spatter pattern in the Zapruder film corresponds in every measurable manner with back spatter replicated in forensic laboratories and described in peer-reviewed publications since the late 1980s.

Film editing specialists apparently possessed the ability to add content to film in 1963. However, the supposition that film or forensic experts were aware of the various characteristics of back spatter at the time of the assassination is impossible. The 1983 and 1986 articles clearly demonstrate the study of back spatter was in its infancy in the early and mid-1980s. No artist or film editor in 1963 was knowledgeable concerning back spatter pattern characteristics. Without the required technical knowledge, it is unreasonable to believe the shape, density, and timing of blood in the Zapruder could be accurately edited into the film. Consequently, the only possible conclusion is the back spatter in the Zapruder film is genuine. As a result, the assertion that the blood in the Zapruder film is faked is absolutely identified as a myth.

CHAPTER 4

THE LIMO STOP

T ime does not stop—at least not technically. Occasionally, however, people experience intense and unique moments, and the rest of the world seems to fade from view. During those moments, the experience is all that matters, and for some, time stands still.

For people in Dealey Plaza, observing the death of President Kennedy may have been one of those moments. The shooting evoked a wide range of emotions, including disbelief, confusion, grief, and fear. Shared memories were imprinted on the minds of witnesses: the sharp sound of gunshots, First Lady Jacqueline Kennedy on the trunk, and Secret Service agent Clint Hill frantically racing to the limousine. However, there are also conflicting memories. A few witnesses recall the limousine coming to a complete stop during the shooting, while most remember the vehicle simply slowed. Certainly, the witnesses who believe the limo stopped are sincere; they have no reason to fabricate a lie. It is not easy to stand firm in dissent to the memories of the majority of their follow witnesses. The Zapruder film, the Nix film, and the Muchmore film do not depict the limousine stopping; consequently, those witnesses are also in conflict with photographic evidence. Nevertheless, those few witnesses are so convincing, many people have come to believe the films are altered to eliminate showing the limousine stop.

When it comes to beliefs, what matters is the pursuit of truth, but how do we know something to be true? For most, truth is based in a belief and justification for certainty. Belief is developed when the experiences of perception are repeated and the resulting information found to be constant. Experience is the basis for many beliefs. Beliefs are informational thoughts with an origin in reliable, recurrent, perceptual experiences such as the five senses.

A belief is trustworthy information we evaluate as accurate because it originates in a reliable cognitive process: primarily that process is vision. Evaluating visual information for reliability is based on perceptional and memorial experiences. The perceptual faculties are our five senses: sight, touch, hearing, smelling, and tasting. Visual experiences are historically reliable; therefore, one can trust what is seen. Justification is knowledge of something in addition to visual experiences that support a belief. For example, looking at a needle one can see, by the tapered point, it is sharp; consequently, the belief about needles is that they are sharp. Pricking the finger with the tip of a needle involves touch, supporting the observed perception that needles are sharp. Therefore, the belief that needles are sharp is justified.

Occasionally, the brain itself is justification for a belief, for example, when it tells someone when he or she is experiencing pain. There is no outside justification or secondary confirmation. However, it is accepted as true. The brain can override the need for justification to confirm a belief as true. Since the awareness of time is a brain function, the brain is the only foundation for interpretation. Does the brain ever err in its evaluation of time?

Why do only a few witnesses remember the limousine stopping? Forensic research indicates the inconsistency in bystanders' observations can be explained by considering how the brain identifies time. The perception of danger can induce a chemical reaction in the brain that increases the ability to remember. The brain floods with the hormone noradrenaline, which amplifies focus and increases the ability to remember explicit moments of lethal danger. As a result, emotionally disturbing events tend to be well remembered after a single experience, and what is remembered is closely connected to time perception. When applying time distortion research to the assassination witnesses' experiences, unquestionably there was an opportunity for variations in time perception.

The assassination witnesses viewed first hand, and some at close range, the horror of murder. They heard the shots, smelled gun smoke, and saw the wounded young President dying in his wife's arms. They witnessed law enforcement brandishing weapons, and the frenzied search for a perpetrator within close vicinity. The eyewitnesses could easily have interpreted the events unfolding before them as highly emotionally and dangerous. Therefore, they were likely deeply affected by the murder of President Kennedy. Perhaps for those few witnesses during the extraordinary moments of the assassination of President Kennedy, the rest of the world did fade away. For those few bystanders in Dealey Plaza, time stood still.

PERCEPTION OF TIME

Humans possess five senses: hearing, sight, touch, smell and taste. The world is observed through the five senses. However, even when senses are prevented from functioning, humans can still detect the passage of time. Unconscious awareness of the passage of time is experienced when awakening from sleep with a general idea of the amount of time that has passed. This is possible because humans possess an internal clock, a unique ability used specifically for detecting the passage of time. This internal clock is called a *pacemaker*.

People recognize familiar events occur over established periods of time. Anticipating how long it takes to drive to the office is an example of associating an event with an established segment of time. Time perception recognizes event duration, synchronization, and order of occurrence. Based upon the volume of data observed and stored, we develop and calculate a sense of passing time. An instinct for evaluating time for a specific activity is developed when one repeatedly engages in that activity. Research supports the existence of an internal clock that equates received data volume as representative of specific time periods (Droit-Volet, 2011).

Research has proven during moments of extreme stress, or life-threatening situations, heightened concentration, and fixated attention alter the perceived passage of time. Enhanced concentration and focused attention on events alter the perceived passage of time and so make it seem longer than it really is (Cole, 1995).

The perception of time depends on many factors, including the importance of the event, past experiences, and behavioral contexts. Our internal pacemaker can slow or accelerate with extreme or unfamiliar, external circumstances. For example, emotionally charged, unusually significant, and more intense stimuli expand estimates of time. Events that are frequent, familiar, and not significant tend to compress perceived time. Time perception research confirms subjective time is particularly sensitive to fear and anxiety, which results in the perception of slowed time (Droit-Volet, 2011).

TIME DILATION

The brain identifies the passage of time by determining if ongoing events are similar to prior experiences. New, emotionally charged, or threatening experiences increase the volume of data absorbed during an event. Increased attention to minute aspects of an experience, results in more information being processed by the brain. This leads to a perception of experiencing a longer interval of time. The emotions we feel in the moment also directly affect our perception of time. During moments of extreme stress, fear, or life-threatening situations, enhanced concentration and focused attention on events alter the apparent passage of time. Fear produces a lengthening effect on time perception, as the brain records more details concerning the experience (Droit-Volet, 2011).

Fear induced distortion of time allows us to remember with specific detail what we experience. The perception of time is based on the quantity of data remembered, therefore, memory experiences inundated with detail are perceived as happening more slowly. The perception of danger can induce a chemical reaction in the brain that increases the ability to remember. The brain is flooded with the hormone noradrenaline, which amplifies focus and increases the ability to remember explicitly moments of lethal danger. As a result, emotionally disturbing events tend to be well remembered after a single experience. This unusual focus and the establishment of in-depth memories are based on the emotional response an event invokes. The more emotionally charged the event, the more detailed the memory becomes, and the longer the moment seems to last. This apparent slowing down of time is called *time dilation* (Holloway-Erickson, 2012).

EXPERIENCING TIME DILATION

Jeff Wise, author of *Extreme Fear: The Science of Your Mind in Danger* (2009), writes survivors of life-and-death situations often report that during near death experiences things seem to take longer to happen; objects appear to move in slow motion. The survivors relate seeing minute details and having complex thoughts in a period represented by the blink of an eye. Their intense fear had a very strange side effect, time dilation. Wise relates an amazing experience submitted by a reader.

> *A car turned left on a red turn arrow right in front of me. I was going 45 and T-Boned the car. I remember thinking many things and logically thinking: Turn left? No other cars are coming, go straight? No, concrete in the center that I will hit, Turn right? Yes, best option, even though I will certainly hit the car. This was slow, but when I hit the car, everything slowed down to a snail's pace. I remember watching the airbag inflate. I watched as violent ripples that normally inflate an airbag in a fraction of a second, took forever to flow across the surface of the bag as it wobbled back and forth like a slow pendulum. When there was finally enough gas in the bag to have it fully inflated, BOOM!!! Everything was back to normal time and I was steering my vehicle to the curb. There was that deadened sound you have just experienced after a large bang and I couldn't tell if it was from the impact or the airbag blowing up in my face. Probably both... but I will never forget what an airbag looks like as it is inflating. That thing that happens in less than a blink of an eye was a several minute production for me to watch and study (Wise, 2010).*

DISTORTED PERCEPTION

> *During a violent shoot-out, I looked over, drawn to the sudden mayhem, and was puzzled to see beer cans slowly floating through the air past my face. What was even more puzzling was that they had the word Federal printed on the bottom. They turned out to be the shell casings ejected by the officer who was firing next to me (Artwohl, 2002, p. 18).*

That statement, given by an officer involved in a shooting, is included in an article by Alexis A. Artwohl, titled *Perceptual and Memory Distortion During Officer-Involved Shootings*. Artwohl is an internationally recognized behavioral science consultant to law enforcement, a researcher, and author. Artwohl's research indicates trauma and other highly emotional experiences can radically affect perception and memory (Artwohl, 2002).

One of Artwohl's research projects indicates perception can be altered during police officer shootings. It described a number of perceptual changes immediately before, during, and immediately after the shootings. The officers all related their emotional state was one of fear, not necessarily for themselves, but still present. The emotion of fear correlates with negative valence. Valence is the psychological term for an instinctual response. The officers reported the unfamiliar ability to see details with unexplainable clarity in eighty two percent of the shootings (Artwohl, 1997).

Reporting officers described the three major components of time dilation during shooting events: attention, arousal, and valence. All officers reported their vision became intensely focused on the perceived threat. This narrowly focused vision and concentration correlates with attention. Heightened visual clarity, causing one to see an astonishing number of details, was reported in sixty-five percent of the shootings. Sixty-three percent of the officers reported events seemed to be taking place in slow motion and seemed to take longer to happen than they actually did (Artwohl, 1997; Klinger, 2002).

ATTENTION, AROUSAL, AND VALENCE

Time perception research indicates the brain is accustomed to processing a certain amount of information during a given time. The brain concludes it requires a longer duration of time to process a greater than normal number of observations. This process advocates a close correlation between time and memory. Several factors can cause distorted perceptions when estimating elapsed time. Three aspects particularly relevant are attention, arousal, and valence. Individually these variables can each increase the retention of memory minutia. The capacity for processing vast amounts of information in a short period is significantly intensified when attention, arousal, and valence are functioning in concert. The more memory details one retains of a complex event, the more likely the brain will interpret the event as requiring a longer duration of time (Angrilli, 1997).

ATTENTION

Attention is the cognitive process of selectively concentrating on one feature of an event while ignoring other things. This narrowly restricted focused concentration becomes fixed as long as the ongoing event is perceived as extraordinary. When this happens, the brain allocates a large amount of processing resources to recording the details of the event. Under normal circumstances, the brain processes a large amount of data at once: noting temperature, listening to conversation, formulating verbal replies, controlling muscle reactions, making cognitive decisions, and assessing visually the environment. This unexpected increase in data fools the brain into thinking an inordinate amount of time has passed (Wise, 2009; Angrilli, 1997).

AROUSAL

Arousal is a psychological state demonstrated by hyper-alertness or reactivity to stimuli. When the stimulus results in a negative emotional response, such as in anger or fear, we experience intensified vigilance. A larger number of details surrounding the event are recorded as memories, during this heightened state of awareness (Angrilli, 1997).

Research addressing the relationship between anxiety and time dilation indicates an anxious state would dramatically increase the opportunity for attention and arousal. While experiencing anxiety, even mildly threatening events could narrowly focus attention and raise arousal in individuals. Research indicates the subjective experience of time can be dramatically affected for anxious individuals when experiencing extreme negative valence (Bar-Haim, 2010).

VALENCE

The psychological term *valence* refers to the instinctive positive or negative emotional response to an event, object, or situation. The emotions popularly referred to as "negative," such as anger and fear, have negative valence. Studies of time perception show greater attention to detail is experienced and recorded by the mind during extreme negative emotional events (Angrilli, 1997).

When experiencing an extremely fearful situation, the amygdala communicates to the brain to cease all nonessential activity and devote all resources to the element causing the fear. Consequently, the brain is suddenly flooded with information concerning one highly focused area of concern. A simple way to explain time distortion is to imagine the brain has a constant meter of incoming information to process that coordinates with a running meter measuring time. For example, one unit of information processed equals one unit of time. The brain's assessment of passing time increases exponentially with an increase in processed information. The brain erroneously concludes increased processed data was a product of a longer time span, creating the illusion that time had slowed (Wise, 2009).

FALSE MEMORIES

The process for creating memories is not a well-understood process. Biases, beliefs, expectations, and prior experiences can all influence people's perceptions of an event. If recollection of an event is not a precise representation of reality, it does not necessarily mean someone is lying. Research specifies memory is not a perfect recording of events, nor are events recalled exactly the same each time a person tries to remember a past event. It is normal for memories to change slightly over time, and the changed, or new memories, may or may not represent reality more accurately than the original memory. Artwohl's research determined twenty-one percent of officers engaged in a shooting saw, heard, or experienced something during the event, later proven false (Artwohl, 2002).

Implicit memory also leads to the *illusion-of-truth effect,* which advocates subjects are more likely to perceive as true statements that they have already heard or that they are familiar with, regardless of their veracity. So the more often the false information is heard, the more real it becomes. Eyewitness testimony can also be distorted by confirmation bias. Hearing or seeing an event occur in a particular fashion can create a false memory or a biased expectation of what will happen if the event is repeated. For example, when repeatedly seeing teenage drivers run a stop sign, an accident observed later at that location will prompt a false memory of observing the involved young driver run the stop sign (Hasher, 1977; Eysenck, 2004).

Some witnesses sincerely and fervently maintain that their memories are accurate when they may not be accurate at all. Interestingly, false memories can feel more real to the witness than what actually took place. A veteran

SWAT officer watched a videotape that conclusively proved he reported things that did not happen during a shooting.

> *Doc, I now intellectually know that what I thought I saw didn't really happen, but it still feels more real to me than what I saw on the tape (Artwohl, p. 18, 2002).*

ASSASSINATION WITNESSES-TIME DILATION

If attention, arousal, or valence can be applied to the Kennedy assassination, it is possible eyewitnesses sustained time distortion. The witnesses would have had to experience (a) a narrowly focused concentration because they perceived the event as extraordinary, (b) a heightened state of awareness, or (c) an extreme negative emotional response to the assassination. Additionally, anxiety may have enhanced the possibility of time dilation for witnesses. Common sense indicates that at least one of these reactions among those present in Dealey Plaza is possible. Witnesses to the murder of the President conceivably experienced time distortion.

It is likely many of the witnesses had never personally seen a sitting President before the day of the motorcade. This exclusive opportunity would have increased the possibility that the attention of bystanders was already focused on the Presidential limousine and its occupants. Certainly, not many people have witnessed a shooting, and even less an assassination of a President. It is conceivable that casual observations suddenly became very narrowly focused concentration, when the spectators realized the President had been shot.

Fear for personal safety would have been a natural response for those near the limousine, especially if they believed they were in the line of fire. If witnesses perceived the event as extraordinary, their focus may have intensified, and a heightened state of awareness, combined with fear, may have resulted in time dilation. Similar to the driver who wrote he would never forget seeing an airbag inflate, or the police officer who thought he was seeing Federal beer cans float by, the limo may have appeared to have slowed or even stopped for some witnesses.

THE PERCEIVED LIMO STOP

President Kennedy, Mrs. Kennedy, and Governor and Mrs. Connally were seated in a 1961 Lincoln Continental convertible at the time of the assassination. Special Agent William Greer was driving the limousine; Special Agent Roy Kellerman was seated in the front passenger seat. It appears the limousine began to slow just before the fatal headshot. In fact, the brake lights are recorded in the Muchmore film for about nine frames, or half a second. Witnesses to the assassination have contradictory opinions concerning whether or not the limousine stopped or merely slowed during the shooting. The majority of the witnesses believe the vehicle slowed; a few have maintained the vehicle came to a complete stop.

Based on the numerous studies of time perception since 1952, it appears the phenomenon of distorted time is more likely to occur when individuals are experiencing a highly charged emotional event, and it can be significantly enhanced if the experienced event is perceived as life threatening. Stimulus that is highly unusual and correspondingly emotionally engaging can trigger the experience of slowing time. Hearing gunshots, being unsure of their origin, and witnessing the homicide of another human being would certainly qualify as a life-threatening, highly charged emotional event. That circumstance creates the perfect opportunity for time perception errors.

BILL NEWMAN

Bill Newman, his wife Gayle, and his sons were on the Grassy Knoll waiting for the Presidential motorcade. As the President's car came into view, Newman heard what he thought were fireworks. However, as the limousine drew closer, Newman said he could see blood on President Kennedy and Texas Governor John Connally, who was in the car with the President. In a 1995 telephone interview conducted by the author, Newman related the following:

> *The car was about 10 feet away from us when I heard the third shot and the side of his head flew off. I remember seeing the blood in front of his face. It was like a very fine red mist or a cloud of blood in about two feet or so in the diameter front of his face, and then it just disappeared.*

The details of Newman's memories were expounded upon in *Crossfire: The Plot That Killed Kennedy* (Marrs, 1992).

> *The car momentarily stopped and the driver seemed to have a radio or phone up to his ear and he seemed to be waiting on some word. Some Secret Service men reached into their car and came out with some sort of machine gun. Then the cars roared off. I've maintained that they stopped. I still say they did. It was only a momentary stop (Marrs, 1992, p. 70).*

Newman described the spatter he witnessed in the same manner blood spatter analysts describe back spatter; as a mist. Looking closely at Zapruder Frame 313, it is readily apparent the film depicts what Bill Newman witnessed and related. The blood spatter was created and dissipated in approximately 1/6 of a second. However, for Newman, time had slowed, providing sufficient opportunity to observe and commit to memory the detail of the back spatter bloodstain pattern created and dispersed from President Kennedy's head wound.

Newman also said the limousine momentarily stopped and the driver seemed to have a radio or phone up to his ear and he seemed to be waiting on some word. Special Agent Roy Kellerman testified to the Warren Commission he had made a radio call just before the headshot, confirming Newman's memory of the event (2H74). Newman also remembers a Secret Service agent with some sort of machine gun. Warren Commission Exhibit 1024 contains a statement from Secret Service Agent George Hinkey concerning the event.

> *At the end of the last report, I reached to the bottom of the car and picked up the AR 15 rifle, cocked and loaded it, and turned to the rear. At this point, the cars were passing under the overpass and as a result, we had left the scene of the shooting. I kept the AR 15 rifle ready as we proceeded at a high rate of speed to the hospital (18H763).*

Newman does not mention Mrs. Kennedy leaving her seat, which means everything he described happened between approximately frame 313 and frame 345 of the Zapruder film. Since the camera Zapruder used filmed at 18.3 frames per second, Newman observed the blood on Kennedy and Connally as they approached, witnessed the gunshot injury to the head, observed the resulting blood spatter, observed Kellerman on the radio and noted the Secret Service agent with the machine gun within 1.77 seconds.

Newman and his family were the closest spectators when the President was killed. A shooting and witnessing a death certainly could be perceived as highly unusual and life threatening. Distorted time perception would explain why Newman believed the limousine had to have stopped in order for him to observe and commit to memory so many details of the shooting. Apparently, for Bill Newman, time did momentarily stand still.

The Films and the Stop

Witnesses to the assassination disagree concerning whether or not the limousine stopped or merely slowed during the shooting. The majority of the witnesses believe the vehicle slowed; however, a few have maintained the vehicle came to a complete stop. Those witnesses may have suffered a distorted since of time; consequently, the films taken during the assassination provide a more accurate view of the limousine's travel. Although detractors of the film believe it has been altered in some fashion, other films taken that day from different locations within Dealey Plaza closely mirror the events depicted in Zapruder's film.

Zapruder Film

Abraham Zapruder stood atop a concrete pedestal along Elm Street, with the Grassy Knoll to his right and slightly behind his position. He began filming as the President's limousine turned onto Elm Street and captured the assassination on color motion picture film. There are other photographs and films of the shooting, but the Zapruder film is the only complete, continuous record of the assassination known to exist.

After the assassination, Zapruder gave the camera to the Federal Bureau of Investigation as part of their investigation. While in the possession of the FBI, they performed several technical tests on the camera. One of the goals of the tests performed by FBI photographic expert Lyndal L. Shaneyfelt was to determine the speed of the camera at the time it recorded the assassination. The results of the tests conducted at the FBI laboratory were later substantiated by the Bell & Howell Company. Shaneyfelt testified, "Yes; we have established that the Zapruder motion picture camera operates at an average speed of 18.3 frames per second" (5H153).

The Warren Report states, "Examination of the Zapruder motion picture camera by the FBI established 18.3 pictures or frames were taken each second, and therefore, the timing of certain events could be calculated by allowing 1/18.3 second for the action depicted from one frame to the next." Since Agent Shaneyfelt numbered 486 frames, the Zapruder film's run time is 26.4 seconds [486 divided by 18.3 equals 26.5] (9WCR:97).

NIX FILM

Orville Nix positioned himself near the curb at the southwest corner of Main and Houston Streets. As the Presidential motorcade traveled down Main Street and turned right onto Houston, Nix began filming. His initial sequence of approximately 115 frames, or just over 6 seconds, recorded the President's limousine moving north on Houston away from Nix's position. His view of the President's car is blocked by nearby spectators. In order to get a better view of the motorcade, Nix hurriedly walked to just west of Houston Street on the south side of Main Street. This position, later determined by the FBI, was approximately 200 feet from the center line of Elm Street, at the point where President Kennedy received the fatal head wound. From this final position, he filmed three sections of the motorcade: the Presidential limousine entering Dealey Plaza, the last portion of the assassination, and the aftermath of the shooting. Nix's film captured the fatal shot to President Kennedy's head, Mrs. Kennedy climbing onto the rear of the limousine, and Secret Service agent Clint Hill jumping onto the rear of the limousine as it left Dealey Plaza. The Nix film shows the limousine slowed, but does not show the limousine completely stopping. Even though the images on his film were discussed by several individuals in the government's final report, Nix was not called to testify before the Warren Commission.

MUCHMORE FILM

Marie M. Muchmore (1909-1990) stood near the northwest corner of Main Street and Houston Street. The Muchmore film consists of seven sequences, six before, and one during the shooting. Muchmore began filming the Presidential motorcade as it turned onto Houston Street from near the northwest corner of Main Street and Houston Street. She walked northwestward to film the President's limousine on Elm Street. The Muchmore film captured the fatal headshot from about 138 feet away from the President. The film ended seconds later, as Secret Service agent Clint Hill climbed aboard the accelerating limousine.

BRONSON FILM

On the day of the assassination, Charles Bronson and his wife stood atop a concrete abutment at the southwest corner of Main and Houston, nearly five feet above street level. This location provided a clear line-of-sight from Bronson's location to the corner of Elm and Houston. When the President's car made the sharp left turn onto Elm, the first 150 feet of Elm was blocked by a large tree and the concrete colonnade located on the west side of Houston Street.

Armed with a Keystone 8 millimeter movie camera loaded with color film, Bronson filmed the President's vehicle in two sequences; one as it made the right turn from Main to Houston Street, then as the limousine came into his view as it traveled west on Elm Street. Bronson kept filming in spite of hearing multiple gunshots being fired within close proximity. His film captured both the President's car and the Secret Service follow-up vehicle at the moment when the President received the fatal headshot. Bronson kept filming until the limousine and the follow-up car disappeared under the triple underpass. Even though Bronson captured less than a few seconds of the President's car on Elm Street, it does not appear it slowed or stopped.

SCIENTIFIC ANALYSIS

Physicist Luis W. Alvarez (1911-1988) received the Nobel Prize in 1968. He is also the recipient of the Presidential Medal for Merit, Albert Einstein Award, National Medal of Science, Michel Award, and the Enrico Fermi Award of the US Department of Energy, among others. Alvarez is considered one of the most prestigious and influential physicists of the twentieth century (Garwin, 1992).

In September 1976, Alvarez published an article in the *American Journal of Physics,* addressing several aspects of the Kennedy Assassination. One portion of the article focused on the speed and possible deceleration of the limousine during the moments surrounding the fatal headshot. The article was entered into the House Select Committee on Assassination records, however Alvarez was not called to testify.

The analysis completed by Alvarez revealed the limousine did not come to a complete stop. Alvarez wrote, "[T]he heavy car decelerated suddenly for about 0.5 sec (10 frames), centered at about frame 299, reducing its speed from about 12 mph to about 8 mph." In the article, Alvarez provides complete analysis techniques and indicates his computations concerning the speed of the limousine had been duplicated by other physicists prior to publication. In the final portion of the article, Alvarez states his work in determining the speed of the limousine was peer reviewed by physicists Sharon "Buck" Buckingham, Don Olson, and Paul Hoch (HSCA 1:428, 440, 441).

CONCLUSION

The assassination witnesses watched helplessly as the brutal murder of our nation's President unfolded. They heard the shots ring out, and saw the fatally wounded President fall toward his horrified wife. They witnessed the police and a crowd of bystanders rush up the Grassy Knoll in search of the killer. The eyewitnesses could easily have interpreted the events unfolding before them as dangerous, and were likely deeply affected by the murder of President Kennedy. The assassination unquestionably provided opportunity for distortions in time perception: focused concentration, fear, and an intensely negative emotional response to the shooting death of President Kennedy.

In the early 1960s, the American public had not been exposed to violent events on television. Censorship for those kinds of scenes was tightly controlled and violence was rarely shown on nightly newscasts. The majority of the population had not been desensitized by the violence we now routinely view in movies, television, and even the evening news. In fact, there were public concerns voiced in the early 1960s about the violence in television series, such as *The Rifleman and The Untouchables* (Cole, 1995).

The basis for believing the limousine stopped rests solely on witness statements; the Zapruder film, the Nix film and the Muchmore film all show the vehicle simply slowing. In order to maintain the claim the limousine stopped one would have to prove all three films are altered, which has not been done. In fact, world renowned physicist Luis Alvarez's analysis of the Zapruder film indicates the limousine slowed from about twelve miles an hour to approximately eight miles an hour. At least three other physicists concur with his results, thereby strengthening the validity of his conclusions.

The assassination witnesses were likely to have been emotionally affected by the murder of President Kennedy. Research has proven during moments of extreme stress or life-threatening situations, heightened concentration and fixated attention alter the perceived passage of time. Enhanced concentration and focused attention on events alter the perceived passage of time and so make it seem longer than it really is (Cole, 1995).

The variance in the statements of witnesses concerning the limousine stopping can be explained forensically by the application of time dilation. Based upon research, Dealey Plaza witnesses may have experienced the extraordinary perception of slowed time; a credible explanation for erroneously believing the limousine stopped. Their brain processed an unprecedented amount of detail in a short period, resulting in a distorted perception of time. As a result, for those few witnesses, during the extraordinary moments of the assassination of President Kennedy, time stood still.

CHAPTER 5

BALLISTICS PROVE ONE SHOOTER

The nearly whole bullet found on Governor Connally's stretcher at Parkland Memorial Hospital, and the two bullet fragments, found in the front seat of the Presidential limousine, were fired from the 6.5-millimeter Mannlicher Carcano rifle found on the sixth floor of the Depository Building to the exclusion of all other weapons (WCR, p. 18).

According to the Warren Commission, Lee Harvey Oswald fired at President Kennedy and Governor Connally using 6.5 millimeter Mannlicher Carcano full metal-jacketed bullets, manufactured by the Western Cartridge Company. One whole bullet was recovered at Parkland Hospital and, according to the Commission, caused seven nonfatal wounds on Kennedy and Connally. This make of bullet is designed to stay intact after striking the target. However, an autopsy confirmed the shot that struck the President in the head splintered into minuscule pieces of metal. Because the bullets reacted differently, there was speculation the two bullets may have been of different makes and perhaps even fired from different weapons. Consequently, the Warren Commission was seeking forensic analysis that would establish proof a single weapon, utilizing a limited number of shots, was used in the shooting death of President Kennedy. If ballistic evidence suggested a second weapon or more than three shots, by definition, the assassination involved a conspiracy; and the Warren Commission would be burdened with proving how Oswald could have used two different types of bullets in killing President Kennedy. In order to assure the American people Lee Oswald was the sole assassin, the Warren Commission needed to resolve the issue.

The Warren Commission utilized ballistic compositional testing to examine fragments recovered from the victims in the limousine and the bullet recovered from the hospital stretcher. A match between the fragments and the bullet would eliminate a second shooter and confirm Oswald acted alone. Forensic analysis of the lead fragments collected as evidence, and the ammunition collected from the weapon, could be proven as coming from the same batch by Neutron Activation Analysis (NAA). Mysteriously, the FBI completed Neutron Activation Analysis, but did not make the results known to the Warren Commission, creating concerns about what it may have proven. Controversy persisted until the House Select Committee on Assassinations completed Comparative Bullet Lead Analysis. Those results specify uniqueness about the Mannlicher Carcano ammunition that indicated all ballistic evidence specimens originated from only two bullets. Although analysis provided what sounded like reasonable conclusions, a later test would show they were not justified.

WARREN COMMISSION BALLISTIC ANALYSIS

The Warren Commission determined the Mannlicher Carcano rifle found on the sixth floor of the Texas School Book Depository fired the shots that killed President Kennedy and wounded Governor Connally. Three spent casings, found adjacent to a window allegedly used by the shooter, suggested only three shots were fired. In an effort to reconcile the number of casings with the injuries to Kennedy, Connally and James Tague, Warren Commission staff attorney Arlen Specter developed the single bullet theory. Therefore, it became essential to develop ballistic evidence to prove only two bullets were necessary to have caused all wounds suffered by President Kennedy and

Governor Connally. There were two types of analyses available to the Warren Commission that could prove that theory: ballistic tool mark analysis and testing the compositional makeup of bullet lead to identify a chemical signature.

BALLISTIC TOOL MARK ANALYSIS

Rifling is a term that refers to the grooves machined into the barrel of a firearm to give a spin to the bullet during flight. This spin helps stabilize the bullet, thereby improving accuracy and increasing the distance the bullet will travel. Raised ridges traveling along the length of the barrel are called *lands*; the spaces between the raised ridges are called *grooves*. These lands and grooves also have a twist or slight rotation to the left or right, depending on make and model which creates the spin. The number, width, direction of twist and the degree of twist can vary between makes and models.

Unintentional, random and distinctive microscopic marks are generated during the manufacture of a firearm's barrel rifling. Additional imperfections can also be produced by excessive use, corrosion, or damage. Firearm materials are harder than ammunition components, therefore the interior of the barrel acts as a tool that leaves unique, impressed or striated marks on the ammunition with which it comes into contact. Mechanisms like the firing pin, extractor and ejector also affect the surfaces of the cartridges as they are fed, fired and ejected from the firearm. Cartridges and cartridge cases are examined for similarities in breech marks, firing pin impressions, extractor marks, ejector marks and other named tool marks associated with firearms.

Forensic examiners measure bullet size to determine caliber, then check the direction of rifling marks and the degree of twist to narrow down the gun's manufacturer. To match a specific firearm to a bullet, a standard must be obtained. Examiners test-fire the weapon and then retrieve the fired bullets to use as known standards during the comparison. The standards and unknown bullets are then examined under a microscope that allows the examiner to observe both bullets simultaneously for identical markings.

Like fingerprints, no two firearms, even those of the same make and model, will produce the same marks on fired bullets and cartridge cases. Furthermore, the manufacturing processes and the use of the firearm leave surface characteristics that cannot be exactly reproduced in any other firearm. This means the tool marks are unique to each firearm.

BULLET CHEMICAL SIGNATURE

When the physical markings of a fired bullet are too mutilated for visual comparison, or the firearm used in the crime is not recovered, the bullet can be compared with other bullets by its elemental composition. Analysis of lead used to manufacture bullets reveals each batch of lead manufactured and contains a unique chemical signature. Antimony, copper, arsenic and other trace metals are commonly found at various levels within lead used to manufacture ammunition. Determining what elements are present in the lead alloy, and quantifying their volume, provides identification of the chemical signature. The chemical signature allows analysts to compare the chemical makeup of different ammunition to determine if they share a common source (Peters, 2002).

ATOMIC ABSORPTION SPECTROSCOPY

In 1952, physicist and metallurgist Alan Walsh (1916-1998) used a process called *Atomic Absorption Spectroscopy* (AAS) for testing metals. Walsh was the originator and developer of this new method of chemical analysis, which is described as the most significant advance in chemical analysis in the twentieth century. Walsh first used this process to test metals in agricultural products and metal mining. Atomic absorption provided a quick, easy, accurate and highly sensitive method of determining the concentrations of more than sixty-five elements in metals, rendering traditional wet-chemical methods obsolete. Atomic absorption has found significant applications worldwide in areas such as medicine, agriculture, mineral exploration, and metallurgy. The analysis of metals quickly moved to forensic testing of bullet lead for law enforcement (Peters, 2002).

Atomic Absorption Spectrometry (AAS) analysis determines the specific chemical elements contained within a manufactured lead bullet using a number of methods. AAS measures the wavelength and spectral line intensity produced by any one of several methods of excitation, such as arc, flame, infrared, and X-Ray. Since 1960, analysis of the chemical makeup of bullet lead has been used by law enforcement for criminal investigations nationwide. Chemical analysis through spectroscopy in 1963 detected minute amounts of trace elements in bullet fragment lead alloys. Atomic Absorption Spectrometry identified and quantified three elements in bullet lead: antimony, copper, and arsenic. It provided a quick, easy, and highly sensitive means of determining the concentrations of components, but often produced unreliable results, due to interference from untested elements (Peters, 2002; Goho, 2004).

NEUTRON ACTIVATION ANALYSIS
In 1936, George Charles de Hevesy (1885-1966) and his assistant Hilde Levi (1909-2003) discovered Neutron Activation Analysis (NAA). Among other achievements, Hevesy received the Nobel Prize for Chemistry in 1943 for his work on the use of isotopes as tracers in the study of chemical processes. Hevesy and Levi found samples containing certain rare earth elements became highly radioactive after exposure to a source of neutrons. This observation led to the use of induced radioactivity for the identification of elements. Researchers at General Atomic, under a federal grant to develop uses for neutron activation analysis, developed comparative bullet lead analysis in the early 1960s. The result of their research was published in the 1970 U.S. Atomic Energy Commission Report (Schlesinger, 1970; Peters, 2002).

In 1975, *The Journal of the Forensic Science Society* published an article by Gary W. Stupian, PhD titled "Lead Isotope Ratio Measurements: A Potential Method for Bullet Identification." In the article, Stupian, a senior scientist with the Aerospace Corporation in California, discussed the potential for the individualization of bullets. Stupian suggested the isotopic composition of lead changes with the place of origin of the lead ore. He suggested the application of isotope ratio analysis could be used to identify trace elements in bullet lead, thereby providing a method of bullet identification. Stupian included results of a limited number of analyses of bullet lead, yet indicated a great deal of additional experimental work was required (Stupian, 1975).

BALLISTIC EVIDENCE

Much of the evidence in the Kennedy assassination is related to firearms. In order to prove a single shooter had fired only three shots, the Warren Commission was hoping to develop an association between the bullets and fragments collected. The following items of evidence, among other items collected, were examined in order to make that association.

1. CE 399: One whole 6.5-millimeter bullet recovered from a stretcher in the emergency area of Parkland Hospital. This is the bullet believed to have struck both the President and Governor Connally

2. CE 543: One Western Cartridge Co. 6.5-millimeter expended shell casing recovered from the sixth floor of the Texas School Book Depository

3. CE 544: One Western Cartridge Co. 6.5-millimeter expended shell casing recovered from the sixth floor of the Texas School Book Depository

4. CE 545: One Western Cartridge Co. 6.5-millimeter expended shell casing recovered from the sixth floor of the Texas School Book Depository

5. CE 567: The nose and base portion of a 6.5-millimeter bullet recovered from the right side of the front seat of the Presidential limousine

6. CE 569: The base portion of a damaged 6.5-millimeter full metal jacket bullet located on the floor near the right front seat of the Presidential limousine

7. CE 840: Three lead fragments recovered from under the left jump-seat of the Presidential limousine

8. CE 842: Four lead fragments, which have been identified as having been surgically removed from the right wrist of Governor John Connally

9. CE 843: Three lead fragments, which have been identified as having been surgically removed from the brain of John Kennedy

10. CE 567: Five lead fragments, and one large copper and lead fragment, with the large copper fragment bearing fibrous debris and the smaller pieces bearing organic material

COMMISSION EXHIBIT 840

November 23, 1963, Special Agent Frazier examined the Presidential limousine at the Secret Service garage in Washington DC. Three small lead fragments were located near the left jump seat. The fragments, described as weighing 9/10 of a grain and two fragments weighing 7/10 of a grain are identified as Commission Exhibit 840. *Grain* is a measurement used to document the weight of bullets. One ounce is comprised of 437.5 grains. The 6.5 millimeter caliber cartridge of Western Cartridge Company, supposedly used in the

Mannlicher Carcano rifle, was designed with 162 grains. The fragments tested were less than 1/162 of the weight of an intact 6.5 millimeter caliber cartridge of a Western Cartridge Company bullet. Originally, Commission Exhibit 840 contained three lead particles.

> *FRAZIER: We found three small lead particles lying on the floor in the rear seat area. These particles were located underneath, or in that area, which would be underneath the left jump seat.*

> *SPECTER: Will you produce them at this time then, please? May we assign to this group of particles Commission Exhibit No. 840?*

> *DULLES: It shall be admitted as Commission Exhibit No. 840 (5H 66).*

Although testimony indicates the FBI originally recovered three particles identified as Commission Exhibit 840, in 1970, the National Archives determined one of the three fragments was missing and unable to be located. The National Archives and Records Administration photographs of Commission Exhibit 840 and FBI C16 now depict two small lead fragments. One of the items of evidence has disappeared.

BALLISTIC TOOL MARK ANALYSIS

A round of ammunition, called a *cartridge* is composed of a primer, a cartridge case, powder, and a bullet. The base of the cartridge contains a primer, a metal cup containing an explosive mixture adjacent to the area loaded with the powder. The bullet, which usually consists of lead, or a lead core encased in a metal jacket, fits into the neck of the cartridge case. To fire the bullet, the cartridge is placed in the chamber of a firearm, located immediately behind the firearm's barrel. The base of the cartridge rests against the breech face or, in the case of a bolt-operated weapon, the bolt face. When the trigger is pulled, a firing pin strikes the primer, detonating the priming mixture. The flames from the resulting explosion ignite the powder, causing a rapid combustion, whose force propels the bullet forward through the barrel. Each of those actions has potential for impressing upon the ammunition unique defects that make tool mark identification possible (AFTE, 1998).

Identification is possible when sufficient agreement exists between two tool marks; meaning the likelihood another tool could have made the mark is so remote as to be considered a practical impossibility. The Association of Firearm and Tool Mark Examiners (AFTE) states examiners either: (1) indicate comparison of the microscopic features are sufficient to conclude individual tool marks on two items are the same and therefore a match; (2) a discrepancy exists in the class characteristics exhibited by two tool marks and therefore the suspect item is excluded from a match; (3) when there is agreement in the class characteristics but insufficient agreement in the fine microscopic marks, an inconclusive response is appropriate; (4) conclude the evidence tool mark is unsuitable for comparison (AFTE, 1998).

WARREN COMMISSION TOOL MARK ANALYSIS

The FBI Laboratory's Firearms Unit was responsible for directing the examination and analysis of the firearm related evidence for the Warren Commission. FBI Special Agents Robert A. Frazier, Cortlandt Cunningham and Charles Killion, together with Joseph D. Nicol, Superintendent of the Illinois State Bureau of Criminal Identification, comprised the panel responsible for examining the firearm evidence. Three experts gave testimony concerning firearms and firearms identification: Robert A. Frazier and Cortlandt Cunningham of the FBI, and Joseph D. Nicol, Superintendent of the Bureau of Criminal Identification and Investigation of the State of Illinois. Testimony concerning the tool mark identification was provided by Frazier, who testified on the rifle, the rifle cartridge cases, and the rifle bullets; and Nicol, who addressed identifying evidence on the bullets and cartridge cases.

After examining the ballistic evidence, the experts presented the results of their investigation to the Warren Commission. They concluded (a) the three spent cartridges found on the sixth floor of the Texas School Book Depository had been fired from the Mannlicher Carcano rifle; (b) Commission Exhibit 399, the bullet found at Parkland Hospital, had been fired through the Mannlicher Carcano rifle; (c) the bullet nose portion and the bullet base portion found on the right side of the front seat of the Presidential limousine had been fired through the Mannlicher Carcano rifle; (d) whether the bullet nose portion and the bullet base portion found in the Presidential limousine were components of the same bullet could not be determined, due to the condition of the bullet (WC Appendix 10:562-568).

HSCA TOOL MARK ANALYSIS

The five members of the House Select Committee on Assassinations Firearm Analysis and Tool Mark Panel were experts nationally recognized for their work in the area of ballistics and firearm identification. They were charged with examining the physical evidence and in answering questions that had arisen following the publication of the Warren Commission Report. Each individual panel member microscopically examined the ballistic evidence and made a separate report. A summary report was provided to the Warren Commission based upon the findings and conclusions of the panel members.

The Firearm Analysis and Tool Mark Panel fired ammunition through the Mannlicher Carcano in anticipation of using the bullets as a standard for comparison identifications. Bullets the firearms panel fired from the rifle did not match either the FBI test cartridges or those found on the sixth floor of the Texas School Book Depository; nor did they match the bullet found on the stretcher at Parkland Hospital. The striking discovery was the test bullets fired by the HSCA panel through the Mannlicher Carcano rifle did not even match each other. Since the rifle had been test-fired numerous times since 1963, the panel assumed its barrel had been altered by wear and deterioration of the rifling surfaces within the barrel over time. Consequently, the panel was forced to use 6.5 millimeter bullets fired from the Mannlicher Carcano rifle by the FBI as a standard for comparisons with class characteristics against (a) Commission Exhibit 399, a 6.5 millimeter bullet recovered from a stretcher in the emergency area of Parkland Hospital; (b) Commission Exhibit 567, the nose and base portion of a 6.5 millimeter bullet recovered from the right side of the front seat of the Presidential limousine; and (c) Commission Exhibit 569, the base portion of a damaged 6.5 millimeter full metal jacket bullet located in the front of the Presidential limousine (HSCA Appendix, 7:365- 383).

The report of the House Select Committee on Assassinations Firearm and Tool Mark Analysis Panel Report included the following; (a) individual characteristics on all three cartridges cases found on the sixth floor of the Texas School Book Depository indicate the cartridges had been fired from the same barrel; (b) Commission Exhibit 399, the bullet found at Parkland Hospital, had been fired through the same barrel as the test-fired bullets; (c) the bullet nose, Commission Exhibit 569, found on the right side of the front seat of the Presidential limousine, had been fired through the same barrel as the test-fired bullets; (d) whether Commission Exhibit 567, the bullet nose portion, and the bullet base portion found in the Presidential limousine, were components of the same bullet could not be determined; (e) Commission Exhibit 399, the stretcher bullet, weighed 158.6 gains when recovered. Its original weight before firing is assumed to have been 160-161 grains. Because all bullet weights are approximate and the exact weight was unknown, the panel was not able to provide a definite opinion as to the possibility the bullet sustained a weight loss of only 1.4 to 2.4 grains during the wounding of President Kennedy and Governor Connally. Minute pieces of metal removed from the victims were too small for tool mark comparisons. Utilizing the same evidence the FBI used, the HSCA findings were the same as the Warren Commission's conclusions (HSCA Appendix, 7:368-383).

BALLISTIC CHEMICAL SIGNATURE ANALYSIS
The Warren Commission needed to establish a strong connection between bullets fired from the Mannlicher Carcano rifle and the wounds inflicted during the assassination. The only method available at that time was to compare the metallic composition of all the ballistic specimens through a scientific process called *spectrographic analysis*. The identifiable bullets and fragments found outside the victims' bodies and tiny pieces of metal removed from the bodies were subjected to spectrographic analysis. The Commission hoped the analyses would provide a conclusive answer to the question of Oswald's guilt: Did the bullets from Oswald's rifle produce the wounds of the victims? If a fragment from a body were not identical in composition with a fragment recovered from the limousine, more than one shooter would have to be considered. The standards for reporting identical composition would necessitate matching elements in exact quantities.

WARREN COMMISSION SPECTROGRAPHIC ANALYSIS
Commission Exhibit 399 was a whole 6.5 millimeter bullet allegedly recovered from a stretcher in the emergency area of Parkland Hospital. This is the bullet believed to have struck both the President and Governor Connally. Traces of copper were found on the bullet holes in the back of the President's coat and

shirt. The copper residue on the clothing and the fragments of lead removed from the Governor's wrist could have been compared with Commission Exhibit 399 using spectrographic analysis. Any variation between the two copper samples would rule out 399 as being the magic bullet capable of traversing the two men and remaining pristine.

In 1963, the FBI analyzed some of the recovered bullet fragments using a process called *Emission Spectrography*. This procedure subjects the samples to intense heat and determines their metallic composition by the color of the gases emitted. Spectrographic analysis was completed by the FBI. There can only be speculation concerning the items analyzed, as the FBI claimed to have arrived at inconclusive results. The Commission took the FBI at its word without ever having looked at the spectrographer's report or entering the relevant documents into the record. The complete results of the spectrographic analysis were never reported to the Commission and no specific testimony relevant to the report was given. One could easily assume, had the spectrographic analysis provided the incontestable proof of the validity of the Warren Report's central conclusions, it would have been included in the Report, eliminating any doubt.

Dallas Police Chief Jesse Curry received a report from FBI Director Hoover summarizing the results of the laboratory examination of the bullet fragments. The Firearms/Spectrographic/Microscopic Analyses report stated the following evidence was available for analysis:

1. Q1 Bullet from stretcher
2. Q2 Bullet fragment from front seat cushion
3. Q3 Bullet fragment from beside front seat
4. Q4 Metal fragment from the President's head
5. Q5 Metal fragment from the President's head
6. Q6 6.5 millimeter Mannlicher Carcano cartridge case from building
7. Q7 6.5 millimeter Mannlicher Carcano cartridge case from building
8. Q8 6.5 millimeter Mannlicher Carcano cartridge from rifle
9. Q9 Metal fragment from arm of Governor John Connally
10. Q14 Three metal fragments recovered from rear floor board carpet
11. Q15 Scraping from inside surface of windshield

The Firearms/Spectrographic/Microscopic Analyses report listed the following conclusions:

1. The bullet, Q1, is a 6.5 millimeter Mannlicher Carcano rifle bullet. Specimen Q1 weighs 158.6 grains. It consists of a copper alloy jacket with a lead core.

2. Specimen Q2 is a portion of the core of a rifle bullet. Q2 weighs 44.6 grains and is composed of a portion of the copper alloy jacket and a portion of the lead core.

3. Specimen Q3 is a portion of the base section of a copper alloy rifle bullet. Q3 weighs 21.0 grains and is composed of a section of the jacket from which the lead core is missing.

4. It could not be determined whether specimens Q2 and Q3 are portions of the same bullet or are portions of two separate bullets.

5. The rifle is a 6.5 millimeter Mannlicher Carcano Italian military rifle Model 91738. Test bullets were fired from this rifle for comparison with specimens Q1, Q2 and Q3. As a result, Q1, Q2 and Q3 were identified as having been fired from the submitted rifle. Specimens Q6 and Q7 were identified as having been fired in this rifle.

6. The lead metal of Q4 and Q5, Q9, Q14 and Q15 is similar to the lead of the core of the bullet fragment, Q2.

Hoover indicated the bullet jackets were composed of copper alloy and the bullet cores were lead. Hoover's vague statement failed to address which specific metallic elements were combined with the copper to form the alloy, which the Emission Spectrographic analysis would have revealed. It is unlikely the submitted fragment specimens were composed solely of lead, since all modern ammunition contains quantities of other elements. Spectrographic analysis would have been specifically quantifying antimony, bismuth, and arsenic, which were commonly found in lead bullets.

The FBI report stated spectrographic analysis was conducted on bullet fragments recovered from President Kennedy's head, Governor Connally's wrist, from inside the limousine, and the metallic scraping from the limousine's windshield. However, the report does not address whether or not the metal fragments removed from Kennedy and Connally were identical to

Commission Exhibit 399, the recovered whole bullet credited with causing seven non-fatal wounds to both men (CE 2003, 24H262-264).

AGENT ROBERT FRAZIER'S TESTIMONY

Robert Frazier, one of the FBI's firearms experts, testified about the spectrograph analysis of ballistic evidence fragments. The first evidence discussed was the copper located on the rear of the President's jacket. Although the nuclear activation testing was cited as being completed on the copper, no results were offered. Of particular interest would have been comparing the copper from the President's clothing spectrographically with the intact copper jacketed bullet found on the stretcher in Parkland Hospital. If the copper from the jacket and from the jacketed Parkland bullet did not match in composition, Frazier would have to concede to the possibility two shooters were involved in the assassination. Perhaps this was not an oversight, because asking that question could have produced an answer specifically capable of dooming the single bullet theory (5H59).

Arlen Specter did not continue to pursue questioning focusing on the copper on the President's jacket. Instead, he asked next about the three small lead particles discovered lying on the rug underneath or in the area of the left jump seat. Frazier testified the fragments had been tested "for spectrographic analysis and comparison with other bullets and bullet fragments." Since the only bullets available for spectrographic analysis and comparison would be Commission Exhibit 399, the bullet removed from the Mannlicher Carcano rifle or ammunition test-fired through the Mannlicher Carcano rifle by the FBI, one would assume the fragments would be directly compared to the most significant evidence, the bullet believed to have injured Kennedy and Connally.

> SPECTER: *Has that comparison been made with a whole bullet heretofore identified as Commission Exhibit 399, which in here proceedings has been identified as the bullet from the Connally stretcher?*

> FRAZIER: *Yes, sir. The comparison was made by comparing Exhibit 399 with a bullet fragment found in the front seat of the Presidential limousine and then comparing that fragment with these fragments from the rear seat of the automobile.*

FRAZIER: That examination was performed by a spectrographer, John F. Gallagher, and I do not have the results of his examinations here, although I did ascertain that it was determined that the lead fragments were similar in composition.

SPECTER: So that they could have come from, so that the fragments designated 840 could have come from the same bullet as fragment designated 567?

FRAZIER: Yes, sir.

SPECTER: Were the tests sufficient to indicate conclusively whether fragments 840 did come from the fragment designated as 567?

FRAZIER: No, sir (5H 66-67).

Within Frazier's testimony, the reader will note several interesting issues are presented; (1) Frazier does not have the final results of the NAA testing in front of him; (2) he is testifying "he ascertained" the results of the NAA testing from Gallagher; (3) Frazier states the fragments identified as CE 840 and CE 567 "could have come from the same bullet", but the test was not conclusive. Similar to Hoover's report to Chief Curry, Frazier told the Warren Commission, "the lead fragments were similar in composition," but said nothing more definitive. Frazier continually reiterated Gallagher completed the spectrographic analysis and had detailed information concerning the results. Then Frazier reveals he actually wrote the formal report for the spectrographic analysis, contradicting either his implied lack of knowledge of the report's details or demonstrating a concerted effort to answer questions concerning spectrographic testing in the most general manner possible.

Specter concluded by asking a summary question concerning the comparisons of Commission Exhibit 399, the bullet collected from Parkland Hospital; Commission Exhibit 842, a fragment of metal identified as coming from Governor Connally; Commission Exhibit 840, the three fragments recovered from the rear floorboard carpet of the limousine; Commission Exhibit 841, the windshield scraping; Commission Exhibit 567, which was found on the front seat of the automobile and Commission Exhibit No. 843, two fragments from Kennedy's head.

> *SPECTER: Is it possible to state with any more certainty whether or not any of those fragments came from the same bullet?*
>
> *FRAZIER: Not definitely, no; only that they are of similar lead composition (5H73-74).*

In the Clay Shaw trial (*State of Louisiana v. Clay L. Shaw*, 1969), Special Agent Frazier testified in regards to the spectrographic analysis of the various bullet fragments recovered during the Kennedy assassination. When asked about similarities in the composition of the various ballistic specimens tested, he testified they all had the same metallic composition as far as the lead core or lead portions of these objects were concerned.

This statement does not quantify the volume of the trace elements used to confirm the fragments as matching or not matching each other, which is unusual, since the primary goal of spectrographic and neutron activation analysis is identifying individual elements and their percentages of the fragment's composition.

WARREN COMMISSION NEUTRON ACTIVATION ANALYSIS

In May of 1964, the FBI performed Neutron Activation Analysis (NAA) on ballistic evidence collected in the assassination to determine its composition in an attempt to prove a common origin, but again, the results were reported as inconclusive. More specific than Emission Spectrographic Analysis, Neutron Activation Analysis identifies the elements within lead and copper alloys, and quantifies the percentage present. Composition of the bullets and fragments should have been specifically determined. If analysis results could have provided a conclusive answer to what fragments had a single origin, then why provide testimony about general similarities in composition? The FBI's 1964, Neutron Activation Analysis findings would not be published until the House Select Committee on Assassinations employed the expert services of UC Irvine chemist Vincent P. Guinn in 1977. The unusual questioning of Special Agent John Gallagher, the scientist who performed the Neutron Activation Analysis, appears to avoid relating the specific results of that test.

AGENT JOHN F. GALLAGHER'S TESTIMONY

The spectrographic examinations and neutron activation analysis on the bullet fragments were performed by FBI Agent John F. Gallagher. The Warren Commission did not immediately call Special Agent Gallagher to clarify Frazier's testimony or to testify concerning the spectrographic analysis results and enter the report into the record. They waited four months, calling Gallagher as their last witness just two weeks before the report was submitted to President Johnson. During Gallagher's testimony, he was not asked to elaborate on FBI ballistics expert Robert Frazier's testimony regarding the spectrographic analysis conducted on the fragments. Providing the results of the spectrographic analysis and neutron activation analysis of the ballistic evidence should have been the primary reason Gallagher was called to testify. However, he seemed to focus more on the paraffin test conducted on Oswald's cheek and hands. Gallagher was asked if he determined the elements barium and antimony were present on the cartridges found on the sixth floor of the Texas School Book Depository. He replied in the affirmative, yet did not provide specifics on the results. This would have been an opportune time to delve into the specifics of the cartridge analysis. Unbelievably, the next question by Redliche abruptly changed the subject, moving from the cartridges back to the previously discussed analysis of paraffin casts. The results of the NAA testing on the cartridges was not revisited, and therefore never recorded in Gallagher's testimony. The reasoning behind the blatant manipulation of the direction of Gallagher's testimony is questionable.

The remainder of the questions asked of Gallagher to elicit his testimony did not focus on, or even allude to, the bullet fragments recovered from Kennedy, Connally or the limousine. The written reports communicating the process of ballistic tests completed by Gallagher were not entered into the official record. The results of the spectrographic test were not reviewed, nor were the neutron activation analysis results conveyed. Specifically, Gallagher was not asked if the bullet fragments recovered from President Kennedy, Governor Connally and the limousine were chemically related to CE399. In failing to do these things, the Commission ignored an ideal opportunity to confirm scientifically the single bullet theory, which was crucial to proving there was a single shooter (15H746-749).

HSCA NEUTRON ACTIVATION ANALYSIS

Warren Commission documents released after the publication of its report revealed, in addition to spectrographic testing, the FBI had arranged for bullet Commission Exhibit 399 and the various fragments found in the car and in Governor Connally's person to be examined using a method known as Neutron Activation Analysis. This technique is a very accurate, non-destructive method of determining the relative concentrations of trace elements in a sample of matter.

In 1977, the House Select Committee on Assassinations (HSCA) consulted with physicist Dr. Vincent P. Guinn (1917-2002) to review the FBI NAA data and conduct new Neutron Activation Analysis. Guinn was renowned in the field of Neutron Activation Analysis. In 1964, he received the American Nuclear Society's Special Award for Novel Applications of Nuclear Energy, a result of his application of NAA to forensic investigations. In 1979, Guinn received the George Hevesy Medal, an international award of excellence honoring outstanding achievements in radio-analytical and nuclear chemistry. He served as an adviser to the Atomic Energy Commission and made a training film on neutron activation analysis, which was in wide use in 1963 (Miller, 2002).

VINCENT GUINN'S TESTIMONY

When Guinn presented his analysis results to the House Select Committee on Assassinations, he stated he initially agreed with the FBI's earlier conclusions. However, after examining the old and new data further, he concluded all the fragments probably came from two bullets, one of which was the whole bullet recovered at Parkland Hospital. This whole bullet was designated as Commission Exhibit 399, and is often referred to as the magic bullet. Guinn also testified the fragment removed from the President's brain (Commission Exhibit 843) and the fragment recovered from the limousine (Commission Exhibit 840) were from one bullet. Guinn stated there was no evidence of a third bullet, which was consistent with the Warren Commission's initial findings that Lee Harvey Oswald acted alone in killing President Kennedy.

The neutron activation analysis results interpreted by Guinn proved the presence of quantified lead, antimony, silver, copper, aluminum, manganese, sodium and chlorine; however, antimony was the prime element considered by Guinn when reaching his conclusions. Guinn stated the antimony content of the evidence fragments was significantly higher than that found in most unhardened bullet lead, and significantly lower than that found in bullet lead of hardened lead bullets. Guinn determined the unusual intermediate range of antimony concentrations was particularly characteristic of the 6.5 millimeter Mannlicher Carcano manufactured ammunition. The test was also interpreted taking the silver concentration into account.

Guinn determined the values for the other six elements did not appear to contribute much useful information, and were not considered. Essentially, only two elements were analyzed to determine the samples originated from only two bullets. Restricted interpretation utilizing only two of the eight elements present in the analysis test did not appear problematic for Guinn, but he did express concern the evidence previously tested by the FBI was not available. When asked if he tested exactly the same particles the FBI tested in 1964, he replied,

> *Well, it turns out, I did not, for reasons I don't know, because as they did the analysis, they did not destroy the samples either. The particular little pieces that they analyzed, I could just as well have analyzed over again, but the pieces that were brought from the Archives-which reportedly, according to Mr. Gear were the only bullet-lead fragments from this case still present in the Archives-did not include any of the specific little pieces that the FBI had analyzed. Presumably, those are in existence somewhere, I am sure nobody threw them out, but where they are, I have no idea (HSCA, 1:491-567).*

UNIQUE AMMUNITION

In 1979, Guinn published an article in the professional journal *Analytical Chemistry* titled "JFK Assassination: Bullet Analysis." The article stated the FBI's 1964 Neutron Activation Analysis report listed 17 different values obtained from various parts of Commission Exhibit 399. The article revealed 1964 FBI neutron activation testing concluded individual Carcano bullets contained wide variances of antimony. This was in direct opposition to Guinn's testimony before the House Select Committee's investigation. It was disturbing that the newly published data conflicted so dramatically with the working theory Guinn used as the basis for his findings.

Based upon his findings, Vincent Guinn developed an atypical profile for Mannlicher Carcano ammunition. Unlike other ammunition, he determined there was a wide variety of measurable level trace elements between Mannlicher Carcano ammunition within the same production lot. As a result, bullets from a single box of ammunition could have widely varying analysis findings. Guinn also determined those same element levels didn't vary within a single individual bullet. That concept suggested the level of antimony, or any other element present, would be uniform throughout each layer of any individual Mannlicher Carcano bullet. Therefore, regardless of where the fragment originated from in a single bullet, the antimony level would be consistent. Guinn proposed rare yet consistent trace metal composition would permit fragments from Mannlicher Carcano ammunition to be matched to a specific bullet.

Guinn's theory concerning the uniqueness of the Mannlicher Carcano ammunition was presented repeatedly in his testimony. He stated the Western Cartridge Company Mannlicher Carcano ammunition presented no uniformity within production lots. Guinn maintained cartridges from a given production lot, packaged in a single box, if analyzed would display widely different results, particularly in their antimony content. He advocated a wide variation in composition from bullet to bullet for Mannlicher Carcano bullet lead. However, within an individual WCC Mannlicher Carcano bullet, Guinn stated his analysis proved there were no composition differences. Thus, finding two specimens that agree closely in chemical composition could only indicate they originated from the same bullet.

Based upon that premise, Guinn concluded the large fragment found in the limousine, the smaller fragments found on the floor of the limousine, and the fragments recovered from President Kennedy at the autopsy all originated from a single bullet. Guinn also determined the fragment recovered from Governor Connally's wrist originated from the bullet recovered from the stretcher at Parkland Hospital. Guinn's results indicated all tested specimens had originated from only two bullets. The inquiries producing that testimony were very specific and Guinn was very definitive in his response. In essence, the questions elicited scientific support for the single bullet theory. Guinn's testimony specified neutron activation analysis had proven the single bullet theory correct and, by default, the Warren Commission's edict that there was a single shooter. For the first time, it appeared scientific evidence would irrefutably deny a conspiracy (HSCA, 1:491-567).

VARIANCE IN TEST RESULTS

The results of the FBI's 1964, Neutron Activation Analysis report were very different from Guinn's. Apparently, Guinn felt the variance needed to be addressed, but his approach was not one anticipated. First, he suggested the data was misinterpreted by the FBI, due to the uniqueness of the Mannlicher Carcano bullet.

> *FITHIAN: Going from this conclusion, could the FBI have been able to draw the conclusion of only two bullets being present if someone, anyone there, did not have the kind of expertise in WCC Mannlicher Carcano ammunition that you have testified or that we understand you possess? Would someone not familiar with that kind of ammunition-could they have drawn the right conclusion?*

> *GUINN. It would have been certainly much more difficult because, as I say, most kinds of ammunition, other kinds that we have looked at over years, have been so uniform that you can't tell-you literally cannot tell one bullet from another out of the same box. WCC Mannlicher Carcano bullet lead, however, is different. The concentration range from bullet-to-bullet is tremendous (HSCA, I:491-567).*

Guinn next suggested Gallagher's inexperience in neutron activation analysis procedures created the differences in his and the FBI report. Guinn proposed the lack of an extensive background in activation analysis and experience with the Mannlicher Carcano bullet may have resulted in erroneous interpretation of the analysis findings.

> *GUINN: Yes, I have subsequently found out most of the details of it. The FBI work was done in May 1964, at which time the FBI laboratory had not done any prior activation analysis work, so far as I am aware. But in the same elemental analysis group, where such work would normally fall, they asked Mr. Jack Gallagher (John F. Gallagher) of their staff, whom I know, to take these bullet lead specimens down to the Oak Ridge National Laboratory, in Oak Ridge, Tenn., where they have all the nuclear facilities, and so on. They*

are quite good, and they do a lot of activation analysis work, although not usually connected with crime investigation, but for other purposes. Two of the people down there, who were highly conversant in activation analysis, but not in forensic work, and Mr. Gallagher, who was highly conversant in forensic work but not in activation analysis work, worked together. He actually did all of the measurements, but with the two Oak Ridge people showing him how to do it and how to calculate the results, et cetera, since this really was his first experience in this field.

FITHIAN: Are you saying this was the first neutron activation analysis work done by the FBI?

GUINN: So far as I am aware, it was; yes (HSCA, I:491-567).

Guinn indicated instead that he had some reservations regarding the evidence he was asked to examine. Perhaps the difference in the FBI report findings and his occurred because they had tested different evidence. Guinn's testimony demonstrates his reservations concerning whether the evidence he used for his analysis was the same evidence previously tested by the FBI, as the fragments received should have been the same weight as the FBI samples, but they were not. It was disconcerting to learn, because this test should have resulted in a loss of weight. This explanation was unusual, as the specimens he received displayed the same exhibit numbers as those tested by the FBI for the Warren Commission. Evidence numbers are intended to assure evidence specificity, yet for Guinn, this was not encouraging.

FITHIAN: Now, then, did you test exactly the same particles that the FBI tested in 1964?

GUINN: Well, it turns out, I did not, for reasons I don't know, because as they did the analysis, they did not destroy the samples either.

GUINN: The particular little pieces that they analyzed, I could just as well have analyzed over again, but the pieces that were brought from the Archives, which reportedly, according to Mr. Gear, were the only bullet-lead fragments from this case still present in the Archives, did not include any of the specific little pieces that the FBI had analyzed. Presumably, those are in existence

somewhere, I am sure nobody threw them out, but where they are, I have no
idea (HSCA, I:491-567).

COMMISSION EXHIBIT 567

Evidence from the Warren Commission had been in the possession of National
Archives and Records Administration (NARA) since 1966. Of specific
interest was Commission Exhibit 567, one larger copper and lead fragment
with adhering fibrous debris, and four smaller pieces of lead containing
organic material. In January 1996, acting Assistant Attorney General John
Keeney contacted FBI Director Louis Freeh requesting the analysis of the
deposits on the bullet fragments. In August of 1998, the NARA agreed to
allow unlimited testing of Commission Exhibit 567 for biological or organic
material (Baker, 2000).

This decision was of major importance, as the results would touch the very
core of the Warren Commission's single shooter theory. If the fiber evidence
embedded in the bullet nose recovered from the front seat of the limousine
were consistent with the President's clothing, the single bullet theory would
be proven flawed. Tests concluded the fibers were of a non-textile origin
and did not come from the clothing of Kennedy or Connally. Instead, the
material was determined to consist of paper fibers and unidentified material
of non-textile origin and, subsequently, did not originate from the clothing of
Kennedy or Connally (Baker, 2000).

The Department of Justice had also speculated the organic fragments might
shed light on the assassination, but DNA analysis proved inconclusive. The
organic material was established to consist of human skin and tissue, but
unfortunately, DNA analyses yielded inconclusive results; consequently, no
comparison of the questioned human tissue with known sources was possible
(Baker, 2000).

COMPOSITIONAL ANALYSIS OF BULLET LEAD

The preservation of the Warren Commission's single shooter, three shot assessment of the assassination rested in Guinn's neutron activation analysis results. Skeptical of Guinn's analysis findings, Dr. Erik Randich and Dr. Pat Grant published the results of a study indicating the metallic composition of lead bullets was misrepresented in Guinn's analysis.

Randich was a metallurgist with the Lawrence Livermore National Laboratory in California and Grant a chemist and director of the Lawrence Livermore Forensic Science Center. Randich and Grant's study originated with research completed by Randich and William Tobin in 2002, addressing FBI procedures in interpreting data from chemical analyses of bullets. Tobin retired as the Chief Forensic Metallurgist in 2000 and initiated research with Randich. Their study showed composition of castings from a single smelting pot sometimes varied, while the composition of lead in different smelting pots sometimes matched. That meant bullets made from two different batches of lead could wrongly appear to have come from the same pot (Randich, 2006).

The bullet evidence in the JFK assassination investigation was reexamined from metallurgical and statistical standpoints by Randich and Grant in 2006. Their research indicated antimony is mixed with lead to assure hardness in a bullet; therefore, manufacturers must strictly monitor the amount of antimony used in the lead of non-jacketed ammunition. In jacketed ammunition however, it is the jacket that provides bullet hardness and not the lead inside the jacket. Because it has no bearing on the bullet hardness, no effort is made to control the antimony levels in jacketed ammunition; subsequently, antimony concentrations can fluctuate widely (Randich, 2006).

Guinn utilized non-jacketed ammunition containing similar antimony levels in his comparison tests. Apparently, Guinn was not familiar with the requirements for the manufacture of jacketed bullets. Consequently, his interpretation of the varying antimony levels being a unique feature of Mannlicher Carcano ammunition was wrong. Actually, varied antimony levels are common in jacketed ammunition. Therefore, the fragments could have originated from other manufactured jacketed ammunition (Randich, 2006).

Comparing those results to jacketed lead resulted in Guinn reaching an incorrect conclusion concerning the source for the samples. The Randich and Grant study concluded their analysis of the material composition of the lead specimens from the assassination by indicating the available evidence is consistent with between two and five bullets being fired in Dealey Plaza at the time of the assassination (Randich, 2006).

Mannlicher Carcano ammunition bullet lead has a crystalline structure that tends to micro-segregate around crystals of lead in casting. The crystals are large enough that a sample taken from one portion of a bullet might have an antimony level very different from one taken from another portion of the same bullet. Guinn found antimony matches within the Mannlicher Carcano ammunition he tested, because he measured samples taken from only a very small portion of his test bullets. Therefore, the fragments with similar antimony levels could have come from one bullet, or more than one, and those with different antimony levels could have come from a single bullet (Randich, 2006).

Guinn did not understand the concept of micro-segregation. As a function of micro-segregation, there may be hotspots of elements, especially antimony, that congregate in very small portions of a bullet or fragment. This can change the antimony level in a fragment, unless multiple measures are taken from multiple locations in the round. Such multiple readings were not made by Guinn (Randich, 2006).

CABL Analysis and MC Ammunition

Following the publication of Tobin and Randich's research in July 2002, as well as other studies including the FBI's own analyses, the FBI reevaluated its analysis methods. The bureau asked the National Academies to put together a committee to formally review the FBI's use of bullet-lead analysis and recommend changes. The Committee on Scientific Assessment of Bullet Lead Elemental Composition Comparison was composed of 14 experts in analytical chemistry, statistics, forensic science, metallurgy, and law. Members were selected from the councils of the National Academy of Sciences, the National Academy of Engineering, and the Institute of Medicine. The members of the committee, accountable for the report, were selected for their special abilities and with regard for appropriate knowledge balance (Spiegelman, 2007).

In 2004, the Committee on Scientific Assessment of Bullet Lead Elemental Composition and Comparison report was published, introducing the new national standards for bullet lead analysis. The report was read by Stuart Wexler, who was in possession of Mannlicher Carcano ammunition manufactured by the Winchester Cartridge company in 1954. Wexler contacted committee member Clifford Spiegelman of Texas A&M University to suggest utilizing the new analysis technique to compare the ballistic evidence collected in the Kennedy assassination. Spiegelman organized a team of experts, which included forensic metallurgist William Tobin, to examine the testimony and analysis results of Guinn. Spiegelman's team found Guinn's findings suspect (Spiegelman, 2007).

To challenge the testing results of Guinn, Spiegelman's team conducted chemical and forensic analysis of bullets purportedly from the same batch as those allegedly used by Oswald to assassinate Kennedy and injure Connally. Their findings showed Guinn's analysis results were indeed flawed. CABL analysis indicated one of the Wexler bullets analyzed matched an assassination fragment. They ultimately discovered the bullet fragments from the assassination could have come from three or more separate bullets. This finding is significant because it strongly suggest a second gunman (Spiegelman, 2007).

In fact, CABL analysis indicated one of every ten test bullets from one box analyzed was considered a match to one or more of the five existing assassination fragments. Their research demonstrated Guinn's testimony concerning the uniqueness of individual bullets from Mannlicher Carcano bullets was erroneous. In direct conflict with Guinn's findings, the team discovered many bullets within a single box of Mannlicher Carcano bullets could have similar composition. This finding proved two-element matches to assassination fragments are not unusually rare, considering they came from the same box. Additionally, the results indicated one of the ten test bullets provided by Wexler is considered a match to one or more of the assassination fragments. This suggests bullet fragments from the assassination could have come from three or more separate bullets, and likely, from more than one shooter, demonstrating the single-gunman theory can't be supported by science (Spiegelman, 2007).

ANALYSIS OF BULLET LEAD

While the 1977 neutron activation analysis by Guinn indicated quantified eight elements, only antimony and silver were considered by Guinn when interpreting the results. This restricted consideration of elements distorted the results, causing Guinn to report the fragments displayed characteristics unique only to Mannlicher Carcano ammunition. Laboratory protocols for interpreting neutron activation analysis were not well established in 1977; meaning Guinn was able to extrapolate results as he wished. Sound forensic guidelines would not be established until 1989. As with other sciences, gradual modifications in laboratory standards occurred as neutron activation analysis testing techniques became more sophisticated.

In 2004, the National Research Council of the National Academies considered recommendations on Forensic Analysis of Bullet Lead Evidence provided by the Committee on Scientific Assessment of Bullet Lead Elemental Composition Comparison. The Committee findings were independently reviewed by a group of specialists for objectivity, evidence, and responsiveness to the study charge. Included in that group was William A. Tobin, the forensic metallurgical consultant whose work with Randich was the impetus for the formation of the Committee on Scientific Assessment of Bullet Lead Elemental Composition Comparison (Peters, 2002).

The National Research Council of the National Academies Compositional Analysis of Bullet Lead (CABL) report provided information regarding association between known bullets and questioned bullets or bullet fragments. CABL uses a chemical technique called *Inductively Coupled Plasma - Optical Emission Spectroscopy* (ICP-OES) and is capable of detecting and measuring the concentration of numerous elements that occur as trace impurities in alloying elements of bullet lead (Peters, 2002).

Manufacturer code standards for lead used in ammunition requires the elements of arsenic, antimony, tin, copper, bismuth, silver and cadmium be contained within the bullet lead. Compositional Analysis of Bullet Lead (CABL) analysis identifies the chemical signature by testing the quantitative concentration of the required elements. Smelters, utilizing recycled lead with various compositions are required to keep the concentrations of the required elements within the particular range set by bullet manufacturers. Because the structure of recycled lead is diverse, it would be particularly difficult for a smelter to duplicate the composition of manufactured lead. Therefore, each batch of lead manufactured contains multiple trace elements in random concentrations, which combine to form a unique chemical signature composition. Discovery of the same concentrations in two samples of bullet lead is an indication the samples were manufactured by the same source (Peters, 2002).

The 2004 Committee's task was to (a) assess the current analytical methods, (b) select elements to be used in comparisons, (c) develop statistics for comparison and interpretation, and (d) make recommendations for the implementation of new lab analysis protocols. Prior to 2004, bullet lead quantitative testing focused on three elements: antimony, copper, and arsenic. The 2004 nationally recognized standards determined the testing and interpretation of seven elements was much more reliable. Guinn's consideration of only two elements is obviously less sensitive than testing for seven elements; subsequently, analysis conducted in 1963 was likely to identify false matches. Utilizing Compositional Analysis of Bullet Lead to determine the lead source, the false-positive probability of a match between two bullet samples that are actually different is less than 0.0004%. The adoption of new lab protocols for the analysis of bullet lead has essentially eliminated erroneous matches, transforming bullet lead analysis nationwide (Peters, 2002).

WEXLER INTERVIEW
Stuart Wexler was interviewed and provided the following information:

> *Actual bullet manufacturers argued that the lead within a vat could produce thousands and thousands of bullets with very, very similar chemical signatures. When bullets are shipped, often regionally, entire shipments of boxes can contain the same profile. Making matters worse, bullet lead from one batch can be recycled into other production lots, even for different bullet types, meaning that there are potentially thousands of bullets that share the same profile. The FBI pretended for years that they could match a bullet to a suspect's box of ammo, but this was killed by Randich, Grant, Tobin, etc. For this reason, no laboratory in the country presently uses Compositional Analysis of Bullet Lead.*

Guinn actually went further than even what the FBI claimed. Claiming unique intra-bullet and inter-bullet properties for the MC round, he said that he could not only match a fragment to a box of ammo, but to the actual individual bullet. Guinn failed on a number of fronts:

1.   *He didn't have Oswald's box of bullets (no one did).*
2.   *His background study was based on a non-random sample, from which he generalized to a population—you can't do that.*
3.   *He used fewer elements than the three he himself recommended, focusing almost exclusively on antimony, which only increases the chances of a false positive.*
4.   *He did not use, and it was not required at the time, a control specimen in his NAA testing.*

And, this is the key of the Spiegelman, et al. study—his very premise, that there is something unique about the way MC bullets are manufactured and packaged, was fundamentally challenged by modern tests. In other words, Spiegelman and others showed more than just a bullet could match a round from a random box, but that MC bullets were just like most bullets in how they were manufactured and packaged.

Now, the above is also limited by the fact that it was a non-random sample. But, as it is consistent with what we know about all other bullets/brands, Occam's Razor suggests that you simply cannot reach the conclusions that Guinn reached, especially with as few elements as he reached them (Wexler, 2012).

FBI DENOUNCES TESTING

In 2002, the FBI requested the National Research Council (NRC) of the National Academy of Science to facilitate the formation of an independent committee of experts to evaluate the scientific validity of comparative bullet lead analysis. The FBI asked the study to address the scientific method, the data analysis, and the interpretation of the results. The NRC found that the FBI Laboratory's analytical instrumentation is appropriate and the best available technology with respect to precision and accuracy for the elements analyzed. It also found the elements selected by the FBI for this analysis are appropriate. The NRC voiced concerns, however, relating to the interpretation of the results of bullet lead examinations.

Following the publication of the report, the FBI Laboratory discontinued testing while initiating a 14-month review to study the recommendations. Ultimately, the FBI officially discontinued the testing stating: "[N]either scientists nor bullet manufacturers are able to definitively attest to the significance of an association made between bullets in the course of a bullet lead examination. While the FBI Laboratory still firmly supports the scientific foundation of bullet lead analysis, given the costs of maintaining the equipment, the resources necessary to do the examination, and its relative probative value, the FBI Laboratory has decided that it will no longer conduct this exam" (FBI, 2005).

CONCLUSION

The Warren Commission did not seek to obtain the FBI's Neutron Activation Analysis report, indicating either they may have been less than meticulous in the documentation of their investigative process, or they may have tried to manipulate the investigative outcome. Subsequently, the HSCA addressed the FBI's missing NAA report by completing new neutron activation tests.

Guinn's HSCA testimony concerning his analysis results can only be characterized as grossly flawed. He did not complete control testing to assure the lead samples provided consistent results, nor was he acquainted with the difference in antimony levels between jacketed and non-jacketed ammunition. Mannlicher Carcano bullets are not unique, as the jacketed bullet's trace levels vary. Non-jacketed bullets have consistent levels of trace antimony. Wrongly, Guinn utilized non-jacketed ammunition containing similar antimony levels as standards in his comparison tests. Guinn's comparing the composition of lead in unjacketed and jacketed ammunition resulted in erroneous deductions concerning the source for the samples. Guinn based his analysis on the erroneous hypothesis Western Cartridge Company Mannlicher Carcano ammunition varied significantly from bullet to bullet, but showed uncommon uniformity within any single Mannlicher Carcano bullet.

Scientific testing in 2006 and 2007 indicates the available evidence is consistent with between two and five bullets being fired in Dealey Plaza at the time of the assassination. This number of bullets would be consistent with more than one shooter and indicates the single-gunman theory can't be supported by science. In direct conflict with Guinn's findings, the Randich and Grant study also concluded the analysis of the material composition of the lead specimens from the assassination indicates the available evidence is consistent with between two and five bullets being fired in Dealey Plaza at the time of the assassination. Moreover, the Spiegelman team specified one of their 10 test bullets is considered a compositional match to one or more of the assassination fragments. This proposes bullet fragments from the assassination could have come from three or more separate bullets, and likely from more than one shooter.

Based on inadequate and erroneous research, Guinn reinforced the single-bullet theory by providing meaningless conclusions. The results of the studies completed by the Randich and Grant study and the Spiegelman team have successfully challenged the reliability of Guinn's analysis, and the Warren Commission's claim of a single shooter.

CABL can neither confirm nor refute the single bullet theory. In fact, in 2005 the FBI denounced comparative bullet lead analysis. Therefore, scientific testing of ballistic evidence in the Kennedy assassination does not support the Warren Commission in their conclusion Oswald was the only shooter in Dealey Plaza.

CHAPTER 6

THE GRASSY KNOLL HEADSHOT

People believing in a conspiracy to assassinate President Kennedy do not agree on all the details surrounding the deadly shooting. Hotly contested issues such as alteration of the Zapruder film and substituted medical evidence appear to divide the conspiracy community. However, they do seem to agree there was a conspiracy manifested by a shooter on the Grassy Knoll. But, what if there was proof the fatal headshot originated elsewhere?

Witnesses observed smoke from that location, heard a shot originating from behind the fence, and spontaneously rushed up the slope in an attempt to locate the shooter. One witness saw a flash of light from near the Grassy Knoll and another witness observed men with a rifle behind the fence. There is even a confession from someone who claimed to have shot the President from behind the picket fence. Police officers also believed the shot originated from that area and rushed in that direction. However, even with such overwhelming evidence, conventional trajectory reconstruction techniques indicate the fatal headshot originated from another location within Dealey Plaza.

Trajectory analysis is an investigative tool that could reveal the shooter's location for Kennedy's fatal headshot. Criminologists nationwide recognize trajectory analysis as a valuable process in crime scene reconstruction. Geometry and trigonometry are the foundation for the procedures used to determine the location of shooters in perforating gunshot injuries. Various entities have employed trajectory analysis to identify the origin of the fatal headshot: including the Warren Commission, the House Select Committee on Assassinations (HSCA) and non-governmental organizations such as the Discovery Channel.

The Warren Commission based their trajectory conclusions upon an unorthodox process. They did not calculate a trajectory angle; instead, the Warren Commission merely identified the downward angle of a preconceived trajectory. The House Select Committee on Assassinations utilized particular points of entry and exit to identify a single line trajectory for the fatal headshot. However, there is no credible evidence to support identification of a specific, definitive point of entry or exit wound to the head. Consequently, developing a single line trajectory is impossible, making their results unacceptable. The Discovery Channel, like the Warren Commission, also confirmed a predetermined angle of trajectory. Additionally, the documentary proposed defects to the fabricated head were consistent with Kennedy's wounds. From that erroneous conclusion, they reasoned the headshot could have only come from the sixth floor window of the Texas School Book Depository, just as the Warren Commission determined in 1964. Comparing the trajectory reconstruction techniques employed by the Warren Commission, The House Select Committee on Assassinations and the Discovery Channel to the current standards for shooting reconstructions will prove they were incorrect.

Physicians and pathologists routinely obtain precise measurements of victims' gunshot wounds to determine the angle a projectile traversed the body. Placing a victim correctly within the crime scene and extending the trajectory away from the victim can help locate the position of the perpetrator. No shooting reconstruction can provide a factual, scientifically based, and reproducible single line trajectory for Kennedy's fatal headshot, because the necessary criterion for that computation does not exist.

Medical personnel at Parkland Hospital, and those who were involved in the Kennedy autopsy are not unanimous concerning entry and exit wound locations. Moreover, they are divided in determining if the fatal shot came from behind or in front of the President. However, reconstruction analysis can calculate a trajectory cone that encompasses all possible single line trajectories. Remarkably, photographic evidence documented the mortal wounding of President Kennedy. Subsequently, locating Kennedy's exact body position within the limousine and the limousine's precise location within Dealey Plaza is possible. Considering all possible angles the projectile may have taken through the head establishes a trajectory cone. Extending the cone against the line of fire and forward of the President into the plaza identifies all possible shooter locations. Surprisingly, that trajectory cone does not include the Grassy Knoll.

TRAJECTORY ANALYSIS

Pulling the trigger on a firearm releases the hammer, which drives the firing pin into the primer of a cartridge. The primer creates a spark that ignites the gunpowder contained within the cartridge case. The gunpowder burns very rapidly, creating expanding gases. When the bullet gets enough pressure behind it, it leaves the casing of the cartridge and begins to travel down the barrel. The gases continue to expand, pushing the bullet out of the gun barrel at high speeds. The *trajectory* is the path the bullet travels once it has left the barrel of the gun. The bullet begins to slow, because of air resistance and lack of continued thrust by the gasses. As the bullet slows, gravity decreases the elevation; this results in a downward curve known as a parabolic arc. In the case of high-speed bullets traveling short distances, the curvature is typically insignificant (Hornady, 2012).

To determine the trajectory of a projectile, either the parabolic arc is determined or the trajectory must be short enough to eliminate parabolic arc computations. Since approximately 300 feet separated the perpetrator and Kennedy, it is reasonable to assume the bullet fired at the President's head followed a straight-line trajectory and trajectory analyst can ignore the parabolic arc of the projectile (Hornady, 2012).

In the event of perforating gunshot wounds, straight-line trajectory analysis requires following a prescribed number of steps. The analyst must define the direction the projectile was traveling and confirm the possible origin of the gunshots within a distance that would embrace a straight-line trajectory.

Connecting the entry and exit wounds establishes a trajectory through the target. Next, the target is oriented within the crime scene. Extending the angle of trajectory through the wounds and back against the line of fire will identify the approximate origin of the shots. The Kennedy autopsy report indicated the entry wound on the rear of the head near the external occipital protuberance. The report did not identify a specific point on the skull as the exit wound. As an alternative, the report categorizes the large defect to the upper right side of the head as the exit wound. Consequently, the Warren Commission could not use conventional techniques in determining the projectile trajectory for the fatal head wound (WCR:85).

WARREN COMMISSION TRAJECTORY

Three pathologists participated in the autopsy performed on Kennedy at Bethesda Naval Hospital on November 22, 1963. Commander James H. Humes officially conducted the autopsy. Colonel Pierre Finck and Commander J. Thornton Boswell assisted Humes. Humes was Director of Laboratories of the Naval Medical School at the Naval Medical Center at Bethesda. Finck was Chief of the Wound Ballistics Pathology Branch at Walter Reed Medical Center of the Armed Forces Institute of Pathology. Boswell was Chief Pathologist at Bethesda Naval Hospital. Fink and Boswell were not forensic pathologists, but were experienced in performing autopsies. Army pathologist Finck arrived after Humes and Boswell initiated the autopsy (Finck, 1969).

The Warren Commission's headshot trajectory reconstruction began with identifying the location of Kennedy's entry wound, provided to the Warren Commission in the Autopsy Report and Supplemental Report. On the night of the assassination, President Kennedy's body was taken to the Bethesda Naval Medical Center for the post-mortem examination. Dr. James Humes, director of the lab at Bethesda, led the three doctors tasked with this responsibility. Army Lieutenant Colonel Pierre Finck, Chief of the Wound Ballistics Branch of the Armed Forces, and Commander J. Thorton Boswell, Navy commander, assisted him. Doctors Finck and Boswell were not forensic pathologists, but each had experience in performing autopsies, though rarely did those post-mortem examinations involve gunshot wounds (Finck, 1969).

THE HEAD WOUND

The Autopsy Report and Supplemental Report Clinical Record/ Autopsy Protocol Report provides information concerning the headshot. Commander James H. Humes wrote the autopsy report; however, it also displayed Colonel Pierre Finck's and Commander J. Thornton Boswell's signatures. The Autopsy Report and Supplemental Report Clinical Record/Autopsy Protocol Report was submitted by Dr. Humes.

> *Situated in the posterior scalp, approximately 2.5 centimeters laterally to the right and slightly above the external occipital protuberance, is a lacerated wound, measuring 15 millimeters by 6 millimeters. In the underlying bone is a corresponding wound through the skull, which exhibits beveling of the margins of the bone, when viewed from the inner aspect of the skull (CE 387; 16H 981).*

On the final page of the autopsy report, Dr. Humes summarizes his findings regarding the head wound:

> *The fatal missile entered the skull above and to the right of the external occipital protuberance. A portion of the projectile transversed the cranial cavity in a posterior-anterior direction, depositing minute particles along its path. A portion of the projectile made its exit through the parietal bone, on the right, carrying with it portions of cerebrum, skull, and scalp. The two wounds of the skull combined with the force of the missile produced extensive fragmentation of the skull, laceration of the superior sagittal sinus, and of the right cerebral hemisphere (CE 387; 16H 981).*

There are several problems with the autopsy report. The text describes the scalp wound, then implies the skull defect was the same size and in the same location as the scalp laceration. Consequently, when the autopsy report refers to an elliptically shaped wound in the scalp and corresponding entry wound through the skull, it appears to substantiate a 15-millimeter by 6-millimeter hole in an unbroken section of bone. However, this is not the case. Later testimony by Finch attests only a portion of the proposed entry wound perimeter was located on the edge of intact occipital bone. One of the two smaller bone fragments that arrived after the autopsy was in progress displayed a similar circular defect. Humes positioned the small bone fragment's curved edge adjacent to the rear skull defect to complete a partial opening in the skull. His assumption the beveling indicated an entry wound, compounded by his bias to a rear shooter, might have affected his judgment as to projectile travel. The same conditions were present in locating the exit wound in the front of the head. The diameter of the bullet allegedly used by Oswald measured 6.5 millimeters in diameter. Humes testified,

> *We had the portion of the perimeter of a roughly- what we would judge to have been a roughly- circular wound of exit. Judging from that portion of the perimeter, which was available to us, we would have judged the diameter of that wound to be between 2.5 and 3 centimeters (2H357).*

It appears Humes located that fragment without an anatomical landmark to confirm the original position of the bone fragment. Therefore, the partially reconstructed circular defect in the skull was simply an assumption by Humes. The three fragments delivered during the autopsy did not complete the large open wound in the skull, nor did placing fragments in the open skull close the hole assumed an entry or exit wound. Moreover, therefore a medical landmark on the small fragment would have been essential for correct reconstruction of the defect. Confirmation that the small fragment used to complete the circumference of the supposed entry wound belonged in that location is impossible. Moreover, the real issue should be that there is no individual measurement of the skull defect. Therefore, using the measurements in the autopsy report is useless when considering trajectory reconstruction.

THE SIZE PROBLEM

The autopsy report describes a 15 millimeter by 6 millimeter skull entry wound. Oddly, the width of the defect measured 0.5 millimeters smaller than the diameter of the 6.5 millimeter bullet purportedly used by Oswald. The Warren Commission questioned Humes on this point. Humes simply stated the measurements were of the scalp defect and disregarded the opportunity to discuss the actual wound in the skull.

> *HUMES: The size of the defect in the scalp, caused by a projectile could vary from missile to missile, because of elastic recoil and so forth of the*

tissues. However, the size of the defect in the underlying bone is certainly not likely to get smaller than that of the missile which perforated it and, in this case, the smallest diameter of this was approximately 6 to 7 mm, so I would feel that that would be the absolute upper limit of the size of this missile, sir (2H246-247, 359).

The Warren Commission Report distorted that information and explained the perceived contradiction with the following statement.

The dimension of 6 millimeters, somewhat smaller than the diameter of a 6.5 millimeter bullet, was caused by the elastic recoil of the skull, which shrinks the size of an opening after a missile passes through it (WCR 86).

There were also problems with the exit wound. The diameter of the bullet allegedly used by Oswald measured 6.5 millimeters in diameter. Humes testified the diameter of the skull defect determined to be the exit wound was roughly half that diameter. Specter asked what enabled Humes to reconstruct a point of exit of the bullet on the skull.

SPECTER: On the reconstruction of the three portions of the scalp which you described...

HUMES: Skull, sir.

SPECTER: Skull; will you state at this point of the record that size of opening or exit path of the bullet?

HUMES: As I mentioned previously, at one angle of this largest pyramidal shaped fragments of bone which came as a separate specimen, we had the portion of the perimeter of a roughly- what we would judge to have been a roughly- circular wound of exit. Judging from that portion of the perimeter, which was available to us, we would have judged the diameter of that wound to be between 2.5 and 3 centimeters (2H357).

Humes does not state the wound in the skull was roughly circular, nor does he state it was a measured diameter. He instead assumes it was circular, and estimates the diameter based on a portion he does not describe as measuring.

The skull vault contains porous cancellous bone sandwiched between two layers of dense, compact cortical bone. Cancellous bone has a sponge like appearance with numerous spaces. It consists of a delicate, vascular fibrous tissue found in the marrow space of a bone. The solid, compact bone is more rigid than cancellous bone. Compact bone encases cancellous bone and is the primary component of bones where greater strength and rigidity are needed. The inner and outer tables of the skull, composed of the compacted bone have a strain limit of 2% of its initial dimensions before fractures occur. Pressure on an area smaller than 15 centimeters creates puncture wounds, as will a projectile with a velocity of greater than nine feet per second. While technically there is a flexible, distortive property to the skull, the deformation would not allow cranial cancellous bone to stretch 0.5 centimeters in order to accommodate a 6.5-millimeter projectile, and then return to its original state (Oehmichen, 2006).

THE LOCATION PROBLEM

The autopsy report was very specific in locating the entry wound to the rear of Kennedy's head: approximately 2.5 centimeters to the right and slightly above the external occipital protuberance. Humes would later state to the HSCA Forensic Pathology Panel the wound was below the external occipital protuberance. In 1967, at the request of Ramsay Clark, Attorney General of the United States, four physicians met in Washington, DC to examine evidence relating to the death of President Kennedy, and evaluate the medical conclusions detailed in the Autopsy Report. The Clark Panel in 1967, and the House Select Committee on Assassinations Forensic Pathology Panel in 1976, disagreed with both assessments. Eventually Humes would surrender his stance on the entry wound location and agree with the House Select Committee on Assassination, testifying the wound was located 10 centimeters above the external occipital protuberance (HSCA 1:327).

THE ENTRY WOUND

The *external occipital protuberance* (EOP), depicted in Figure 6, is the prominent projection of the bone at the bottom of the skull. The autopsy report

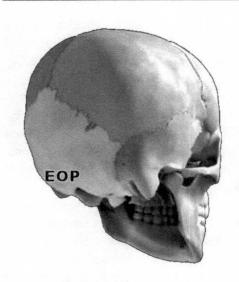

(FIGURE 6) External Occipital Protuberance

describes the entry wound as measuring 6 millimeters by 15 millimeters and approximately 2.5 centimeters to the right and slightly above the external occipital protuberance. In 1968, Attorney General Ramsey Clark charged a panel of physicians to review medical evidence concerning the assassination of President Kennedy. The panel consisted of four physicians: Russell S. Fisher, William H. Carnes, Russell H. Morgan, and Alan R. Moritz. Forensic pathologist Russell Fisher directed the Clark Panel. The panel determined one bullet struck the back of Kennedy's head well above the external occipital protuberance. Their conclusions raised the entry wound located at the rear of the head approximately 10 centimeters higher than reported in the original autopsy report (Fisher, 1968).

The back of the skull only measures approximately 19 centimeters, therefore, a 10-centimeter discrepancy is significant. The House Select Committee on Assassinations (HSCA) Forensic Pathology Panel sought to rectify the inconsistency between the Clark Panel conclusions and the autopsy report. To facilitate reaching a better understanding of the autopsy and its findings, the Forensic Pathology Panel interviewed the three pathologists, Humes, Boswell, and Finck, and John Ebersole, assistant Chief of Radiology at Bethesda Naval Hospital. Addendum 1 of the HSCA Report contains the published interviews of Humes, Boswell, and Finck, who all maintained the entry wound was located near the external occipital protuberance. Based upon the medical evidence, the HSCA Forensic Pathology Panel interpreted the entry wound was 10 centimeters above the occipital protuberance; four inches higher than Humes and Boswell claimed. Eventually, this would become the HSCA Forensic Pathology Panel's entry wound of record.

THE ANGLE PROBLEM

If a round projectile penetrates the skull at a perpendicular angle, the resulting defect is circular. If the projectile strikes the skull at a more oblique angle, the resulting deflect becomes more elliptically shaped. The angle of impact can be determined using a calculator with an arc sine function or a trigonometry table. By measuring the width and length of the elliptically shaped defect, the angle at which the projectile penetrated the skull can be determined. The width of the skull defect, 6 millimeters divided by the length of the skull defect, 15 millimeters, equals 0.40. The arc sine of 0.4 is 23.578; which means the defect indicates the projectile struck Kennedy's head at an approximate 24° angle.

The elliptically shaped hole can indicate the trajectory angle of the impacting projectile using the computed degree of impact. Correctly positioning Kennedy's head and extending the calculated trajectory angle forward into the plaza indicates possible positions for the shooter. Utilizing an entry and exit provides a trajectory traversing the head. Humes testified as to how the trajectory through the head was established.

> *HUMES: Yes, sir; there is one difficulty, and that is the defect of exit was so broad that one has to rely more on the inclination of the entrance than they do connecting, in this instance, entrance and exit, because so much of the skull was carried away in this fashion (2H360).*

During the autopsy, Humes testified that he placed a small bone fragment adjacent to the intact bone of the skull to reconstruct a partial entry and exit defects in the skull. Based upon those defects, Humes generated a trajectory he felt was plausible. Certainly, he had no actual point of exit, and no documentation indicates he mathematically determined the angle of trajectory. Either Humes employed the scalp defect to dictate the angle of impact, or he opted to use a fractional skull defect reconstructed with a loose fragment placed without proper location confirmation. Either choice results in a skewed angle of impact and an inaccurate trajectory determination (2H361).

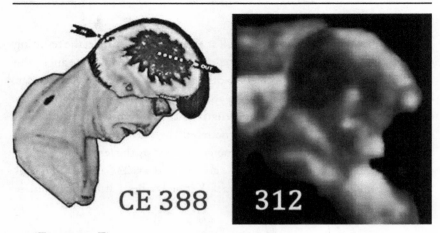

(**FIGURE 7**) Comparison of Head Position between CE388, the Rydberg Drawing, and Zapruder Frame 312

RYDBERG ILLUSTRATIONS

Humes and Boswell employed medical illustrator Harold A. Rydberg to produce a drawing that would indicate the estimated trajectory. Under the direction of doctors Humes and Boswell, Rydberg sketched two drawings that depicted the entry wound near the EOP. See Figure 7.

The Warren Commission accepted the Rydberg drawings as Commission Exhibits 386 and 388. Commission Exhibit 388 depicts Kennedy's tilted downward, with an arrow entering near the EOP and traversing the head indicating the proposed trajectory of the bullet. The downward tilt was supposedly a replication of Kennedy's head position shown in Zapruder Frame 312. The Warren Commission final report states,

> *Based on information provided by the doctors who conducted the autopsy, an artist's drawing depicted the path of the bullet through the President's head, with his head being in the same approximate position [as Zapruder Frame 312] (WCR 109).*

The trajectory given for the alleged rear entry wound is incompatible with a shot from the southeast corner window on the sixth floor of the Texas School Book Depository Building. The Warren Commission knew the angle depicted in Commission Exhibit 388 needed to closely correspond with

Zapruder Frame 312, but ignored the fact it obviously did not. Rotating the Rydberg diagram counterclockwise to agree with President's head position in Zapruder Frame 312, results in an upward trajectory, eliminating Oswald as the shooter.

The House Select Committee on Assassinations asked if a trajectory established using the entry and exit wounds was possible.

> *COOPER: Did you establish them [the point of entry and point of exit] so exactly that they could be related to the degree of angle of the trajectory of the bullet?*
>
> *HUMES: Yes, sir; to our satisfaction we did ascertain that fact (2H360).*

However, Humes neglected to mention what the angle was. The dimensions provided in the autopsy report indicate a wound measuring 6 millimeters by 15 millimeters; indicating a 24° angle of impact by the projectile for the fatal headshot. The trajectory angle based on those wounds would be calculated at 5° downward and 18.6° right, relative to Kennedy's head position in Zapruder Frame 312 (WR:110).

AN UNCONVENTIONAL TRAJECTORY METHOD

The Warren Commission failed to complete a conventional trajectory analysis of Kennedy's shooting injuries. Regardless, they did reach conclusions concerning trajectory of the fatal head wound. The FBI and Secret Service conducted a reenactment of the assassination on May 24, 1964 to determine the trajectory angle of the bullet that struck Kennedy in the head. The reconstruction team determined the location of the limousine within Dealey Plaza by utilizing individual frames of the Zapruder, Nix, and Muchmore films. A surveyor employed by the FBI and Secret Service identified a 3° 9' downward grade in Elm Street. The reenactment team positioned the vehicle in a location that corresponded with Zapruder Frame 312. An FBI agent, with similar physical characteristics to Kennedy, replicated his position within the limousine. Cardboard boxes positioned in the Texas School Book Depository window supported a Mannlicher Carcano rifle. The surveyor concluded the entry wound was 265.3 feet from the end of the rifle muzzle. The surveyor then computed the angle from the end of the rifle muzzle to the precise point of entry on the back of President Kennedy's head. The reenactment computed trajectory angle of 15° 21' did not match the 24° elliptically shaped reconstructed entry wound in the skull, a difference regarded as troublesome by the Clark Committee and the House Select Committee on Assassinations (WCR 96-110).

On April 14, 1964, Warren Commission staff members Redlich, Specter, and Robert Eisenberg; along with Humes, Boswell, Finck; Dr. F. W. Light, Jr. Deputy Chief of the Biophysics Division at Edgewood Arsenal, Maryland, and Chief of the Wound Assessment Branch of the Biophysics Division; Dr. Oliver, Chief of the Wound Ballistics Branch of the Biophysics Division at Edgewood Arsenal; and several FBI and Secret Service agents met to study the Zapruder film. Melvin A. Eisenberg added the consensus of the group to the official record in a memorandum dated April 22, 1964. The group determined the following concerning the trajectory (Eisenberg, 1964b).

Pictures should be made showing the car (positioned under paragraph 2) from the following vantage points: (a) the spots at which the photographers were standing; (b) a point in the TSBD approximating the point at which the muzzle of the rifle was located; and (c) several points on the overpass. Still pictures and moving pictures taken through the cameras actually used by Zapruder, Nix, and Muchmore should be taken from vantage point (a). Two sets of still pictures, one through a 4 x telescopic sight, should be taken from vantage points (b) and (c).

The position of the tapes and all marked points thereon should then be mapped on a survey, and the lengths of the various possible trajectories should be measured by the surveyor on a trigonometric basis, measuring from the point at which the muzzle was probably located to the beginning, end, and marked points of each tape. The surveyor should also determine the angle each trajectory makes with the horizontal. Copies of the surveyor's work-sheets and calculations should be sent to us (Eisenberg, 1964b).

From each of the ground points established in parts I [Kennedy's back and throat shot] and II [Kennedy's headshot] trigonometric readings should be taken from a point on either end of the overpass to chart the path which a bullet would travel if fired from those points on the overpass to the rear seat of the car. It should be determined whether a bullet could reach the rear seat without hitting the windshield, and the angle with the horizontal which would be made by a bullet fired from these points to a car located at each of the points to a car located at each of the points on the ground as determined in parts I and II (Rankin, 1964).

Obviously, the triple overpass was a consideration in determining trajectory in the minds of the men meeting on April 14, 1964. Why was the directive of the Warren Commission not followed? Perhaps the answer lies in the fact at that same meeting, the foundation of the Single Bullet Theory was discussed. Several attendees strongly opposed the supposition Commission Exhibit 399 penetrated the wrist of Governor Connally. Even more significant, those in attendance unanimously agreed, with one exception, the timing of Connally's chest wound did not support a single bullet creating all injuries. Arlen Spector was the lone dissenter. All others agreed that at no time after frame 236 was Connally in a position to sustain a chest injury from a bullet fired from the Texas School Book Depository. Spector would later be instrumental in the reenactment proposing the Single Bullet Theory was viable (Eisenberg, 1964).

The acceptable method of calculating trajectory would include (a) precisely locating the limousine within Dealey Plaza, (b) determining the orientation of victims within the limousine, (c) establishing the angle between entry and exit wounds, and (d) extending that angle in the appropriate direction to establish trajectory. Instead, the Warren Commission located the President and measured the angle from Kennedy to the unverifiable point believed to be the end of the shooter's rifle muzzle. The Warren Commission's technique eliminates any trajectory indicating any location other than the Texas School Book Depository sixth floor window as the origin of the shots.

Thomas Canning was a staff engineer for the Space Project Division of the National Aeronautics and Space Administration (NASA). Canning testified before the House Select Committee concerning the trajectory reconstruction completed by the Warren Commission.

DODD: Would you care to comment on the type of test that the Warren Commission used in that year to determine trajectory?

CANNING: Well, in a sense I feel that they were not testing the ability to determine a trajectory. They were testing the inconsistency of a trajectory with a hypothesis. The hypothesis was that a bullet was in fact fired from the southeast corner of the school book depository at the sixth floor, and that they were then observing the consistency of the facts with that hypothesis.

DODD: In other words, they had reached a conclusion and they were trying to determine or prove that conclusion.

CANNING: That is the way I read it, yes (HSCA 2 0912:192).

HSCA TRAJECTORY

Thomas Canning completed trajectory analysis of Kennedy's gunshot wounds for the House Select Committee on Assassinations. Canning listed three essential steps in determining trajectory: establish wound locations, establish the location of the Presidential limousine, and establish the orientation or relative alignment of the limousine occupants within the vehicle. In addition to the three steps listed by Canning, his trajectory analysis also addressed the direction the projectile was traveling and the nature of the projectile path. These five elements encompass traditional trajectory analysis used today (HSCA 2:161).

The House Select Committee on Assassinations based their trajectory analysis on the premise that the fatal headshot originated from behind the President Kennedy. They fashioned that opinion based on the evidentiary bullet cartridges and Mannlicher Carcano rifle collected from the sixth floor of the Texas School Book Depository and further noted there was no evidence that suggested a shooter was in any other location (HSCA 6:30, 34).

THE ENTRY WOUND

The HSCA Forensic Pathology Panel interviewed James J. Humes and J. Thornton Boswell at the National Archives September 16, 1977 to facilitate reaching a better understanding of the autopsy and its findings. The HSCA Forensic Pathology Panel likely realized a bullet fired from the sixth floor of the Texas School Book Depository Building did not support a trajectory angle based on the entry wound described by the autopsy doctors. Consequently, the HSCA Forensic Pathology Panel concluded the autopsy pathologists incorrectly positioned the wound. The Forensic Pathology Panel determined the fatal bullet entered the back of Kennedy's head approximately 9 centimeters above the external occipital protuberance, and 1.8 centimeters right of the skull's midline. The exit wound was identified as located right of the coronal suture and 11 centimeters forward of the entry wound, and 5.5 centimeters right of the midline; suggesting the autopsy physicians misjudged the entry wound location by approximately four inches. Forensic pathologist Michael Baden testified before the HSCA as a representative of the as Forensic Pathology Panel indicating the entry wound documented in the autopsy report was incorrect (HSCA 1:184, 234).

KLEIN: In what ways was the autopsy report not consistent with the other evidence available to the panel?

BADEN: The location and placement of the gunshot wound of entrance was significantly different on examination by the panel members than the autopsy pathologists had indicated. The panel members unanimously placed the gunshot wound of entrance in the back of the President's head approximately 4 inches above the point indicated in the autopsy report prepared by Drs. Humes and Boswell.

KLEIN: So the panel concluded that the autopsy report placed the wound in the back of the head 4 inches too low?

BADEN: That is correct; as recorded in the original autopsy.

KLEIN: Doctor, on the basis of the foregoing evidence, the photographs and X-Rays taken of the autopsy, the reports of the radiologists and the autopsy report, did the panel unanimously conclude that a bullet entered the President high on the back of his head and exited on the right side toward the front of his head?

BADEN: All nine members of the panel so unanimously concluded (HSCA 1:250).

Ultimately, the HSCA concluded entry point was 9.0 centimeters above the external occipital protuberance, 1.8 centimeters to the right of the midline (HSCA 6:35).

THE EXIT WOUND

Dr. J. Lawrence Angel (1982) prepared interpretations of the skull X-Rays for the HSCA Forensic Pathology Panel. Regarded as one of the most prestigious and influential physical anthropologists in the United States, Angel was the Curator of Physical (Biological) Anthropology at the National Museum of Natural History, Smithsonian Institution. Renowned in his field, Angel placed the exit wound through the right frontal bone, corresponding with a small semicircular notch 35 millimeters above the right orbit, just in front of the coronal suture above the stephanion. Figure 8 indicates the stephanion is the point on the side of the skull where the temporal line crosses the coronal suture. The HSCA Forensic Pathology Panel accepted the defect in front of the coronal suture above pterion as the official exit wound (HSCA Addendum E 7:230; Buikstra, 2012).

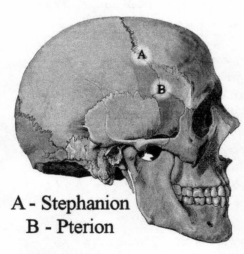

A - Stephanion
B - Pterion

(FIGURE 8) Exit Wound Placed in Front of the Coronal Suture above Stephanion

BADEN: And this would place the exit gunshot wound just anterior and almost incorporated into the lateral aspect of the coronal suture line.

ANGEL: A little in front of it, yes.

BADEN: Then it's slightly in front of and just superior to the temporal bone.

ANGEL: Apparently above the hairline. His hairline was fairly low; he wasn't getting bald like me. So, I think an exit wound about there would fit, then, the fragment that you have.

BADEN: Just anterior to the coronal suture line?

ANGEL: Just anterior to the coronal suture line. Yes. Well above pterion, far above pterion near the point where the temporal line crosses the coronal suture.

BADEN: Do you have a name for it?

ANGEL: Stephanion (HSCA Addendum 1:251).

Designating specific entry and exit wound locations establishes a single-line trajectory through the head. The HSCA Forensic Pathology Panel located the entrance wound on the back of the head about 3.9 inches above the external occipital protuberance, and 0.7 inches to the right of the midline. An exit wound was determined to be near the right temple at the right coronal suture 11 centimeters forward of the entry wound, 5.5 centimeters to the right of the midline, and 1.0 centimeter lower than the entry wound. The trajectory angle was determined to be 5° downward and 18.6° right, relative to Kennedy's head position in Zapruder Frame 312. The next step to trajectory reconstruction was to orient the position of Kennedy's head within Dealey Plaza (HSCA 6:32-35).

POSITIONING THE HEAD

Photogrammetric analysis conducted by a geological survey established placement of Kennedy and the Presidential limousine within Dealey Plaza at the time of the shooting. Zapruder Frame 312, exposed approximately 0.055 seconds before the headshot, allowed precise placement and orientation of Kennedy's head within Dealey Plaza. The Civil Aeromedical Institute of the FAA's Aeronautical Center prepared a series of calibrated photographs of replicas of Kennedy's head. Comparing facial features in the calibrated photographs to Zapruder Frame 312 generated a three dimensional positioning of Kennedy's head. The distance between Kennedy and Zapruder was about seventy feet, with a line of sight of 10° downward. Kennedy's head was turned away from Zapruder approximately 25° past profile, tilted to his left and away from Zapruder about 15°, and was nodding forward about 11° (HSCA 6:36-38; HSCA 6:34-40).

TRAJECTORY CONCLUSIONS

The geometric relationship between Zapruder's camera and Kennedy represents an angle. The trajectory line established by the entry and exit wounds in Kennedy's head represents another angle. Physically reconstructing Kennedy's position and the trajectory angle of the projectile required placing these two angles in the correct position within the plaza. A flat piece of wood represented Kennedy's head. An affixed dowel represented Zapruder and his camera's line of sight. Two short posts on the flat piece of wood indicated the location of the established entry and exit wounds. The posts were fastened to the wood 11 centimeters apart and extended 1.8 centimeters and 5.5 centimeters outward to represent the three-dimensional wound placement of Kennedy's head. A scale drawing developed from a survey of Dealey Plaza incorporated the data. Positioning the limousine and Kennedy's head as in the scaled drawing of Dealey Plaza replicated Zapruder Frame 312. The virtual trajectory line through the head extended rearward, indicating the path of the bullet striking President Kennedy. The trajectory computed by the House Select Committee on Assassinations was 18.6° left to right and 5.5° downward relative to the President's facial axis (HSCA 6:35, 39-40).

When extending the computed trajectory line rearward, it intercepts the face of the southeast corner of the Texas School Book Depository approximately eleven feet west of the southeast corner of the building and approximately fifteen feet above the sixth floor windowsill. The House Select Committee on Assassinations explained the disparity in the trajectory as the result of the revision of the wound locations in Kennedy's head. Even slightly altering the precise position of the body or the location of the wounds alters the extended trajectory considerably, which changes the point of origin. The panel thereby adopted as acceptable a 5° margin of error. That adjustment resulted in the extended trajectory including a twenty-three foot radius around the intersecting trajectory point, thereby encompassing the sixth floor window believed to have been used by Oswald (HSCA 6: 40-42).

TRAJECTORY ISSUES

The House Select Committee on Assassinations purported there was no evidence suggesting a shooter was in any other location than the Texas School Book Depository. Their trajectory analysis was based on that premise. Based on the FBI reenactment, the Warren Commission determined the projectile struck Kennedy's head at an approximate 15° 21' off horizontal. This photographic record would be hard to dispute; however, the wound description was not aligning with that angle. Suggesting the autopsy physicians misjudged the entry wound location, HSCA moved it upward approximately four inches. Based on those measurements a trajectory of 5.5° downward relative to the President's facial axis was calculated. Added to the 11° downward tilt of his head, the official HSCA trajectory became 18.5° off horizontal; much closer to the 15° downward angle documented in the FBI reenactment.

DISCOVERY CHANNEL TRAJECTORY

The House Select Committee's Analysis began with the assumption the headshot originated from a shooter in the Texas School Book Depository. However, critics of the Warren Commission and the House Select Committee on Assassinations were not convinced the headshot originated from behind. They pointed to the backward movement of Kennedy following the headshot and apparent back spatter in the Zapruder film as indications of a front shot. To challenge the suppositions of a conspiracy, the Discovery Channel resolved to re-create the shooting death of President Kennedy.

In November 2008, a Discovery Channel documentary united a team of experts in a quest to re-create the assassination of President John F. Kennedy. *JFK: Inside the Target Car* hoped to address the number of shots fired and the number and location of the shooters by using the following investigative team:

1. Gary Mack, Curator of the Sixth Floor Museum in Dallas
2. Michael Yardley, British shooting expert, author and graduate of the Royal Military Academy of Sandhurst
3. Wesley Fisk, Chief operating officer of Adelaide T&E Systems, an engineering company that specializes in creating exact human specimens utilized in military weaponry development
4. Steve Schliebe, a blood spatter specialist with the Los Angeles Sheriff's Department
5. Tom Bevel, blood spatter expert, author and retired police captain (Erickson, 2008).

Adelaide T&E Systems constructed a head and torso mannequin that was an accurate anatomical replica of Kennedy. The mannequin torso and head design provides accurate human tissue response as ballistic projectiles impact it. The mannequin head contained a substance similar to ballistic gelatin that facilitates blood spatter analysis following ballistic impact. The Discovery Channel team addressed the assassination reconstruction in two parts. The most likely possible locations of an assassin were determined while in Dealey Plaza; and the reconstruction of the shooting from those locations took place at a gun range in California (Erickson, 2008).

DUPLICATING THE TRAJECTORY

A vehicle was positioned within Dealey Plaza at a location corresponding with the Presidential limousine at the time of the headshot. Occupants representative of the Kennedys and Connallys were seated in the appropriate positions. Yardley and Mack contemplated various locations within Dealey Plaza as possible origins for the headshot. Yardley's and Mack's assessment of viable locations for the shooter identified two possibilities: the Grassy Knoll and the sixth floor of the Texas School Book Depository. Yardley agreed the Grassy Knoll would provide a good shot, but expressed concern an exiting bullet would strike Jackie Kennedy (Erikson, 2008).

The documentary team reproduced the angles, distances, and wind speeds of those two locations on a California firing range. A wooden replica of the interior of the Presidential limousine was constructed and the Adelaide T&E Systems replicated head placed in a position representing President Kennedy. Yardley first fired from the simulated Grassy Knoll position utilizing two types of projectiles. A Winchester rifle using non-jacketed ammunition resulted in extensive fragmentation of the simulated head. The second shot from the replicated knoll utilized a Mannlicher Carcano rifle. The full metal-jacketed ammunition perforated the simulated head exiting on the left side. Neither of the two shots produced wounds consistent with those of President Kennedy, consequently eliminating the Grassy Knoll as the shooter's location for the fatal headshot (Erikson, 2008).

The documentary team then duplicated the shot Oswald allegedly made by recreating the necessary height, angle, and distance from Yardley to the simulated head. A surveyor calculated the trajectory distance and angle. The narrator suggests upon firing, the viewer would see the effects of a bullet on a human skull. However, the narrator also stipulated the viewer would not necessarily see the back and to the left movement observed in the Zapruder film. Evidently, the documentary team did not consider Kennedy's head movement the result of a bullet striking the skull, and did not want the viewer to anticipate duplication of the Kennedy's movements (Erikson, 2008).

Yardley fired a shot from the position representing the Texas School Book Depository using a Mannlicher Carcano rifle and full metal-jacketed ammunition. The projectile from that shot perforated the artificial head, exited without fragmentation, and became embedded in the dashboard of the replicated vehicle. The documentary narrator declared the obviously incorrect defects to the fabricated head as consistent with Kennedy's wounds. From that erroneous conclusion, the documentary team obstinately extrapolated the headshot could have only come from the sixth floor window of the Texas School Book Depository, just as the Warren Commission determined in 1964 (Erikson, 2008).

DUPLICATING BLOOD SPATTER
The second portion of the reconstruction entailed utilizing experts in blood spatter analysis to confirm the Yardley trajectory matched the Kennedy trajectory. The documentary investigative team employed recollections of blood in the   Presidential limousine provided by Jack McNairy and H. B. McLain, a Dallas Motorcycle Police Officer. An 18-year-old high school student and *Dallas Times Herald* employee in 1963, McNairy saw the motorcade on Stemmons Freeway and gave an official a ride to Parkland

Memorial Hospital, where he and McLain briefly viewed the limousine. During the documentary, McNairy and McLain proclaimed the spatter created in the reconstruction shooting consistent with the blood spatter they observed within the limousine at the Parkland Hospital main entrance. The ability to differentiate between different types of bloodstain patterns and recognize the directionality of individual bloodstains within a pattern requires specialized training. The two witnesses nevertheless proclaimed the simulated brain matter pattern indistinguishable with what they had observed 45 years earlier (Erickson, 2008).

The projectile used to produce the simulated spatter lodged in the dashboard of the replicated vehicle. Blood spatter experts Steve Schliebe and Tom Bevel used a laser to illustrate the trajectory from the embedded projectile to the replicated head, and extended the trajectory to the location from which Yardley had fired. Schliebe and Bevel next examined the simulated brain matter expelled from the manufactured heads. The experts concluded the spatter indicated a shot from the rear. Inconceivably, the Discovery Channel team concluded an assassin fired from the sixth floor of the Texas School Book Depository based exclusively on a re-created shooting incident structured around the memories of two unqualified observers (Erickson, 2008).

PROBLEMS WITH THE CONCLUSIONS

The procedure used by the Discovery Channel's documentary team to determine the trajectory is highly unorthodox and inaccurate in both methodology and findings. Shooting a manufactured replicated head creates defects dissimilar to shooting injuries sustained by a human skull. Kennedy's hat size was the basis for the head model. The replication lacked blood, sutures, and the variable bone thicknesses found in individual human skulls. The substance contained within the replicated head was not blood, nor was it a liquid with the viscosity of blood. The simulated head contained no liquid, only a type of ballistic gelatin incorporated to simulate biological brain tissue.

In essence, the documentary team created a gelatin spatter pattern then asked if the experts could determine where the shooter for that gelatin pattern was located. The analysts used basic shapes of the dispersed gelatin to determine a general direction of travel. Since the shooter for the current pattern was behind the target, the experts recognized and correctly stated the shooter was behind the target. The experts did not state a blood spatter pattern they had never seen proved a shot from the rear of Kennedy.

The Discovery Channel reconstruction team should have conferred with their bloodstain pattern analyst experts to determine if witnesses matching patterns was a realistic method of confirming trajectory. They should have asked the experts if untrained observers could reliably make comparisons between patterns. Instead, the documentary team accepted the statements of the witnesses as support for their preconceived conclusion of a rear shooter without knowing if they were using a valid procedure.

The program incorrectly portrays this convoluted, pseudo-science methodology as a reliable, forensic technique. Establishing ballistic trajectory through the visual resemblance of head wounds is not an acceptable scientific method; and visual similarity in blood spatter patterns does not confirm identical trajectory. Nothing the Discovery Channel's team accomplished provides results that upon analysis would provide a factual, scientifically based trajectory conclusion. The narrator implies scientific neutrality; unfortunately, evaluation of the documentary reconstruction and subsequent trajectory declaration reveals an inadequate understanding of the forensic fields applied and a poorly concealed bias and manipulation of the results.

Forensic procedures are consistently reproducible, and therefore, considered reliable. The Discovery Channel did not prove they could consistently reproduce identical defects by shooting numerous replicated heads. Therefore, their results are unreliable. They did not prove the defects created in the simulated head were identical to Kennedy's injuries. The exact location of President Kennedy's entry and exit wounds are areas of contention. Therefore, Mack's indication of the entry wound location on the simulated head is also questionable. Moreover, the defects visualized in the replicated head do not correspond to the well-defined, single entry wound and a larger exit wound that the documentary states Kennedy suffered.

The experts merely replied that the forward scattering of gelatin debris is consistent with a shot from the rear; not that Kennedy's assassin was located in the sixth floor window of the Texas School Book Depository. Proclaiming the apparent defects as displaying sufficient uniformity with Kennedy's wounds to identify a single line trajectory is irrational and unquestionably not based on acceptable forensic trajectory analysis techniques. The Discovery Channel's documentary team may have shown reason to discount a Grassy Knoll shooter, but they did not prove the headshot originated from the sixth floor window.

STANDARD TRAJECTORY ANALYSIS

Bullet trajectories follow a downward curve known as a parabolic arc; however, in high velocity bullets traveling short distances the curvature is typically slight. The distance the bullet path begins to decline due to air resistance and gravity. Projectile identification provides velocity and weight information that allows the parabolic arc to be calculated. Short-range distance shootings with high velocity projectiles usually have straight-line trajectories. Three steps are essential to computing straight-line trajectories using a single bullet hole.

1. The location of the bullet hole and impact site
2. The vertical angle of the bullet path as viewed from the side
3. The horizontal angle of the bullet path as viewed from above (Haag, 2011).

The location of the bullet hole must be associated with fixed locations. For example, if the bullet hole were on a wall, the distance from a specific corner and the floor would indicate the location. Demonstrating the results of mathematically computed vertical and horizontal angles is challenging. Crime scene analysts typically reconstruct and demonstrate angles using a laser or trajectory rods. Using lasers fitted into hollow rods for trajectory reconstruction is most common, and documentation using photography is easily accomplished. A plum bob hanging adjacent to the trajectory rod will provide the vertical angle of the bullet path when viewed at a 90° angle to the wall. A zero edged protractor placed parallel to the floor will assist in establishing the horizontal angle when the plum bob rests against the outer edge of the protractor. In cases where the bullet perforates the wall, there will be two points for the laser to intersect (Haag, 2011).

Trajectory is also determined using the trigonometric relationship of right triangles. Drop the plumb bob to the floor a few feet from the wall. Measure the distance from the point of the floor indicated by the plumb bob to the wall. Locate the height at which the laser beam intersects the plumb bob line. The height of the laser intersection, divided by the distance to the wall measured on the floor represents the tangent of the vertical angle. The arctangent function on a scientific calculator will provide the vertical angle of the bullet (Haag, 2011).

This process works well in interior shooting scenes; however, exterior scenes do not always have surfaces with well-defined bullet holes. Exterior scenes usually mean longer trajectories and increased distances, which necessitates the consideration of the parabolic arc. All scenes can have degraded bullet holes, with fragmented surfaces and irregular edges. Therefore, in all shootings, the single line trajectory should include a calculated margin of error; usually determined to be 5° (Haag, 2011).

PARABOLIC ARC

Before calculating a straight-line trajectory or a trajectory cone, the bullet parabolic arc must be considered. Bullet trajectories follow a downward curve known as a parabolic arc; however, in high velocity bullets traveling short distances the curvature is typically slight. The HSCA alleged the projectile that struck President Kennedy was traveling at a velocity of 2000 feet per second. Since the sixth floor window was approximately 265 feet from Kennedy at the time of the headshot, it is reasonable to assume the bullet fired at the President's head followed a straight-line trajectory path (HSCA A6:27).

> *GOLDSMITH: What type of trajectory is involved in the case of a bullet that travels a distance of less than 100 yards?*
>
> *CANNING: For a high-speed bullet, the effects of the aerodynamics and of the gravity are very small, so that we can consider the trajectory essentially a straight line (HSCA 2:154).*

Most rifle ammunition has a velocity of well over 2000 feet per second, and as a result, the parabolic arc does not affect the trajectory until the distance is beyond 400 feet or more. Most locations that could have concealed a shooter within Dealey Plaza were well within that range. Therefore, it is reasonable to use a straight-line trajectory (Hawks, 1212).

STEP ONE:

DETERMINE WOUND LOCATIONS

By applying standard trajectory analysis procedures, an accurate determination for possible shooter locations for the headshot is established. Steps in trajectory analysis by the Warren Commission, the House Select Committee on Assassinations, and the Discovery Channel were either incomplete, failed to consider a point of origin in front of the President, or both.

The entry wound and exit wound points used to determine trajectory do not appear to be consistent when reviewing information published by the Warren Commission, Clark Panel, or House Select Committee on Assassinations. Based upon his observations of the beveling effect in Kennedy's skull, Finck concluded the bullet entered at the back of the head and exited on the right side; proving the shots originated from above and behind Kennedy. Pathologists Humes, Boswell, and Finck signed the autopsy report and testified before the Warren Commission the projectile entered the skull approximately 2.5 centimeters laterally to the right and slightly above the external occipital protuberance (WCR:86; 16:CE 387).

In 1968, Attorney General Ramsey Clark charged four physicians to review medical evidence concerning the assassination of President Kennedy: William H. Carnes, Russell S. Fisher, Russell H. Morgan, and Alan R. Moritz. The Clark Panel determined the projectile entered the head in the occipital region 25 millimeters to the right of the midline and 100 millimeters above the external occipital protuberance (ARRB MD 59: 12).

The House Select Committee on Assassinations Forensic Pathology Panel determined the fatal bullet entered the back of Kennedy's head 9 centimeters above the external occipital protuberance, and 1.8 centimeters right of the skull's midline (HSCA 1:184, 234).

The autopsy report indicated a portion of the projectile made its exit through the parietal bone on the right, carrying with it portions of cerebrum, skull, and scalp. This general description became more specific under The House

Select Committee on Assassinations Investigation. The HSCA Forensic Pathology Panel relied upon the expertise of panel member Lawrence Angel to identify the exit wound. Angel placed the exit through the right frontal bone, corresponding with a small semicircular notch 35 millimeters above the right orbit, just in front of the coronal suture above the stephanion. The stephanion is the point on the side of the skull where the temporal line, or upper edge of the temporal fossa, crosses the coronal suture. The HSCA Forensic Pathology Panel accepted the defect in front of the coronal suture above pterion as the exit wound (16HCE 387; HSCA Addendum E 7:230).

Various entities and individuals have issued statements concerning the entry wound location. Confirmation of an entry or exit is determined with intact skull defects; however, no skull defects displayed intact circular or elliptically shaped perforations. The autopsy photographs depicted intact skull with portions of bones with semicircular edges., However, the location and orientation of the photographs is uncertain. Moreover, the presumption the projectile entered the posterior skull affects the determinations concerning entry and exit wounds. The most accurate description of wound locations may be to simply state the entry or exit was located in the right front quadrant of the head, with an exit wound in the right rear quadrant.

STEP TWO:

DETERMINE PROJECTILE DIRECTION OF TRAVEL
Beveling, fracture sequencing and projectile fragmentation in gunshot wounds to the head are methods of assessing the projectile direction of travel. In the case of the Kennedy assassination, head movement and blood spatter recorded in the Zapruder film also suggest a particular direction. However, before extending a trajectory through entry and exit wounds into the crime scene, there must be no doubt as to what defect classifies as an entry wound and what defect classifies as an exit wound.

BEVELING
Historically, beveling determines projectile directionality in bone. Bullets traveling through bone create marginal conical shaped fractures adjacent to the entry or exit site. The conical beveling characteristically appears as

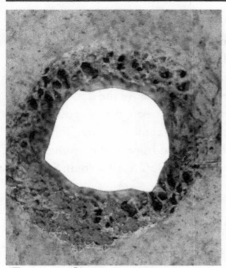

(FIGURE 9) Defect in Skull with Symmetrical Beveling

a symmetrical chipping out of bone forming an indentation surrounding the entry or exit point on the opposite side of impact. An entry wound creates a defect that appears as a punched hole on the outer table of the skull with concentric internal beveling on the inner table. The small end of the cone touches the interior or exterior bone table from which the bullet entered. Figure 9 depicts the coning observed at the exit portion of bone (Levy, 2012).

There is an exception to these patterns; tangential gunshot wounds to the head create elliptically shaped defects resembling an old-fashioned keyhole. The resulting keyhole entry wound contains both internal and external beveling, such as in Figure 10. The keyhole wound displays a clean-edged, elliptically shaped opening opposing a larger, circular opening with exposed beveling. Therefore, the tangential gunshot wound interacting with the curvature of the skull can show beveling characteristics of entry at one side of the defect and characteristics of exit at the other side of the same defect. For many years pathologist believed all entry wounds generated only keyhole or internal beveling, however recent research shows that is incorrect (Levy, 2012).

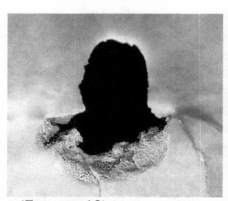

(FIGURE 10) Asymmetrical or Keyhole Beveling In Tangential Wound

Scientists describe beveling as symmetrical or asymmetrical. Symmetrical beveling has marginal fractures evenly distributed around a wound. Asymmetrical beveling has more pronounced beveling only on one side of the wound. Round entry wounds can display a variety of beveling characteristics, including no beveling, symmetrical beveling, or asymmetrical beveling. Elliptically shaped holes can have symmetrical beveling or asymmetrical beveling. The shapes of the entry wounds may be circular, ovoid, triangular, diamond, or rectangular with rounded corners (Quatrehomme, 1998).

Beveling is not common in the thinner temporal bone. Skull bones are not uniform plates and display variations in thickness at different points. The average thickness of skull bones in males is frontal bone: 6.3 millimeters, temporal bone: 3.9 millimeters, occipital bone: 7.7 millimeters, parietal bone: 5. millimeters, central frontal bone: 8.1 millimeters, and lower occipital bone: 9.35 millimeters. The occipital bone and frontal bone are the thickest skull bones (Quatrehomme, 1998, Mahinda, 2009).

Some entry wounds can present both internal and external beveling. External beveling of an entry wound often results in a wound misidentified as an exit wound. Researchers attribute this external pseudo-beveling in high velocity distance shots to the transference of kinetic energy to the skull. The transference of kinetic energy fractures the adjacent bone resulting in dislodged chips flaking off entry wound edges, producing the effect of beveling. Exit wounds occasionally display the phenomenon of chipped edges that may be mistaken for beveling. Without careful examination, misinterpretation of an entrance wound as an exit wound is possible in all types of entries (Quatrehomme, 1998).

Tangential entry and exit wounds can easily be confused, especially with extensive fragmentation and expelled bone fragments. Complete reconstruction of disconnected skull fragments is necessary to observe the characteristics of skull beveling used to determine the bullet's path. Partial reconstruction of the beveled defect diminishes the opportunity for correct direction interpretation. A fragment can splinter off an irregular break, leaving what only appears to be beveling. Based upon current forensic research, it appears beveling cannot provide conclusive evidence of projectile direction. Incorrect assessment of direction can occur with tangential entries or exits, mistaken orientation, insufficient beveling, or the failure to recognize external beveling on entry wounds (Coe, 1981; Prahlow, 2010; Adams, 2010).

Beveling, once considered the gold standard for determining the direction of travel for a projectile perforating the skull, is proving to be less reliable than previously thought. However, that is the process used by the House Select Committee on Assassination Forensic Pathology Panel to determine projectile direction. The HSCA Forensic Pathology Panel located two small edges located within intact bone displaying a curved edge and beveling. The first was the entry wound Humes described, which the HSCA Forensic Pathology Panel moved to 10 millimeters above the external occipital protuberance. The second is a small curved notch 35 millimeters above the right orbit, just in front of the coronal suture above the stephanion. HSCA Forensic Pathology Panel member Angel placed the exit wound through the right frontal bone corresponding with that notch. The medical evidence in the Kennedy assassination does not document an intact circular defect in the skull with appropriate beveling to indicate direction. Keyhole beveling resulting from a tangential gunshot wound is possible since the projectile injuring Kennedy likely struck at an acute angle. No medical evidence in the Kennedy assassination documents a completely circular defect with beveled edges within intact bone. Moreover, no dislodged fragment with medical landmarks completes a beveled circular or elliptical hole in the skull. External beveling from transference of energy in entry wounds via high velocity distance shots is also a factor to consider in the Kennedy shooting (HSCA Addendum E 7:230).

The beveled nick observed in the frontal bone or the beveled portion of bone observed rear of the head might represent a tangential wound. The beveled portion of bone observed in the frontal bone could also be an entry wound with pseudo-beveling. Partially reconstructing the beveled defect, as Humes did, diminishes the opportunity for correct direction evaluation. Current scientific research focusing on beveling suggests the direction of travel adopted by the HSCA is unverifiable.

FRACTURE SEQUENCING

It is always possible to recognize fracture sequencing when two fracture lines of a solid surface such as glass intersect. That same principle applies to skull fractures resulting from gunshot wounds to the head. The first impact from the projectile creates *radial fractures* that extend out from the wound. *Concentric fractures* surround the entry wound and are perpendicular to the radial fractures. Secondary radial fractures created by a second impact, such as the exit wound, will terminate at previously formed fractures. Fracture sequencing can determine the progression of multiple gunshot injuries, the direction of fire, and differentiate entrance from exit wounds in the absence of specific distinguishing features, such as beveling. In the 1980s, researchers who addressed the sequencing of radial and concentric skull fractures in gunshot injuries established a secondary method of determining projectile direction (Viel, 2009).

The first fractures formed are radial fractures that originate from the entry wound and travel outward from the impact site primarily in the continued direction of the force of the projectile. Radial fractures travel faster than a perforating bullet. These long linear fractures often cross suture lines as they radiate outward from the entry wound. Increased internal pressure then creates concentric or heaving fractures. The concentric fractures appear as a series of parallel-arced fractures surrounding the point of impact and connecting the radial fracture lines. Each successive group of concentric fractures is called a *generation*. While they may appear to be connected, the concentric fractures are essentially a series of independent arcs between radial fractures. The preponderance of concentric fractures is closer to the point of entry (Viel, 2009; Karger, 2008; Smith, 1987; Leestma, 2009).

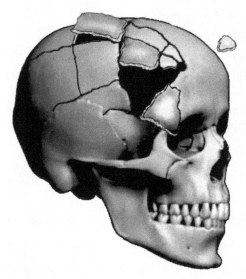

With sufficient internal pressure, fractures can separate, create bone avulsions or dislodge and expel bone fragments from the skull. This is demonstrated in Figure 11. Radial fractures extending out from the entry wound and the adjacent concentric fractures occur while the bullet is still traveling within the head. Occasionally, the exit of the

(**FIGURE 11**) Fracture Sequencing - Radial and Concentric Fractures with Avulsion and Expelled Fragment

projectile produces a second series of radial and concentric fractures. Exit wounds produce fewer and shorter radial fractures with little concentric fracturing, because less energy is available by the time the projectile reaches the exit point. Comparison of the radial fractures and concentric fractures can help to differentiate between entry and exit wounds. Fracturing sequencing research indicates the radial fractures stem from a point of entry (Viel, 2009; Karger, 2008; Smith, 1987; Leestma, 2009).

The Kennedy autopsy report stated multiple fracture lines radiated from both the large defect and the smaller defect at the occiput. They varied considerably in length and direction, the longest measuring approximately 19 centimeters. The Clark Panel observed extensive fracturing in the autopsy X-Rays. The panel report specified there was extensive fragmentation "of the bony structures from the midline of the frontal bone anteriorly to the vicinity of the posterior margin of the parietal bone behind." The report goes on to state, "throughout this region, many of the bony pieces have been displaced outward; several pieces are missing." The Clark Panel report indicates the majority of the fracturing and displaced bones fragments are closer to the location they described as the exit wound; this is in direct conflict with scientific research concerning skull fractures resulting from gunshot injuries (CE 387 16H978; ARRB MD 59:10).

This fracturing pattern was discussed in the Assassinations Records Review Board deposition of Jerrol Francis Custer on October 28, 1997. Custer was the X-Ray technician on call at Bethesda Hospital the night of the Kennedy autopsy. Custer testified the fragments increased in size as the force moved forward.

> *GUINN: So, it's your opinion that the trauma to the head began at the front and moved towards the back of the head?*
>
> *CUSTER: Yes, sir. Absolutely (Custer, 1997).*

Kennedy's X-Rays depict radial fractures that appear to originate in the frontal bone. Concentric fractures are located predominately near the front of the head. Kennedy's autopsy X-Rays have distinct radial fractures propagating from the front of the head, with the preponderance of concentric fractures located at the front. This results in smaller fragments nearer the point of entry, enlarging in size as they move toward the exit wound. Current research indicates Kennedy's fracturing pattern corresponds with an entry wound located in the frontal bone, which correlates to a projectile striking the front of the head (Karger, 2008; Smith, 1987; Leestma, 2009).

MOVEMENT

When examining the Zapruder film frame by frame, it is readily apparent the President Kennedy's head moves forward slightly for one frame before his head and shoulders move backward in response to the gunshot wound to the head. The sudden forward movement occurring between frames 312 and 313 is restricted to the head; as the torso does not move. Conversely, the head, neck, and upper torso move together in backward rotation to the left in frames 314 through 320. Josiah Thompson first published research concerning this forward movement in *Six Seconds in Dallas: A Micro-Study of the Kennedy Assassination* (1967). Like many who observe the contrasting movements of Kennedy in the Zapruder film, Thompson proposed they were indicative of nearly simultaneous, opposing projectile impacts to the skull. Consequently, the scenario of two entry wounds was suggested to the House Select Committee on Assassinations, but it was dismissed (Thompson, 1967).

The House Select Committee on Assassinations Report states a single bullet struck Kennedy in the rear of the head. This conclusion was not unanimous, however, as noted in the accompanying footnote:

> *In many of its conclusions, the forensic pathology panel voted 8 to 1, with the dissenting vote being consistently that of Cyril H. Wecht, M.D., coroner of Allegheny County, Pa. In all references to conclusions of the panel, unless it is specifically stated that it was unanimous, it should be assumed that Dr. Wecht dissented (HSCA Report 1A-LHO: 43).*

Wecht did not agree with several of the conclusions of the HSCA Forensic Pathology Panel. The single bullet theory concerning the torso injuries of Kennedy and Connally is likely the most familiar conclusion in dispute; however, Wecht also vehemently opposed a single gunshot to the rear of Kennedy's head. Wecht strongly attributed the President's movement immediately following the head wound to a second projectile entering the right front portion of Kennedy's skull (HSCA 7:201).

The slight forward head movement followed by the prolonged rear movement was obviously disconcerting to the HSCA Forensic Pathology Panel. The panel concluded that forward movement:

1. Was the result of the initial impact of the projectile.
2. An immediate stiffening of muscles resulting in a backward lunge explained the subsequent rear movement of Kennedy's head and shoulders. They determined a massive downward rush of neurologic stimulus triggered the lunge. The Forensic Pathology Panel cited the phenomena known as Sherrington rigidity, as a possible cause of the rearward movement. However, the Forensic Pathology Panel conceded Sherrington does not normally present until several minutes after brain damage occurs.
3. Finally, the panel suggested the motion of the vehicle might have created the backward movement of the President.

The Forensic Pathology Panel's official conclusion is the rear movement was the result of a "reverse jet effect, a neuromuscular reaction, or a combination of the two." They referenced the short interval between the two observed movements as support for their conclusions. Ultimately, the HSCA Forensic Pathology Panel determined that the rearward movement of the President Kennedy's head was consistent with a bullet entering the rear of Kennedy's head and exiting at the front of the head (HSCA 7:173-174, 178).

FORWARD MOVEMENT

Ballistics involves the study of the scientific properties of projectiles, their behavior, and their terminal effects on biological tissues and other materials. Wound ballistics deals with the analysis of injuries caused by projectiles and the behavior of projectiles within human or other biological tissues. When studying terminal ballistics, engineers and scientists are interested in determining the effects of a projectile on a target. *Forensic Ballistics* (2008) by German researcher Bernd Karger, addresses gunshot wounds to the head. The important factors to consider are energy, penetration, and expansion. The energy in a moving bullet is energy of motion, or kinetic energy. When a bullet hits a target and stops, the majority of the kinetic energy transfers to the target, creating a vast amount of tissue damage, and the balance converts to heat energy. The ideal bullet hits the target with as much energy as possible and stops as rapidly as possible. The higher a projectile's velocity upon impact, the more kinetic energy is available to transfer to the target. The amount of Kinetic energy transferred to a target increases with faster projectile deceleration. The more kinetic energy transferred to the target, the greater tissue damage. This initial transfer of energy causes the target to move minutely into the force and against the line of fire, prior to movement with the force of the moving bullet. The greater the transferred energy, the more pronounced the forward movement (Karger, 2008).

In *Wound Ballistics: Basics and Applications* (2011), author Robin Coupland, et al, uses high-speed photography to document the forward movement into the line of fire referenced by Karger (2008). Coupland secured model skulls filled with ballistic gelatin to a surface to prevent movement upon impact by a 9 millimeter Luger, full metal-jacketed bullet. However, the target continued to display the phenomenon of moving into the force, or line of fire, by creating a bulge in the skull. In the eight frames published, the bullet approached the target, perforated the skull, and exited. Karger photographed the pressure from the temporary cavity as it created a visible and measurable bulge where the bullet entered. Radial fractures extended to the rear of the model skull before the bullet exited the head. As the cavitation pressure increased, the skull reached its maximum bending capacity and the radial and concentric fractures appeared. Sustained pressure waves from the temporary cavitation increases the number of fractures and may dislodge and expel bone fragments. Coupland noted the fracturing and bulge created by a higher velocity bullet would exceed that created by the 9 millimeter handgun used in the experiment (Coupland, 2011).

REARWARD MOVEMENT

To determine how targets reacted when impacted by a projectile, the Warren Commission had research physical scientist Larry M. Sturdivan conduct experiments. Sturdivan, one of only a few wound ballistics experts worldwide at that time, was associated with the Wounds Ballistics Branch of the Aberdeen Proving Ground Vulnerability Laboratory. Aberdeen Proving Grounds conducts research, tests and evaluates weapons for governmental agencies.

The Laboratory's evaluations encompassed wound ballistics, which focused on studying the behavior of bullets inside tissue and tissue simulants. In 1964, Aberdeen Proving Grounds implemented research and tests for the Warren Commission in connection with their investigation of the assassination of President Kennedy. Sturdivan testified that they completed air retardation and gelatin tissue simulants retardation tests of cadaver wrists, skulls, and anesthetized animals (HSCA 1:384-385).

Unbelievably, it appears the Warren Commission suppressed both the experiments and the results and did not call Sturdivan to testify. However, the House Select Committee on Assassinations was not so cautious and questioned him about the 1964 experiments. Sturdivan testified that while using Mannlicher Carcano 6.5 millimeter ammunition, Aberdeen Proving Grounds scientists had shot 10 goat skulls filled with ballistic gelatin. The skulls were also covered with a film of gelatin and, at the point of impact, a piece of goatskin simulating skin and hair. Sturdivan's testimony then related the following results of the shooting (HSCA1:402-403).

> *STURDIVAN: As you can see, each of the two skulls that we have observed so far, have moved in the direction of the bullet. In other words, both of them have been given some momentum in the direction that the bullet was going. This third one also shows momentum in the direction that the bullet was going, showing that the head of the President would probably go with the bullet. In fact, all 10 of the skulls that we shot did essentially the same thing (HSCA 1:404).*

Sturdivan's testimony and filmed exhibits of the skulls moving with the direction of the projectile obviously challenged the Warren Commission's conclusion concerning the direction of the headshot. Sturdivan countered his earlier divulgence of "the head of the President would probably go with the bullet" by providing several explanations.

1. The deposit of momentum from the bullet was not sufficient to cause significant movement in any direction
2. The movement was diminished by the connection of the head with the neck and body

3. The lack of appropriate movement was due to a neuromuscular reaction
4. The heavy back muscles predominate over the lighter abdominal muscles would have thrown him backward no matter where the bullet came from (HSCA 1:414- 415,421).

Regardless of the convoluted rationalizations offered by Sturdivan, it is still a matter of physics. Objects behave in predictable manners. Newton's Laws of Motion help us to understand how objects behave when they are standing still, when they are moving, and when forces act upon them. Newton's First Law of Motion states an object in motion will stay in motion unless an external force acts upon it. Similarly, if an object is at rest, it will remain at rest unless an unbalanced force acts upon it. A resting object will not start moving unless a force causes it to do so. Moving objects will not change their direction unless a force causes them to move from their trajectory. Newton's Second Law of Motion states when a force acts on an object, it causes the object to move. The larger the mass of the object, the greater the force will need to be to cause it to move. Another way to state the Second Law is that it takes more force to move a heavy object than it does to move a light object (Helmenstine, 2012).

The Zapruder film depicts Kennedy's moving slowly forward when suddenly between frames 312-313 there is a sudden forward movement of approximately 2 inches. Frame 312 also reveals blood spatter leaving the head because of a gunshot wound to the head. The successive frames show the back and to the left movement that is recognizable to anyone who is familiar with the film. There appears to be no question as to the mechanism of wounding; the President suffered a fatal gunshot to the head. However, no one knows with certainty what caliber projectile inflicted the wound. However, the explosive nature of the wounds suggests high velocity ammunition.

BULLET FRAGMENT DISTRIBUTION
Some projectile designs cause bullets to fragment or deform upon contact with the target. Fully jacketed ammunition does not usually fragment and has little deformity, while hollow point, non-jacketed and soft point bullets tend to deform or fragment, leaving a trail of fragments through soft tissue. The fragments may be extremely small and with increased number have a snowstorm appearance on X-Rays. The fragment distribution pattern

identifies the projectile's direction of travel. The fragment pattern begins near the point of entry and continues in the direction of the bullet trajectory in an ever-widening path as they move away from the entry wound. When observing X-Rays of lead fragments at the same angle as the trajectory of the perforating bullet, the fragments appear to radiate around the bullet path. A lateral view of the same pattern will reveal a conical shape to the fragment distribution. The apex of the pattern is closest to the entry wound and the wider portion of the fragment cone is closest to the exit wound (Rushing, 2008; Fung, 2008; Wilson, 1999; DiMaio, 1998).

The House Select Committee on Assassinations heard testimony concerning the characteristics of bullet fragment patterns. Larry Sturdivan testified the majority of metallic fragments are typically deposited nearest the entry wound.

> *STURDIVAN: In those cases, you would definitely have seen a cloud of metallic fragments very near the entrance wound. So, this case is typical of a deforming jacketed bullet leaving fragments along its path as it goes. Incidentally, those fragments that are left by the bullet are also very small and do not move very far from their initial, from the place where they departed the bullet. Consequently, they tend to be clustered very closely around the track of the bullet (HSCA 1: 402).*

The Clark Panel Report describes the bullet fragments observed in Kennedy's X-Rays.

> *Distributed through the right, cerebral hemisphere are numerous small, irregular, metallic fragments, which are less than 1 millimeter in maximum dimension. The majority lay anteriorly (the top of the head) and superiorly (toward the front of the head). None can be visualized on the left side of the brain and none below a horizontal plane through the floor of the anterior fossa of the skull. The metallic fragments visualized within the right cerebral hemisphere fall into two groups. One group consists of relatively large fragments, more or less randomly distributed. The second group consists of finely divided fragments, distributed in a postero-anterior direction in a region 45 millimeter long and 8 millimeter wide. As seen on lateral film #2,*

this formation overlies the position of the coronal suture; its long axis,
if extended posteriorly, passes through the above-mentioned hole. It
appears to end anteriorly immediately below the badly fragmented
frontal and parietal bones, just anterior to the region of the coronal
suture (ARRB MD59:10-11).

There are two significant statements in the Clark Panel Report. In human anatomical usage, anterior refers to the "front" and superior refers to the top; therefore, the Clark Panel Report states the majority of fragments are located in the front and top of the head. Secondly, the panel determined the second grouping of fragments is located below the badly fragmented frontal and parietal bones, just in front of the coronal suture.

BLOOD SPATTER

A bloodstain pattern is a distribution of blood droplets with identifiable characteristics. Bloodstain pattern analysis refers to the examination of the shape, location and distribution of blood droplets to interpret the events connected with bloodshed, in particular, the forces that created them. Analysis incorporates information gathering, observation, documentation, analysis, assessment, conclusion, and technical review. Bloodstain pattern studies are based on general principles of physics, chemistry, biology, and mathematics and have been a widely recognized as reliable and credible evidence in a court of law.

BLOOD SPATTER IN GUNSHOT WOUNDS TO THE HEAD

Blood spatter from gunshot wounds include forward spatter and back spatter. *Forward spatter* is blood ejected from the exit wound and travels in the same direction as the bullet. *Back spatter* is blood ejected from the entry wound and travels against the line of fire, back towards the shooter. Although forward and back spatter patterns display some common features, there are also dissimilarities. Studying forward and back spatter patterns created during a singular incident identifies those differences. By differentiating between forward and back spatter in shooting incidents, the identification of the direction of the origin of force is possible (James, 2005).

When a projectile strikes a human head, it begins the progression of specific events. The bullet enters the skull by forming a small entrance hole. The force of the bullet striking the skull creates fractures moving away from the impact site. These fractures, called radiating fractures are complete before the bullet exits the skull. When the bullet strikes the skull, the velocity slows and kinetic energy transfers to the target. This initial transfer of energy causes the target to move minutely into the force and against the line of fire, prior to movement with the force of the moving bullet (Karger, 2008).

Pressure builds as temporary cavitation begins, and increases as the projectile traverses the head. It has also been suggested that as a bullet traverses tissue, backward streaming of blood and other fluid or tissue particles may transpire. These particles flow along the sides of the bullet in the opposite direction to which it is traveling. There are only the entrance wound and any consequent fractures for release of that pressure. The resulting back spatter, created within three to five milliseconds, spews from the hole from which the bullet entered (Karger, 2008; Fackler, 1987).

If the bullet leaves the skull, it typically creates an irregularly shaped exit hole that is normally larger than the corresponding entry wound. Blood and brain matter will exit the skull from the exit hole in the same path of the bullet until the head bursts from the accumulated pressure, creating an even larger and more irregularly shaped exit wound. Brain matter ejects out all available openings as forward spatter, the largest of which is usually the expanded exit wound, with its final size depending on how large the internal pressures become (DiMaio, 1999).

FORWARD AND BACK SPATTER PATTERNS

During the experimental shooting of bloody targets, dispersed blood travels back toward the shooter and forward in the continued direction of travel of the projectile. The forward spatter and back spatter in all circumstances consistently produce patterns with specific characteristics, regardless of changing variables, such as expressed blood volume and projectile velocity. The consistency of patterns produced in actual shootings and lab settings make practical comparisons of the two individual patterns created from a single incident possible. The forward and back spatter patterns produced in the field and the forward and back spatter patterns produced in the lab were identical in characteristics. The study of blood spatter is therefore is determined to be reproducible, reliable and credible (James, 2005).

SIMILAR CHARACTERISTICS OF FORWARD AND BACK SPATTER

Some elements of forward and back spatter patterns are identical; those similarities include:

1. Shape of stains: On targets capturing expelled forward and back spatter patterns, the stains near the center of the pattern were circular in shape, a result of the spatter striking the target surface at or near a perpendicular angle. At the perimeters of both forward and back spatter patterns, the stains are more elliptical in shape, a result of striking the target at an angle.

2. Stain distribution: The distribution of the droplets was more concentrated when the target surface was near the bloody target, with the distance between the droplets increasing as the droplets moved away from the bloody target.

3. Pattern shape: Both types of patterns leave the injury site and travel outward in a basic conical shape, moving in every possible direction. A slight difference is back spatter patterns tend to move to the side forming a wide cone, while forward spatter has a more forward travel with the cone shape developing more slowly, due to the presence of increased velocity, larger stains and increased blood volume (James, 2005).

DISSIMILAR CHARACTERISTICS OF FORWARD AND BACK SPATTER

Forward and back spatter patterns also exhibit divergent characteristics:

1. Distance: Forward spatter consistently travels farther than back spatter created in the same incident. In some cases, forward spatter travels well in excess of fifteen feet. Back spatter consistently travels a shorter distance than forward spatter created in the same incident. Back spatter normally travels four feet or less.

2. Blood volume: Forward spatter patterns held a larger volume of blood, expressed as individual stains, when compared to back spatter created in the same incident.

3. Tissue dispersement: Tissue fragments frequently permeate forward spatter pattern. Fragments in the forward spatter varied in

size and were occasionally large. When observed in head wounds, the fragments consisted of both soft tissue and bone fragments. Occasionally, back spatter contains tissue fragments; however, they are markedly smaller in size and fewer in quantity than tissue fragments in forward spatter.

4. Pattern dimensions: Increased blood volume resulted in increased pattern dimensions, therefore back spatter patterns are smaller than forward spatter patterns created in the same incident. Pattern dimensions for back spatter are approximately four feet; conversely, large exit wounds can result in forward spatter with sufficient projectile velocity traveling ten to twenty feet.

5. Velocity of blood: Videotape with a recording speed of 30 frames per second captured blood spatter patterns as they are created in shooting instances. The video utilized approximately 4-5 frames to capture the forceful impact blood spatter when a low velocity, large caliber projectile with a high kinetic energy rate struck a large volume of blood. This means in 1/6 of a second that particular pattern was created. Some patterns require less than 1/6 of a second. Back spatter dissipates faster than forward spatter, due to air resistance and gravity acting on the small stain volume.

6. Stain size: Forward and back spatter targets displayed a multitude of minuscule blood droplets, some resembling an atomized spray or mist. No single stain size is exclusive to a particular range of impact velocity. However, forward spatter is likely to result in predominantly larger stains than back spatter (James, 2005).

INDICATING DIRECTION OF TRAVEL

With the assistance of a Law Enforcement Assistance Administration grant, Herbert MacDonell conducted research to re-create and duplicate bloodstain patterns commonly observed on crime scenes. In 1971, MacDonell documented his research in *Flight Characteristics and Stain Patterns of Human Blood,* published by the US Department of Justice. MacDonell, widely recognized as the "father" of bloodstain pattern analysis in the Western hemisphere, continued to expand upon the analysis of blood spatter patterns, including back spatter. With an expanded and technical look at individual stains and patterns, MacDonell's work captured the attention of law enforcement and crime labs nationwide (James, 2005).

Scientific journals, books, and research published since the late 1980s indicate the blood observed in the Zapruder film displays the pattern shape of back spatter. It also extends from the wound area a distance characteristic of back spatter, particularly when correlated to blood documented elsewhere on the scene. The timing for the pattern creation and the dissipation rate identifies it as back spatter. In fact, all available information concerning the blood spatter pattern in the Zapruder film corresponds in every measurable manner with back spatter replicated in forensic laboratories and described in peer-reviewed publications since the late 1980s. Consequently, the only possible conclusion is the back spatter in the Zapruder film is genuine. Identifying the blood in the Zapruder film as back spatter signifies a shot from the front of President Kennedy.

Projectile Direction Conclusion

Once considered the benchmark for determining the direction of travel for a projectile perforating the skull, beveling is proving to be less reliable than previously thought. Without careful examination, misinterpretation of an entrance wound as an exit wound is possible, especially with extensive fragmentation and expelled bone fragments. Examination of beveling to determine the direction of travel for the projectile is inconclusive in the assassination of President Kennedy.

Kennedy's autopsy X-Rays have distinct radial fractures propagating from the front of the head, with the preponderance of concentric fractures located at the front of the head. Concentric fractures are located predominately near the front of the head. Current research indicates fracturing patterns of this nature correspond with an entry wound located in the front of the head.

The energy in a moving bullet is energy of motion, or kinetic energy. The majority of the kinetic energy transfers to the target when a bullet hits a target and stops. This initial transfer of energy causes the target to move minutely into the force and against the line of fire, before moving with the force of the bullet. The greater the transferred energy, the more pronounced the forward movement. The minute forward motion followed by more pronounced rearward movement is consistent with a shot from the front.

Kennedy's autopsy X-Rays depict the majority of bullet fragments in the front and top of the head. Multiple forensic publications indicate fragment patterns display the majority of fragments near the entry wound.

STEP THREE:

DETERMINE KENNEDY'S LOCATION AND POSITION

It is necessary to correctly position Kennedy within Dealey Plaza, in order to complete the trajectory analysis. Thomas N. Canning was an engineer with the Space Project Division of NASA engaged by the House Select Committee on Assassinations to determine Kennedy's location within Dealey Plaza. Photogrammetric analysis conducted by a geological survey established placement of Kennedy and the Presidential limousine within Dealey Plaza at the time of the shooting. Zapruder Frame 312, exposed approximately 0.055 seconds before the headshot, allowed precise placement and orientation of Kennedy's head within Dealey Plaza.

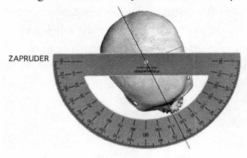

(**FIGURE 12**) Kennedy's Line of Sight Reference to Zapruder

The FAA's Aeronautical Center Civil Aeromedical Institute prepared a series of calibrated photographs of replicas of Kennedy's head. Comparing facial features in the calibrated photographs to Zapruder Frame 312 generated a three dimensional positioning of Kennedy's head. The distance between Kennedy and Zapruder was about seventy feet, with a line of sight of 10° downward. Kennedy's head was turned away from Zapruder approximately 25° beyond profile, tilted to his left and away from Zapruder about 15°, and was nodding forward about 11°. Figure 12 indicates that degree of turn from Zapruder (HSCA 6:36-38; HSCA 6:34-40).

Dale Myers is a computer animator who received an Emmy for his 2004 animated recreation of the Kennedy assassination. Myers' computer reenactment found the orientation of JFK's head relative to Zapruder's view at frame 312 turned away from Zapruder 25.7° past profile, tilted to the left 18.1°, and nodding forward 27.1°. The computer calculations, which contain a 2° margin of error, are comparable with the HSCA findings, with the exception of the pitch or forward nodding of Kennedy's head. The computer recreation shows the angle to be about 16° steeper than Canning's calculations. A 2003 impartial review of Myers' computations found the 27.1° forward nod correct (Myers, 1995).

In 2003, ABC News hired independent experts from Z-Axis Corporation, one of the nation's leading forensic animation companies, to assess Myers' computations. Z-Axis Corporation produces computer-generated animations of events, including recreations for major litigations in the United States and Europe. Established in 1983, Z-Axis Corporation has participated in most major air crash litigations in the U.S. over the past fifteen years, including the crash of Delta Flight 191 in Dallas, the crash of USAir 427 in Pittsburgh, the crash of American 965 in Cali, Colombia and the crash of Korean Air 801 in Guam. They also performed work for the prosecution in the Oklahoma City bombing trials of Timothy McVeigh and Terry Nichols. Axis Corporation determined Myers did "an excellent job" and provided opportunity for the assassination sequence examination "from any point of view with absolute geometric integrity" (Treibitz, 2003).

EXTEND THE LINE OF SIGHT

Kennedy's line of sight is the direction he would be facing if he looked forward relative to his body and head position. Based upon the assessment by Axis Corporation, the Myers computer recreation represented a closer match to the actual orientation of JFK's head than the position proposed by the HSCA Photographic Panel. Therefore, the direction Kennedy would face is determined to be a 115° turn from Zapruder.

(**FIGURE 13**) Extending Kennedy's Line of Sight into Dealey Plaza

In Figure 13, with a protractor placed at a 90° angle to Zapruder's location, a line represents the 115° turn relative to Zapruder. Obviously "front" of Kennedy is not the Grassy Knoll, but toward the south end of the triple overpass on the opposite side of Dealey Plaza.

STEP FOUR:

DETERMINE POSSIBLE ANGLES OF TRAJECTORY

If there are entry and exit wounds in a victim, a single straight-line trajectory through the victim can be determined. If one of the wounds can then be properly located within the shooting scene, a trajectory through the victim extending out into the crime scene can be determined. In the Kennedy assassination, the location of the victim is well established; on the other hand, there is no uncontested, precise entry or exit wound. Consequently, determining a single trajectory line reconstruction for the fatal shot is impossible. Analysis of a more encompassing entry area and exit area would provide a trajectory cone. Trajectory cones encompass all possible projectile trajectories, and subsequently, all shooter locations (Haag, 2011).

TRAJECTORY CONES

Analysis of fracture sequencing, Kennedy's movement immediately following the headshot, bullet fragmentation and blood spatter conclusively support a frontal shot. Since the autopsy photographs and X-Rays show no significant damage left of the midline of the President's skull, a viable trajectory must incorporate an entry wound in as much of the right front quadrant as possible without the exit crossing the midline.

If a projectile were to enter the head in the right front quadrant, just to the right of midline, and exit in the right rear quadrant, just right of midline, that line would represent one possible straight-line trajectory along which, at an undetermined distance and coordinating elevation, a shooter was located. Repeating the straight-line trajectory from every plausible direction creates a three-dimensional trajectory cone, along which, at an undetermined distance and coordinating elevation, a shooter was located.

The straight-line trajectories must enter the right front quadrant and exit within the right rear quadrant of the head. Straight-line trajectories indicating extreme entry points from both right and left of Kennedy delineate the trajectory cone approximate horizontal angle. The capacity to accommodate a shooter restricts the vertical angles of the trajectory cone. If the shooter's elevation is too low, the limousine becomes an intermediate target; too high an elevation suspends the shooter off the ground. Concealment and the ability to exit the area is also a consideration.

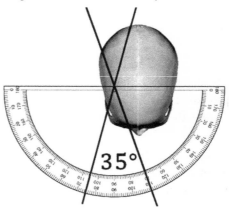

(FIGURE 14) 35° Trajectory Cone

Figure 14 demonstrates the computed angles for a horizontal trajectory cone by establishing two approximate straight-line trajectories restricted to entry in the right front quadrant of the head. If a projectile were to enter the head in the right front quadrant right of midline and exit in the right rear quadrant, that line would represent one possible straight-line trajectory. Repeating the process of establishing straight-line trajectories from every reasonable angle creates a horizontal trajectory cone.

A second straight-line trajectory represents a projectile entering the right front quadrant and exiting at the right rear quadrant right of midline. The extreme right and left trajectories form an angle that represents the possible trajectories for the projectile in the headshot. The computed angle from a shooter at the extreme angles to Kennedy would have a horizontal trajectory angle of approximately 30°. The shooter could be located anywhere within the 35° angle defined by the extreme right and left straight-line trajectories.

The proposed trajectory must not cross the midline, and should not exit close enough to the ear as to create damage to the head in that area. This creates a straight-line trajectory representing a shooter that would be as far as possible to Kennedy's left. That process is repeated on the opposing side of the skull, thereby forming an angle that, when considered in a three dimensional manner, generates a cone. Please note the computed angles are approximate. The exact measurements of President Kennedy's head are not available; however, the skull graphic is anatomically correct and proportional.

The average skull width for males is 5.7 inches, and the average skull length is 6.9 inches. Therefore, the projectile is restricted to a possible path that is approximately 2.85 inches wide and 6.9 inches in length. The probability of the projectile striking the median of the head itself while confining damage to the right side of the head is unlikely; therefore, considering entry or exit approximately one-half inch off the median is realistic. The 35° angle accommodates a front shot that would restrict damage to the right side of the head, entering at the right front quadrant, and exiting at the right rear quadrant.

EXTENDING THE TRAJECTORY CONE

The next step in determining the trajectory is to extend the trajectory angle into Dealey Plaza. Photogrammetric analysis conducted by a geological survey established placement of Kennedy and the Presidential limousine within Dealey Plaza at the time of the shooting. Zapruder frame 312, exposed approximately 0.055 seconds before the headshot, allowed precise placement and orientation of Kennedy's head within Dealey Plaza.

The distance between Kennedy and Zapruder was about seventy feet, with a line of sight of 10° downward. Relative to Zapruder, frame 312 illustrates

Kennedy's head turn of approximately 25° past profile. By superimposing a protractor over a photograph of Dealey Plaza, Kennedy's line of sight, or the turn of 25° past profile relative to Zapruder, can be visualized (HSCA 6:36-38; HSCA 6:34-40).

The Grassy Knoll is located on the north side of Dealey Plaza. Kennedy's line-of-sight, had he raised his head and looked directly forward, would have been toward the south end of the triple overpass.

The vertex of a protractor approximates a 90° angle from Zapruder. The line in the graphic represents the 25° turn beyond profile relative to Zapruder. The 35° angle representing all possible frontal trajectories is determined using the protractor and extended into the plaza. The extreme right and left straight-line trajectories created by restricting damage to the right side of President Kennedy's head establish the horizontal perimeter of the trajectory cone.

The calculated trajectory cone demonstrated in Figure 15 eliminates the muted area in the photograph as possible locations for the shooter. The

(**FIGURE 15**) The Muted Area is Excluded as an Origin for the Headshot

clear 35° angle in the photograph represents an area that encompasses all possible trajectories for the fatal headshot. The Grassy Knoll is eliminated mathematically as a possible location for the shooter.

VERTICAL TRAJECTORY

While horizontal trajectory is imperative for locating possible shooter positions, one must disregard locations with insufficient elevation to miss the highest points of the Presidential limousine. When determining the possible vertical trajectory, elevation, concealment, and egress are considered. At Kennedy's location in Zapruder frame 313, the street elevation is 421.75 feet. The roadway has a declining angle of 3°, or about one foot drop per 20 linear feet; therefore, the street level at the triple underpass is a little more than 24 feet lower than at the Houston Street level. The Warren Commission determined the elevation of Elm Street at locations corresponding to various frames of the Zapruder film. Elevation at street level at frame 313 is 421.75 feet. The highest point on the limousine is 57 inches, added to street elevation equals 426.5 feet. Elevation at the top of the overpass handrail is 428.4 feet. The 2.1-foot elevation difference is sufficient for firing a shot over the highest point of the limousine (CE 844, 18H902).

Persons standing on the overpass would not have been able to see someone positioned at the angled end of the overpass. The large concrete buttresses obstruct the view. At the time of the shooting, the adjacent parking lot was open to the public and was not fenced, thereby allowing the shooter easy access to a parked vehicle.

SOUTH KNOLL WITNESS

> *Q: Where were you on November 22, 1963?*
>
> *A: I was observing the attempt on Kennedy's life. I was at Dealey Plaza on the South Knoll (Dankbaar, 2003).*

That statement is a reply by William Robert "Tosh" Plumlee to an interview question by Wim Dankbaar in 2003. Plumlee is a Florida native and retired commercial pilot, who worked for the United States Government. Plumlee states in November 1963, he was the co-pilot on a top-secret mission, attached to a Military Intelligence unit and supported by the CIA. The men assigned understood the assignment was to abort an imminent attempt on the President's life in Dallas (Plumlee, 2004).

Several men flew into Dallas with Plumlee, and one was an acquaintance named Sergio. Upon arrival, he and Sergio went to Dealey Plaza and determined the fence behind the south knoll was a good location for a shooting team. Seeing nothing suspicious, they walked down and across the grassy expanse to a place about 5 feet up from the roadway near the triple overpass. Then he and Sergio heard shots (Plumlee, 2004).

Q: Could you tell the direction of those shots?

A: I couldn't tell the direction of the shots, but however, but my memory is that I feel a shot went over our head to the left of us. I'm familiar with gunfire. Also, when we left the area, we got a taste of gunpowder when we went over the railroad tracks [at the south end of the triple overpass] which would have been south of the north Grassy Knoll (Dankbaar, 2003).

Plumlee and Sergio were not the only witnesses in Dealey Plaza that believed shots originated from the triple overpass.

DELORES KOUNAS, Texas School Book Depository employee: Kounas was standing on the south side of Elm near the intersection of Houston. Kounas told the FBI she heard three shots. She also stated it sounded as though the shots were coming from the triple underpass (CE 1436, 22H 846).

VIRGIE BAKER: Bookkeeper at the Texas School Book Depository and located in front of the depository building, Baker indicated he heard three shots. He stated it sounded as though these sounds were coming from the direction of the triple underpass (7H 510).

OCHUS CAMPBELL: Vice President of the Texas School Book Depository and located in front of the book depository, Campbell stated he heard shots being fired from a point which he thought was near the railroad tracks located over the viaduct on Elm Street (CE 1381, 22H 638).

WESLEY FRAZIER: Texas School Book Depository employee, Frazier was located on the depository front steps. In his March 11, 1964 Warren Commission testimony, he indicated he heard three shots. Concerning the origin of the shots, Frazier stated, "well to be frank with you, I thought it come from down there, you know, where that underpass is" (2H 234).

BOBBY HARGIS: Dallas Police Department Motorcycle Officer Hargis recalled hearing two shots. Concerning the origin of the shots, he stated, "At that time there was something in my head that said that they probably could have been coming from the railroad overpass" (6H 294).

PAUL LANDIS: Secret Service Agent Landis was in the Secret Service follow-up car. Landis said, "my reaction at this time was that the shot came from somewhere towards the front, but I did not see anyone on the overpass and looked along the right-hand side of the road." Concerning the number of shots, Landis stated he did not recall hearing a third shot (18H 759).

DAVID POWERS: Powers, a Presidential aide, was located in the Secret Service follow-up car. Powers said, "My first impression was that the shots came from the right and overhead, but I also had a fleeting impression that the noise appeared to come from the front, in the area of the triple overpass" (7H 473).

CONCLUSIONS

Nonprofessionals dedicate their lives to putting pieces of seemingly unrelated assassination information research together. Scientists and criminologists apply the latest technical knowledge to arrive at new pieces of the assassination puzzle, and researchers seek to develop a comprehensive or new insight surrounding Kennedy's death.

In the years since President Kennedy's death, various technical fields have made great strides in understanding ballistics. Developing accurate methods to establish projectile trajectories and establishing a better understanding of wound ballistics continues to be the focus of new research and technical publications. That new knowledge has prompted renewed efforts to determine what really happened on that dismal November day in 1963. Nevertheless, despite all of these gains, disputes about basic evidence still trouble us: Where was the shooter for the headshot located?

Nonprofessionals have not been able to address correctly the trajectory of the fatal headshot. The Discovery Channel documentary did not correctly apply forensic investigative techniques to discover the truth. They manufactured evidence and manipulated experts to guarantee an inevitable outcome. However, shooting from the Grassy Knoll did provide ballistic and trajectory information. Utilizing both fully jacketed ammunition and fragmenting ammunition, the replicated heads were targeted. When firing from the Grassy Knoll, the left side of the artificial heads displayed substantial defects regardless of the type of ammunition used. This eliminated the trajectory for the fatal headshot as coming from that location because the injuries sustained by Kennedy did not include the left side of the head.

A close look at the Discovery Channel's analysis methods reveal a subtle bias (as opposed to their implied scientific neutrality), an inaccurate replication of evidence to be examined by experts and the manipulation of experts to arrive at conclusions designed to support preconceived opinions.

Preconceived opinions also permeated official trajectory reconstruction. The Warren Commission failed to insure a conventional trajectory analysis of Kennedy's shooting injuries was complete. The overpass was a Warren Commission consideration in April 1964 when discussing trajectory. In fact, the FBI was instructed by the Warren Commission to include the overpass as a possible location for the shooter for both the throat wound and the headshot. However, when the FBI conducted the reenactment of the assassination on May 24, 1964 to determine the trajectory angle of the bullets that struck Kennedy, the overpass trajectory study was excluded.

The primary problem with the Warren Commission's trajectory procedure is that it does not identify the shooter's location; it merely measures the angle between the presumed location of the shooter and President Kennedy at the time of the headshot. The reenactment team did not perform a trajectory analysis nor did they truly re-create the shooting. They simply provided a measurement for a trajectory they falsely asserted to be true.

Ammunition does not have to be of an explosive nature to create the type of trauma seen in Kennedy's headshot. Fragmenting bullets break up into many small pieces almost immediately. This means that all the kinetic energy from the bullet transfers instantaneously into the target. As a result, the closed and inelastic skull experiences extensive fragmenting, occasionally dislodging, and the internal pressures can explosively expel bone, blood, and tissue.

The House Select Committee on Assassinations, like the Warren Commission, determined in its 1979 report that Lee Harvey Oswald fired three shots, successfully killing the President. Although experts in various fields support the official finding, additional shooting locations and the possibility of co-conspirators remain in debate. In fact, the HSCA Forensic Pathology Panel had dissenting opinions within their own ranks; specifically the differences of opinion centered on trajectory reconstruction.

There are standardized procedures for trajectory reconstruction that provide an accurate method to define where shooters are located. However, neither the Warren Commission, nor the House Select Committee on Assassinations used those uniform processes for trajectory analysis.

By following the currently recommended steps for reconstructing shooting trajectories, an angle of possible projectile paths can be established for President Kennedy's fatal headshot. Utilizing those recommended and recognized standards, the results indicate the shooter was likely near the south end of the triple overpass or the parking lot adjacent to that portion of the overpass. Addressing the location for the shooter, for that shot, with proven scientific concepts, proves mathematically what areas are viable for locating a potential shooter, and it does not include the Grassy Knoll.

CHAPTER 7

TWO HEADSHOTS

The eruption of shots started with someone pulling a trigger. It ended with a fatal head wound to the President of the United States. The reaction of President Kennedy to that final shot has become the mantra for conspiracists: *"Back and to the left, back and to the left."* Nevertheless, careful study of the Zapruder film shows before the head and shoulders began moving back, the head moved forward. That movement has generated several decades of questions concerning the possibility of two headshots.

The subtle forward movement of Kennedy's head prior to the more exaggerated back and to the left movement is troublesome for supporters of both a single shooter and for conspiracists. Several explanations have been offered to reconcile the anomaly. Some purport a gunshot to the back of the Kennedy's head initiated the forward movement, followed immediately by backward movement created by an almost simultaneous second gunshot from the front. Some maintain the movement is the result of a propulsive jet effect created by blood exiting the front of the head from a rear shot. Others believe in a rear shot and insist neuromuscular spasms created the rear movement. The study of wound ballistics reveals the truth concerning Kennedy's opposing movements.

BALLISTICS

There are four types of ballistic studies: internal, external, terminal, and wound ballistics.

INTERNAL BALLISTICS

Simply stated, the process starts when the trigger on a weapon is depressed and the firing pin strikes the primer. The priming compound explodes, resulting in a flame entering the flash hole in the weapon and contacting the propellant charge. This flame ignites the propellant, which burns at a very rapid rate, generating a large volume of gas. The propellant is contained within a confined space, which produces tremendous pressure. The pressure grows until it becomes sufficient to eject the bullet down the barrel and out of the mouth of the muzzle (Hornady, 2012).

EXTERNAL BALLISTICS

External ballistic studies focus on trajectory, or the flight path of the bullet from the muzzle of the weapon to the target. The trajectory for the majority of projectiles is parabolic in shape. Once a projectile leaves a barrel, two other forces begin to influence its flight; the first is air resistance and the second gravity. Regardless of muzzle velocity, a bullet will lose velocity from air resistance and lose height because of gravity, resulting in a parabolic arc trajectory. The design of a projectile will also influence the loss of velocity. Bullets with a pointed shape preserve their velocity longer than round nose or flat point bullets. Regardless of design shape and air resistance, a projectile traveling over 2000 feet per second has a flat trajectory until about 300 yards (Hornady, 2012).

TERMINAL BALLISTICS

Terminal ballistics is the study of how a projectile performs when striking a target and transferring its kinetic energy to the target. The bullet's design and impact velocity affects that transference. Projectiles may remain intact, perforating the target, thereby transferring little kinetic energy. Other projectiles are designed to remain within the target, resulting in a rapid velocity deceleration and a corresponding rapid transfer of kinetic energy (Hornady, 2012).

WOUND BALLISTICS

Wound ballistics is the study of a missile's effect on living tissue. The mechanics of projectile wounding includes penetration, the creation of temporary and permanent cavities and projectile fragmentation. Opportunity for extreme damage to the brain occurs when the maximum amount of kinetic energy transfers to the tissue rapidly, from a fragmented projectile with high velocity. Projectile injuries violently disrupt inelastic tissue, such as the brain. The bullet enters the skull by creating a small entrance hole. The force of the bullet striking the skull generates fractures stemming from the impact site. The fractures take a straight line from the point of impact, on the vault, to the base of the skull. These fractures, called *radiating fractures,* form before the bullet exits the skull (Karger, 2008).

When the bullet strikes the skull, the velocity abruptly slows, thereby transferring kinetic energy to the target. This primary transfer of energy causes the target to move minutely into the force and against the line of fire, quickly followed by movement with the force, and in the continued direction, of the moving bullet (Karger, 2008).

High velocity, fragmenting projectiles have the capacity to impart a greater amount of kinetic energy than slower traveling bullets. The higher a projectile's velocity upon hitting a target, and the faster the forward momentum is disrupted, the more energy is transferred into the target. This results in increased damage. Velocity and mass determine the bullet's kinetic energy, and the wounding potential relies on the efficient transfer of that kinetic energy to tissues. Pressure builds, and as the projectile navigates the head, there are only the entrance wound and any consequent fractures for release of that pressure. Therefore, within three to five milliseconds, blood is expelled out of the hole from which the bullet entered as back spatter (Karger, 2008).

The bullet, which may expand, fragment, or tumble, continues through the brain, creating a permanent cavity by crushing tissue. If the bullet fractures, each fracture has the ability to create additional permanent cavities (Fackler, 1987).

Bullet design, and its propensity for fragmentation, combined with tissue resistance relative to elasticity and density, slows the projectile. This rapid deceleration transfers kinetic energy to the surrounding tissues, producing a temporary cavity within the tissue that dramatically moves backward, forward, and sideward. The transmitted energy generates a series of tissue pulsations moving at right angles to the bullet path. This movement is called temporary cavity formation. Over a period of five to ten milliseconds, the cavity enlarges and then collapses until all of the kinetic energy is expended. Consequently, tissues as far away as forty times the diameter of the bullet are stretched, torn, and sheared. As the brain becomes incompressible, the increased internal pressure of the temporary cavity causes the tissues to seek an avenue to alleviate that pressure. As a result, blood is forcefully ejected from both entry and exit wounds (DiMaio, 1999; Karger, 2008).

The force of the temporary cavitation pushes against the fractured skull, resulting in additional fractures called *concentric fractures*. These fractures are perpendicular to the radial fractures and appear to circle the entry site. This occurs as cavitation is in process and may hinder propagation of radial fractures. The skull is a closed and inflexible structure, therefore only fracturing can relieve the temporary cavity pressure. The fractured skull may or may not remain intact. If the scalp tears from the force of the temporary cavitation, dislodged bone fragments are sometimes ejected. In this event, blood, tissue, and occasionally, bullet fragments will forcefully exit from the opening created by the missing bone fragment (Fackler, 1987; Karger, 2008).

If a portion of the scalp adheres to the dislodged bone fragment, a bone avulsion results. Fragmented bullets cause a much larger permanent cavity by detaching tissue segments between multiple fragment paths. Thus, projectile fragmentation can turn the energy used in temporary cavitation into a vastly destructive force, because it focuses on areas weakened by various fragment paths, rather than being absorbed evenly by the tissue mass. Cavitation begins before the bullet has reached the point of exiting the skull (Fackler, 1987; Karger, 2008).

If the bullet leaves the skull, it typically creates an irregularly shaped exit hole that is normally larger than the corresponding entry wound. Blood and brain matter will exit the skull from the exit hole in the same path of the bullet until the head bursts from the accumulated pressure and creates an even larger and more irregularly shaped exit wound. Brain matter ejects out all available openings as forward spatter; the largest opening is usually the expanded exit wound, with its final size depending on how large the internal pressures become (DiMaio, 1999).

FORWARD HEAD MOVEMENT

The subtle and rapid forward movement of President Kennedy's head before moving markedly rearward is not readily observed when viewing the Zapruder film at normal speed. Figure 16 displays Zapruder Frames 312 and 313. A close examination of the individual frames indicates an unmistakable forward

and slight downward movement. The forward movement is best realized by comparing the back edge of Kennedy's head in frames 312 and 313 of the Zapruder film.

JOSIAH THOMPSON

Josiah Thompson provided the most familiar measurements of President Kennedy's front and rear movements in his 1967 publication,

(FIGURE 16) Kennedy's Head Moves Forward in Zapruder Frame 313

Six Seconds in Dallas: A Micro-Study of the Kennedy Assassination. He and physics graduate student William Hoffman precisely measured the positions of the back of Kennedy's head relative to two fixed points in the limousine. Thompson used 8x10-inch enlargements of Frames 301–330, in the offices of *Life Magazine,* to compute the measurements. Thompson's research indicates, in frames 301–312, Kennedy's head slowly travelled backwards about one inch. Between Zapruder Frames 312 and 313, the President's head suddenly moves forward by about 2.2 inches. The forward movement lasts for only one frame, about 1/18 second, or 55 milliseconds. President Kennedy's head and shoulders then begin to move backward for seven more frames (Thompson, 1967).

DAVID LIFTON

David Lifton also addresses the forward movement of Kennedy's head in *Best Evidence* (1988). Lifton met with 1965 Nobel Prize laureate, Richard P. Feynman at the California Institute of Technology in 1966. Lifton provide Feynman with an aerial photograph of Dealey Plaza, and summarized the assassination events. He also provided information concerning conspiratorial evidence such as footprints behind the fence, and the smoke observed and smelled by bystanders. Using large photographs of Zapruder Frames 312 through 323, the eminent physicist examined the movement of President Kennedy's head. Feynman determined Kennedy's head did in fact move forward and then back, and suggested the two movements were not unrelated (Lifton, 1988).

THE FORWARD MOVEMENT

Once the forward movement was noted, an assortment of possible reasons was offered as explanation. Some people believe there were two simultaneous headshots, one from the rear followed by a shot from the front. Others believe a neuromuscular reaction created the rear movement. Still others adopted the jet effect as an explanation. Those who are proponents of an altered Zapruder film point to the forward movement as proof of missing frames or poorly executed alteration. In order to use the movement in the film as a valid concept, the suggestion of film alteration of frame 312 must be disproven.

ALTERED FRAME 312

A bloodstain pattern is a distribution of bloodstains with identifiable characteristics that can be consistently reproduced and studied to form dependable determinations concerning the manner in which the pattern was produced. Bloodstain pattern analysis refers to the examination of the shape, location and distribution of blood stains for interpreting the events connected with bloodshed. This is based on the principle that bloodstain patterns have characteristics that are suggestive of the forces that created them. Analysis incorporates information gathering, observation, documentation, analysis, assessment, conclusion, and technical review. Bloodstain pattern analysis is based on general principles of physics, chemistry, biology, and mathematics and is widely recognized as reliable and credible evidence in a court of law.

Many published studies support the acceptance of spatter analysis in the scientific community; there is, as well, case law to support its validity. Studies and publications date its use back to the late 1800s, with routine use on crime scenes internationally since the 1970s. Scientific meetings hosted by professional organizations and government agencies in the United States and other countries offer the principles and procedures of analysis.

Professional organizations that recognize bloodstain pattern analysis include the International Association of Bloodstain Pattern Analysts (IABPA), International Association for Identification (IAI) and Association for Crime Scene Reconstruction (ACSR).

The Federal Bureau of Investigation organizes and sponsors Scientific Working Groups to address issues arising within specific forensic disciplines. The Scientific Working Group on Bloodstain Pattern Analysis (SWGSTAIN) formed in the spring of 2002. SWGSTAIN members come from both nationally and international fields including: law enforcement; federal, state, and local laboratories; the private sector ; and academia. SWGSTAIN provides a professional environment in which bloodstain pattern analysts can discuss and evaluate procedures, techniques, protocols, quality assurance, education, and research. SWGSTAIN's ultimate goal is to use these professional exchanges to address practical issues within the field of bloodstain pattern analysis and to build consensus-based, best practice guidelines for the discipline (Federal Bureau of Investigations, 2009).

Other researchers working under the same conditions can validate bloodstain pattern analysis conclusions. Analysts have effectively reconstructed patterns utilizing various means of force directed toward a variety of target surfaces with dependable results. The ensuing patterns are documented with video, photographs, and written accounts. Patterns and individual stains are documented by noting stain distribution, shape, diameters, and directionality. When blood is impacted with sufficient force, blood droplets are dispersed with reproducible characteristics that assist with categorizing patterns into possible methods used to disperse the blood. Analysts can then differentiate between blood spatter patterns shed during a bludgeoning as opposed to a shooting.

KODAK TECHNICAL REPORT

The Assassination Records Review Board first met with the Eastman Kodak Company in June 1996, in Washington, to address potential issues with the Zapruder film. Kodak technical expert Roland J. Zavada, a retired Kodak film chemist and former leading 8-millimeter film expert, was charged with analyzing the film. Specific attention was given to purported film irregularities, which some believed to be proof of alteration. While the report provides no succinct conclusions concerning film authenticity, it does document numerous aspects in which the film's characteristics are consistent with authenticity. The Assassination Records Review Board considered the Zapruder film alteration allegations unfounded (Tunheim, 1998).

FORWARD SPATTER AND BACK SPATTER

Blood spatter from gunshot wounds are divided into two categories, forward spatter and back spatter. Forward spatter, ejected from the exit wound, travels in the same direction as the bullet. Back spatter, ejected from the entrance wound, travels against the line of fire, back towards the shooter. Although forward and back spatter patterns display some common features, there are also some dissimilarities. By studying forward and back spatter patterns created during a singular incident, differences in patterns are identified. Once the characteristics of the patterns are recognized, the distinction between forward and back spatter can be made. By differentiating between forward and back spatter in shooting incidents, the identification of the direction of the origin of force is possible (James, 2005).

Blood spatter patterns created on shooting crime scenes and blood spatter patterns from shooting bloody targets in a lab setting prove patterns are reproducible with consistent characteristics. The forward spatter and back spatter in all circumstances produce patterns with specific characteristics, regardless of changing variables, such as expressed blood volume and projectile velocity. The lab studies, like the crime scene shootings, utilized a wide range of weapons and calibers and at various distances. Consequently, blood spatter is unquestionably determined to be reproducible, reliable, and credible evidence (James, 2005).

Laber, Epstein, and Taylor took the adjacent photograph of forward and back spatter during research. Figure 17 is a video capture of a .44 caliber bullet striking a bloody sponge wrapped in tape. The video

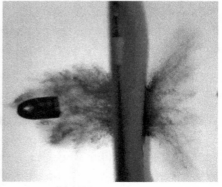

(**FIGURE 17**) Forward Spatter and Back Spatter

is a part of the Bloodstain Pattern Analysis Video Collection completed by Midwest Forensics Resource Center (MFRC) and produced by U.S. Department of Energy by Iowa State University. Note the difference in the overall shape of the two patterns. A slight difference is that back spatter patterns tend to move to the side quickly, forming a wide cone, while forward spatter has a more pronounced forward travel with the cone shape developing more slowly, due to the presence of increased velocity, larger stains and increased blood volume (James, 2005; MFRC, 2008).

SIMILAR CHARACTERISTICS

1. Shape of stains: On targets capturing expelled forward and back spatter patterns, the stains near the center of the pattern were circular in shape, striking the target surface at or near a perpendicular angle. At the perimeters of both forward and back spatter patterns, stains are more elliptically shaped, reflecting the more acute striking angle.
2. Stain distribution: The distribution of the droplets was more concentrated when the target surface was near the bloody target, with the distance between the droplets increasing as the droplets moved away from the bloody target.
3. Pattern shape: Both types of patterns leave the injury site and travel outward in a basic conical shape, moving in every possible direction. A slight difference is that back spatter patterns tend to move to the side, forming a wide cone, while forward spatter has a more forward travel with the cone shape developing more slowly, due to the presence of increased velocity, larger stains and increased blood volume (James, 2005).

DISSIMILAR CHARACTERISTICS

1. Distance: Forward spatter consistently travels farther than back spatter created in the same incident. In some cases, forward spatter has been observed traveling well in excess of fifteen feet. Back spatter consistently travels a shorter distance than forward spatter created in the same incident. Back spatter travels approximately four feet.
2. Blood volume: Forward spatter patterns held a larger volume of blood, expressed as individual stains, when compared to back spatter created in the same incident.

3. Tissue dispersement: Tissue fragments frequently permeate forward spatter pattern. Fragments in the forward spatter varied in size and were occasionally large. When observed in head wounds, the fragments consisted of both soft tissue and bone fragments. Tissue fragments observed in back spatter are markedly smaller in size and fewer in quantity than tissue fragments in forward spatter.

4. Pattern dimensions: Increased blood volume resulted in increased pattern dimensions, therefore back spatter patterns are smaller than forward spatter patterns created in the same incident. Pattern dimensions for back spatter are approximately four feet; conversely, large exit wounds can result in forward spatter with sufficient projectile velocity traveling ten to twenty feet.

5. Velocity of blood: The videotape used to capture patterns records 30 frames per second. The video utilized approximately 4-5 frames to capture the forceful impact pattern when a low velocity, large caliber projectile with a high KE rate struck a large volume of blood. This means that particular pattern was created in its entirety in 1/6 of a second. Some patterns were created in less than 1/6 of a second. Back spatter dissipates faster than forward spatter, due to air resistance and gravity acting on the small stain volume.

6. Stain size: Forward and back spatter targets displayed a multitude of minuscule blood droplets, some resembling an atomized spray or mist. No single stain size is exclusive to a particular range of impact velocity. However, forward spatter is likely to result in predominantly larger stains than back spatter (James, 2005).

The prominent blood spatter pattern in Zapruder Frame 313 corresponds in every measurable manner with back spatter. The blood observed displays the pattern shape of back spatter. It also extends from the wound area a distance that is characteristic of back spatter. The timing for the pattern creation, and the dissipation rate, identifies it as back spatter. In fact, all available information concerning the blood spatter pattern in the Zapruder film corresponds in every measurable manner with back spatter replicated in forensic laboratories and described in peer-reviewed publications since the late 1980s.

Falsifying that particular type pattern through film alteration requires not only the ability to edit the film, but demands an accurate knowledge of back spatter pattern characteristics. However, an appropriate understanding of back spatter pattern characteristics was unavailable to film experts in 1963. The earliest mention of this phenomenon was in the 1980s.

BACK SPATTER RESEARCH

Experimental research directed towards the examination of back spatter was first published in 1982. Analysts affiliated with six Florida Regional Crime Laboratories wrote the Summary Report of the Bloodstain Pattern Analysis Research Group. The scientists utilized .22 caliber, .38 caliber, 30.06 caliber and 12 gauge #1, 16 pellet ammunition to shoot bloody sponges. Paper targets placed alongside, behind and in front of the sponges captured the static aftermath of the dispersed blood. The research revealed back spatter patterns have some unique characteristics, and share some characteristics with forward spatter (Parker, 1982).

The Journal of Forensic Sciences published a 1983 article entitled "Back Spatter of Blood From Gunshot Wounds" by Forensic Pathologists and Chief Medical Examiner Dr. Boyd G. Stevens of the San Francisco Medical Examiner's-Coroner's Office in California and Dr. Terrence B. Allen, a forensic pathology fellow. The authors recognized the occurrence of minute droplets of blood from gunshot entry wounds traveling back against the line of fire. They also conceded back spatter of blood from gunshot wounds was a poorly understood and complex phenomenon. The authors acknowledged the occurrence of back spatter was not widely recognized but commonly seen in gunshot wounds to the head. To reproduce back spatter patterns, the researchers fired through a blood-soaked sponge encased in various materials, such as plastic, rubber, and tape. They determined back spatter expelled from the bloody sponges was more common with large caliber handguns. In conclusion, Stephens and Allen indicated, "back spatter of blood from gunshot wounds should not be considered an anomaly, but a common characteristic of gunshot wounds to the head" (Stephens, 1983, p. 439).

In a 1986 *Journal of Forensic Sciences* article, authors Peter Pizzola, Steven Roth and Peter DeForest refer to the new study of back spatter. They dictated precaution when making interpretations from bloodstain patterns at crime scenes, citing a number of complexities. They noted the existence of blood spattered backward from an entrance wound and called on the scientific community for additional research (Pizzola, 1986).

ALTERATION IS REPUDIATED

Film editing specialists may have possessed the ability to add content to film in 1963. However, the possibility that film or forensic experts were aware of the various characteristics of back spatter at the time of the assassination is doubtful. The 1983 and 1986 articles clearly demonstrate the study of back spatter was in its infancy in the early and mid1980s. Faking the blood in the Zapruder film would have required a working knowledge of back spatter to replicate accurately the pattern. However, that pattern was not considered for forensic study until twenty years after the assassination. Therefore, it is impossible for any person falsifying the blood in the Zapruder film to have created an accurate representation of the back spatter pattern. If the forgers of the Zapruder film could not have been aware of blood spatter attributes, we can only conclude the blood is genuine. This defines the assassination film, at least at the time of the headshot, as the authentic "in camera" original taken by Abraham Zapruder. Moreover, the Kodak Technical Report does not support a finding of alteration.

BLURRED FILM

The forward head movement demonstrated in the Zapruder film has been called an illusion, a glitch in the film, a blur that has been misconstrued and interpreted as movement. Nevertheless, based on the two movements, many researchers concluded there must have been two shots to the head. The first shot supposedly originated from the rear, creating minute forward head movement, quickly interrupted by an almost simultaneous shot from the front that pushed the head rearward. However, apparently claims that the medical evidence did not support such a conclusion, forced another explanation. In an attempt to reconcile the conflicting information, the suggestion that the frames were blurred and the forward movement was an anomaly began to replace the simultaneous shot theory. Josiah Thompson, like many, revised his position on the forward movement.

However, the most dramatic results of studying the photo record from Dealey Plaza may come from new insights into the timing and character of the wounds to the President. Many years ago, I concluded that the President had been struck twice in the head within approximately one-ninth of a second between Zapruder Frames 312 and 314. The first shot pushed his head forward approximately two inches between frames 312 and 313. The second shot bowled him over backwards and to the left.

Although it remained a remarkable coincidence that two shots would arrive on their target from different locations and distances within one-ninth of a second, this conclusion was compelled by what I measured on sequential frames of the Zapruder film. Using two points on the back of the limousine, I measured the distance between these points and the back of the President's head. Between frames 312 and 313, this distance increased dramatically by two inches. The only way to explain this extraordinary acceleration of the President's head was to suppose he had been hit by a bullet fired from the rear.

In the years since those measurements were made, I've learned I was wrong. Z312 is a clear frame while Z313 is smeared along a horizontal axis by the movement of Zapruder's camera. The white streak of curb against which Kennedy's head was measured is also smeared horizontally and this gives rise to an illusory movement of the head. Art Snyder of the Stanford Linear Accelerator staff persuaded me several years ago that I had measured not the movement of Kennedy's head but the smear in frame 313. The two-inch forward movement was just not there (Thompson, 2005).

JOHN COSTELLA

In an effort to determine the truth, Thompson consulted film expert, John Costella to determine if it was possible to ascertain if the forward movement was genuine or a result of camera panning by Zapruder. John Costella of Australia has a degree in both Engineering and Science and has completed a Ph.D. in theoretical physics, specializing in high-energy physics, Einstein's theory of relativity, and quantum electrodynamics. Costella designed a program to correct blurring due to camera movement during video recordings.

Although he is a proponent of an altered Zapruder film, Costella confirmed the movement originally reported by Thompson in the Zapruder film is not a blur (Costella, 2011).

> *What the Z film shows is not in dispute. I think Lifton pointed out in Best Evidence that he took the film frames to Richard Feynman in 1965, who pointed out the forward movement. This is what I found when I deblurred Z-313 in 2001: the forward movement is unmistakable (Costella, 2011).*

ITEK CORPORATION

Itek Corporation is a corporation located in Massachusetts that stemmed from a research group developing aerial surveillance cameras for the Pentagon at Boston University. Itek Corporation was a United States defense contractor that specialized in camera systems for spy satellites and later developed cameras for the Apollo space program. Itek Corporation previously performed Zapruder film studies for United Press International and *Time-Life*. As the leading experts in film image analysis, Itek Corporation analysis contributors had expertise in physics, photographic science, special photographic processing, photo interpretation, image analysis, coherent optical image processing, photogrammetry, and digital image processing. In 1975, CBS News asked Itek to study the original Zapruder film, using the most advanced techniques and equipment available. Over a period of several months, Itek studied the film, conducted precision measurements, and provided their conclusions in a 94-page report. The analysis used the original Zapruder film, and nowhere in the report did Itek suggest any frame appeared altered or edited in any manner. The Itek Corporation report concluded Kennedy's head moved forward approximately 2.3 inches and his shoulder about 1.1 inches at frames 312 and 313. Following that forward movement, Itek reported President Kennedy's head moved rearward from Zapruder 314 to 321 (Itek, 1976).

BLURRED FILM RENOUNCED

Film expert John Costella has denied the suggestion that blurring is misinterpreted as movement. Moreover, both Costella and Itek Corporation state there is actual forward movement, with Itek providing the distance moved. Nobel Prize laureate, Richard P. Feynman, at the California Institute of Technology, examined the movement of President Kennedy's head and determined Kennedy's head did in fact move forward and then back, and suggested the two movements were related.

JET EFFECT

Physicist Luis W. Alvarez (1911-1988) received the Nobel Prize in 1968. He is also the recipient of the Presidential Medal for Merit, Albert Einstein Award, National Medal of Science, Michel Award, and the Enrico Fermi Award of the US Department of Energy, among others. Alvarez is considered one of the most prestigious and influential physicists of the twentieth century (Garwin, 1992).

In September 1976, Alvarez published an article in the *American Journal of Physics* addressing several aspects of the Kennedy Assassination. In that article, remarkably Alvarez theorized the backward snap of the President's head was consistent with a shot fired from the rear due to what he called the jet effect. *Jet effect* is a term used to describe the force created when a concentrated stream of matter exits an object with sufficient force to move the object in the opposing direction. In order for the stream to move the object, the matter must be exiting primarily from a single opening, and other openings must be dampened or restricted in some manner (Alvarez, 1979).

> *The simplest way to see where I differ from most of the critics is to note that they treat the problem as though it involved only two interacting masses: the bullet and the head. My analysis involves three interacting masses: the bullet, the jet of brain matter observable in frame 313, and the remaining part of the head. It will turn out that the jet can carry forward more momentum than was brought in by the bullet, and the head recoils backward, as a rocket recoils when its jet fuel is ejected. The jets visible in frame 313 were what suggested this mechanism to me (Alvarez, 1979, p.434, 436).*

Alvarez assumed the rearward movement of the head was against the line of fire, but could be explained as being consistent with the law of conservation of momentum and the conservation of energy. Alvarez indicated the equal and opposite reaction to the expelled brain matter was similar to the thrust developed in a jet engine. He advocated the simple example of releasing an untied balloon filled to capacity and watching the balloon be propelled by the escaping air. However, this may have been misleading and incorrect (Alvarez, 1979).

In order for a jet effect to have occurred, a pressure would have to be built up inside the head, acting at least rearward as well as forward, which was then relieved on the forward side allowing the rearward pressure to dominate and create an unbalanced force in that direction. This change in momentum is directly related to the forward acting pressure opposite that of the exhaust gases, since their initial pressure values are the same, but one is allowed to escape. A jet effect requires a pressure opposite that of the exhaust (Szamboti, 2012A, p. 4, 5).

Proponents of the jet effect erroneously believe Kennedy's head movement is the result of Newton's third law of motion at work, with the head being pushed back due to the exiting material in the jet pushing against the air. Newton's third law is at work here, as it is when any force is applied, but not the way those who believe in the jet effect think. Newton's third law states that for every reaction there is an equal but opposite reaction (Szamboti, 2012).

Once it exits, the forward moving jet is not pushing against anything in relation to the skull or melon, but since it is relieved, it allows the rearward component of the pressure to act on the skull. The skull applies an equal and opposite reaction by absorbing the rearward acting component of the pressure over a specific area, which is a force. Since it is ultimately not restrained, it accelerates in the direction of the force (Szamboti, 2012, p. 8).

Alvarez recognized that for a jet stream of matter to move an object, the matter must be exiting primarily from a single opening, and other openings must be dampened or restricted in some manner. He experimented by shooting melons that were wrapped in fiberglass tape. Alvarez suggested the kinetic energy of the bullet was transferred to the target slowly and in a conical pattern as it traversed the melon. In other words, he indicated little energy was transferred near the entry site; however, an increasingly larger amount of kinetic energy was transferred to the experimental melons as the bullet moved toward the exit site. Alvarez correctly believed the melon's subsequent movement was associated with the transference of kinetic energy. However, he did not calculate and credit the force developed due to the temporary cavity pressure and neglected to consider the difference in the shear force needed to perforate the melon as opposed to a skull (Alvarez, 1979).

> *If one wants to know more about the details of the transfer mechanism of kinetic energy from the bullet to kinetic energy of the fragments thrown forward, he will have to ask someone more knowledgeable in the theory of fluid mechanics than I am. My intuitive feeling is that the conical shape of the interaction zone is the key to the nonnegligible efficiency of energy transfer (Alvarez, 1979, p. 436).*

Another problem with the shooting experiments conducted by Alvarez was the melon itself. For his tests, Alvarez covered a melon with fiberglass tape to, in his words, "mock up the tensile strength" to that of a human skull. However, it is not the tensile strength that is important to the direction the impacted melon or skull would take, but the shear strength. The tape did nothing to cause the melon to have similar shear strength to that of a human skull. The force required for a 6.5-millimeter projectile to penetrate and shear through a taped up melon is significantly lower than it is for that same projectile to penetrate and shear through a human skull. The shear strength of melon rinds is approximately 70 pounds per square inch (psi). In comparison, the shear strength of live human bone is approximately 17,000 psi perpendicular to its grain and 7,100 psi parallel to its grain. The force required to penetrate and shear through the same thickness of live human bone, compared to that required to penetrate a melon rind, is at least one hundred times greater. This tremendous variance in the shear strength resulted in skewed test results for Alvarez (Szamboti, 2012, Piersol, 1987).

As explained above, the substance exiting from an exit point is not pushing against anything in relation to the skull or melon. It simply relieves pressure in one direction, allowing the opposing pressure to move the object. Specific requirements must be met for the jet effect to generate movement in the opposite direction of the projectile's travel.

1. Sealing or dampening of the entry wound or the permanent trajectory cavity near the point of entry when compared to the exit area

2. Creation of a temporary cavity occurring relatively soon after penetration
3. A target with a very low shear strength requiring a lower penetrating force than the force generated by the temporary cavity pressure (Szamboti, 2012).

Interestingly, the human skull and melon rinds are both approximately 0.300 inches thick, but the density and shear strength are very different. A projectile traveling at 2,000 feet per second travels 0.300 inches in 0.0125 milliseconds, or 1/80,000th of a second. A projectile weighing 0.35 ounces with a velocity of 2,000 feet per second affects a hard target, such as a human skull, with a force of 1,700 pounds, whereas it influences the soft melon rind with a force of 17 pounds.

Another issue with Alvarez's tests as it relates to the assassination is that Alvarez did not produce a jet effect in the melon with copper-jacketed ammunition, like that used with a 6.5-millimeter Mannlicher Carcano rifle. He used soft-nosed lead ammunition, designed to distort on entrance, which creates a large temporary cavity almost immediately. Copper-jacketed ammunition does not generate a significant temporary cavity until it has penetrated over 17 centimeters or 6.69 inches. The human head is approximately 17 centimeters in diameter and most melons are not much larger, therefore, a skull or melon shot with jacketed ammunition would generate limited temporary cavity pressure until it had almost exited the target, if at all. This clarifies why others who have also performed the experiment on melons only reproduced the jet effect when using soft-nosed lead ammunition and could not get it to occur when using jacketed ammunition similar to the 6.5-millimeter Mannlicher Carcano ammunition (Szamboti, 2012).

The direction the target moves after projectile entry and exit is dependent upon the net force, or the sum of all of the forces involved. Wound ballistics research concludes the size of a temporary cavity is about twelve times the diameter of the projectile. Therefore, the temporary cavity for a 6.5-millimeter projectile would be approximately three inches in diameter, creating a temporary cavity area of about 7 square inches. If the four atmosphere (59 psi) temporary cavity pressure acted on this full circular area, it would generate a 413 foot-pound force within the melon, both forward in the continued direction of the projectile, and rearward towards the shooter, so it is neutral relative to the skull or melon before exit. The shear force developed by a 6.5-millimeter projectile passing through a 0.300 inch thick melon rind is only 17 foot pounds. Since the projectile passes through both sides of the melon, the shear force is experienced twice, totaling 34 pounds. This 34-foot pound force is pushing the melon away from the shooter. The temporary cavity pressure generates a balanced force of 413 foot pounds both forward and rearward until the larger exit wound creates a larger opening for that pressure than the entry wound. The 413 foot pounds of pressure pushing back toward the shooter then overcomes the shear force of 34 foot pounds, driving the melon back toward the shooter (Szamboti, 2012).

That same formula can be applied to demonstrate why President Kennedy's head was driven back in the continued direction of force. As stated earlier, the shear force of a 6.5-millimeter projectile through a human skull would generate approximately 1,700 pounds of force in the direction the projectile is moving. For comparison purposes, if the temporary cavity pressure is estimated at the same 413 pounds, and is pushing against a shear force of 1,700 pounds, the head is going to move in the direction of the greater force, which is the continued direction of the projectile (Szamboti, 2012).

JET EFFECT DISPROVEN

The conservation of momentum, the conservation of energy, and the conservation of mass are fundamental concepts of physics. Newton's laws embody these concepts. Unbalanced force acting on a body results in acceleration in the direction of that force. Utilizing physics to interpret the movement of President Kennedy's head also necessitates a good understanding of the mechanics of terminal ballistics, wound ballistics, and blood spatter patterns. Alvarez failed to appreciate the difference in the force required to penetrate the skull as opposed to the melon, and how that force would correspond with the conservation of momentum. He admittedly was lacking in the application of fluid mechanics and how that relates to gunshot wounds to the head. More importantly, the study of back spatter had not been introduced at the time of the adoption of the jet effect. Alvarez erroneously assumed the blood in the Zapruder film was exiting matter from a gunshot originating behind the President. The jet effect became a method of explaining movement based on a flawed premise: the shot originated from behind the President, not in front.

NEUROMUSCULAR REACTION

Neurology is the branch of medicine that addresses the nervous system and skeletal musculature. The nervous system is a complex, sophisticated system consisting of the brain and spinal cord. If you think of the brain as a computer that controls all bodily functions, then the nervous system is like a network that relays messages back and forth from the brain to different parts of the body via the spinal cord. The nervous system regulates and coordinates both conscious movements and reflex movements. A muscular reflex is an automatic response facilitated by the nervous system; for example, a bright light causes the pupils to contract. This involuntary reflex action differs from normal muscle control, as the brain does not initiate the muscle movement, and the reaction is observed even without consciousness. The involuntary reflex action is much faster than voluntary movements, since the muscle contraction response is initiated at the spinal cord, through reflex pathways. In the time it takes the stimulus to reach the brain, the muscle contraction has already responded to the stimulus (Rohkamm, 2004).

Trauma literature shows 50% of all trauma deaths are secondary to traumatic brain injury (TBI), and gunshot wounds to the head cause 35% of all brain injuries. Firearm-related violence and the subsequent increase in penetrating head injury is a concern to neurosurgeons in particular. Despite the frequency of these injuries, the morbidity and mortality of gunshot wounds to the head remains high (Vinas, 2011).

Located in the back of the head and just above the spinal cord, the brain stem controls involuntary functions such as breathing and heartbeat. A bullet that travels along the brain's midline can damage both hemispheres, along with the brain's central core, which controls many of the body's functions (Bor, 2006).

Victims of traumatic brain injuries (TBI) occasionally display abnormal posturing called *spastic hypertonia,* stemming from damage to the brain stem, cerebellum or mid-brain. Two types of spastic hypertonia are decorticate posturing and decerebrate posturing. The damage affects the reflex centers in the brain, interrupting the flow of messages along various nerve pathways. This disruption of signals can cause changes in muscle tone, movement, sensation and reflex. However, it does not occur instantaneously (Greenberg, 2004).

Patients with decorticate posturing display arms that are flexed, or bent inward to the chest, hands are clenched into fists, and legs extended with feet turned inward. Decerebrate posturing is also called decerebrate response, decerebrate rigidity, or extensor posturing. It describes extension of the upper extremities in response to external stimuli. In involuntary decerebrate posturing, the head arches back, the arms extend by the sides, and the legs are extended. The arms and legs are extended and rotated internally, the patient is rigid, and the teeth clenched. This is not congruent with the position of Kennedy in the Zapruder film. Since the Zapruder film shows President Kennedy seated, with his hips flexed neither of these conditions are applicable (Greenberg, 2004).

ABERDEEN PROVING GROUND FINDINGS

To determine how targets reacted when impacted by a projectile, the Warren Commission asked research physical scientist Larry M. Sturdivan to conduct shooting experiments. Sturdivan, one of only a few wound ballistics experts worldwide at that time, was associated with the Wounds Ballistics Branch of the Aberdeen Proving Ground Vulnerability Laboratory. Aberdeen Proving Grounds conducts research and evaluations of weapons for governmental agencies. The laboratory's evaluations also encompassed wound ballistics, which focuses on studying the behavior of bullets inside tissue and tissue simulants. Aberdeen Proving Grounds implemented research and tests for the Warren Commission, in connection with their investigation of the assassination of President Kennedy in 1964. Sturdivan testified they completed "air retardation, gelatin tissue simulants retardation, tests of cadaver wrists, some skulls, and into some anesthetized animals" (HSCA 1:384-185).

Unbelievably, it appears the Warren Commission suppressed the Aberdeen Proving Grounds experiments and results and did not call Sturdivan to testify. However, the House Select Committee on Assassinations was not so cautious, and questioned him about the 1964 experiments. Sturdivan testified that while using Mannlicher Carcano 6.5 millimeter ammunition, Aberdeen Proving Grounds scientists had shot 10 goat skulls filled with ballistic gelatin. The skulls were also covered with a film of gelatin and at the point of impact, a piece of goatskin simulated skin and hair. Sturdivan's testimony then related the following results of the shooting (HSCA1:402-403).

> *STURDIVAN: As you can see, each of the two skulls that we have observed so far have moved in the direction of the bullet. In other words, both of them have been given some momentum in the direction that the bullet was going. This third one also shows momentum in the direction that the bullet was going, showing that the head of the President would probably go with the bullet. In fact, all 10 of the skulls that we shot did essentially the same thing (HSCA 1:404).*

Sturdivan's testimony and corresponding filmed exhibits of the skulls moving with the direction of the projectile obviously defied the Warren Commission's conclusion concerning the direction of the headshot. Sturdivan countered his earlier divulgence of *"the head of the President would probably go with the bullet"* by providing several explanations.

1. The deposit of momentum from the bullet was not sufficient to cause significant movement in any direction.
2. The appropriate movement was diminished by the connection of the head with the neck and body.
3. The lack of appropriate movement was due to a neuromuscular reaction.
4. The heavy back muscles predominate over the lighter abdominal muscles would have thrown him backward no matter where the bullet came from (HSCA 1:414- 415,421).

The decisive test for any theory comes with rigorous, replicable experiments. Research shows penetration of targets with higher shear force move in the continued direction of the projectile. Therefore, regardless of the convoluted rationalizations offered by Sturdivan, it is still a matter of physics.

Neuromuscular Movement Unsound

While victims of traumatic brain injuries sometimes display atypical posturing, the distinctive body positions are the result of damage to the brain stem, cerebellum or mid-brain. The frames immediately following the headshot in the Zapruder film indicate President Kennedy is seated, with his hips flexed, which is not characteristic of posturing stemming from a traumatic brain injury. Although he lacked medical expertise, it appears Sturdivan introduced that explanation in an attempt to reconcile Kennedy's movement with a preconceived origin for the headshot. There is no credible medical foundation for considering the rear movement of Kennedy's head and shoulders is a result of abnormal posturing.

HEAD WOUND CHARACTERISTICS

Over the past ten years, gunshot wounds to the head have dramatically increased in number. Current statistics indicate gunshot wounds to the head have become the leading or second leading cause of head injury in many United States cities. Gunshot wounds to the head are also the most lethal of all firearm injuries, with an estimated fatality rate of 90% for United States civilians. Consequently, forensic research focusing on the mechanics of gunshot wounds to the head has become more prevalent. Research has provided major advances in understanding bone beveling and fracturing sequencing to determine projectile trajectory. The mechanics of blood spatter have been more completely determined, as has cavitation and its role in target movement. President Kennedy's head, as visualized in the Zapruder film, displays movement into the direction of force followed by movement in the continuing direction of the force. This dual movement is addressed in several studies, all of which include that dynamic as a part of the characteristic of gunshot wounds to the head (AANS, 2011).

CURRENT RESEARCH

From a physical point of view, an impact between a bullet and a target is a highly complex process occurring over a very short time span, and involving large forces and pressures. The wounding process of a gunshot injury to the head is best understood by conducting research experiments. Research experiments must be reproducible and must always yield the same results in order to be considered reliable. The experiments must meet three requirements in addition to the reproducibility and reliability.

1. Analysts must be able to observe the experimental process as it is conducted

2. Bullet dynamics and the response of the test medium must correspond very closely to the real-life situation of a bullet in biological tissue

3. The values of the physical parameters along the wound channel (deceleration, force, penetration depth and timing) must correspond to those encountered in real life (Coupland, 2011).

Numerous experiments in various countries have resulted in the widespread adoption of two materials for simulating soft tissue in wound ballistics experiments over the last few decades: ballistic gelatin and ballistic glycerin soap. Experience has shown these materials possess the physical characteristics needed to simulate biological tissue, including the required response under high pressure. The validity of these two materials has been confirmed through experiments on animals and in comparing results to victims of bullet wounds in war surgery and forensic pathology (Cronin, 2010; Coupland, 2011).

There is one fundamental difference between the two simulants; the deformation that a bullet causes in soap remains apparent, whereas gelatin returns to almost the same state as before bullet impact. The temporary cavity is permanently depicted in soap and can readily be studied and analyzed. In gelatin, the temporary cavity collapses, as it does in biological tissue. Bullets behave in both media as they do in human tissue, displaying similar penetration depth, deformation and velocity. Wound ballistics results can vary with different types of weapons. The fundamental differences between handguns and long barrel weapons are the type of projectile used. The projectile structure and potential for energy affects their behavior once the target is penetrated and with the formation of the wound channel. The determining factor is not the weapon, but the ammunition (Cronin, 2010; Coupland, 2011).

The most significant features from rifle bullets are the temporary cavity and the effect it has on the body. Rifle bullets carry between 1,100 to 3,300 foot-pounds of force; more than enough to cause devastating injury. Handgun bullets generally carry 185 to 560 foot pounds of force, which is significantly less energy. The circumstances of the assassination and the resulting wound to the head indicate the use of a rifle. However, debate over the number of shots remains, due to lesser understood blood spatter and movement. Categorizing President Kennedy's head wound as the result of a single gunshot from the front, requires understanding the fundamentals of gunshot wounds to the head, including the development and characteristics of the resulting trauma.

BEVELING

A specific sequence of events begins when a bullet strikes a human skull, starting with the bullet entering the skull by creating a small entrance hole. The basic shape of an entry wound in the skull can be round or elliptical, depending on the angle of the impacting projectile as it relates to the skull surface. Bullets traveling through bone create marginal conical shaped fractures adjacent to the entry or exit site. The conical beveling characteristically appears as a symmetrical chipping out of bone, forming an indentation surrounding the entry or exit point on the opposite side of impact. See Figure 18. An entry wound creates a defect that appears as a punched hole on the outer table of the skull with concentric internal beveling on the inner table. The small end of the cone touches the interior or exterior bone table from which the bullet entered. The graphic depicts the coning observed on a bone fragment (Levy, 2012).

Scientists describe beveling as symmetrical or asymmetrical. Symmetrical beveling has marginal fractures evenly distributed around a wound. Asymmetrical beveling has more pronounced beveling only on one side of the wound. Round entry wounds can display a variety of beveling characteristics, including no beveling, symmetrical beveling, or asymmetrical beveling. Elliptically shaped holes can have symmetrical beveling or asymmetrical beveling. The shape of an entry wound may be circular, ovoid, triangular, diamond, or rectangular with rounded corners (Quatrehomme, 1998).

(FIGURE 18) Beveling in Bone Fragment

Beveling is not common in entry wounds located in the thinner temporal bone. Skull bones are not uniform plates and display variations in thickness at different points. The average thickness of skull bones in males is (a) frontal bone: 6.3mm, (b) temporal bone: 3.9 millimeter, (c) occipital bone: 7.7mm, (d) parietal bone: 5.8mm, (e) central frontal bone: 8.1mm, and (f) lower occipital bone: 9.35mm. The occipital bone and frontal bone are the thickest skull bones (Quatrehomme, 1998, Mahinda, 2009).

Historically, beveling determines projectile directionality in bone, but some entry wounds can present both internal and external beveling. External beveling of an entry wound often results in a wound misidentified as an exit wound. Researchers attribute this external pseudo-beveling in high velocity distance shots to the transference of kinetic energy to the skull. The transference of kinetic energy fractures the adjacent bone resulting in dislodged chips flaking off entry wound edges, producing the effect of beveling. Exit wounds occasionally display the phenomenon of chipped edges that may be mistaken for beveling. Without careful examination, misinterpretation of an entrance wound as an exit wound is possible in all types of entries (Quatrehomme, 1998; Levy, 2012).

Tangential entry and exit wounds can easily be confused, especially with extensive fragmentation and expelled bone fragments. Complete reconstruction of disconnected skull fragments is necessary to observe the characteristics of skull beveling used to determine the bullet's path. Partial reconstruction of the beveled defect diminishes the opportunity for correct direction interpretation. A fragment can splinter off an irregular break, leaving what only appears to be beveling. Based upon current forensic research, it appears beveling cannot provide conclusive evidence of projectile direction. Incorrect assessment of direction can occur with tangential entries or exits, mistaken orientation, insufficient beveling, or the failure to recognize external beveling on entry wounds (Coe, 1981; Prahlow, 2010; Adams, 2010).

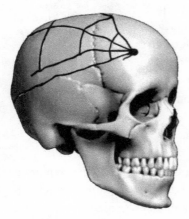

(FIGURE 19) Radial Skull Fractures
Originate at the Entry Wound

RADIAL FRACTURES

Although the skull is resilient, the severe impact of a projectile results in fractures of the skull. A skull fracture is a break in the complete thickness of one or more of the bones that form the cranial portion of the skull. Projectiles that penetrate the skull create bone fractures with specific characteristics. The first fractures formed are linear fissures called *radial fractures*, since they radiate outward from the entry wound in relatively straight lines. These fractures often extend from the point of entry to the base of the skull, as in Figure 19 (Viel, 2009; Vinas, 2011).

The direction of force is determined by examination of radial fractures, as these bone fractures begin at the point of impact and continue in the same direction as the penetrating object. Exit wounds strike the skull interior with less force than the original impact; therefore, the secondary radial fractures are markedly shorter in length and will terminate at previously formed fractures. Fracture sequencing can determine the progression of multiple gunshot injuries, the direction of fire, and differentiate between entrance wounds and exit wounds in the absence of specific distinguishing features, such as beveling (Viel, 2009; Vinas, 2011).

MOVEMENT INTO THE FORCE

Once the bullet enters the skull, if the design of the projectile limits penetration by distortion or fragmentation, the bullet immediately loses velocity. The loss of velocity results in the transfer of kinetic energy, demonstrated by the instantaneous generation of temporary cavitation. The higher a projectile's velocity upon impact, the more kinetic energy is available to transfer to the target. The amount of kinetic energy transferred to a target increases with faster projectile deceleration. This initial transfer of energy causes the target to swell or move minutely into the force and against the line of fire. The greater the transferred energy, the more pronounced the forward movement (Karger, 2008; Coupland, 2011; Radford, 2009).

Karger (2008) photographed the pressure from the temporary cavity as it created a visible and measurable bulge where the bullet entered. Robin Coupland, author of *Wound Ballistics: Basics and Applications* (2011) employed high-speed photography to document shooting into ballistic gelatin. The forward movement into the line of fire referenced by Karger is demonstrated in those frames. The same reaction is addressed by Radford (2009) and is displayed in photographs accompanying her research. The immediate transfer of a greater amount of kinetic energy results in a more dramatic initial forward movement of the target into the direction of force, or

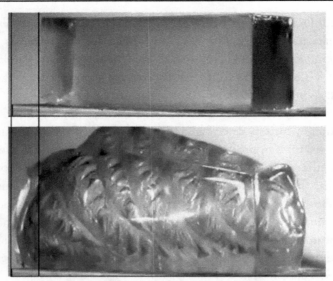

(**FIGURE 20**) The Gelatin Moved Almost Two Inches
into the Direction of the Force

against the line of fire. This initial movement against the line of fire transpires one to two milliseconds after impact. When the bullet strikes the surface, the immediate cavitation adjacent to the entry wound causes the target tissue to bulge or swell against the line of fire. A bulge may not be created in smaller targets with less weight; under those conditions, the entire target may move into the force, instead of simply bulging in the direction of the shooter (Karger, 2008; Coupland, 2011; Radford, 2009).

The internet has numerous videos of ballistic gelatin moving initially into the direction of force when penetrated by projectiles designed to transfer kinetic energy upon impact. John Ervin, owner of Brass Fetcher Ballistic Testing, is a research and development engineer of ballistic gelatin, who tests firearms for private and governmental agencies. His recording of a .308 Winchester Federal 150 grain bullet with a velocity of 2691 fps striking ballistic gelatin shows dramatic movement into the force, or toward the shooter.

Movement into the force and back toward the shooter is exemplified in Figure 20. The 6 X 6 X 12 inch ballistic gelatin block located at the top of the photograph depicts the stationary target prior to the bullet impact at the left end of the gelatin block. The lower photograph is at the peak of cavitation and after the projectile has exited the right end of the target; but before the forward momentum is initiated. Note the rear of the gelatin has moved almost 2 inches into the direction of the force, and back toward the shooter (Ervin, 2011).

This movement back toward the shooter was also demonstrated in experiments completed by wound ballistic expert Larry Sturdivan and presented in testimony before the House Select Committee on Assassinations.

> *STURDIVAN: The bullet will be coming in from the left, will strike the can and you will see pieces of the can moving toward the right, in the direction of the bullet, but you will also see pieces of the can moving in other directions. Notably, the top of the can will be moving back toward the left, in the direction from which the bullet came (HSCA 1:403).*

BACK SPATTER

The target movement into the direction of travel is accompanied by blood expelled from the entry wound. Blood spatter from gunshot wounds include forward spatter and back spatter. Forward spatter is blood expelled from the exit wound, and travels in the same direction as the bullet. Blood ejected from the entry wound, traveling against the line of fire and back towards the shooter is called *back spatter*. Spatter is expelled from the wounds primarily as a result of cavitation. As the projectile transfers kinetic energy to the target tissue, temporary and permanent cavitation is generated. As pressure from the cavitation builds, there are only the entrance wound and any consequent fractures for the release of that pressure. Research indicates that within 3 to 5 milliseconds blood is expelled as back spatter out the hole from which the bullet entered. It has also been suggested that as a bullet traverses tissue, backward streaming of blood and other fluid or tissue particles may transpire. These particles flow along the sides of the bullet, in the opposite direction to which it is traveling. Some of this material is then projected out of the entry wound. This phenomenon, called *tail splashing*, may be considered an early stage of temporary cavitation, as it is said to occur as soon as the bullet enters the target (Karger, 2008; MFRC, 2008; Coupland, 2011).

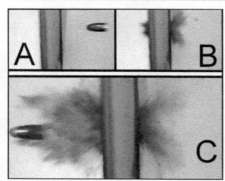

(FIGURE 21) Forward and Back Spatter
Expelled from a Bloody Sponge

Figure 21 contains three frames from a video capture taken during blood spatter research by Terry Laber, Bart Epstein and Michael Taylor. The top left section, photograph A, depicts a bullet approaching a 1.5-centimeter thick bloody sponge. The top right section, photograph B, shows the bullet captured within the sponge. Note in photograph B, back spatter and forward spatter are already being expelled from the target. The lower section, photograph C displays both the forward spatter and back spatter. The high-speed video is a part of the Bloodstain Pattern Analysis Video Collection completed by Midwest Forensics Resource Center (MFRC) and produced by U.S. Department of Energy by Iowa State University (MFRC, 2008).

TEMPORARY AND PERMANENT CAVITATION

As the bullet traverses the target, it leaves a permanent wound cavity by crushing and cutting the tissue. Depending on the bullet's design, it can be quite large in diameter or hardly noticeable. Pointed or round nose non-expanding, non-tumbling bullets make the smallest permanent cavities. If the bullet fractures, each fracture has the ability to create additional permanent cavities. Permanent wound cavities geometrically resemble hollow cylinders. Additional damage is created by temporary cavitation, which, when located in the incompressible skull, can be devastating (Fackler, 1987; DiMaio, 1999; Karger, 2008; Coupland, 2011).

Once the bullet enters the skull, bullet design and its propensity for fragmentation, combined with tissue resistance, demonstrated in elasticity and density, slows the projectile. This rapid deceleration transfers kinetic energy to the surrounding tissues, which dramatically move backward, forward, and sideward, producing a temporary cavity within the tissue. As energy from the slowing projectile is transmitted to the target, a series of tissue pulsations moving at right angles to the bullet path is created. This movement is called *temporary cavity formation*. Over a period of 5-10 milliseconds, the cavity enlarges then collapses. Tissue elasticity perpetuates this process until all of the kinetic energy is expended. Consequently, tissues as far away as 40 times the diameter of the bullet are stretched, torn, and sheared. The energy in a moving bullet is energy of motion, or kinetic energy. The extremely rapid deceleration of bullet velocity instantaneously transfers the majority of the kinetic energy to the surrounding tissue, dramatically moving it away from the bullet in all directions, creating a temporary cavitation. The higher a projectile's velocity upon impact, the more kinetic energy is available to transfer to the target. The amount of kinetic energy transferred to a target increases with faster projectile deceleration, which is controlled by bullet design. The kinetic energy is calculated employing the formula $1/2mv^2$, where m is the bullet mass and v is the impact velocity. In shooting incidents concerning a living being, it is more accurate to describe a temporary cavity as a temporary wound cavity, since the temporary cavity creates a wound. The temporary cavity is the most important feature in higher-velocity bullet wounds, especially gunshot wounds to the head. The temporary cavity in the wound channel is created as the tissue flows away from the contact surface of the bullet. At the same time, tissue is deformed as it is accelerated radially away from the bullet channel, or permanent cavity (Fackler, 1987; DiMaio, 1999; Karger, 2008; Coupland, 2011).

Research indicates the characteristics of temporary cavities generated by fragmenting or deforming projectiles differ from those of fully jacketed ammunition. Fully jacketed projectiles display a conservative temporary wound cavity that is created after the projectile has penetrated the target for some distance; therefore, a longer narrow permanent wound channel is observed. Fragmenting projectiles generate very short permanent wound channels preceding the formation of the temporary wound channel generated by cavitation. Temporary cavitation is initiated approximately 0.1 millisecond after impact, a point at which the bullet has penetrated the target only two to four centimeters. The cavity collapses after a few milliseconds, as part of the bullet's energy is transferred into the adjacent tissue. In most cases, that energy is not fully expended in creating the cavity and a second temporary cavity is created. This second cavity is smaller than the first, as less energy is available. This process of creating cavities is repeated until all the energy is expended. Finally, the energy is converted into heat, through pressure waves and internal friction, and the cavity pulsation ceases (Karger 2008; Coupland, 2011).

CONCENTRIC FRACTURES

The radial fractures are formed microseconds before the cavitation begins. Radial fractures, extending out from the entry wound, and the perpendicular concentric fractures are generated while the bullet is still traveling within the head, meaning the fractures are produced microseconds after the bullet impacts. Figure 22 depicts the fractures. The pressure of the temporary cavitation pressing against the skull interior creates a second fracture pattern, heaving or concentric fractures. Concentric fractures are perpendicular to radial fractures and move in a circular or semicircular manner around the entry site. The majority of concentric fractures are located near the point of entry. Radial fractures combined with concentric fractures create a fracture pattern resembling a spider web (Smith, 1987; Karger, 2008; Leestma, 2009; Coupland, 2011).

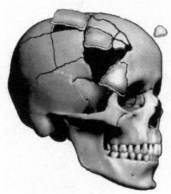

(FIGURE 22) Radial and Concentric Fractures Microseconds after Bullet Entry

A temporary cavity produced in tissue that has been damaged by a fragmented bullet causes a much larger permanent cavity by detaching tissue segments between the multiple fragment paths. Thus, projectile fragmentation can turn the energy used in temporary cavitation into a truly destructive force, because it is focused on areas weakened by fragment paths rather than being absorbed evenly by the tissue mass. This happens before the bullet has reached the point of exiting the skull. The brain responds as a fluid from a ballistics point of view, and is therefore incompressible. Since the brain is encased by the closed and inflexible structure of the skull, only breaking the skull open can relieve the temporary cavity pressure. The fractured skull may or may not remain intact. If the scalp tears from the force of the temporary cavitation, bone fragments may be ejected from the skull. In this event, blood and tissue will forcefully exit from the opening created by the missing bone fragment. If a portion of the scalp adheres to the dislodged bone fragment, a bone avulsion is produced (Fackler, 1987; Karger, 2008; Smith, 1987; Leestma, 2009; Coupland, 2011).

Occasionally, a second series of radial and concentric fractures are produced when the projectile exits the head. However, exit wounds produce fewer and shorter radial fractures with little concentric fracturing, because less energy is available by the time the projectile reaches the exit point. Comparison of the radial fractures and concentric fractures can help to differentiate between entry and exit wounds (Karger, 2008; Smith, 1987; Leestma, 2009; Coupland, 2011).

FORWARD SPATTER

Blood is expelled in a conical fashion from any available opening in the skull and expands in width as the spatter is projected from the head. If the only openings on the skull are the entry and exit points, the blood is projected from those wounds. If the skull fractures and the bones separate because of interior pressure from cavitation, blood is forcefully expressed from those openings. If bone fragments are ejected from the skull, or if bone avulsions are created, the blood will exit from those areas. Forward spatter blood velocity is gained from the force of the temporary cavity combined with the larger force created by the conserved momentum of the projectile being transferred to the displaced blood and tissue (DiMaio, 1999; Karger, 2008; Smith, 1987; Leestma, 2009; Coupland, 2011).

Itek Corporation, located in Massachusetts, stemmed from a research group developing aerial surveillance cameras for the Pentagon at Boston University. In 1975, CBS News asked Itek to study the original Zapruder film using the most advanced techniques and equipment available. Over a period of several months, Itek studied the film, conducted precision measurements, and provided their conclusions in a 94-page report stating the following:

> *It is hypothesized that in fact the several outlines shown are actually two or three major particles. They would appear as several particles here if they were spinning as they moved and if one side was highly reflective. For example, a particle with a wet and a dry side would act as a specular reflector when the wet side reflected sunlight towards the camera. The distances between the President's head and the further*

most particles of each trajectory are such that calculations reveal they were traveling at velocities on the order of 80 mph. For a particle to hold together at such a velocity it would quite likely have to be composed of a cohesive substance such as a bone fragment. The velocity calculations were made from the plane of the photograph and therefore represent minimum velocities.

The velocities of the particles were computed from measurements on the three furthermost particles visible in frame 313 which were associated with the three separate trajectories defined in Figure 3.3.15. The velocity of the median velocity particle was = 87 mph. The particles which are evident in frame 314 are traveling at velocities slower than the upper particles (Itek, 1976, p. 59, 62).

The Midwest Forensics Resource Center (MFRC) is a National Institute of Justice sponsored facility at Iowa State University. The mission of the MFRC Research and Development Program is to provide research and technological advances in forensic science for the benefit of the forensic community. It studied the formation of common bloodstain patterns by using a high-speed digital video (HSDV) camera. The project, a collaborative effort between Laber with the Forensic Science Laboratory, Minnesota Bureau of Criminal Apprehension; Epstein a Forensic Consultant; and Taylor of the Institute of Environmental Science and Research, published their findings in 2008 and made the videos available for viewing online. The videos provided valuable information which allowed scientists to measure when patterns are initially formed, and the speed of blood droplets and spatter patterns being generated (MFRC, 2008).

Examination of the high speed videos of blood dispersed as the result of gunshots allows the measurement of distance and time in impact spatter. The research revealed blood droplets projected from a shooting occurs within hundreds of thousands of a second, not tenths of a second. The research recordings film speed is 10,000 frames per second, meaning each frame represents 1/237000 a second. The research video taken as a .44 caliber bullet strikes a bloody sponge indicates back spatter starts 0.000400 seconds after the bullet strikes the target. The emerging forward spatter is observed at 0.000500 seconds. The video frame time stamped at 0.000700 indicates the forward spatter has already moved twice the distance from the sponge as the back spatter created in the same shooting incident. This indicates the forward spatter moves at a greater velocity than the back spatter (MFRC, 2008).

REARWARD MOVEMENT

Physics is the key to understanding the forward head movement of President Kennedy as demonstrated in comparing Zapruder Frame 312 and 313. Newton's first law of motion states an object at rest stays at rest and an object in motion stays in motion with the same speed and in the same direction unless acted upon by an unbalanced force. The velocity of a body, or more accurately, its momentum remains constant unless a force acts upon it. An object at rest has zero velocity, and in the absence of an unbalanced force will remain with a zero velocity. In other words, a vase sitting on a table will not move unless some outside event takes place. The physical parameter responsible for a change in the movement or deformation of that vase is known as force. An applied force is energy that engages or affects an object, such as a bullet.

In physics, it is often useful to express impact force as a function of the area on which it is acting. When a force, such as a bullet, strikes perpendicular to a target surface, it is described as a tensile or a compressive force. That force per unit area is known as stress. In order to move a target, a force is required that corresponds to the weight of the body. If, however, the body undergoes acceleration because of the force acting upon it, the work completed results in movement. The work completed on a body therefore results either in an increase in distance within the gravitational field, or in movement. The ability to perform work is generally referred to as energy. In the case of a moving body, the term is kinetic energy; in physics, therefore, work and energy are equivalent. Neither work nor energy can be created or destroyed. All that can happen is that the one is converted into the other.

Although physics is a complicated subject, it is the only method for explaining the movements of President's Kennedy head movements subsequent to the headshot. Newton's first law of motion states an object at rest stays at rest and an object in motion stays in motion with the same speed and in the same direction, unless acted upon by an unbalanced force. An object at rest has zero velocity

(FIGURE 23) Balanced Forces

and momentum, and in the absence of an unbalanced force will remain in that state. Figure 23 indicates balanced forces.

The process of moving an object requires applied force, or pressure applied to an object by a person or another object. When sufficient force is applied to an object, it accelerates or moves; this movement, or acceleration, is the result of unbalanced forces. An unbalance force is one that is not opposed by an equal and opposite force operating directly against the force intended to cause a change in the object's state of motion or rest.

If the application of an applied force strikes a stationary object that possesses a lesser opposing force, it creates an unbalanced net force and the object moves in the direction of the greater force, as in Figure 24. The direction the larger portion of the unbalanced force is applied, dictates the direction the object will move. For example, if you are pushing a heavy carton, it is also pushing back against you. However if you apply more force than the opposing force generated by the carton, the carton will move in the direction you are pushing it., An object's mass, velocity, or both mass and velocity must change to change the object's momentum.

When a bullet strikes a target and does not exit, the object mass is increased. However, the weight of a bullet is so small, greater change is evident in velocity change rather than increased mass, the unbalanced force evidenced as velocity produces acceleration. In shootings, this unbalanced force is the basis for movement in target movement that is in the continuing direction of the projectile's trajectory (Karger 2008; Coupland, 2011)

Wounding occurs when energy is converted into work. This process is demonstrated when energy transferred from the projectile velocity deforms and destroys tissue. In other words, this energy performs work on the molecular structure of human tissue. The amount of energy imparted to the tissue is estimated as the kinetic energy upon impact, minus the kinetic energy upon exit. If there is no exiting bullet, some kinetic energy transfers to the target as it creates the permanent

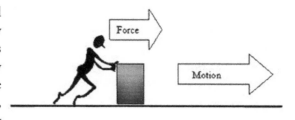

(FIGURE 24) Unbalanced Forces

and temporary cavities; the residual energy is conserved as momentum (Karger 2008; Coupland, 2011).

The human head is equal to approximately 1/8 of total body weight; therefore, an adult weighing 170 pounds has a head weight of approximately 13 pounds. If a force acts on a system capable of rotation, at a point away from its axis of rotation, the system will begin to rotate. The angular velocity will depend on the force and on the distance between the point of application and the axis of rotation. Therefore, a bullet strike on the side of the head will result in an angular rotation combined with a rearward movement (Louw, 2002; Coupland, 2011)

The United States War Department tasked Major Louis Anatole LaGarde, a surgeon with the Medical Corps, and Colonel John T. Thompson of the Infantry Ordnance Department with choosing the most effective cartridge and handgun combination from among those available in 1904. Firing was conducted at approximately three feet into targets consisting of ten human cadavers, sixteen live oxen and two horses. Longer ranges of approximately 35 meters and 70 meters were simulated by reducing the propellant loads. The cadavers were suspended by the neck, and the experiment consisted of measuring the displacement when the cadaver was struck by various caliber bullets. Both individual limbs and entire cadaver bodies were documented as moving in varying degrees in the continued direction of the bullet force, dependent upon the projectile used. In physics terms, what Thompson measured was the momentum of the bullet. The cadavers effectively formed a ballistic pendulum; the measured displacement was proportional to the momentum of the bullet (Thompson, 1904; Coupland, 2011).

The Warren Commission asked research physical scientist Larry M. Sturdivan to conduct shooting experiments to determine how targets reacted when impacted by a projectile. Sturdivan, one of the world's few wound ballistics experts at that time, was associated with the Wounds Ballistics Branch of the Aberdeen Proving Ground Vulnerability Laboratory. Aberdeen Proving Grounds conducts research and evaluates weapons for governmental agencies. The laboratory's evaluations focused on studying the behavior of bullets inside tissue and tissue simulants for the Warren Commission in connection with their investigation of the assassination of President Kennedy in 1964. Sturdivan testified they completed "air retardation, retardation in a gelatin tissue simulants, tests of cadaver wrists, some skulls, and into some anesthetized animals (HSCA 1:384-185).

Apparently, the Warren Commission concealed both the experiments and the results: neglecting to ask Sturdivan to testify. However, the House Select Committee on Assassinations was not as guarded and heard testimony on the 1964 experiments. Sturdivan testified Aberdeen Proving Grounds scientists shot 10 goat skulls filled with ballistic gelatin while using Mannlicher Carcano 6.5 millimeter ammunition. The skulls were covered with an additional film of gelatin, and a piece of goatskin simulated skin and hair was attached at the point of impact. Sturdivan's testimony concerning the shooting addressed the movement of the skulls when impacted by the bullets (HSCA1:402-403).

> *STURDIVAN: As you can see, each of the two skulls that we have observed so far have moved in the direction of the bullet. In other words, both of them have been given some momentum in the direction that the bullet was going. This third one also shows momentum in the direction that the bullet was going, showing that the head of the President would probably go with the bullet. In fact, all 10 of the skulls that we shot did essentially the same thing (HSCA 1:404).*

Sturdivan's testimony included filmed exhibits that showed the skulls moving with the direction of the projectile. Obviously, the recorded movements challenged the Warren Commission's conclusion concerning the direction of the headshot. Sturdivan softened his earlier declaration of *"the head of the President would probably go with the bullet"* by providing several possible explanations.

1. The deposit of momentum from the bullet was not sufficient to cause significant movement in any direction.
2. The movement was diminished by the connection of the head with the neck and body.
3. The lack of appropriate movement was due to a neuromuscular reaction.
4. The heavy back muscles predominate over the lighter abdominal muscles would have thrown him backward no matter where the bullet came from (HSCA 1:414- 415,421).

Careful analysis of the accelerations of JFK's torso seems to reveal the effect of gravity on the torso as soon as it begins to lean backwards.

CONCLUSIONS

For many years, the mantra for conspiracists touting a frontal shot was *"Back and to the left, back and to the left."* However, with study, the subtle forward movement of Kennedy's head prior to the more exaggerated back and to the left movement has become evident. That slight forward movement between Zapruder Frames 312 and 313 is troublesome for supporters of a single shooter and for conspiracists.

Numerous rationalizations have been offered to reconcile the perceived irregularity of trajectory and movement. Film alteration is suggested as one explanation for the two movements. Some reason a gunshot to the back of the Kennedy's head initiated the forward movement, followed by an almost simultaneous second gunshot from the front that created the backward movement. Others assert the rear movement is the result of a propulsive jet effect created by blood exiting the head from a rear shot. Others accept a rear shot, insisting a neuromuscular spasm created the rear movement. However, the truth concerning Kennedy's opposing movements is revealed in the application of physics and the study of terminal and wound ballistics.

Regardless of their ability, it is improbable that film-editing specialists faking the blood in the Zapruder film would have mandated a functioning knowledge of back spatter to replicate accurately the pattern; that pattern was not considered for forensic study until 20 years after the assassination. Therefore, it is impossible for any person falsifying the blood in the Zapruder film to have created an accurate representation of the back spatter pattern. If the alleged forgers of the Zapruder film could not have been aware of blood spatter attributes, we can only conclude the blood is genuine. This defines the assassination film, at least at the time of the headshot, as the authentic "in camera" original taken by Abraham Zapruder.

The suggestion that blurring has been misinterpreted as movement has also been suggested. However, film experts John Costella and Itek Corporation have determined the movement is genuine, and state there is actual forward movement. Physicist Richard Feynman also determined Kennedy's head did in fact move forward and then back, and suggested the two movements were not unrelated. The ability of that movement to be measured by Itek Corporation also supports the film displaying actual movement, not blurring.

The jet effect became a method of explaining movement based on the faulty proposition of a shot originating from behind the President. Alvarez failed to appreciate the variance in the force required to pierce the skull, as opposed to the melon, and how force would correspond with the conservation of momentum. Moreover, he admittedly was deficient in the application of fluid mechanics and how that transmits to gunshot wounds to the head. More importantly, the study of back spatter had not been introduced at the time of the assumption of the jet effect. Alvarez erroneously assumed the blood in the Zapruder film was exiting matter from a gunshot originating behind the President, which resulted in a faulty conclusion. The jet effect is proven unsubstantiated.

Victims of traumatic brain injuries sometimes display atypical posturing called spastic hypertonia. The distinctive body positions are the result of damage to the brain stem, cerebellum or mid-brain. The frames immediately following the headshot in the Zapruder film indicate President Kennedy is seated, with his hips flexed, which is not characteristic of posturing stemming from a traumatic brain injury.

Although he lacked medical expertise, it appears Sturdivan introduced that explanation in an attempt to reconcile Kennedy's movement with a preconceived origin for the headshot. There is no credible medical foundation for considering the rear movement of Kennedy's head and shoulders is a result of abnormal posturing.

Current forensic research indicates the forward movement of Kennedy's head follow by a rearward movement is consistent with a single gunshot to the head from the front. Research by Karger (2008), Radford, (2009) and Coupland (2011) prove initial transfer of energy causes the target to swell or move minutely into the force and against the line of fire. This phenomenon is readily observed in internet videos depicting high-speed recordings of ballistic gelatin, and explained in forensic research that addresses wound ballistics.

The concepts of a faked Zapruder Frame 313, a blurred frame misconstrued as movement, two almost simultaneous gunshots to the head, blood pushing the head backward, or a neuromuscular spasm as responsible for the two head movements are wrong. Current forensic research supports a single gunshot originating in front of the President. All other explanations are myths and are to be discounted as such.

CHAPTER 8

THE SINGLE BULLET THEORY

The remarkable flight of Warren Commission Exhibit 399 is mysterious and convoluted. The Warren Report states the bullet struck President John Kennedy in the back of the neck, passed through the neck without striking bone, and then exited at the front of his throat. The bullet then entered Texas Governor John Connally's back at the right armpit, damaging four inches of his fifth rib before it exited his chest below the right nipple. Continuing forward, the bullet then struck Connally's right wrist and shattered the radius bone before exiting at the base of his palm. The still moving bullet then struck Connally's left thigh just about the knee, penetrating about three inches beneath the surface of the skin. The bullet struck the femur, depositing a small lead fragment before stopping its forward movement. If the trajectory is not mysterious enough, consider the bullet was expelled from the wound in Connally's thigh, somehow escaped capture by his clothing, and was curiously deposited on a stretcher to be found in a hallway of the Parkland Memorial Hospital.

According to the "Single Bullet Theory", generally credited to Warren Commission staffer Arlen Specter (1930-2012), a single bullet, known as Commission Exhibit 399, caused five wounds to the governor, and two non-fatal wounds to the President. This 3-centimeter, copper-jacketed, 6.5

millimeter bullet was allegedly fired from a Mannlicher Carcano bolt-action rifle operated by Lee Harvey Oswald, who was stationed on the sixth floor of the Texas School Book Depository. This bullet passed through fifteen layers of clothing, seven layers of skin, and approximately fifteen inches of tissue, struck a necktie knot, removed 4 inches of rib and shattered a radius bone, and remained nearly in pristine condition when found in the hospital. Critics of the Commission's findings claim after passing through several layers of clothing and flesh, breaking dense bones and shedding metal fragments, it could not be in such pristine condition, especially since supposedly the same type of bullet struck Kennedy in the head and completely broke apart after passing through only two layers of skull. Regardless of the questions, the Warren Commission concluded there was persuasive evidence a single bullet caused the President's neck wound and all the wounds in Governor Connally.

The Commission did acknowledge there was a "difference of opinion" among members of the Commission as to this probability, but stated the theory was "not essential to its conclusions" and all members had no doubt all shots were fired from the sixth floor of the Texas School Book Depository. This bullet would eventually become the foundation of the Warren Commission's theory that a single assassin was responsible for the shooting of the President. Any deviation from this preconceived conclusion would suggest a second assassin. The Commission, however, did not declare they had proven the Single Bullet Theory. In fact, Representative Hale Boggs, Senators Richard Russell, and John Cooper thought the theory unconvincing. Nevertheless, that did not stop the official report from stating the assassination was executed by one man with three bullets. To circumvent the problem of having no proof, the Warren Commission just declared their inability to prove the validity of the Single Bullet Theory as inconsequential (WCR:19)

> *Although it is not necessary to any essential findings of the Commission to determine just which shot hit Governor Connally, there is very persuasive evidence to indicate that the same bullet which pierced the President's throat also caused Governor Connally's wounds (WCR:19).*

THE WARREN COMMISSION DILEMMA

In December 1963, the FBI provided a report concerning President Kennedy's assassination. Based on the three casings recovered from the Texas School Book Depository, the report correlated Kennedy and Connally's wounds to three bullets. The report indicated one bullet caused all of Governor Connally's wounds by passing through his torso and shattering his right wrist. One bullet caused President Kennedy's fatal head wound; and one bullet caused one of Kennedy's non–fatal wounds by entering his back, but did not cause his throat wound. The Warren Commission modified this explanation in March 1964 by assuming the same bullet that caused Kennedy's back wound his caused throat wound (FBI, 1963).

In April of 1964, the Warren Commission held two single day long conferences to examine the Zapruder film and determine which frames in the Zapruder film portray the times at which the first and second bullets struck Kennedy and Connally. Warren Commission staff; autopsy physicians James J. Humes, J. Thornton Boswell and Pierre A. Finck; FBI and Secret Service agents; and various ballistic experts provided input. The conclusion indicated Kennedy was injured by bullet number one, Connally was struck by bullet number two, and then Kennedy was fatally wounded by bullet number three. The assemblage determined that President Kennedy had already been hit when he emerged from behind the Stemmons sign. No consensus was reached concerning the exact time Connally had been injured, but it was determined frame 230 was consistent with film observations and corresponded with medical testimony (Eisenberg, 1964).

Initially, the shooting of Kennedy and Connally seemed to mesh perfectly with the three casings found in the Texas School Book Depository: Kennedy's back and neck injury accounted for one bullet, Connally's injuries accounted for the second shot, and Kennedy's head wound accounted for the third. Then, it was discovered there was a problem: the wounding of bystander, James Tague. The discovery that a missed shot marked the south curb of Main Street, and ricocheted, causing the injury to James Tague, reduced the number of possible projectiles responsible for the injuries to Kennedy and Connally. In addition, a home movie taken by Abraham Zapruder showed too little time had elapsed between the apparent shots that hit both men in the back for Oswald to have fired, re-acquired his target, and fired again. The Warren Commission either had to admit to a fourth shot, and thereby a conspiracy, or they had to offer a plausible explanation that would account for all of the wounds having been inflicted by just three bullets with a plausible timing sequence.

The three casings discovered in the Texas School Book Depository buttressed the Warren Commission's supposition of a single shooter; having no other expended casings in evidence, they were forced to stick to that scenario. President Kennedy and Governor John Connally suffered eight wounds, suggesting more than three projectiles would have been necessary to explain all the damage. The Single Bullet Theory solved both the timing problems and number of required shots to injure Kennedy and Connally. It speculated a single, nearly whole bullet later recovered at Parkland Hospital had caused all seven of the non-fatal wounds sustained by both men: one bullet caused Tague's wound, one bullet caused President Kennedy's fatal head wound, and one bullet caused all of Kennedy and Connally's non–fatal wounds. That bullet supposedly entered Kennedy's back, exited through his throat, entered Connally's back, exited his chest, passed through his right wrist, and pierced his left thigh. The hypothesized bullet trajectory became known as the *Single Bullet Theory*: the means of securing a single shooter (WR:116-117).

KENNEDY'S WOUNDS

The Warren Report states the bullet struck President John Kennedy in the back of the neck, passed through the neck without striking bone, and then exited at the front of his throat before continuing its path to Connally. The placement of Kennedy's rear wound is crucial to the Single Bullet Theory, because it is the initiating point of the Single Bullet Theory trajectory. If the trajectory from the rear wound to the throat wound does not align with the trajectory from the TSBD sixth floor window, and then continue seamlessly into the trajectory through Connally, then the Single Bullet Theory is not sustainable. Without the Single Bullet Theory, there can be no lone gunman.

THE REAR WOUND
Three physicians performed the autopsy on President John F. Kennedy. In command was James J. Humes, Commander of the Medical Corps United

States Navy and Director of Laboratories Naval Medical School. He was certified in Anatomic and Clinical Pathology. Assisting were J. Thornton Boswell and Pierre A. Finck. Boswell was Commander in the Medical Corps United States Navy and Chief of Pathology at the Naval Medical School. Boswell was certified in Anatomic and Clinical Pathology. Finck, a Lieutenant Colonel Medical Corps United States Army, was Chief of the Military Environmental Pathology Division and Chief of the Wound Ballistics Pathology Branch Armed Forces Institute of Pathology Walter Reed Medical Center. Finck was certified in Anatomic Pathology and Forensic Pathology. These three pathologists were responsible for documenting the location of the wounds on President Kennedy (Humes, 1967).

The autopsy report was written by Humes, but signed by all three pathologists. Portions of the report, included in Appendix 9 of the Warren Report, are provided here (Humes, 1967).

> *Situated on the upper right posterior thorax, just above the upper border of the scapula, there is a 7 x 4 millimeter oval wound. This wound is measured to be 14 centimeters from the tip of the right acromion process and 14 centimeters below the tip of the right mastoid process. Beneath the skin, there is ecchymosis of subcutaneous tissue and musculature. The missile path through the fascia and musculature cannot be easily proved.*

> *Situated in the low anterior neck at approximately the level of the third and fourth tracheal rings is a 6.5 centimeter long transverse wound with widely gaping irregular edges. The wound presumably of exit was that described by Dr. Malcolm Perry of Dallas in the low anterior cervical region. When observed by Dr. Perry the wound measured "a few millimeters in diameter", however it was extended as a tracheostomy incision and thus its character is distorted at the time of autopsy. However, there is considerable ecchymosis of the strap muscles of the right side of the neck and of the fascia about the trachea adjacent to the line of the tracheostomy wound. The third point of reference in connecting these two wounds is in the apex (supra-clavicular portion) of the right pleural cavity. In this region, there is contusion of the parietal pleura and of the extreme apical portion of the right, upper lobe of the*

lung. In both instances, the diameter of contusion and ecchymosis, at the point of maximal involvement, measures 5 centimeters. Both the visceral and parietal pleura are intact overlying these areas of trauma.

The other missile entered the right superior posterior thorax above the scapula and traversed the soft tissues of the supra-scapular and the supra-clavicular portions of the base of the right side of the neck. This missile produced contusions of the right apical parietal pleura and of the apical portion of the right, upper lobe of the lung. The missile contused the strap muscles of the right side of the neck, damaged the trachea and made its exit through the anterior surface of the neck. As far as can be ascertained, this missile struck no bony structures in its path through the body (Humes, 1963a; WR Appendix 9).

Originally, when the pathologists performing the autopsy discovered the rear entry wound in the President's back, they determined it had no corresponding exit wound. The wound was repeatedly probed, but Humes declared the end of the wound track was short enough to have been accessible by his finger. When the pathologists discovered a bullet had been recovered from a Parkland Hospital stretcher, Humes decided the retrieved bullet must have been pushed from Kennedy's back wound during external heart massage. When Humes learned Parkland physicians had observed a bullet wound in the throat prior to making the tracheotomy incision, he explained the lack of wound track by stating the bullet passed between two major muscles, bruising them but not leaving a channel (AARB MD 44:555-556, WCR 88).

A FBI teletype dated December 13, 1963 from the Special Agent in Charge in Dallas to the FBI Director and Special Agent in Charge in Baltimore, included the following comment concerning the autopsy findings referencing the rear wound.

Autopsy findings at the Bethesda Hospital as reported on page 284 of the report of AS Robert P. Gemberling at Dallas of December ten, last, which reflects an opening was found in the back, that appeared to be a bullet hole, and probing of this hole determined the distance travelled by the missile was short, as the end of the opening could be felt by the examining doctor's finger (ARRB MD 161:1407).

On the autopsy face sheet, the rear wound is described as affecting three thoracic vertebrae lower than the neck. The face sheet was signed by Admiral George Gregory Burkley, personal physician to the President. He verified the location of the rear wound and signed the Kennedy autopsy sheet at Bethesda on November 24. Burkley filled out and signed John F. Kennedy's official death certificate on November 23, 1963, and positioned the rear wound in the death certificate as being located at the President's third thoracic vertebra (Humes, 1967).

The rear wound would later be described as located in the cervical area of the neck, which the face sheet called imprecise and not representative of the wound location. There can be no other explanation for adjusting the entry wound than to adjust height to accommodate the needed trajectory from the sixth floor of the Texas School Book Depository. Otherwise, the trajectory would be traveling upward, perhaps indicating a shot separate from Connally's wounding.

WITNESS PLACE THE REAR WOUND
Several persons have provided varied testimony concerning the location for Kennedy's rear wound.

1. Secret Service Agent Clint Hill, who was called to the morgue for the specific purpose of viewing Kennedy's wounds, said the entrance point was about six inches below the neckline to the right-hand side of the spinal column (AARB MD 50:608).
2. Agents James Sibert and Francis O'Neill, who attended the autopsy, located the back wound below the shoulder (AARB MD 44:556).
3. James Jenkins was present at the autopsy. He states the rear wound was just below the collar to the right of midline (AARB MD 65:888).
4. Paul O'Connor was present at the autopsy, and testified the wound was midline in the neck at about cervical vertebra 5 (AARB MD 64:878).
5. X-Ray technician Edward Reed wrote he observed a large, 1 1/2 inch apparent exit wound right between the scapula and thoracic column (AARB MD194:1590).

6. Floyd Riebe, one of the photographers who took pictures at the autopsy, recalls the rear wound was in the right hand side of the upper back (ARRB Riebe Deposition, p. 93).

7. J. Lee Rankin, in the transcript of the January 27, 1964 Executive Session of the Warren Commission, said the bullet entered Kennedy's back below the shoulder blade. Rankin even referred to a photograph showing the bullet entered below the shoulder blade (WC Executive Session 0127:193).

8. Dr. George Burkley, the President's personal physician, signed President Kennedy's death certificate. The death certificate places the bullet wound to Kennedy's back at the third thoracic vertebra (Burkley 1963).

9. The House Select Committee on Assassinations Forensic Pathology Panel believed the autopsy photos and autopsy X-Rays show a bullet hole at the first thoracic vertebra (ARRB MD 6:90).

The signed autopsy sheet described the back wound as measuring four millimeters by seven millimeters, located fourteen centimeters (5.5 inches) below the tip of the right Mastoid Process behind the right ear, and fourteen centimeters (5.5 inches) from the right acromion. This detailed description locating the wound in Kennedy's back was reiterated and confirmed by Humes, Boswell and Finck in January 1967, during a five-hour examination of evidence for the ARRB. Analyzing each of the two measurements separately illuminates the problems in understanding the wound location (Humes, 1967).

Boswell testified before the Assassination Records Review Board (ARRB) in February 1996. During his testimony, he was questioned by Jeremy Gunn, general counsel for the Assassination Records Review Board. Boswell was shown the face sheet he completed at the autopsy and asked by Gunn if the wound location Boswell depicted was correct. Boswell replied the face sheet stipulated the third thoracic vertebra location described in the Autopsy Report; however, he believed it incorrect. Boswell stated the Autopsy Report was inaccurate in placing the back wound at the President's third thoracic vertebra, and emphasized a fourteen centimeters (5.5 inches) drop below the right Mastoid Process would correctly place the entry wound in the base of the neck (AARB Boswell:72-75).

Boswell testified the accuracy of the Autopsy Report was carefully considered prior to it being signed by Humes, Bowell and Finck.

> *Jim (Humes) and Pierre (Finck) and I went over it quite carefully, item by item, and discussed everything in it, as to contents, accuracy, and so forth. I do remember that we spent quite a bit of time just preliminary to signing it (AARB Boswell:127).*

Warren Commission Exhibit 386, a drawing by medical illustrator H. I. Rydberg to show the entrance wound in the neck, was also discussed. Boswell maintained Exhibit 386 was a better example of the actual location of the rear wound than the Autopsy Report (AARB Boswell Deposition, p. 77).

James J. Humes was questioned by the Assassination Records Review Board on February 1996. Humes was shown the death certificate for President John Kennedy completed by George Gregory Berkley on November 23, 1963. Although Boswell did not testify to any changes, Humes stated minor alterations were made, but did not detail the modifications. Importantly, Humes and Boswell agreed the location of the rear wound is best determined by the measurement from the right Mastoid Process (AARB Humes Deposition p. 141-143).

SKULL LANDMARKS TO LOCATE THE REAR WOUND

The first landmark located the wound vertically: fourteen centimeters (5.5 inches) below the tip of the right Mastoid Process behind the right ear. The problem with this measurement was the location of the wound changes with the location of the Mastoid Process as the head is tilted forward or back. By placing the thumb on the top of the shoulder and the little finger on the Mastoid Process, the variation in distance can be appreciated by facing forward and then tilting the head back. Therefore, the first measurement using the Mastoid Process as a landmark is vague, and can be easily misinterpreted. Figure 25 demonstrates the location of the Mastoid Process, the Acromion, and the first Thoracic Vertebrae of the spine.

Finck testified in the Clay Shaw trial in New Orleans on February 24, 1969. Shaw was charged by the State of Louisiana for conspiracy to murder John

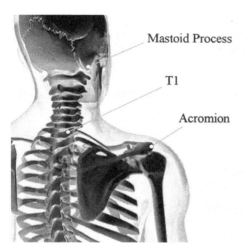

Mastoid Process

T1

Acromion

(FIGURE 25) Mastoid Process, Acromion, and T1 Vertebra

F. Kennedy. During Finck's cross examination, he was asked if altering the position of the head would change the measurements from the Mastoid Process. Finck conceded movement of the head would change the distance from the Mastoid Process to the wound location. He also testified he could not recall the body position of President Kennedy at the time the measurements were taken. The size of the entry and exit wounds was also called into question. Finck testified he personally measured the rear wound and found it to be seven by four millimeters; just one millimeter larger than the five-millimeter supposed exit wound described by the Dallas physicians. This is unusual, as entry wounds are characteristically recognizably smaller than exit wounds. It is also problematic that the entry wound is described as elliptical and the exit wound is described as round; this suggests a deflection to change the trajectory, which is not supported in the medical evidence. Interestingly, when asked if he could have closed the tracheotomy and thereby exposed the exit wound, Finck failed to answer the question (Finck, 1969).

The second landmark located the wound horizontally: fourteen centimeters (5.5 inches) from the right acromion—described in the 1967 review report to the ARRB as the extreme tip of the right shoulder bone. The neck contains cervical vertebra of the spine denoted as C1 through C7. Beneath the last cervical vertebra are the 12 vertebrae of the thoracic spine. These are abbreviated T1 through T12. The acromion is the lateral extension of the spine of the scapula, forming the highest point of the shoulder. The acromion is not aligned horizontally with cervical vertebrae; it is aligned horizontally with T1 or T2. Therefore, if the acromion was intended as a landmark for a horizontal measurement, the rear wound has to align with thoracic vertebrae (Humes, 1967; Cramer, 2005).

AN ALTERED REPORT

The Warren Commission final report concluded a bullet entered the base of the back of his neck slightly to the right of the spine and, traveling downward, caused a nick in the left lower portion of the knot in the President's tie. The key word here is downward, because, if the wound location were on the neck, the trajectory would have been in an upward direction. The autopsy located the rear wound at approximately T3, suggesting that the wound location in the cervical portion of the neck appears suspect. The House Select Committee on Assassinations determined a bullet had injured the first thoracic vertebrae and it fractured because of the bullet passing through the President's body. This necessitates the entry wound being adjacent to the first thoracic vertebrae and does not readily correspond with Ford's descriptive use of neck.

Seconds later shots were heard in rapid succession. The
President's hands moved to his neck and he stiffened in his seat.
A bullet had entered ~~the~~ back, *the* *of his neck* at a point slightly ~~above the shoulder and~~
to the right of the spine. It traveled a downward path, and exited from
the front of the neck, causing a nick in the left lower portion of the
knot in the President's necktie. When the shooting started, Governor

(**FIGURE 26**) Altered Draft of Warren Commission Report

In 1997, the Assassination Records Review Board (ARRB) released a document revealing Gerald R. Ford had altered the first draft of the Warren Commission report. See Figure 26. Ford elevated the location of the wound from its original location in the back to a location in the neck, ostensibly to support the single bullet theory. The staff of the Warren Commission had written, "A bullet had entered his back at a point slightly above the shoulder and to the right of the spine." Ford suggested, "A bullet had entered the back of his neck at a point slightly to the right of the spine." This change was likely made because a neck wound adjacent to the spine sounds higher on the body than a shoulder wound adjacent to the spine. However, Ford denies changing the wording to support a single assassin (HSCA 1:199; Ford, 2004, p. xxi).

THE THROAT WOUND

Unknown to the pathologists performing the autopsy, Malcolm O. Perry, a surgeon who treated President Kennedy in Dallas, discussed the wound on the President's throat at a 2:16 PM press conference, calling it an entry wound. Perry was experienced with gunshot wounds, having treated between one hundred fifty to two hundred gunshot victims. He was also an instructor in surgery at the Southwestern Medical School. Perry noted the wound to the throat, and confirmed no one had previously attempted a tracheotomy incision. The President was making ineffectual attempts to breathe; therefore, a tracheotomy incision was required. The throat wound was the normal location chosen to execute a tracheotomy, therefore, Perry cut through the wound. Perry noted the trachea was deviated slightly to the left. In his Warren Commission testimony, Perry described the throat wound as in the lower anterior one-third of the neck, approximately five millimeters in diameter, and roughly circular in shape with clean edges. Perry later changed his opinion concerning the trajectory of the wound, identifying the throat wound as a wound of exit; thereby, supporting the official autopsy report findings (3H366-374; Perry, 1963).

WHEN DID HUMES LEARN OF THE THROAT WOUND?

Humes telephoned Perry to discuss the tracheotomy incision on Saturday morning, November 24, the day following the autopsy. Handwritten notes by Humes appearing to document portions of the conversation, describe the throat wound as being three to five millimeters in diameter. However, it appears Humes may have been aware of the possibility of a throat wound prior to Kennedy's body arriving at Bethesda. The Assassination Records Review Board Medical Exhibits contains the November 19, 1993 testimony given in deposition by Dr. Robert B. Livingstone in connection with the Crenshaw, et al v. Sutherland civil suit. The deposition indicates Humes received a telephone call from Livingstone, advising there was an entry wound in the throat, before the autopsy was conducted (2H362-363; Livingston, 1993).

WOUND DOCUMENTATION

Humes reported he examined the area of the incised surgical tracheotomy wound and observed bruising of the muscles of the neck, as well as laceration, or a defect, in the trachea. He also reported bruising of the muscles of the right, anterior neck inferiorly, the right parietal pleura, and the upper portion of the right lung. Based on the trauma, Humes and the other pathologists concluded the missile crossed the neck and slid between these muscles and other vital structures, such as the carotid artery, the jugular vein, and other structures of the neck. If Humes actually observed those bruises during the autopsy, one has to wonder why he did not immediately suspect the bruising represented a bullet path and identify the throat wound as a corresponding exit to the rear wound.

Concerning the tracheotomy incision, later to be identified as an expanded exit wound, Finch wrote to Brigadier General J. M. Blumberg, MC, USA, stating he examined the throat wound and did not observe a bullet wound (2H362-363; Livingston, 1993).

> *The tracheotomy wound was examined by the three prosectors. None of us noticed a bullet wound along its course. I examined the tracheotomy skin wound and the trachea and did not find evidence of a bullet wound (Finch, 1965).*

The House Select Committee on Assassinations Forensic Pathology Medical Panel stated the semicircular shaped wound was observed and felt it unusual the wound was not detected by the pathologists performing the autopsy. They also addressed the odd lack of dissection concerning both the back and throat wounds.

> *There is a semicircular missile defect near the center of the lower margin of the tracheotomy incision, approximately in the midline of the neck, with margins which are slightly denuded and reddish-brown (HSCA 7:93).*

> *It is conspicuously unclear from the autopsy report alone that during autopsy, the pathologists were unaware and failed to recognize that there was a missile preformation in the anterior neck. This may account*

for the fact that the neck, trachea, strap muscles, and spine were not dissected and examined (HSCA 7:93).

There is no photographic evidence available that shows any of the internal injuries described by the pathologists within the trunk of the body. Dr. Humes recalled directing that a single photograph of the upper interior aspect of the right thoracic (chest) cavity be taken to illustrate the hemorrhage just exterior to the pleura (lining) of this cavity, adjacent to the missile track (HSCA 7:95).

Humes' abandoned hypothesis, suggesting the bullet penetrating Kennedy's back had been forced from the rear wound during external cardiac massage, was addressed in his Warren Commission testimony. He indicated the bruising along the proposed bullet path was made when the circulatory system function was more dynamic than when the tracheotomy was performed. Humes does not address why, if the bruising was the result of the bullet traveling from the rear wound to the throat, he did not reach that conclusion during the autopsy. Ultimately, Humes, and the other pathologists determined the back wound was a wound of entry and the exit was at the front of the neck—incorporated within the tracheotomy wound (2H368).

The adult trachea measures about 11 centimeters in length. This structure starts from the inferior part of the larynx in the neck, opposite the sixth cervical vertebra, to the intervertebral disk between T4 and T5 vertebrae in the thorax, where it divides into the right and left bronchi. The trachea has 15-20 u-shaped rings of hyaline cartilage responsible for the lateral rigidity of the organ. In adults, the trachea's diameter is between nine and fifteen millimeters and it is ten to thirteen centimeters long. A tracheotomy is the procedure undertaken when making an incision between the third and fourth cartridge rings to allow placement of a tube to re-establish an airway. Tracheal tubes measure approximately eleven to thirteen millimeters in diameter and thirty centimeters in length (Walls, 2012).

Perry, in his Warren Commission testimony, described President Kennedy's throat wound as a roughly circular wound, about five millimeters in diameter. Handwritten notes recorded by Humes during the November 23 telephone conversation with Perry, document the throat wound as being three to five millimeters (0.12 inches to 0.20 inches) in diameter. This measurement corresponds with the testimony of Dr. Robert McClelland, who assisted with the tracheotomy. McClelland testified before the Assassinations Records Review Board, stating Perry contemporaneously described the wound as less than .25 inches in diameter. Ultimately, the throat wound was described as a spherical to oval shaped wound, roughly five millimeters in diameter, and four to six millimeters by Perry; a spherical wound four to five millimeters in diameter by Dr. Charles R. Baxter; a round wound four to seven millimeters, and five to eight millimeters in diameter by Charles J. Carrico; and a wound no greater than .25 inches in diameter by Jones. However, this same wound in Kennedy's throat was not recognized, not described, and not documented by the autopsy report. When Perry testified to the Assassinations Records Review Board, he indicated he had enlarged the original wound to accommodate a cuffed tracheotomy tube. It is unknown what size tracheotomy was used in 1963; however, 1961 medical guidelines dictate making an incision corresponding to the tracheotomy tube diameter. Astonishingly, the autopsy report does not indicate the dimensions of the throat wound; however, the autopsy face sheet completed by Boswell indicates the incision as 6.5 centimeters (2.56 inches) in length. Since the tracheotomy tube used likely was no larger than thirteen millimeters (0.51 inches) in diameter, one has to wonder who enlarged the tracheotomy incision from a .51 inch incision to one five times that size. More importantly, for what purpose was the wound enlarged so dramatically (6H3, 9, 42, 53; 3H53; HSCA 7:300;3H368; ARRB MD 5; ARRB MD 38; ARRB MD 57; ARRB MD 159; Hewlett, 1961)?

Other Parkland doctors also believed the neck wound to be an entrance, not an exit. Carrico, the first doctor to see the President, states the wound was approximately a 4-7 millimeter wound, almost in the midline, slightly to the right of midline, and below the thyroid cartilage, round with no jagged edges or stellate lacerations. Carrico said he observed a ragged wound of the trachea immediately below the larynx (6H6, 42).

Malcolm Perry was an assistant professor of surgery, attending surgeon and vascular consultant for Parkland Hospital and John Smith Hospital in Fort Worth. Perry also testified concerning the throat wound.

PERRY: The trachea was noted to be deviated slightly to the left and I found it necessary to sever the exterior strap muscles on the other side to reach the trachea.

I noticed a small ragged laceration of the trachea on the anterior lateral right side (3H366, 370).

SUIT COAT DEFECTS

President's Kennedy's grey suit was lightweight, tropical worsted wool. The sleeves were cut up the inside of the arms and across the jacket front to facilitate quick removal at Parkland Hospital. Examination of the President's suit jacket revealed the presence of a small hole in the back of the coat. Figure 27 is a portion of the photograph of the defects in the jacket. The FBI located the defect in the suit jacket at approximately 5⅜ inches below the top of the collar and 1¾ to the right of the mid-seam. The HSCA located the hole approximately 5.3 inches from the top edge of the collar and approximately 2 inches from the middle of the back panel. The hole in the back of the coat

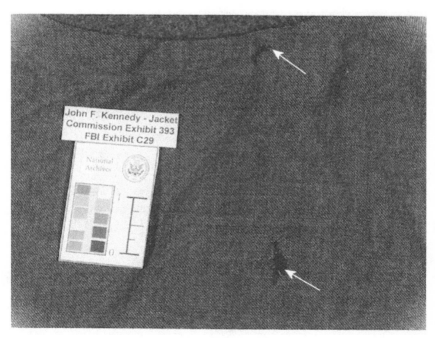

(FIGURE 27) Bullet Holes in Suit Coat

was identified as a defect caused by a bullet, and measured the hole as 1.5 centimeters vertically and 1 centimeter horizontally. The ends of the torn threads around the hole were bent inward, characteristic of a bullet entrance. Spectrographic examination of the material surrounding the defect by the Warren Commission revealed minute traces of copper (HSCA 7:81-83).

SPECTER: Commission Exhibits Nos. 393, being the coat worn by the President, 394, being the shirt, and 395, being the President's tie, and at this time move for their admission into evidence.

CHAIRMAN: It may be admitted. (The articles of clothing referred to were marked Commission Exhibits Nos. 393, 394 and 395 for identification, and received in evidence.)

SPECTER: Taking 393 at the start, Doctor Humes, will you describe for the record what hole, if any, is observable in the back of that garment, which would be at or about the spot you have described as being the point of entry on the President's back or lower neck.

HUMES: Yes, sir. This exhibit is a grey suit coat stated to have been worn by the President on the day of his death. Situated to the right of the midline, high in the back portion of the coat, is a defect, one margin of which is semicircular. Situated above it, just below the collar, is an additional defect. It is our opinion that the lower of these defects corresponds essentially with the point of entrance of the missile at Point C on Exhibit 385.

SPECTER: Would it be accurate to state that the hole, which you have identified as being the point of entry, is approximately 6 inches below the top of the collar, and 2 inches to the right of the middle seam of the coat?

HUMES: That is approximately correct, sir. This defect, I might say, continues on through the material.

Attached to this garment is the memorandum which states that one half of the area around the hole which was presented had been removed by experts, I believe, at the Federal Bureau of Investigation,

and also that a control area was taken from under the collar, so it is my
interpretation that this defect at the top of this garment is the control
area taken by the Bureau, and that the reason the lower defect is not
more circle or oval in outline is because a portion of that defect has been
removed apparently for physical examinations.

SPECTER: *Now, does the one which you have described as the entry*
of the bullet go all the way through?

HUMES: *Yes, sir; it goes through both layers.*

SPECTER: *How about the upper one of the collar you have described,*
does that go all the way through?

HUMES: *Yes, sir; it goes all the way through. It is not--wait a minute,*
excuse me, it is not so clearly a puncture wound as the one below.

SPECTER: *Does the upper one go all the way through in the same course?*

HUMES: *No.*

SPECTER: *Through the inner side, as it went through the outer side?*

HUMES: *No, in an irregular fashion (2H365).*

MCCLOY: *Before you go, may I ask a question? In your examination*
of the shirt, I just want to get it in the record, from your examination
of the shirt. There is no defect in the collar of the shirt which coincides
with the defect in the back of the President's coat, am I correct?

HUMES: *You are correct, sir. There is no such defect (2H366).*

SHIRT DEFECTS

The shirt Kennedy was wearing is white, with a thin triple gray stripe
alternating with a thin triple brown stripe. There is a defect in the shirt back
measuring 1.2 centimeters vertically by 0.8 centimeters horizontally. This is
congruent with a bullet entry angle of 42°. It is in a location corresponding

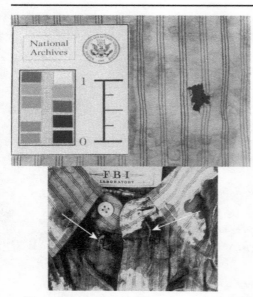

(FIGURE 28) Bullet Holes in Kennedy's Shirt

to the defect in the jacket, with its upper margin fourteen centimeters (5½ inches) below the upper margin of the shirt collar and 2½ centimeters (approximately one inch) to the right of the midline of the shirt. The FBI report describes this defect as 5¾ inches below the top of the collar and 1⅓ inches to the right of midline.

The left front panel of the shirt has a slit-like defect beginning in the lower part of the neckband, extending into the front of the shirt, 1.4 centimeters below the top buttonhole. This defect measured 1.4 centimeters vertically. There was a corresponding defect 1.5 centimeters below the center of the button on the right front panel of the shirt. The shirt defects are indicated in Figure 28. While all the defects in the back of the clothing did not necessarily align perfectly, they appeared to coordinate nicely with a wound location depicted on the face sheet, a wound located below the shoulder (HSCA 7:83, 89).

CONNALLY'S WOUNDS

Robert Roeder Shaw treated Connally's chest wounds. Shaw was Professor of Thoracic Surgery at the University Of Texas Medical School at the time of the assassination. In September 1963, Shaw started working full time with the University of Texas Southwestern Medical School as professor of thoracic surgery and chair of the division of thoracic surgery. He was also Chief of Thoracic Surgery at Parkland Memorial Hospital in Dallas. Importantly, Shaw had been in the US Army Medical Corps during WWII and stationed in both England and France. Shortly before joining the team at Parkland Memorial Hospital, Shaw had served with the MEDICO team at Avicenna Hospital in Kabul, Pakistan (1961-1963). By the time he treated Connally, Shaw had experience with over 1,000 gunshot wounds (4H101, 102).

THE BACK AND CHEST WOUNDS

Shaw described the wound in Connally's back as an entry wound, a small elliptical puncture injury that corresponded readily to the 1.5 centimeter or 5/8 inch defects in his shirt and jacket. The entry wound was positioned just inside the auxiliary fold or the crease of the armpit. The delineated path of the bullet entered Connally's back at the right armpit and exited slightly below and medial to his right nipple. Shaw specified the projectile had not pierced the shoulder blade; however, it stripped away approximately 10 centimeters of Connally's fifth rib, and punctured his lung. The rib fragments acted as secondary missiles and contributed to the damage to the anterior chest wall and to the underlying lung. The bullet trajectory was determined to have generally followed the slanting direction of the fifth rib. Shaw determined the projectile trajectory was not altered, indicating deflection would have been minimal due to the portion of the rib impacted (4H104, 107; 5H64; 6H83-88).

WRIST WOUND

At the time of the Kennedy assassination Charles Francis Gregory was professor of Orthopedic Surgery and chair of the Division of Orthopedic Surgery at the Southwestern Medical School, University of Texas. Gregory testified before the Warren Commission, stating his experience with the treatment of gunshot wounds began with his training in orthopedic surgery; was expanded in 1953 and 1954 in the Korean Theatre of Operations with the U.S. Navy; and with treating victims of gunshot injuries at Parkland Hospital in Dallas. Gregory was consulted to treat the wrist wounds of Governor John Connally. The wounds on the wrist of Connally were described by Gregory as one large wound on the volar or palmar surface of the right arm and a small wound on the dorsum or back of the right wrist. Gregory described the dorsal wound, the wound in the back of the hand, as about two centimeters in length, ragged, somewhat irregular, and located about an inch and a half or two inches above the wrist joint. It was a little to the thumb side of the wrist area. Gregory identified the wound on the back of the hand as a wound of entry and the wound on the palmar side of the hand as a wound of exit (6H95-97).

THIGH WOUND

George T. Shires, at the time of the assassination, was Professor of Surgery and Chairman of the Department of Surgery at the University of Texas,

Southwestern Medical School. Shires treated Governor Connally's leg wound. In his Warren Commission testimony, he described the wound as a one-centimeter gunshot wound over the junction of the middle and lower third of the leg and the medial aspect of the thigh. X-Rays of the left leg disclosed a one to two millimeter bullet fragment imbedded in the femur of the left leg (6H104-106).

COUNTERFEIT TRAJECTORY

Shooting incidents are dynamic and the Kennedy assassination is no exception. The victims were moving as individuals, and seated within a traveling vehicle, more than one shot was fired and both victims had more than one injury. Projectile paths, called *trajectories*, can be reconstructed with appropriate information. In some circumstances, the trajectory of the projectile may be determined to assist in determining possible positions from where a shot originated. Accurate reconstruction characteristically requires the identification and collection of related evidence and its subsequent analysis. Therefore, meticulous documentation of bullet impact on surfaces and victims including penetrating, perforating, or non-penetrating points of impact is essential for later reconstruction. Generally, pathologists and treating physicians provide precise locations of wounds and indicate wound tracks with probes. This information is then translated to victim locations within the scene. The premise is to begin with known angles of wounds and wound tracks, and utilize shooting reconstruction techniques to reveal the location of the shooter. The Warren Commission did just the opposite.

The Warren Commission based their trajectory conclusions upon an unorthodox process. They did not calculate a trajectory angle. Instead, the Warren Commission used the FBI reenactment to calculate the downward angle of a preconceived trajectory while attempting to prove the Single Bullet Theory correct. Conventional trajectory analysis begins with correct placement of the victims, locating more than one wound, and extending a line through each wound into the surroundings to identify the shooter's location. In a distorted version of identifying trajectory, the FBI, and by extension the Warren Commission, began with a preconceived location for the shooter. The FBI then determined where the limousine had to be located for the bodies of Kennedy and Connally to be aligned and clearly visible from the sixth floor of the Texas School Book Depository while not recorded by the Zapruder film. Once they located a possible alignment, they measured the angle and pronounced it the correct trajectory for the Single Bullet Theory. The actual angle of the entry of wounds, the trajectory from one victim to another, and the trajectory of wound tracks through the victim's bodies were completely discounted. If the FBI shooting reenactment had identified the correct trajectory angle, everything would have aligned perfectly; predictably, it did not (HSCA 2:139-142).

TRAJECTORY FROM TSBD

The Single Bullet Theory relies on the straight trajectory of a single bullet from the Texas School Book Depository (TSBD) through Kennedy and through Connally, without deflection or deviation from its linear path.

FBI TRAJECTORY FROM THE TSBD

On May 7, 1964, J. Lee Rankin, General Counsel for the Warren Commission, sent a letter to J. Edgar Hoover, Director of the Federal Bureau of Investigation. The letter addressed the Warren Commission's study of various videos taken in Dealey Plaza the day of the assassination (Rankin, 1964).

On May 24, the FBI and Secret Service re-enacted the shooting in Dallas, and the Warren Commission tested the validity of the Single Bullet Theory. Agents acting as the President and the Governor sat in a vehicle of approximately the same dimensions as the Presidential limousine. The agents were positioned within the vehicle to re-create particular frames of the Zapruder film. With the agents in position, photographs were taken from the sniper's nest of the Texas School Book Depository (TSBD). An oak tree partially obscured the line of sight until frame 210, so the Commission concluded the President was not hit until after frame 210 and before frame 225 (WCR:105-106).

The FBI reenactment of the shooting revealed the fired bullet entering the President's back was between Zapruder Frame 210 and Frame 225. The FBI concluded those frames placed the stand-ins for the President and the Governor in direct alignment for a single projectile to have struck both men. A rifle with a camera and telescopic sight allowed photographs to be taken from the window, believed used by the assassin, which depicted the projectile trajectory. A surveyor then placed his sighting equipment at the location the reenactment participants determined to be the precise point of entry on the back of the President's neck, and measured the angle from the end of the muzzle of the rifle to the wound location. The downward angle measured 21.34° at Frame 210, and 20.11° at Frame 225, providing an average downward angle of 20.5° between Frame 210 and Frame 225. Allowing for a downward street grade of 3°9', the angle through the President's body was calculated at 17.43°, assuming he was sitting in a vertical position (WCR:105-106).

WOUND ANGLE INDICATING TSBD TRAJECTORY

The entry angle of the projectile was estimated at the autopsy. The autopsy report states the dimensions of the entrance wound were 7 millimeters by 4 millimeters. There is a relationship between the length and width of a wound and the angle at which the projectile penetrates the target tissue. It is possible to calculate the angle of impact measuring the length and width of a wound. The sine of the angle of impact equals width divided by the length. The result of the division is a ratio. The inverse sine or the arc sine function on a scientific calculator converts the ratio to an angle. Based on the dimensions of the wound, an entry angle of the projectile struck Kennedy at a 34.84 angle, very different from the 17.43° angle determined feasible in the FBI reenactment. The FBI Summary Report provided to the Warren Commission in December 1963 also indicated a possible angle of impact of 45° to 60° (Humes, 1967; Haag, 2006; WC:105-106; FBI, 1963).

> *Medical examination of the President's body revealed that one of the bullets had entered just below his shoulder to the right of the spinal column at an angle of 45 to 60 degrees downward, that there was no point of exit and that the bullet was not in the body (FBI, 1963, p. 18).*

The November 1963 report by Sibert and O'Neill also described the back wound:

> *This opening was probed by Dr. Humes with the finger, at which time it was determined that the trajectory of the missile entering at this point had entered at a downward position of 45 to 60 degrees. Further probing determined that the distance travelled by this missile was a*

short distance inasmuch as the end of the opening could be felt with the finger (AARB MD 44:4).

Based on the dimensions of the wound documented in the Kennedy autopsy, an entry angle of the projectile struck Kennedy at a 34.84 angle. The FBI Report provided by agents Sibert and O'Neill stated during the autopsy Humes estimated the entry angle of the projectile as 45° to 60°. In an effort to bring clarity, the FBI determined trajectory in a shooting reenactment. The FBI reenactment did not actually re-create the shooting; it simply determined a position along the motorcade when the bodies of Kennedy and Connally aligned and then measured the angle from the tip of the weapon muzzle to the point on Kennedy in which the projectile struck his back. The FBI reenactment was completed on May 1964, after the introduction of the Single Bullet Theory and the need to prove it correct. The FBI reenactment revealed a bullet fired from the TSBD sixth floor window meeting the requirements of striking both Kennedy and Connally, would have to have entered the President's body at 17.43°. Predictably, a 17.43° angle is much different from the wound angle of 34.84°. Additionally, the approximate 17°angle and 35° angle are different from the estimated projectile entry angle of 45° to 60° estimated by Humes, which was determined before the need for confining all injuries to two projectiles was identified (HSCA 2:139-142; AARB MD 44:4).

The Warren Commission proposed an assassin fired at the President from a window more than 60 feet above and behind the President. A downward trajectory angle would naturally result in an entry wound location on the President being higher anatomically than the established exit wound in his throat. In January 1967, Humes, Boswell, and Finck reviewed the medical exhibits and concluded the photographs verified the location of the wound as stated in the Autopsy Report. By comparing various photographs, the Warren Commission determined the wound in the back of the neck to be higher than the wound in the throat on the horizontal plane. There is also information suggesting the bullet was traveling upward (Humes, 1967; AARB Sibert:13-14).

A red-brown to black area of skin surrounds the wound, forming what is called an abrasion collar. It was caused by the bullet's scraping the margins of the skin on penetration and is characteristic of a gunshot wound of entrance. The abrasion collar is larger at the lower margin of the wound, evidence that the bullet's trajectory at the instant of penetration was slightly upward in relation to the body (HSCA 7:175).

The HSCA Forensic Panel also documented the wound and abrasion ring orientation. Their conclusions were the wound was oval with the top portion oriented between two o'clock and three o'clock and the bottom portion oriented between eight o'clock and nine o'clock. The abrasion ring was found to be most prominent between one o'clock and seven o'clock. From the abrasion, wound shape, and the apparent wound track, the panel deduced the projectile was traveling upward and right to left. Several members of the panel felt an upward trajectory would not be a problem if Kennedy were leaning forward at the time of the rear injury. However, there is no indication he was leaning forward; Kennedy was upright when the Zapruder film captured him moving behind the Stemmons Freeway sign; and he was upright and, obviously injured, when he was once more visible. The House Select Committee on Assassinations also confirmed the entry wound in the back of the neck to be higher or equal to the exit wound in the throat on a horizontal plane. That new wound location, became the basis for the HSCA trajectory analysis completed by Canning (HSCA 1:192; HSCA 2:170-171).

HSCA TRAJECTORY FROM THE TSBD

Thomas Canning testified before the House Select Committee on Assassinations concerning a possible trajectory of a single bullet through Kennedy's neck and into Connally's back. The House Select Committee on Assassinations Pathology Panel supplied the wound information for the trajectory analysis. However, Canning did not construct a single trajectory; he constructed three. When asked why three, he replied, "We determined three trajectories in order to examine the validity of the single bullet theory that has received so much attention" (HSCA 2:156).

The HSCA Panel determined Kennedy was shot between Zapruder Frames 190 and 193. In a scaled graphic, entered as JFK Exhibit 142, Canning placed a drawing representing Kennedy in a position relative to the limousine. He identified the wound location relative to the horizontal plane of the limousine.

Transferring that angle to the lower portion of the graphic, Canning has drawn a line, which intersects the top of the Texas School Book Depository. The margin of error is a circle 26 feet in diameter. The 22° trajectory is determined by superimposing a protractor over the exhibit as depicted in Figure 29 (HSCA 2:176, 177-178).

Curiously, the graphic identified as JFK Exhibit 142 does not position the entry wound as described in Canning's corresponding testimony, nor does it comply with the wound locations provided by the House Select Committee on Assassinations Pathology Panel for

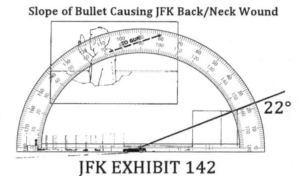

Slope of Bullet Causing JFK Back/Neck Wound

JFK EXHIBIT 142

(FIGURE 29) JFK Exhibit 142, Canning's 22° Trajectory from the TSBD to a Wound in the Back

the trajectory through President Kennedy's neck. Canning's testimony states, the bullet "entered just to the right of his neck, just to the right of his center plane, and exiting the forward part of his neck." A position he indicated was interpreted from the forensic pathologists report.

If the source is the autopsy report, or the HSCA, the entry wound should be located 5.5 inches from the Mastoid Process; placing the wound much higher—at about the first thoracic vertebrae. The estimated 28° trajectory angle with a higher entry wound is compared to the 22° lower wound as demonstrated in Figure 30 (HSCA 2:178).

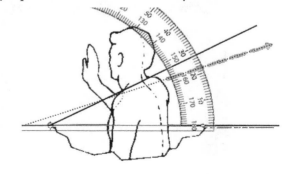

(FIGURE 30) Trajectory based on Entry at Approximately Thoracic Vertebra 1 and Exiting at Throat

TRAJECTORY THROUGH KENNEDY

The Warren Commission did not attempt to calculate a trajectory through Kennedy using the wounds on his body. Instead, they used the predetermined 17° trajectory from the FBI reenactment to establish a single line trajectory from the Texas School Book Depository sixth floor window, through Kennedy and into Connally.

Placing substitutes for Kennedy and Connally in a vehicle, Spector attempted to demonstrate the 17° angle from the Texas School Book Depository wound aligned with the wounds in the men. White chalk marks on the rear of Kennedy and Connally's suit coats indicated the wounds. If the throat wound and the highlighted chalk wounds aligned with a single trajectory, the Single Bullet Theory would appear plausible.

However, as demonstrated in Figure 30, the 17° angle did not work. The rod illustrates a downward angle of approximately 20°, not 17°. The rear entry wound for Kennedy in the photograph appears to be at the cervical

(**FIGURE 31**) Demonstrating the Single Bullet Theory

portion of the spine when, at that time, the back wound was supposedly below the top of the shoulder. The arrow in the lower photograph indicates the chalk mark representing Kennedy's entry wound in other segments of the FBI reenactment, a mark obviously several inches lower than the trajectory being demonstrated. The photograph suggests the rear entry for Connally as slightly higher than the actual back wound. By manipulating the downward trajectory angle and adjusting wound placement in both men, the trajectory in Figure 31 appears to support the viability of the Single Bullet Theory.

THE BACK WOUND ANGLES

Sibert reported Humes stated the trajectory entering the back was 40° to 60°. The Warren Commission Report, and autopsy report, state Kennedy's back wound was oval and measured approximately seven millimeters by four millimeters with well-demarcated edges. Mathematically those measurements indicate a 34.84° angle of impact for the projectile as it entered Kennedy's back. Projectiles entering or exiting a target at a 0° (completely horizontal) angle create round wounds.

As the angle of impact becomes more acute, the wound becomes elliptically shaped. Therefore, a description of a spherical or round throat wound is an indication the wound was not as elliptically shaped as the back wound. The adjacent graphic represents the elliptical shape of Kennedy's back wound, 34.84°. The first mentioned, 40° by Humes, is fairly close to the 34.84°angle of entry the wound dictates. The 17° and approximate 35° angles of entry for the projectile are demonstrated in Figure 32.

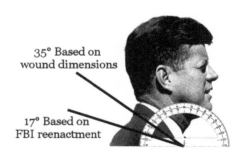

35° Based on wound dimensions

17° Based on FBI reenactment

As the Warren Commission Report states, there was no deflection of the bullet striking Kennedy in the back. The bullet trajectory should be a straight line. This means the angles indicated by the entry and exit wounds should be identical.

(FIGURE 32) Trajectory Angles Based on Wound Dimensions and the Exit Wound

Additionally, the bullet should strike Governor Connally with the same angle of trajectory.

Humes declared at the autopsy the entry wound trajectory appeared to be between 40° to 60°. The 40° to 60° angle downward trajectory indicates the first bullet to strike the President did so when the limousine was considerably closer to the Texas School Book Depository Building than the Warren Commission endorsed. The only other explanation is the projectile was fired from a higher location with a similar trajectory: the Dal-Tex Building may be a possibility.

THE HSCA TRAJECTORY THROUGH KENNEDY

The second trajectory by Thomas Canning for the House Select Committee on Assassinations was based on the President's back and neck wounds as provided by the House Select Committee on Assassinations Pathology Panel. The rear wound was determined to be 0.9 centimeters by 0.9 centimeters, reflecting a round wound. The entry wound is slightly below the base of the neck at the back, and very close to the seventh cervical vertebra and near the first thoracic vertebra. The exit wound was determined to be through the front of the neck. In the frontal view shown in Figure 33, the entry wound on the back was 4.5 centimeters to the right of the mid-plane of the body, and the neck wound was about one-half centimeter to the left of mid-plane. As shown in Figure 33, the trajectory is approximately 0°, relative to the horizontal plane (HSCA 2:170-171; HSCA 7:85).

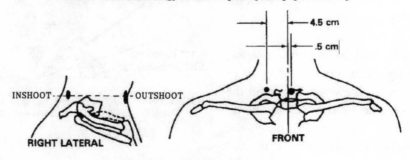

JFK Wound Locations
Deduced From Pathology Panel Report (Autopsy Position)

JFK EXHIBIT F-376

(FIGURE 33) The HSCA Throat Trajectory was Approximately 0°

KENNEDY'S THROAT WOUND SHAPE

Perry described Kennedy's throat wound as spherical or oval, while Baxter and Carrico described it as spherical or round. The throat wound was described as roughly five millimeters in diameter, and four to six millimeters by Perry; four to five millimeters in diameter by Baxter; four to seven millimeters, and five to eight millimeters in diameter by Carrico (6H3, 9, 15, 423, 3H359; HSCA 7:300).

Carrico, the first doctor to see Kennedy at Parkland Hospital, stated the wound was approximately a 4-7 millimeter in diameter, slightly to the right of midline and below the thyroid cartilage. He described the wound as round, with no jagged edges or stellate lacerations (6H6, 42).

If the throat wound followed the same trajectory as the back wound, they would have had the same elliptical shape. In addition, cutting through an elliptically shaped wound would have been more noticeable than making a tracheotomy incision through a smaller round wound. Moreover, it is impossible to believe a 35° elliptically shaped wound could be mistakenly described as round or spherical.

Perry testified before the Assassinations Record Review Board Kennedy's throat wound was a circular wound, and measured about five millimeters in diameter, or the size of a pencil eraser, before he performed the tracheotomy. This measurement corresponds with the testimony of McClelland, who assisted with the procedure (ARRB Parkland Doctors: 553-54).

In an interview, McClelland was asked if it were possible the throat wound was a shored exit wound. Shored exit wounds are encountered when the skin is supported by a firm surface, in this case, Kennedy's necktie. The exiting bullet pushes the skin into the supporting surface, which scrapes and abrades it, much like an entry wound's abrasion collar. As a result, occasionally, a shored exit wound can closely resemble an entrance wound. McClelland was emphatic in his answer, stating, "Absolutely not" (McClelland, 2012).

THE TRAJECTORY THROUGH KENNEDY PROBLEM

Trajectory through Kennedy is a problem. The exact location of the entry wound in the back may be in dispute, but the exit wound in the throat wound is established as below the Adam's apple, and within the lower one third of the cervical vertebra. Using that wound as a known location, wounds with dimensions that indicate an entry angle can create estimated trajectories through the President's neck.

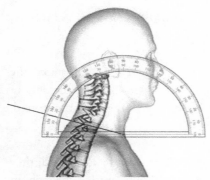

(FIGURE 34) An Estimated 15° Trajectory from Thoracic Vertebra 1 to the Throat Wound

The House Select Committee on Assassinations determined the first thoracic vertebra was fractured as the bullet passed through the President's body. Utilizing the fractured vertebra T1 and the throat wound as points of entry and exit, the bullet trajectory would be similar to Figure 34. This 15° trajectory obviously places the wound adjacent to the top of the shoulder and is similar to the 17° trajectory developed in the FBI reenactment. It also creates a wound similar to the circular shape the House Select Committee on Assassinations designated the entry wound to the rear of Kennedy. A bullet travelling at a 15° to 20° angle of impact creates a wound that has an approximate 75° elliptical shape. While it may appear the wounds and trajectories are beginning to align, the original autopsy specifically indicates an entry corresponding to a 35° elliptically shaped wound.

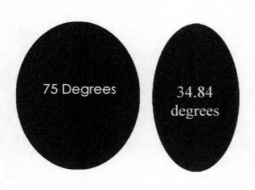

(FIGURE 35) 75° and 34.84°

The autopsy report provides proportions for a 34.84° elliptical shaped rear entry wound. The FBI reenactment developed a 17° trajectory angle suggesting a 75° entry wound. Figure 35 depicts the two angles and corresponding shapes. Normally, a bullet creates entry and exit wounds exhibiting the proper dimensions to match the trajectory angle. However, in this particular instance there are no corresponding elements.

There are components of the trajectory through Kennedy that should synchronize with each other: the trajectory angle with a fixed exit wound in the throat, the wound dimensions, and the subsequent shapes of the wounds. There is no synchronization between the trajectory and the wounds.

1. The trajectory is defined as 17° by the FBI reenactment.
2. The entry wound should represent the 17° impact angle by displaying measurement coordinating to approximately a 75° elliptical shape.
3. The autopsy measurements for the back entry wound, seven by four millimeters, compute to a 35° oval shaped wound instead of the expected 75° shaped wound.

The challenge in understanding the trajectory through Kennedy's neck is to reconcile the inconsistent components; unfortunately, it appears reconciliation of the trajectory angles and wound shapes is impossible.

KENNEDY TO CONNALLY TRAJECTORY

Trajectory has a three dimensional aspect. The standard technique for measuring three-dimensional movements is vertical, horizontal, and forward. Trajectory for vertical and forward movement was addressed by the Warren Commission trajectory reenactment. They failed, however, to address the horizontal angle. Fortuitously, the FBI re-reenactment photographs documented the horizontal angle in each photograph they took.

THE FBI TRAJECTORY FROM KENNEDY TO CONNALLY

The Warren Commission was unable to determine the exact point in time the President was first shot. When studying the Zapruder film, it appears Kennedy showed no sign of injury before frame 210. Yet, he was obviously hit at frame 225. The Warren Commission determined, while no photographic evidence recording the specific moment of the shot to the President's back was known to exist, trajectories should be considered. This was accomplished by first determining the position of the limousine between Zapruder Frames 210 and 225. Agents seated in the limousine represented Kennedy and Connally. At each intervening frame, an FBI agent located in the sixth floor window of the Texas School Book Depository lined up a telescopic sight on the points of entry wounds marked on stand-ins for the President and Governor Connally. The next step was to have a surveyor measure the angle from the end of the muzzle of the rifle in the sixth floor window to the mark representing the back wound on President Kennedy. This was completed for each Zapruder Frame between 210 and 225. All angles were averaged to calculate a downward estimated trajectory angle of 17°, 43 minutes, 30 seconds (HSCA 2 0912:139-140).

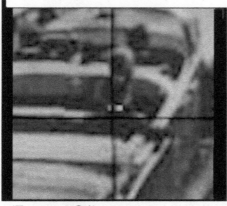

Frame 210 CE 893 (above)

Frame 222 CE 894 (below)

(FIGURE 36) CE 893 and CE 894 Trajectory through Kennedy and Connally

Trajectory for vertical and forward movement was addressed by the Warren Commission trajectory study. Mysteriously, the horizontal, or right to left, angle was not adequately addressed. Telescopic sights for firearms, generally just called scopes, magnify the target area for the shooter. The cross hairs within the scope provide the shooter greater accuracy.

Tree branches obscuring the field of view combined with Zapruder Frames depicting an injured President, make Zapruder Frame 210 the earliest Kennedy could have been shot. Figure 36 is a cropped version of Warren Commission Exhibits 893 and 894; photographs taken through cross hairs on a scope. The vertical cross hairs on rifle scopes indicate the forward and horizontal trajectory of a projectile. By following the vertical line of the scope, one can establish a possible forward trajectory as the projectile would continue through Kennedy into Connally.

In Frame 210, although Connally appears slightly turned to his right, it is not clear if Connally is far enough to the left of the President for a projectile striking Kennedy to exit his throat and strike Connally's back near the right arm pit. The limousine was advanced down the street to coordinate with positions in frames of the Zapruder film. The photographs indicate the angle between Kennedy and Connally changes as the vehicle moves away from the shooter. Each progressive forward movement of the limousine has a corresponding adjustment in the relationship of Connally to Kennedy: Connally progressively moves to the right of Kennedy. This makes the trajectory alignment through Kennedy and into Connally, more difficult with each successive frame (CE 893 18:89; CE 894 18:90).

HSCA TRAJECTORY FROM KENNEDY TO CONNALLY

The third trajectory calculated by Thomas Canning for the House Select Committee on Assassinations was from Kennedy to Connally. The location of Connally's rear wound was determined by the House Select Committee on Assassinations Pathology Panel and Canning's examination of medical reports from Parkland Hospital. Canning determined the distance between Kennedy's throat exit wound and Connally's back entry wound was about sixty centimeters. The photographic panel provided the height difference between the men at 8 centimeters. Canning drew a line between Kennedy's throat exit wound and the entrance wound on Connally's back. Although Canning did not use the President's back wound, just the exiting neck wound and Governor Connally's entry back wound, Canning declared the line the trajectory between the two men (HSCA 2:179-193).

The trajectory through Kennedy and the trajectory from Kennedy to Connally did not align; Canning dismissed the difference but found them "close enough so that they fell within a reasonable error of one another" (HSCA 2:179-193).

> *CANNING: Yes, those two angles are different. Our interpretation of the data tells us that if we were to determine one trajectory based on the two pieces of information, one the Governor's wound, and the President's neck wound, that that will give us one line. The other wound, the other wound pair in the President, will give us a second line. Those two lines do not coincide (HSCA 2: 191).*

The House Select Committee recognized the slope, or the downward angle of the trajectory and the horizontal or right to left direction was different in all three trajectories. From the Texas School Book Depository to Kennedy, the slope reference to horizontal was 22°, through Kennedy it was 0°, and it was 20° from Kennedy to Connally.

> GOLDSMITH: Mr. Canning, each of the three trajectories that you constructed had different slope, different direction, and a different margin of error. What consequence, if any can you attribute to these differences?

> CANNING. The differences may well arise simply because all measurements are imprecise, and it would simply be unrealistic to expect the slopes and directions to be identical (HSCA 2: 191).

One could expect some minor variations in measurements, which would result in minor differences in wound angles. However, a 22° angle trajectory from the TSBD suddenly becoming a 0° angle traversing Kennedy's neck, followed by a 20° angle downward into Connally is more than a minor deviation from a single trajectory. It is a second trajectory.

TRAJECTORY THROUGH CONNALLY

The FBI reenactment did not appear to be concerned with reconstructing a trajectory through Connally's wounds. However, the Warren Commission needed precise placement of Connally's wounds to facilitate a trajectory for the Single Bullet Theory.

WARREN COMMISSION TRAJECTORY THROUGH CONNALLY
Governor John Connally was riding in the Presidential limousine in a jump seat in front of the President. Connally's wounds included an entry wound in the back near the right shoulder, a broken rib, an exit wound in the chest, a shattered wrist caused by a bullet entering from the dorsal (back) side, and a fragment lodged in his thigh. Robert Shaw was the treating physician for Connally's chest wounds. Shaw depicted the entry wound to Connally's back as positioned just inside the auxiliary fold or the crease of the armpit. The

(**FIGURE 38**) Discovery Channel Trajectory

bullet trajectory was described as entering Connally's back at the right armpit and exiting slightly below and medial to his right nipple. Shaw testified the projectile had not penetrated the shoulder blade; however, it stripped away approximately 10 centimeters of Connally's fifth rib, and punctured his lung. The rib fragments acted as secondary missiles and contributed to the damage to the anterior chest wall and to the underlying lung. The bullet trajectory was determined to have generally followed the slanting direction of the fifth rib. Shaw determined the projectile trajectory was not altered, indicating deflection would have been minimal due to the portion of the rib impacted (4H104, 107; 5H64; 6H83-88).

When depicting the entry and exit wounds on an anatomically correct drawing and adding a protractor as an overlay, the approximate 22° angle for the trajectory is appreciated. Figure 37 indicates this angle of trajectory.

DISCOVERY CHANNEL SHOOTING RECREATION

On November 14, 2004, the Discovery Channel aired the program *Unsolved History: JFK, Beyond the Magic Bullet.* The program duplicated the trajectory

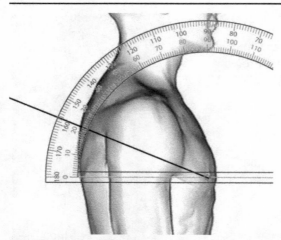

(FIGURE 37) Trajectory through Connally's Chest

of the Single Bullet Theory. State-of-the-art anatomical recreations of Kennedy and Connally's torso were utilized, with additional ballistic gelatin blocks to represent Connally's wrist and thigh.

The angle from the sixth floor of the Texas School Book Depository was meticulously re-created based upon the measurements published by the House Select Committee on Assassinations. The height of the firearm muzzle in the shooting reconstruction was sixty feet; the distance from the end of the weapon muzzle to the torso representing President Kennedy was one hundred eighty feet. The entry wound on Kennedy's back was located at a point corresponding with fourteen centimeters (5.5 inches) from the right acromion and fourteen centimeters (5.5 inches) below the tip of the right Mastoid Process. The entry wound on the torso representing Kennedy is forty-seven inches from the ground. The Connally torso was positioned to represent the three-inch difference in height and at a distance ensuring the back entry wound was sixty centimeters from the President's throat exit wound. Using the same type weapon and ammunition allegedly used by Oswald, the program duplicated the trajectory mandated by the Single Bullet Theory.

A high-speed video camera recording at 3,000 frames per second captured the projectile as it traversed Kennedy and struck Connally. The bullet entered the torso representing Kennedy just below, and to the left of, the point designated as the entry wound. One would expect, therefore, for the projectile to exit the surrogate torso at a corresponding point just below and to the left of the anticipated throat wound. Astonishingly, as observed in Figure 38, the bullet exits the chest. Predictably, the show's producers did not acknowledge this significant finding.

In the high-speed video, the producers highlight the projectile's 20° trajectory through Kennedy and Connally. Despite the careful calculations to insure they were firing from the same height and distance the Warren Commission determined correct, the angle does not correspond with the 17.43 downward trajectory the FBI reached in its reconstruction. The highlighted trajectory depicted by the Discovery Channel indicated an exit in the Kennedy surrogate torso chest, followed by an entry in the substitute Connally torso. Incredibly, the narrator then falsely declares, "Amazingly, Alex has replicated the magic bullet shot." It is obvious to the viewer the highlighted trajectory is not replicating the trajectory proposed by the Single Bullet Theory. The trajectory is not discussed further; instead, all emphasis is directed to the wounds depicted on the torso representing Connally. The viewer is left wondering why the exit wound in the Kennedy torso is not in the throat (Erickson, 2004).

THE PARKLAND BULLET

The bullet recovered at Parkland Hospital is a three-centimeter or 1.2-inch long, copper-jacketed, lead-core, 6.5-millimeter rifle bullet. After passing completely through Kennedy and Connally, Specter alleged the bullet had fallen out of the Governor's clothes and onto a stretcher at Parkland Hospital where Darrell C. Tomlinson discovered it. Analysis conclusions show this bullet was fired from Oswald's Mannlicher Carcano to the exclusion of all other weapons. See Figure 39.

DISCOVERY

An emergency room head nurse, Ruth Jeanette Standridge, received word President Kennedy and Governor Connelly were enroute to Parkland Hospital, at approximately 12:30 PM. Nurse Standridge prepared Trauma Room two for Governor Connally's arrival. Once Connally was in the room, Standridge, orderly David Sanders, hospital aid Rosa Majors, and physicians Fueishier and

(**FIGURE 39**) Parkland Hospital Bullet, CE 399

Duke removed Connally's clothing to facilitate medical treatment. Standridge testified Rosa Majors removed the money from Connally's pants, but at no time did Standridge notice a bullet. Standridge collected the Governor's clothing and gave them to Cliff Carter, while Connally was being taken to surgery by Fueishier, Duke, and Shaw (6H115-117).

Jane Carolyn Wester was a registered nurse assigned as assistant supervisor in the operating room at Parkland Hospital when the attending physicians brought Governor Connally into the operating room. Outside of operating room five, Wester helped transfer Connally from the stretcher onto an operating table. Wester testified she rolled the sheets up on the stretcher into a small bundle. Wester, in contrast to Standridge, stated she collected the Governor's clothing and gave them to Cliff Carter. Wester stated Connally's clothes were removed from the bottom of the stretcher and placed on the bottom of the cart in a paper sack located in the hallway by the operating table. Wester stated several glassine packets, small packets of hypodermic needles, some alcohol sponges, and a roll of 1-inch tape were also located on the cart. Wester then watched as orderly, R. J. Jimison took the cart and proceeded to the elevator. She attested the last time she saw Jimison he was standing at the elevator with the cart (6H120-122).

Orderly R. J. Jimison testified before the Warren Commission on March 21, 1964. He stated the orderly typically placed the used cart and dirty linen in the elevator, but not to accompany the elevator down to the emergency room. Jimison testified he placed only one cart on the elevator during his shift; and he did not recall another cart placed on the elevator. He did not recall items other than the sheet on the cart (6H125).

Darrell C. Tomlinson was a senior engineer in charge of the power plant at Parkland Hospital. In his testimony before the Warren Commission, Tomlinson stated at approximately 1:00 PM, he was asked to manually run the emergency elevator to limit access to the ground floor, and the second floor, where the operating rooms were located. When he opened the elevator door, he observed a stretcher, which he removed and placed against a second stretcher already located in the hallway. After making several trips between the floors, Tomlinson noticed a man had pushed one of the stretchers away from the wall. Later, the stretcher appeared to have been moved and was obstructing the hallway, so Tomlinson pushed it back against the wall. When he did, a bullet fell to the floor. During his Warren Commission Testimony, Tomlinson was asked approximately fifteen times if he could positively identify the stretcher from which the bullet fell. Mysteriously, he was never asked to describe the bullet or confirm it was similar in appearance to Commission Exhibit 399 (6H128-134).

> *SPECTER: You say you can't really take an oath today to be sure whether it was stretcher A or stretcher B that you took off the elevator?*

> *TOMLINSON: Well, today or any other day, I'm just not sure of it, whether it was A or B that I took off.*

> *SPECTER: And, then, when—*

> *TOMLINSON (interrupting): Here's the deal—I rolled that thing off, we got a call, and went to the second floor, picked the man up and brought him down. He went on over across, to clear out of the emergency area, but across from it, and picked up two pints of, I believe it was, blood. He told me to hold for him, he had to get right back to the operating room, so I held, and the minute he hit there, we took off for the second floor and I came back to the ground. Now, I don't know how many people went through that—I don't know how many people hit them—I don't know anything about what could have happened to them in between the time I was gone, and I made several trips before I discovered the bullet on the end of it there (6H131-133).*

THE CHAIN OF CUSTODY

The FBI developed and reported a chain of custody accepted as Warren Commission Exhibit 2011 dated June 7, 1964. Reportedly, Tomlinson gave the bullet to O. P. Wright, Personnel Director of Security at Dallas County Hospital. Mr. Wright gave the bullet to Secret Service Agent Richard E. Johnsen. Johnsen gave the bullet to Secret Service Chief James Rowley. Chief Rowley gave the bullet to FBI Agent Elmar Lee Todd. Later, the persons who handled the bullet were asked if they could identify the bullet marked as Commission Exhibit 399 as the bullet they had received and passed on to someone else. FBI Agent Bardwell D. Odum showed Tomlinson and Wright Commission Exhibit 399. The report indicated Tomlinson "cannot positively identify this bullet as the one he found and showed to Mr. O. P. Wright." Wright, when shown the bullet identified as Commission Exhibit 399, advised he "could not positively identify" Commission Exhibit 399 as the bullet. Agent Johnsen also stated, "He could not identify this bullet as the one he obtained from O. P. Wright," when shown the bullet by FBI Agent Todd. Todd showed Secret Service Chief Rowley the bullet Commission Exhibit 399, who also advised he "could not identify the bullet as the one he received from Secret Service Agent Richard E. Johnsen and given to Special Agent Todd on November 22, 1963."

The Warren Commission obviously received and accepted as evidence a report identified as Exhibit 2011, which was clearly fabricated. Furthermore, the report conspicuously omitted descriptive details, or identifying comments, regarding the evidentiary bullet. The FBI reported in Warren Commission Exhibit 2011, both Tomlinson and Wright stated to Special Agent Bardwell D. Odum, Commission Exhibit 399 resembled the bullet found at Parkland Hospital. However, neither of the Secret Service Agents stated Commission Exhibit 399 appeared to be the same bullet, which should have immediately raised concerns (CE 2011, 24H412-413).

One would expect one, or both agents, to state Commission Exhibit 399 looked like the same bullet, even if unable to make a positive identification. One would expect a Secret Service agent holding a bullet used in the assassination of President Kennedy to give special attention to the size, shape, and condition of the projectile. One would also expect a Secret Service agent to be cognizant of the importance of maintaining a proper chain of custody for physical evidence. Given the importance of this case, it seems one might even expect a Secret Service agent to initiate some chain of custody, which would include a physical description of the evidence being transferred, and the signatures of both parties with appropriate dates and times. This apparent poor handling of physical evidence, combined with Special Agent Johnson and Secret Service Chief James Rowley's failure to indicate a similarity of the bullet they handled as Commission Exhibit 399, was a conspicuous omission. Also questionable is the lack of reference to Odum, who had the bullet in Dallas, as participating in the chain of custody.

The FBI reported in Warren Commission Exhibit 2011 both Tomlinson and Wright stated to Special Agent Bardwell D. Odum that Commission Exhibit 399 resembled the bullet found at Parkland Hospital. In an attempt to obtain additional information concerning the bullet discovered at Parkland Hospital, Josiah Thompson interviewed O. P. Wright in November 1966. Prior to seeing photographs of Commission Exhibit 399, Wright provided the following description (Thompson, n. d.):

> *"That bullet had a pointed tip." Wright then presented the photograph of a .30 caliber bullet in "Six Seconds in Dallas" (Thompson, 1967). As Thompson described it in 1967, "I then showed him photographs of CE's 399, 572 (the two ballistics comparison rounds from Oswald's rifle) (sic), and 606 (revolver bullets) (sic), and he rejected all of these as resembling the bullet Tomlinson found on the stretcher. Half an hour later in the presence of two witnesses, he once again rejected the picture of 399 as resembling the bullet found on the stretcher" (Thompson, 1967).*

The statement by Wright in the Thompson interview is in direct opposition to the FBI report identified as Commission Exhibit 2011. During an attempt to confirm the June 24, 1964 FBI Report, Thompson discovered a FBI memo from the FBI's Dallas field office dated June 20, 1964, just four days earlier than the Commission Exhibit 2110 report was published. This memo stated Tomlinson and Wright were unable to identify Commission Exhibit 399 as the bullet found at Parkland Hospital, and did not mention the men as reporting similarities in the two bullets. To determine the validity of the statements given to Special Agent Bardwell D. Odum by Tomlinson and Wright, Thompson interviewed Odum in 2002. Odum said he "had never, at any time, had any bullet" related to the Kennedy assassination in his possession. Asked whether he might have forgotten the incident, Mr. Odum stated he doubted he would have ever forgotten such an important piece of evidence (Thompson, n. d.).

The projectile identified as Commission Exhibit 399 was first presented as evidence and entered into the official record on March 16, 1964 when Humes testified before the Commission. Spector, subject to later proof, introduced the projectile as the missile recovered from the stretcher occupied by Governor Connally. Fifteen days later, the authenticity of Commission Exhibit 399 had mysteriously been proven. Eisenberg declared Commission Exhibit 399 was "for the record", the "bullet which was found in the Parkland Hospital following the assassination." Frazier confirmed Commission Exhibit 399 was the same bullet he had received from Special Agent Todd the day of the assassination. However, that does not verify whether it was the same bullet recovered from the stretcher in Dallas, or that it was associated with Connally. Inexplicably, Todd, Johnsen, and Wright—all of whom handled the bullet and were a part of its chain of custody—were not called to testify before the Warren Commission (2H374; 3H428).

Tomlinson was questioned extensively concerning what stretcher may have held the bullet introduced as Commission Exhibit 399. However, he was never shown the bullet or asked if he could identify it as the bullet he discovered the day Kennedy was assassinated. Furthermore, it appeared no one could positively establish if Kennedy or Connally occupied the stretcher where the bullet was discovered. Supposedly, Tomlinson gave the bullet to O. P. Wright, who gave it to Johnsen, who gave it to Rowley, who gave it to Todd. Each man should have been questioned by the Warren Commission in order to establish a proper chain of custody. However, the FBI report identified as Commission Exhibit 2011 designated a chain of possession for Commission Exhibit 399 beginning with the bullet's discovery in the hallway, and then skipped ahead to Frazier, bypassing the other men in the process. According to the FBI, the two hospital employees who discovered and physically handled the bullet originally identified it as the same bullet six months later in an FBI interview. This was flatly denied by O. P. Wright, and by Special Agent Bardwell D. Odum, who furthermore denied ever interviewing the hospital employees. Which begs the question, why did the FBI report intentionally and deceptively state the men at Parkland Hospital recognized similarities in the 6.5-millimeter rifle bullet (CE 2011, 24H412-413)?

PRISTINE CONDITION

Providing a proper chain of custody and confidently connecting Commission Exhibit 399 to either Kennedy or Connally was not accomplished by the Warren Commission. Additional trepidation is produced by the fact the bullet was not found in or around either victim. Even disregarding those issues, the condition of the bullet promoted skepticism in its capability to traverse both men with so little damage and brings doubt to the Single Bullet Theory. Commission Exhibit 399 is the bullet allegedly found on the stretcher, which supposedly held Governor Connally, was virtually undamaged, and displayed no blood or tissue on its surface.

Humes was asked in his Warren Commission testimony if Commission Exhibit 399 could have made the wound on Connally's wrist. His answer was "I think that highly unlikely." Humes was then asked if Commission Exhibit 399 could have lodged in Connally's thigh. He replied, "I think that extremely unlikely." Finck was also questioned concerning Commission Exhibit 399. When asked if it could have been the bullet inflicting the wounds to Connally's wrist, he replied, "No, for the reason that there are too many fragments described in that wrist." Shaw was asked similar questions (2H374; 2H382).

> *SPECTER: What is your opinion as to whether bullet 399 could have inflicted all of the wounds on the Governor, then, without respect at this point to the wound of the President's neck?*

> *SHAW: I feel that there would be some difficulty in explaining all of the wounds as being inflicted by bullet Exhibit 399 without causing more in the way of loss of substance to the bullet or deformation of the bullet (4H114).*

Larry Sturdivan is the author of numerous professional articles and a consultant in wound ballistics for such agencies as the Law Enforcement Assistance Administration, the Department of Justice, and NATO. He has studied mathematics and computer sciences at the Ballistics Institute of the Ballistic Research Laboratory, Aberdeen Proving Grounds, Md., and was a physical scientist with the Wounds Ballistics Branch of the Aberdeen Proving Ground Vulnerability. Sturdivan is degreed in statistics and physics. One of just a handful of experts on wound ballistics, Sturdivan was called to testify before the House Select Committee on Assassinations. His testimony provided the conclusion Commission Exhibit 399 could have injured both Kennedy and Connally without distortion (HSCA 1:383, 385).

Sturdivan testified research indicated the Mannlicher Carcano bullet would begin to deform, nose on, at approximately 1,400 feet per second. Sturdivan affirmed the muzzle velocity when the projectile left the muzzle was approximately 2,000 feet per second, and had decelerated to approximately 1,800 feet per second when it entered the back of President Kennedy. When exiting the President's throat, the velocity would have decelerated to approximately 1700 feet per second. Entering the back of Connally, striking a rib, and exiting at the chest would have added a minimum of 400 feet per second loss in velocity, meaning the bullet would have entered the wrist at 1,300 feet per second or less. The total loss in velocity would result in a projectile traveling 700 feet per second or less impacting Connally's thigh, which is well below the deformity threshold defined by Sturdivan. The question becomes, how could a bullet traveling only 700 feet per second strike the femur and not be deformed (HSCA 1:386, 407-409).

On April 14, 1964, Warren Commission staff members Redlich, Specter, and Eisenberg; Humes, Boswell, Finck; Dr. F. W. Light, Jr. Deputy Chief of the Biophysics Division at Edgewood Arsenal, Maryland, and Chief of the Wound Assessment Branch of the Biophysics Division; Dr. Oliver, Chief of the Wound Ballistics Branch of the Biophysics Division at Edgewood Arsenal; and several FBI and Secret Service agents met to study the Zapruder film. Melvin A. Eisenberg added the consensus of the group to the official record in an April 22, 1964 memorandum. The group determined the following concerning the condition of Commission Exhibit 399 (Eisenberg, 1964):

> *The bullet recovered from Governor Connally's stretcher does not appear to have penetrated a wrist and (2) if the first bullet did not hit Governor Connally, it should have ripped up the car, but apparently did not. Since the bullet recovered from the Governor's stretcher does not appear to have penetrated a wrist, if he was hit by this (the first) bullet, he was probably also hit by the second bullet (Eisenberg, 1964a).*

Alfred G. Oliver was a Supervisory Research Veterinarian for the Department of the Army at Edgewood Arsenal and Chief of Wound Ballistics Branch. Frederick W. Light, Jr. was the Chief of the Wound Assessment Branch and assistant chief of the Biophysics Division at Edgewood Arsenal. At the request of the Warren Commission, Oliver and Light participated in a series of experiments to determine wound ballistics comparable to those Kennedy and Connally suffered. The tests were completed using Commission Exhibit 139, a 6.5-millimeter Mannlicher Carcano rifle, and Winchester Western ammunition. Ballistic gelatin, animals, and human cadavers were used in the experiments. In one instance, a goat was covered with clothing similar to what Connally wore at the time he was injured. The bullet was retrieved and marked as Commission Exhibit 853. When comparing Exhibit 399 with Exhibit 853, Oliver stated Exhibit 853 was "quite flattened" along the "whole length" of the bullet. He stated Exhibit 399 had a "suggestion of flattening." A cadaver was similarly clothed and shot through the wrist, creating a wound Oliver characterized as "for all purposes identical" to Connally's injury. The experimental testing bullet was recovered and marked as Commission Exhibit 856. Spector asked Oliver how the experimental bullet Exhibit 856 compared with Exhibit 399.

Oliver testified,

> *"It is not like it at all. I mean, Commission Exhibit 399 is not flattened on the end. This one is very severely flattened on the end." Light was asked what about Commission Exhibit 399 suggested it caused the President's neck wound and all of the wounds on Governor Connally. He replied, "Nothing about that bullet" (5H75, 95, 80-82).*

Robert Frazier testified before the Warren Commission that the current weight of Commission Exhibit 399 was 158.6 grains. He testified 6.5 mm. Mannlicher Carcano cartridges, manufactured by the Western Cartridge Company weighed between 160 and 161 grains. Frazier later added examination of several standard or known bullets revealed bullet weights of 160.85, 161.5 and 161.1 grains. Frazier estimated the weight loss of CE 399 at 3 to 4 grains. However, Guinn weighed the projectile prior to any analysis and found Commission Exhibit 399 weighed 160.62 grains. This weight parallels the bullet weight of 161 grains as quoted by the Western Cartridge Company. Two samples were removed from the bullet for testing and the bullet reweighed. The new weight was determined to be 160.15 grains. Three lead fragments from Connally's arm, designed as Commission Exhibit 842 and FBI Exhibit Q9, weighed 0.5 grains. This would make the total weight of Commission Exhibit 399, prior to analysis, 160.65 grains. The weights of the fragments remaining within Governor Connally are unknown. Subsequently, there is no definite method to compute the original weight of Commission Exhibit 399; and thereby no method to either confirm, or exclude, the total weight as falling within the rage of Western Cartridge Company 6.5 mm. Mannlicher Carcano cartridges (3H399, 430; HSCA 1:518).

TIMING

On April 14, 1964, a conference was held to determine which frames in the Zapruder film portray the instants at which the bullets struck Kennedy and Connally. Participants included: Humes, Boswell, Finck, Dr. F. W. Light, Jr. Deputy Chief of the Biophysics Division at Edgewood Arsenal, Maryland, and Chief of the Wound Assessment Branch of the Biophysics Division, Dr. Oliver, Chief of the Wound Ballistics Branch of the Biophysics Division at Edgewood Arsenal, Redlich, Specter and Eisenberg of the Warren Commission staff; and FBI and Secret Service Agents (Eisenberg, 1964).

> *The President may have been struck by the first bullet as much as two seconds before any visible reaction began. In all likelihood, however, the maximum delay between impact and reaction would be under one second, and it is possible that the reaction was instantaneous. Putting this in terms of frames, the President may have been struck as much as 36 frames before any visible reaction is seen. If the visible reaction begins at 199, the President may have been struck as early as 163; if the visible reaction begins at 204-206, he may have been struck as early as 168-170; if the visible reaction begins while the President is behind the sign, he may have been struck as early as 179-188 (Eisenberg, 1964a).*

FBI weapons expert Robert Frazier testified before the Warren Commission on March 31, 1964 as to the time required to rapid fire the Mannlicher Carcano. Frazier testified on November 27, 1963, accompanied by agents Charles Killion and Cortland Cunningham; he participated in experiments to determine how fast the weapon could be fired. In the first test, at a distance of fifteen yards, Killion fired three shots in 5.9 seconds, Cunningham fired three shots in approximately 7 seconds, and Frazier fired three shots in 6 seconds. The second test was performed at twenty-five yards. The three shots were fired in 5.9 seconds, 6.2 seconds, and 5.6 seconds. In both tests, the shots were striking the target high and to the right of the aimed point on the target. This was determined to be due to the scope, which could not be properly sighted or stabilized. Frazier also testified a moving target would add approximately one second to the firing time (3H390, 403-405, 407).

The Warren Commission assembled expert shooters who were all rated as Master by the National Rifle Association. Experiments by those marksmen were provided to the Warren Commission in testimony by Ronald Simmons, Chief of the Infantry Weapons Evaluation Branch of the Ballistics Research Laboratory of the Department of the Army. In the tests, three targets were set up at 175, 240, and 365 feet from a 30-foot high tower and the shooters attempted to hit the three targets within as short a time interval as possible. Each shooter fired two series of three shots using a scope-mounted rifle. Shooter Hendrix fired at 8.25 and 7.0 seconds, Staley fired at 6.75 and 6.45 seconds, and Miller fired in 4.6 and 5.15 seconds. In the first experiment in the series, all three men hit the first and third targets, but missed the second target. Results varied on the next series, although in all cases but one, at least two targets were hit. In only two instances during the experiment were the Master rated experts able to fire three aimed shots in less than 5.6 seconds (3H441-446).

FBI marksmen, who test-fired the rifle for the Warren Commission, concluded the minimum time for getting off two successive, well-aimed shots was approximately 2 .25 seconds or 41 to 42 Zapruder Frames. The Zapruder film shows Kennedy waving to the crowd in frame 205 of the Zapruder film as he disappears behind the Stemmons Freeway sign. When he emerged from behind the sign at frames 225-226, Kennedy appeared to be reacting to a gunshot injury. The earliest Connally appears to react to being injured is Frame 235. Given the earliest possible frame at which Kennedy could have been struck, (Frame 210 according to the reenactment), and the minimum 42 frames (2.3 seconds) required between shots, Connally reacting at Frame 225 is insufficient time for separate bullets to be fired from a rifle. However, assuming a delay in the reaction of Connally is also problematic (5H153, 154).

Prior to providing testimony to the Warren Commission, one of Connally's treating physicians, Robert Shaw had opportunity to review the Zapruder film and slides made from frames of the Zapruder film. In Shaw's April 21,

1964 Warren Commission testimony, he described Connally complaining bitterly of difficulty in breathing, and of pain in his right chest. Shaw was also asked if he could identify the Zapruder Frame in which the Governor was injured. Shaw responded he believed Frame 236 through 237 indicated Connally was reacting to a gunshot wound to the chest. Shaw was then asked if there could have been a delayed reaction by Connally. Shaw responded, "Yes; but in the case of a wound which strikes a bony substance, such as a rib, usually the reaction is quite prompt." In other words, Shaw felt Connally reacted immediately (4H103, 114, 115).

Concerning the sequence of injuries to Kennedy and Connally, timing was also considered by the House Select Committee on Assassinations. For photographic evaluation of the film evidence, the House Select Committee on Assassinations assembled a photographic panel of photography scientists who served either as contractors or as members. Calvin McCamy was a member of the panel. McCamy was chair of the American National Standards' Working Group on Print Quality for Optical Character Recognition, chair of the American Society of Photogrammetry Standards Committee, and adviser to the U.S. delegation to the International Organization for Standardization Committee on Photography. His testimony was clear in outlining the directives of the Photographic Panel. The panel used other analytical photogrammetry methods to place the limousine in Dealey Plaza (HSCA 2:141-143, 149-150).

> *MCCAMY: Our first purpose was to ascertain from the photographic evidence, if possible, the first signs that the President or Governor Connally were in distress. The second objective was to ascertain from the photographic evidence, if possible, whether or not the President and the Governor were in positions in the limousine that would be consistent with the single bullet theory (HSCA 2:143).*

McCamy's testimony indicated twelve of seventeen HSCA Photographic Panel members agreed President Kennedy first showed signs of injury prior to Zapruder Frame 207. This meant Kennedy was shot before being obscured from Zapruder's view by the Stemmons Freeway sign. Eleven of fourteen panel members agreed Connally first showed distress at Frame 226, which is immediately after he came from behind the freeway sign. The positions of

Kennedy and Connally were examined just prior to the time the limousine went behind the sign. Fifteen of sixteen panel members agreed the men were in positions consistent with the Single Bullet Theory (HSCA 2:143).

McCamy attested a portion of the rear seat of the limousine was observed between Kennedy and Connally at Frame 193. The panel concluded, at this point, Connally was well inside the automobile and Kennedy seated adjacent to the edge of the limousine. The panel determined their position was maintained until Frame 193, when a projectile entered the President's back, exited through his neck, and then travelled downward to cause all Connally's wounds (HSCA 2:146).

The HSCA Photographic Panel believed Connally reacted to hearing a gunshot at a point that coordinated with Zapruder Frame 166 or 167. The panel believed the second shot struck Kennedy and Connally at Frame 207. Their conclusions placed the first two shots within forty frames. However, the FBI marksmen, who test-fired the rifle for the Warren Commission, concluded that the minimum time for getting off two successive, well-aimed shots on the rifle is approximately two and a quarter seconds or 41 to 42 Zapruder Frames. The findings of the House Select Committee on Assassinations Photographic Panel conflict with the physical time restraints of actually firing the weapon (HSCA 2:151, 5H153, 154).

Could Oswald have fired the shots within the allotted time with any degree of accuracy? The Marine Corps asserts the reasonable application of shooting instructions provided to a Marine should translate to at least a marksman certification and perhaps the next step up as sharpshooter, and then expert. Consequently, a low marksman qualification indicates a rather poor aptitude for shooting and a sharpshooter qualification indicates a fairly good ability. Oswald's last qualification was as sharpshooter. The faster firing sequences were completed by men with Master certifications by the National Rifle Association. When asked if a Master certification by the National Rifle Association was a grade higher than sharpshooter in the Army, Simmons replied, "There really is no comparison" (19H16-18; 3H449).

TIMING CONCLUSION

The Zapruder film established timing of the shootings by coordinating individual frames with the speed of the recording. The FBI reenactment proved Zapruder Frame 210 was the earliest frame that could represent the shot entering Kennedy's back. The HSCA panel determined the shot was at Frame 207. Unfortunately, at Frame 207, the FBI reenactment proved the victims were not in the field of view. The FBI claims the minimum firing time for the murder weapon was 2.3 seconds or forty-two film frames, yet the HSCA Photographic Panel concluded both Kennedy and Connally were hit in a forty-frame time span. The FBI had no motive to make the minimum time needed to fire two successive shots from the Mannlicher Carcano as short as possible, therefore the 2.3 seconds between shots is likely correct and it coordinated with the visual determinations of the shooting sequence.

DECEPTION OR DELUSIONS

Connally was certain he had been struck by a bullet separate from the one striking Kennedy, as was Mrs. Connally. The Warren Commission determined Kennedy reacted immediately to a bullet which went through his neck without hitting bone, yet decided Connally did not react immediately to the same bullet penetrating his chest, smashing a rib, shattering his wrist and puncturing his thigh. Choosing to believe Governor and Mrs. Connally could have been mistaken concerning what shot struck the Governor, and believing Connally could have had such a dramatically belated reaction, revealed the Warren Commission's philosophy concerning the assassination. Regardless of the available evidence, the Warren Commission maintained a single assassin firing from the sixth-floor window of the Texas School Book Depository fired all the shots.

JIM TAGUE

Clyde A. Haygood was a solo motorcycle officer for the Dallas Police Department on the day of the assassination. In his April 9, 1964 Warren Commission testimony, Haygood said he was approached by a man, shortly after the shooting, with a shallow cut on his upper right cheek, just to the right of his nose. The man was James Thomas Tague (6H298-299).

Tague was traveling into Dealey Plaza on Commerce Street when traffic was stopped due to the Presidential Motorcade. The car was parked halfway out from underneath the underpass when Tague exited his vehicle and stood by the bridge abutment (3H 552).

> *TAGUE: And I says, "Well, you know now, I recall something sting me on the face while I was standing down there." And he looked up and he said, "Yes; you have blood there on your cheek." And I reached up and there was a couple of drops of blood. And he said, "Where were you standing?" And I says, "Right down here." We walked 15 feet away when this deputy sheriff said, "Look here on the curb." There was a mark quite obviously that was a bullet, and it was very fresh (3H 552).*

Two photographers recorded a mark on the curb twenty-one feet, eleven and one half inches east of the Triple Underpass, James Underwood, a newsman for MD-TV Dallas, and Tom Dillard of *The Dallas Morning News*. Underwood and Dillard each stated it was definitely a mark and not a nick in the curb. Both men also emphasized the concrete was not broken and the mark appeared to have possibly been made recently (Hoover, 1964).

Incredibly, the FBI did not reference Tague's cut or the curb mark in its five-volume report to the Warren Commission on the assassination. In July 1964, the Warren Commission requested additional information concerning the mark on the curb. Included with the request was a photograph of the curb made by Tom Dillard of *The Dallas Morning News,* which had been forwarded to the President's Commission by Martha Joe Stroud, Assistant United States Attorney, Dallas, Texas. The response from the FBI to the Warren Commission was dated July 15, 1964. The report specified two unnamed Special Agents of the FBI, accompanied by Tom C. Dillard, a Photographer for The *Dallas Morning News*, and James Underwood, a Newsman for KRLD-TV, searched the area, but were unable to locate any mark on the curb. The report then suggested rain or perhaps street sweepers had erased the mark (21H472-474).

The Warren Commission ultimately sent investigators to Dallas. Predictably, they had no trouble finding the mark on the curb. The piece of curbing containing the mark was eventually removed on August 5, 1964. The mark was determined to contain metal smears and, spectrographically determined to be lead with a trace of antimony. The lead could have originated from the lead core of a Mannlicher Carcano cartridge. It was also determined, from a microscopic study, the lead object striking the curb was moving in a general direction away from the Texas School Book Depository Building (21H 475-476).

On August 5, 1964, a piece of curbing was removed from the south side of Main Street twenty-three feet four inches from the abutment of the Triple Underpass. The curbing, designated as item C321 by the laboratory, was analyzed and spectrographically found to have traces of lead, but no copper. The absence of copper prohibits the possibility the mark on the curbing section was made by a full metal-jacketed bullet. This missed shot would force the issue of a fourth shot, confirming a second shooter, or all injuries to Kennedy and Connally would have to be explained with two bullets (Hoover, 1964).

THE BEGINNING OF DECEPTION

In the January 27, 1964, Warren Commission Executive Session, General Counsel J. Lee Rankin introduced a serious inconsistency with the medical evidence. The autopsy face sheet depicted the back wound entrance lower than the throat wound exit. The Zapruder film showed Kennedy sitting upright in his seat when first hit in the back, with the bullet believed to have come from sharply upwards of the President, and specifically from the sixth floor of the School Book Depository. The location of Kennedy's back wound—as measured by the shirt and jacket holes, medical witnesses, autopsy photos, and other evidence—is too low for a shot fired from the sixth floor of the TSBD to exit at the neck wound. Rankin told the Commission he would be seeking help from the doctors concerning the problematic trajectory inconsistency (WCEX 0127:193-194).

THE RYDBERG ILLUSTRATIONS

On the evening of the assassination, during the autopsy of President Kennedy, pathologist Boswell designated the location of the President's wound on the printed outline of a body, on the autopsy face sheet. The back wound dimensions were noted as seven by four millimeters, and located 14 centimeters below the tip of the right Mastoid Process. In March 1964, Humes learned he was to testify before the Warren Commission without the use of autopsy photographs or X-Rays. Humes contacted a medical illustrator to provide drawings for his use. Harold Alfred "Skip" Rydberg completed the schematic drawings of Kennedy's head and upper back wounds known as Warren Commission Exhibits 385, 386 and 388. Rydberg had no access to photographs or X-Rays and produced the drawings completely from verbal descriptions given to him by Humes and Boswell. Commission Exhibit 385 depicts the rear wound as high on the neck, at a position above the alleged exit wound in the throat. Humes likely used the highest possible location for the entry wound he felt would be accepted as coordinated with the well-observed location of the exit wound deformed by the tracheotomy incision (16H977; 16H984). Figure 40 illustrates Commission Exhibits 385 and 386.

Special Agent Francis O'Neill, Jr. contended the trajectory angle determined by Humes in the Rydberg drawing during autopsy was bogus. He insisted the entry wound on the President's back was well below the shoulder. O'Neill made the following statements in an affidavit provided to the House Select Committee on Assassinations.

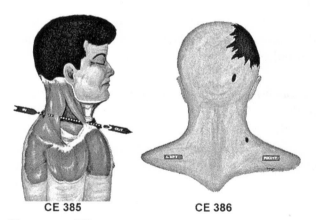

CE 385   CE 386

(**FIGURE 40**) Humes uses Rydberg Drawing to Locate Neck Wound

The medical illustrator that the Commission employed did not accurately depict the President's wounds. I do not see how the bullet that entered below the shoulder in the back could have come out the front of the throat. During the interview on January 10, 1975, I disagreed

with Dr. Boswell's depiction of the location of the back (thorax) wound that Dr. Boswell had drawn on a diagram during an interview with this Committee in the fall of 1977. I heard Humes say that the bullets entered from a 45-60° angle. Pierre Finck seemed to be more attuned to the angle of the bullets that entered JFK's body. I do not recall anything about the tracheotomy incision that indicated a bullet had damaged the area. When shown a tracing of the tracheotomy during the HSCA interview, I had no recollection or comment concerning the apparent bullet wound perimeter. It was, and is, my opinion that the bullet that entered the back came out the back.

Although I was interviewed at length by Arlen Specter, an attorney for the Warren Commission, I felt it was odd that I was not called upon to give oral testimony (ARRB MD47: 1-9).

Lt. Colonel Pierre A. Finck wrote a letter to Brigadier General J. M. Blumberg dated February 1, 1965, concerning his personal notes on the Kennedy autopsy. The National Museum of Health and Medicine, Armed Forces Institute of Pathology is conservator for the original document in the Otis Historical Archives, National Museum of Health and Medicine Archives. The letter included the following information:

There is another wound, in the region of the right trapezius muscle, at 140 millimeters from the right acromion and at 140 millimeters from the tip of the right Mastoid Process, (I took these measurements). The wound is oval, seven by four millimeter, and shows well demarcated edges. This wound cannot be probed with the soft probe available. There is subpleural hemorrhage in the right apical mesial region. The apex of the right lung is hemorrhagic, without laceration of the pleura. There is a recent tracheotomy wound (transversal incision) with moderate hemorrhage in the subcutaneous tissue. Thanks to a telephone call from CDR Humes to Dallas, I found out later that the surgeon in Dallas had extended the exit wound in the anterior aspect of the neck to make his tracheotomy. The tracheotomy wound was examined by the three prosecutors. None of us noticed a bullet wound along its course (Finck, 1965).

HUMES WARREN COMMISSION TESTIMONY

In March 1964, Humes was called to testify before the Warren Commission. Humes stated when he learned he was to testify before the Commission, he was unsure if the autopsy photographs would be available. To assist in making his and Boswell's testimony more understandable, Humes had medical drawings prepared under his and Dr. Boswell's supervision. He stressed the drawings were made without the benefit of autopsy photographs or X-Rays, and suggested the photographs were the best and most accurate evidence. Humes emphasized the drawings were lacking scale and bony references stating "These exhibits, again, are schematic representations of what we observed at the time of examining the body of the late President" (2H348-351).

Humes located the back wound as in the low posterior neck, fourteen centimeters from the tip of the Mastoid Process, and fourteen centimeters from the acromion at its central point. Humes expanded on his procedures by asserting the pathologists present were unable to probe a definite path through the tissue (2H361).

> *Examined carefully the bony structures in this vicinity, as well as the X-Rays, to see if there was any evidence of fracture or of deposition of metallic fragments in the depths of this wound, and we saw no such evidence, that is, no fracture of the bones of the shoulder girdle, or of the vertical column, and no metallic fragments were detectable by X-Ray examination. Attempts to probe in the vicinity of this wound were unsuccessful without fear of making a false passage (2H361).*

EISENBERG MEMORANDUM

Following the April 1964 Warren Commission meetings to examine the Zapruder film and determine which frames portrayed the times at which the bullets struck Kennedy and Connally, Melvin A. Eisenberg wrote a memorandum on April 22, 1964 addressing the condition of the bullet recovered from Parkland Hospital. Eisenberg questioned the ability of the projectile recovered at Parkland Hospital to have maintained its condition and still have penetrated Connally's wrist.

> *The velocity of the first bullet would have been little diminished by its passage through the President. Therefore, if Governor Connally was in*

the path of the bullet, it would have struck him and (probably) caused the wounds he sustained in his chest cavity. Strong indications that this occurred are provided by the facts that (1) the bullet recovered from Governor Connally's stretcher does not appear to have penetrated a wrist and (2) if the first bullet did not hit Governor Connally, it should have ripped up the car, but apparently did not. Since the bullet recovered from the Governor's stretcher does not appear to have penetrated a wrist, if he was hit by this (the first) bullet, he was probably also hit by the second bullet.

In a discussion after the conference, Drs. Light and Dolce expressed themselves as being very strongly of the opinion that Connally had been hit by two different bullets, principally on the ground that the bullet recovered from Connally's stretcher could not have broken his radius without having suffered more distortion. Dr. Oliver withheld a conclusion until he has had the opportunity to make tests on animal tissue and bone with the actual rifle (Eisenberg, 1964).

THE REDLICH MEMO
Regardless, the Warren Commission Report, partly based on the FBI shooting reconstruction, determined President Kennedy's wounds were as follows:

"The nature of the bullet wounds suffered by President Kennedy and the location of the car at the time of the shots establish that the bullets were fired from above and behind the Presidential limousine, striking the President as follows: President Kennedy was first struck by a bullet which entered at the back of his neck and exited through the lower front portion of his neck, causing a wound which would not necessarily have been lethal. The President was struck a second time by a bullet which entered the right, rear portion of his head, causing a massive and fatal wound" (WCR:19).

Although, the methods utilized during the shooting reconstruction were unorthodox, some clarity may be found when scrutinizing the reasoning behind the reenactment. The April 27, 1964 ominous memo by Norman Redlich to J. Lee Rankin, suggested the Warren Commission was seeking evidence to support their preconceived conclusions concerning the timing and number of shots (Redlich, 1964).

The purpose of this memorandum is to explain the reasons why certain members of the staff feel that it is important to take certain on-site photographs in connection with the location of the approximate points at which the three bullets struck the occupants of the Presidential limousine.

Our report presumably will state that the President was hit by the first bullet, Governor Connally by the second, and the President by the third and fatal bullet. The report will also conclude that the bullets were fired by one person located in the sixth floor, southeast corner window of the TSBD building.

As our investigation now stands, however, we have not shown that these events could possibly have occurred in the manner suggested above. All we have is a reasonable hypothesis, which appears to be supported by the medical testimony, but which has not been checked out against the physical facts at the scene of the assassination.

Our examination of the Zapruder films shows that the fatal third shot struck the President at a point which we can locate with reasonable accuracy on the ground. We can do this because we know the exact frame (no. 313) in the film at which the third shot hit the President and we know the location of the photographer. By lining up fixed objects in the movie fram [sic] where this shot occurs, we feel that we have determined the approximate location of this shot. This can be verified by a photo of the same spot from the point where Zapruder was standing.

We have the testimony of Governor and Mrs. Connally that the Governor was hit with the second bullet at a point which we probably cannot fix with precision. We feel we have established, however, with the help of medical testimony, that the shot which hit the Governor did not come after frame 240 on the Zapruder film. The Governor feels that it came around [frame] 230, which is certainly consistent with our observations of the film and with the doctor's testimony. Since the

President was shot at frame 313, this would leave a time of at least four seconds between two shots, certainly ample for even an inexperienced marksman.

Prior to our last viewing of the films with Governor Connally, we had assumed that the President was hit while he was concealed behind the sign which occurs between frames 215 to 225. We have expert testimony to the effect that a skilled marksman would require a minimum of time of 2 1/4 seconds between shots with this rifle. Since the camera operates at 18 1/3 frames per second, there would have to be a minimum of 40 frames between shots. It is apparent therefore, that if Governor Connally was hit even as late as frame 240, the President would have to have been hit no later than frame 190 and probably even earlier.

We have not yet examined the assassination scene to determine whether the assassin in fact could have shot the President prior to frame 190. We could locate the position on the ground which corresponds to this frame and it would then be our intent to establish by photography that the assassin could have fired the first shot at the President prior to this point. Our intention is not to establish the point with complete accuracy, but merely to substantiate the hypothesis which underlies the conclusions that Oswald was the sole assassin.

I had always assumed that our final report would be accompanied by a surveyor's diagram, which would indicate the appropriate location of the three shots. We certainly cannot prepare such a diagram without establishing that we are describing an occurrence which is physically possible. Our failure to do this will, in my opinion, place this Report in jeopardy, since it is a certainty that others will examine the Zapruder films and raise the same questions which have been raised by our examination of the films. If we do not attempt to answer these questions with observable facts, others may answer them with facts which challenge our most basic assumptions, or with fanciful theories based on our unwillingness to test our assumptions by the investigatory methods available to us.

I should add that the facts which we now have in our possession, submitted to us in separate reports from the FBI and Secret Service, are totally incorrect and, if left uncorrected, will present a completely misleading picture.

It may well be that this project should be undertaken by the FBI and Secret Service with our assistance instead of being done as a staff project. The important thing is that the project be undertaken expeditiously (Redlich, 1964).

The memo made it abundantly clear the truth concerning the shooting of President Kennedy and Governor Connally was not the paramount goal of the Warren Commission. They simply sought to validate a preconceived conclusion identifying Oswald as the sole assassin. Stating, "The important thing is that the project be undertaken expeditiously" and not "revealing what really happened" exposed the true nature of the Warren Commission agenda (Redlich, 1964).

PATHOLOGIST PHOTOGRAPHIC REVIEW

In November 1966, pursuant to a request by the Department of Justice, Humes and Boswell had an opportunity to review, examine, identify, and inventory the photographs the autopsy photographs for the first time at the National Archives. In January 1967, Humes, Boswell, and Finck examined the autopsy photographs together. The results, published in ARRB MD 14, verified the locations of the wounds as stated in the autopsy report, Warren Commission Exhibit 397. They addressed the low marking of the back wound on the face sheet by stating the drawing was misleading as to the location of the wound, making it appear at a point lower than it was actually located. The report specifically stated the location of the wound was 14 centimeters (5.5 inches) from the tip of the Mastoid Process (behind the right ear) and 14 centimeters from the tip of the right acromion (the extreme tip of the right shoulder bone). They conceded no one photograph illustrated both the wound at the back of the neck and the wound in the throat; but by comparing photographs, they concluded the wound in the back of the neck is higher from the horizontal plane than the wound in the throat (7H45; Humes, 1967).

HOUSE SELECT COMMITTEE ON ASSASSINATIONS FORENSIC PANEL

The House Select Committee on Assassinations Forensic Panel was instructed within the appointing letter of August 8, 1977 to complete precise tasks:

1. To determine whether there are fundamental conclusions within the field of forensic pathology on which all or most of the consultants can agree.
2. To write a report containing descriptions and interpretations of the medical evidence and detailed explanations supporting any conclusions.
3. To compile recommendations regarding those matters deemed to be outside the expertise of forensic pathologists.
4. To conduct a detailed, objective critique of the professional manner in which the autopsy on President Kennedy was conducted (HSCA 17:75).

Concerning the back and throat wounds, The House Select Committee on Assassination's Forensic Panel determined there was no photographic evidence indicating the internal injuries described by the pathologists. Norman Chase, M.D., professor and chairman of the Department of Radiology of New York University School of Medicine-Bellevue Hospital Medical Center, examined the X-Rays and their computer assisted enhancements. He noted the presence of a metal fragment, or artifact in the area of the transverse process was definitely not a bone fragment. William B. Seaman, M.D., professor and Chairman of Radiology of Columbia Presbyterian Hospital and Physicians and Surgeons Medical School in New York City, concurred with the assessment. Testimony of Humes revealed he did not consider a dissection of the throat to confirm a bullet path (HSCA 17:98-102).

THE CLARK PANEL

At the invitation of Ramsey Clark, Attorney General of the United States, four physicians met in Washington, D.C. on February 26 and 27, 1968 to examine photographs, X-Rays, films, documents and other evidence pertaining to the death of President Kennedy. The group of physicians, commonly referred to as the Clark Panel, was mandated to evaluate the evidence in relation to the medical conclusions chronicled in the President John Kennedy's Autopsy Report and Supplemental Autopsy Report.

The four physicians constituting the Clark Panel were:

1. Carnes, William H., MD, Professor of Pathology, University of Utah, Salt Lake City, UT, Member of Medical Examiner's Commission, State of Utah, nominated by Dr. J. E. Wallace Sterling, President of Stanford University.

2. Fisher, Russell S., MD, Professor of Forensic Pathology, University of Maryland and Chief Medical Examiner of the State of Maryland, Baltimore, MD, nominated by Dr. Oscar B. Hunter, Jr., President of the College of American Pathologists.

3. Morgan, Russell H., MD, Professor of Radiology, School of Medicine and Professor of Radiological Sciences, School of Hygiene and Public Health, The Johns Hopkins University, Baltimore, MD, nominated by Dr. Lincoln Gordon, President of The Johns Hopkins University.

4. Mortiz, Alan R., MD, Professor of Pathology, Case Western Reserve University, Cleveland, OH and former Professor of Forensic Medicine, Harvard University, nominated by Dr. John A. Hannah, President of Michigan State University (Carnes, 1968).

The panel findings included an elliptical penetrating wound of the back located approximately 15 centimeters medial to the right acromial process, five centimeters lateral to the mid-dorsal line, and fourteen centimeters below the right Mastoid Process. This wound was approximately 5.5 centimeters below a transverse fold in the skin of the neck. This fold can also be seen in a lateral view of the neck, which showed an anterior tracheotomy wound. This view makes it possible to compare the levels of the two wounds in relation to the horizontal plane of the body. The wound, including marginal abrasion, measures approximately seven millimeters in width and ten millimeters in length (Carnes, 1968).

A well-defined zone of discoloration of the edge of the back wound, most pronounced on its upper and outer margins, identified it as having the characteristics of an entrance wound of a bullet. The dimensions of this cutaneous wound are consistent with those of a wound produced by a bullet similar to exhibit CE 399. At the site of, and above the tracheotomy incision in the front of the neck, there can be identified the upper half of the circumference of a circular cutaneous wound the appearance of which is characteristic of an exit wound of a bullet. The lower half of this circular wound is obscured by the surgically produced tracheotomy incision that transected it. The center of the circular wound is situated approximately nine centimeters below the transverse fold in the skin of the neck as described in a preceding paragraph. This indicated the bullet that produced the two wounds followed the course downward and to the left in its passage through the body. Films eight, nine, and ten allowed visualization of the lower neck. Subcutaneous emphysema is present just to the right of the cervical spine immediately above the apex of the right lung. Also, several small, metallic fragments are present in this region. There is no evidence of a fracture of either scapula or of the clavicles, or of the ribs, or of any of the cervical and thoracic vertebrae. The foregoing observations indicated the pathway of the projectile involving the neck was confined to a region to the right of the spine and superior to a plane passing through the upper margin of the right scapula, the apex of the right lung and the right clavicle. Any other pathway would have almost certainly fractured one or more bones of the right shoulder girdle and thorax (Carnes, 1968).

ROBERT B. LIVINGSTONE

In April 1992, Doctor Charles A. Crenshaw, J. Gary Shaw, and Jen Hansen published *JFK: Conspiracy of Silence*, later released as *Trauma Room One: The JFK Medical Coverup Exposed*. The book states President Kennedy was shot twice from the front; resulting in an entry wound to his throat, and a fatal shot to his head. In May 1992, the editor of the *Journal of the American Medical Association* (JAMA) published an article personally and professionally defaming Crenshaw. As a result, a civil suit was filed as Charles Crenshaw, M.D. and Gary Shaw v. Lawrence Sutherland, et al in the 18th Judicial District Court of Johnson County, Texas, Cause No. 73-93. The suit was settled in October 1994, but not before depositions were taken (Crenshaw, 2001).

The Assassination Records Review Board Medical Exhibits contains the November 19, 1993 testimony given in deposition by Dr. Robert B. Livingston in connection with the Crenshaw, et al v. Sutherland civil suit. When Livingston was deposed, he was a retired professor of Neurosciences at the University of California in San Diego. In 1963, Livingstone was Scientific Director for the National Institute of Health and the National

Library of Medicine in Washington DC. He was in the process of forming the National Institute of Neurological Diseases and Blindness, and was certified to the Bureau of Narcotics and the United Nations for the identification of narcotic addicting drugs. Livingston attested he heard radio reports quoting physicians Perry, Crenshaw and Clark describing the throat wound as a clean round hole of entry. Having extensive experience with projectile wounding, and considering the physician's descriptions and his extensive experience, Livingston believed the throat wound to be one of entry (Livingston, 1993).

Before the President's body was received at Bethesda Hospital, Livingston telephoned and spoke with Humes. Humes related to Livingston he had not heard much news from Parkland concerning the President's wounds. Livingstone attests he told Humes the reason he was making the call was to stress the Parkland Hospital physicians' examination revealed a small wound to the neck, adjacent to and to the right of the trachea. He also specifically discussed with Humes the need to dissect the wound. Livingstone stated the conversation was abruptly concluded when Humes said the FBI would not allow him to continue (Livingstone, 1993).

CUSTER ARRB DEPOSITION
The Assassinations Records Review Board deposed Jerrol Francis Custer on October 28, 1997. Custer was the X-Ray technician on call at Bethesda Hospital on the night of the Kennedy autopsy. Custer testified he took X-Rays of Kennedy during the autopsy, stating Ebersole had no technical part in taking the autopsy X-Rays. Custer indicated Edward E. Reed, Jr. assisted him in taking and developing the autopsy X-Rays. Custer testified, concerning the back wound designations, he took five or six exposures of the neck. He also attested to seeing a bullet fragment (Custer, 1997).

> *When I lifted the body up to take films of the torso, and the lumbar spine, and the pelvis, this is when a king-size fragment —I'd say—I estimate around three, four sonometers—fell from the back. And this is when Dr. Finck come over with a pair of forceps, picked it up, and took —That's the last time I ever saw it. Now, it was big enough—That's about, I'd say an inch and a half. My finger—my small finger. First joint. That's when I picked him up, and the bullet dropped out of there. There was a small wound (Custer, 1997, p. 54, 90).*

Gunn questioned Custer concerning X-Rays of the area.

> *GUNN: Are you certain you took X-Rays that included the—included C3 and C4?*
>
> *CUSTER: Yes, sir. Absolutely.*
>
> *GUNN: How many X-Rays did you take that would have included that?*
>
> *CUSTER: Just one. And that was all that was necessary, because it showed - right there.*
>
> *GUNN: And what, as best you recall, did it show?*
>
> *CUSTER: A fragmentation of a shell in and around that circular exit—that area. Let me rephrase that. I don't want to say "exit", because I don't know if it was an exit or entrance. But all I can say, there were bullet fragmentations all around that area - that opening.*
>
> *GUNN: Around C3/C4?*
>
> *CUSTER: Right.*
>
> *GUNN: And do you recall how many fragments there were?*
>
> *CUSTER: Not really. There was enough. It was very prevalent.*
>
> *GUNN: Did anyone make any observations about metal fragments in the C3/C4 area?*
>
> *CUSTER: I did. And I was told to mind my own business (Custer, 1997, p. 168-169).*

Custer testified three X-Rays taken that night by him were not a part of the official autopsy record: the two tangential views, and the AP cervical spirit.

Custer stated it was his opinion the X-Rays were not included because they showed massive amounts of bullet fragments. When asked if he had ever heard of anyone destroying X-Ray material, Custer stated he overheard a conversation between Ebersole and Loy Brown, Head of the Radiology Department. Ebersole was telling Brown certain pertinent things were taken care of (Custer, 1997).

CONCLUSIONS

The Warren Commission Report states,

> *The alignment of the points of entry was only indicative and not conclusive that one bullet hit both men. The exact positions of the men could not be re-created; thus, the angle could only be approximated. Had President Kennedy been leaning forward or backward, the angle of declination of the shot to a perpendicular target would have varied. The angle of 17°43'30" was approximately the angle of declination reproduced in an artist's drawing. That drawing, made from data provided by the autopsy surgeons, could not reproduce the exact line of the bullet, since the exit wound was obliterated by the tracheotomy. Similarly, if the President or the Governor had been sitting in a different lateral position, the conclusion might have varied. Or if the Governor had not turned in exactly the way calculated, the alignment would have been destroyed (WR: 107).*

The Single Bullet Theory is a manufactured resolution of problems stemming from a biased investigation that obviously attempted to manipulate the findings supporting a single shooter. By its own admission, the Warren Commission did not demonstrate a trajectory that proves the Single Bullet Theory correct; yet, the Single Bullet Theory hinges on trajectory. Computed projectile trajectories from wound measurements and clothing defects, and the FBI and HSCA reconstructed trajectory are wildly varied.

- Humes at the autopsy estimated Kennedy's rear wound trajectory at 40° to 60°
- The HSCA Forensic Panel indicates Kennedy's throat trajectory is 0°
- The FBI reenactment estimated the trajectory to Kennedy at 17°

- Rear wound measurements at autopsy indicate a trajectory of 34.84°
- The defects in the rear of Kennedy's clothing indicate a trajectory of 41° to 42°
- Connally's wounds indicate a trajectory of 22°
- HSCA trajectory with regards to Kennedy is computed by extending the Connally trajectory
- HSCA found two separate right to left trajectories for Kennedy and Connally
- HSCA trajectory through Kennedy is 0° in one graphic and 20° in another

Other considerations speak to the Single Bullet Theory. The chain of custody of the bullet is highly suspect. The pristine condition of the bullet is questionable, since a similar bullet supposedly fragmented in Kennedy's head. The bullet velocity generated severe damage to Connally's radial bone, yet suddenly lost sufficient velocity to remain embedded in Connally's thigh. The Warren Commission Report and autopsy report stated Kennedy's back wound measured approximately seven millimeters by four millimeters. Mysteriously, that wound became a 0.9-centimeter or nine-millimeter round wound. The rear wound in Kennedy alone has enough contradictions to hamper belief in the Single Bullet Theory. Combined with the other variants, the trajectory becomes a guess at best.

When scientific methods prove a theory true, it becomes a fact. When scientific methods prove a theory false, it becomes a myth. Myths have no place in the historical record and should be abandoned. Instead, single shooter devotees, regardless of the evidence, incongruously and resolutely support the Single Bullet Theory. One thing is certain: if the Single Bullet Theory is correct, the trajectory of the bullet is a single, straight line originating at the muzzle of the weapon terminating in the entry wound in Connally's back. That trajectory should be reproducible and supported by evidence, but it is not reproducible and is not supported by medical evidence. The possibility of aligning the muzzle of a weapon in the Texas School Book Depository sixth floor window with the two wounds in Kennedy and the back wound in Connally has not been proven, because it is impossible. Because it is impossible, the Single Bullet Theory remains a myth.

THE WITNESSES

The great majority of people in the world are merely spectators to the events of history. Although events can deeply influence us emotionally, and even be considered life changing, we are still the outsiders looking in. However, occasionally ordinary people find extraordinary roles in history thrust upon them. They move from being observers of history into the role of participants in history, albeit reluctantly.

Standing in Dealey Plaza on November 22, 1963, a group of men and women observed the shooting death of President John F. Kennedy. I have been privileged to share some time with a few of those people in the writing of this book. People, who throughout the research community have become known simply as *The Witnesses*.

MARINA OSWALD

I do not know how many people have sat in Marina Oswald's living room and discussed the Zapruder film with her; I'm guessing there haven't been many, however, unbelievably, I have. The day began with my sister Debra Conway driving me to Marina's home in Texas in 1995. I remember Marina's long driveway led to a modest, ranch style house with a hodgepodge of plants scattered about the yard. Marina stepped out of the kitchen door, greeting us with her infamous cigarette in hand. I could see she was nervous, and perhaps apprehensive concerning the topic of the scheduled conversation. Debra and Marina greeted each other warmly, and exchanged small talk for a second or two before Debra introduced me. It gave me a moment to observe Marina unobtrusively. She was thin and, although she moved gracefully, not especially feminine. Marina's facial features were stern, however, her piercing blue eyes were captivating. She was casually dressed in slacks, flats and a simple shirt; her hair was pinned up and she wore no makeup. She held a pack of cigarettes and a lighter in her hand, although she was already smoking. I soon learned why. As soon as the cigarette she drew deeply on was completed, she lit another, pushing the spent butt into the ground with the toe of her shoe. We stood in the yard for five minutes or so with Debra and Marina making small talk before being welcomed through the kitchen door into her home.

As she and Debra continued their conversation at the kitchen table, Marina would occasionally give me a quick glance, although I had said little more than hello since arriving. When a break in the conversation occurred, I mentioned I loved the homey, eclectic look of her kitchen, commenting I preferred decorating that reflected the life and personality of the occupants, as opposed to an "out of a magazine" contrived look. Her face suddenly became animated with a smile—the first I had seen. She asked if I wanted to tour the house and, of course, I accepted. We walked about the house as she pointed out the history behind favorite mementoes, photographs, and furniture. The house was modest and clean, not finished in a particularly sophisticated decor, but with a comfortable lived-in feeling. I admired her children's photographs and the homemade gifts offered during their childhood. There were also some antique possessions and items from Russia that I liked and she talked warmly and in detail about them, indicating she clearly honored and respected her heritage.

We returned to sit around the kitchen table like most southern women do, sans the normal hospitality of offering coffee or tea. I remember Debra asking her some questions about Lee, in particular questions about the backyard photographs. She responded saying she definitely remembered taking the photographs and spoke about the incident briefly. As the subject matter progressed into Lee Oswald's activities, I was completely lost, since I knew very little about the Kennedy assassination at that time. I kept silent and tried to affect the look of one knowledgeable of one of the most significant events in our lifetimes. I was terrified she would ask my opinion on any of the topics they were discussing, not wanting to reveal my lack of familiarity with such an historic event.

Thankfully, talk soon returned to mundane things as it became apparent she was not ready to discuss my reason for being there. Marina wanted to walk outside. It was a sunny but windy day, and we walked around the yard with her pointing out different flowers and plants that she enjoyed. Some were in various handmade or unusual containers and had a history behind them that she wanted to share. How the conversation turned to children, I do not really remember. Nevertheless, Marina began to talk about her children and the burden they had growing up with Lee Harvey Oswald as their father. She stressed that she had always tried to protect them and provide them with the home that was as normal as possible. This was the first time during the day's conversation that Marina had revealed personal emotions and given us insight into her life. It was obvious she loved her children and cherished their family life; it was also apparent that it had been a continual struggle to protect them from the backlash of people who hated Lee Harvey Oswald.

Suddenly, Marina's demeanor changed as she realized she had become vulnerable by exposing information so personal. Sensitive to the situation, Debra quickly changed the subject, indicating she was hungry, and suggested going into town for lunch. Marina indicated she thought that was a great idea and would like to stop at a store. So after gathering our things, we left in Debra's car and drove to a small restaurant Marina said she liked.

Marina obviously went to the restaurant frequently as she was greeted warmly and by name. We sat in a booth, Debra and I on one side and Marina on the other. Since Marina and Debra had an established relationship, most of the conversation centered between them, with the majority of the conversation about mundane things that were just meant to pass the time. Occasionally they would talk about some detail of the assassination. Again, I was unable to participate, because I was not familiar with many of the subjects they discussed. So much of my time was spent just watching Marina.

When conversation topics centered on Texas weather, flowers or food, I noticed her relaxed posture and an occasional smile. As the topic became more serious, her posture became more rigid and those blue eyes became fixed on the speaker. There is something about Marina that commands respect. When she is looking at you, you can almost feel the gaze, it is so intense. However, regardless of the topic, I was surprised at her ability to eat and smoke at the same time; she had a burning cigarette in her hand continually.

When lunch was over, we made a quick trip to a nearby grocery store for Marina to pick up a few items, before we returned to her home and the kitchen table. While in the store, Debra and I had an opportunity to speak privately. Debra was concerned that we had already spent hours with Marina without ever discussing why I was there. She told me that once we returned to the house, she was going to direct the conversation to my work reconstructing the Kennedy shooting, and in particular my findings of a shooter located in front of the President.

Back in the car, it amazed me that there were so many safe topics that could be used for small talk. No one was discussing any detail of the assassination. Once back at the house, we again settled around the kitchen table. After just a few moments, Debra stood, asking if she could have a glass of water. Debra walked over to the kitchen sink and after having a drink, leaned against the counter, and broached the subject of why I was there. Marina instantly became quiet, her clear blue eyes glued to mine. Debra continued to talk, but Marina never looked at her. I do not remember exactly what Debra was saying, but I vaguely remember her indicating I had a forensic background. I knew Debra had spoken to Marina in advance of my analysis techniques and of my findings, so I knew she had some idea of what I was going to say. After a few moments of uncomfortable silence in the room, I begin to explain my field of expertise—blood spatter interpretation and crime scene reconstruction. I focused on analysis procedures and the information it can reveal, I had yet to mention the assassination or the Zapruder film.

I stopped to allow Marina to ask any questions, but she had none. Instead, without a word, she rose from her chair and walked to a phone hanging in the hall just beyond the open kitchen door and placed what appeared to be an overseas call. Debra never moved from her position against the kitchen counter. We just looked at each other, neither of us daring to speak. Once the call was connected, Marina spoke in what I assumed was her native language, Russian. After approximately five minutes of conversation, she returned to her chair and said she had checked out this field of study and had determined it was authentic. Without any sign of embarrassment from her behavior or without any reference to or explanation of her telephone call, she announced she was ready to hear what I had to say.

I explained how this type of analysis was used on crime scenes, and how I had applied it to the Kennedy assassination. She then asked a few questions to insure she had good comprehension of what I was telling her. She is very bright and immediately grasped the significance of what I was saying. Brazenly, I said I wanted her to watch the Zapruder film with me. I think for the first time since our arrival Marina was anxious. Her hand was shaking mildly as she lit her next cigarette from the butt of the one she was smoking. She stalled, saying her VHS player was not working properly. Debra assured her all would be fine, that she was mechanically minded and could make the player work.

Debra bravely went into the living room and placed the tape we had brought with us into the tape player. As if sleepwalkers, Marina and I silently went into the other room and sat adjacent to each other on her sofa as the Zapruder film begin to play on her television. Other than the slow movement of the cigarette moving to her mouth and the escape of the blown smoke, Marina was motionless and watched the film attentively. With Debra pausing and rewinding the tape as necessary, I pointed out a few things and she asked a few questions. Then there was nothing but a deathly quiet. I felt like I was in the twilight zone. On the outside I was the professional expert explaining the details of my work, while inside my head I was screaming, "Oh, my gosh! I am in Marina Oswald's home discussing the possibility of her deceased husband firing the fatal headshot that killed President Kennedy!"

Then Marina snapped me back to the present by asking, "Did my husband kill the President?" I responded, "I don't know who killed the President. But, I do know it wasn't Lee Oswald unless he was firing from the front of the President." She continued to look at me for a second or two and then silently got up and walked into the kitchen with Debra close behind. When I finally got up and went into the kitchen, she and Debra had changed the subject to gardening. I do not remember the details of the conversation; I was still amazed that I had been so brazen and definitely less than gracious by making this woman return so vividly to a time in her life she obviously wanted so desperately to forget.

There was no more discussion of the Zapruder film, the assassination or of Lee. For the next hour, gardening, children, and Texas weather once again dominated the conversation. Debra skillfully directed the topics of conversation until it was apparent Marina was once more at ease. Then Debra said it was time for us to go and Marina walked with us to the car. She gave each of us a long hug and thanked us for coming. As Debra backed slowly out of the drive, Marina stuck her head and arm into the car window walking alongside the slowly moving car while beseeching us to stay longer. We both recognized it could not be an invitation she offered often, but it was a request impossible for us to honor at that time. As we drove away, Marina was left standing midway down the long driveway from her house watching us go. She was the first person I met that was directly associated with the Kennedy assassination. I found her a complicated, outspoken, fascinating, and intelligent woman. I liked her immensely and still wish we could have stayed longer.

BILL NEWMAN

Debra and I were in the first office JFK Lancer occupied. JFK memorabilia was mixed between the books, documents, and photographs stacked about the room. Blood spatter in the Zapruder film was the topic of our conversation. The significance of this spatter was becoming more evident; it supported a frontal shot, and established the authenticity of the Zapruder film at that portion of the film. During the conversation, I used the term mist when describing back spatter. "That is the word Bill uses when he describes what he saw", Debra said.

Bill and Gayle Newman, both just 22 years old, along with their two young sons were perhaps the closest observers to the Presidential limousine at the time of the shooting. I was familiar with photographs of the Newman family lying on the ground the day of the shooting—the parents shielding their children from possible stray bullets. Immediately after the assassination, the Newman family was driven to WFAA-TV, a Dallas television station, to be interviewed. Approximately 20 minutes after the President had been assassinated, Bill and Gayle Newman were telling their story on live television.

Bill Newman had two television interviews that day. During the interviews, Newman said he heard only two shots fired during the assassination. Both

Bill and Gayle Newman stated on live WFAA-TV that they both saw blood coming from the right side of President Kennedy's head. Gayle Newman offered graphic details in her interviews with WFAA's Jay Watson stating, "President Kennedy reached up and grabbed—looked like grabbed his ear— and blood just started gushing out." I took that to believe she was referring to the blood spray depicted in the Zapruder film, blood I knew to be back spatter.

"You know him?" I inquired. In answer, Debra took out her cell phone and simply dialed his number. After a brief dialogue, she handed the phone to me. I initiated the conversation by asking Newman to describe what he had witnessed the day of the assassination.

Newman begin by saying he, Gayle, and his young sons were on what is now called the Grassy Knoll waiting for the President to come by. The Newman family had been to Love Field to see the President and First Lady Jacqueline Kennedy as they arrived in Dallas but did not have a good view of President and Mrs. Kennedy. After leaving Love Field, they hastened to Dealey Plaza and positioned themselves near the curb on Elm Street in front of what would become known as the Grassy Knoll. Bill and Gayle were eagerly awaiting the President and Mrs. Kennedy's arrival in the motorcade. As the President's car came into sight, at a distance of about 50 feet from them, Bill Newman heard the first shot. At first, he thought it was fireworks. However, as the limousine drew closer, Newman said he could see blood on Kennedy and Texas Governor John Connally, who was also in the Presidential limousine. As the limousine came abreast of their position, an additional shot rang out. Bill Newman said he was looking directly at the President when he was hit by the fatal gunshot to the head.

I remember in the beginning of our conversation Newman's voice was clear, almost methodical in the telling of the event, as if he had said the same thing many, many times. Now, there was a little hesitation, and then he continued by saying, "The car was about 10 feet away from us when I heard the third shot and the side of his head flew off. I remember seeing the blood in front of his face."

I asked him to be as specific as possible in describing the blood. Newman said, "It was like a red mist or a cloud of blood in front of his face, and then it just disappeared." When questioned concerning the overall size of the mist, he replied "about two feet or so in diameter."

I had been writing down his statements, realizing the significance of having an eyewitness to the Kennedy assassination describe the high velocity blood spatter generated by a fatal shot to the President's head. Newman described the spatter he witnessed in the same manner blood spatter analysts describe back spatter, as a mist. Looking closely at the Zapruder Frame 313, it is readily apparent that the film depicts exactly what Bill Newman witnessed and related.

Since that time, I have had opportunities to meet Bill Newman on several occasions. He is a quiet, unassuming, but confident individual. His story has not been embellished over the years, nor does he discount the importance of what he witnessed. But, since blood spatter was likely the first scientific discipline introduced to prove a front headshot, I believe him to be one of the most important witnesses I have met. Certainly, he is the one who singularly motivated me to apply forensics to the assassination.

BOBBY HARGIS

It was January and JFK Lancer was hosting its annual educational meeting for students. Debra had lured me there by telling me Bobby Hargis would be speaking. As a police officer, I was intrigued with meeting one of the motorcycle cops assigned to President's Kennedy's motorcade and was looking forward to the event.

Hargis, his wife, and I spoke briefly before the event began. They are a charming couple, gracious and very approachable. Mrs. Hargis was obviously proud of her husband and in retrospect seemed almost protective of him. Hargis is a big guy, like many who enter the field of law enforcement. That breed of man is principled, exudes confidence and trust, Hargis was no exception. Even retired, he had that no nonsense attitude and demeanor. After a few minutes of introductory conversation, I told him my profession and asked him to describe the blood spatter from JFK's fatal headshot. He became instantly still. A solemn look filled his face and, for a moment, he was silent.

Hargis's petite wife held onto his arm as he began to tell me of that fateful day, her eyes never leaving his face. He described to me how the blood left the back of the President's head in a copious amount. He stated that as the expelled blood hung in the air, he drove into it, thereby getting blood and bits of bone and brain on his motorcycle, clothing, and person. I pressed for a more specific description of the blood leaving the President's head and he said, "It was as if a bucket of blood was thrown from the back of his head; it spread out and hung in the air for a minute."

He went on to talk about how bits of solid matter had been deposited on him and was noticed by his wife when he returned home. He talked about the confusion of the moment, and how the reality of the event did not really hit him until he went home from that day's tour of duty. Tears welled in his eyes at one point, the emotion from that day so many years ago still fresh for him.

Later, after his presentation to the students attending the educational conference, several of the adults in the audience, parent-chaperones of the attending students, asked questions. There were some thoughtless and accusatory comments made. One of them harshly asked Hargis why he did not do something to stop the President from being killed. Hargis tearfully stammered his answer. He had done all he could. Debra quickly stopped the question and answer segment and I walked to the front of the room. I wanted to yell at them, wanted to insist they put themselves in the shoes of a man who saw what they could only imagine. Instead, I just looked at the audience slowly letting my gaze travel from face to face, the night ruined, my heart broken by the few unsympathetic attitudes toward Hargis, my brother in blue.

"Have you ever been in the same room when your child hurt themselves in a fall? Why didn't you stop your child from falling?" I probed. "For that matter, why can't you stop milk from being spilled when you sit next to your child at dinner?"

Their silence was a sign of their shame. Calmer, I continued. "Wearing a uniform doesn't make you able to stop a speeding bullet. Neither Bobby Hargis nor anyone else in that motorcade could have stopped that bullet."

Softly, I asked the audience to imagine how hard it was for a person who had committed his life to the protection and service of others to have that type of incident in his past. I asked them to consider that just as our nation was altered with the murder of the President, so was the life of Bobby Hargis. It was a man who endured having JFK's blood flung onto him and it was a man who had just endured reliving it to appease their curiosity. If our nation cried out in pain for an incident they could only imagine, how much more traumatic was it for a police officer on the job to have experienced it first hand? The difference, I reminded them, was that the nation just heard about it; he lived it.

Bobby Hargis and his wife spoke very briefly with me subsequent to my addressing that now subdued and silent group. I told him I was privileged to have had an opportunity to meet him. He thanked me for my comments; I thanked him for a lifetime dedicated to others.

ROBERT FRAZIER

As I began to expand on my investigation on blood spatter analysis in the assassination, I thought a lot about Special Agent Robert Frazier. On the morning of November 23, Frazier had been directed to conduct a search of the Presidential limousine, which was stored under guard at the White House Garage. Frazier testified in the February 1969 Clay Shaw trial in Louisiana that he examined the Presidential limousine following the assassination. During his testimony, Frazier discussed what he found when the limo was searched at one o'clock a.m. on November 24, 1963. Of particular importance is his description of blood volume.

> *We found blood and tissue all over the outside areas of the vehicle from the hood ornament, over the complete area of the hood, on the outside of the windshield, also on the inside surface of the windshield, and all over the entire exterior portion of the car, that is, the side rails down both sides of the car, and of course considerable quantities inside the car and on the trunk lid area.*

This seemed to indicate Frazier believed the greater volume of blood and tissue was located inside and on the trunk of the vehicle. A large volume of the blood and tissue inside the vehicle is documented in photographs; yet, no photographs of the blood located on the vehicle exterior have been published.

I wanted to determine exactly what he meant by "considerable quantities" on the trunk. I spoke with Mr. Frazier over the telephone in January 2002. I found him cordial, a little guarded, and very astute. I explained that I wanted clarification on something in his testimony that touched on my field of expertise. I then read the statement to him and asked what his rationale was concerning that phrase. He did not reply immediately, so there was a moment of silence on the telephone. I did not press, just allowed him to think for a moment about what he wanted to say. Then he slowly replied.

> *It has been 30 years since that happened, and I may have made a contemporaneous statement then with more detail. I just do not remember all the bloodstains. We were more concerned with examining blood clots and such, as we were looking for bullet fragments in the car.*

I could relate to that type of search, and told him so. I had processed many bloody scenes created as the result of gunshot injuries. In order to locate fragments mixed with expelled blood, you gently press the congealed blood against the surface it is on, in order to feel the fragments. I shared with him my investigation experience, and my expertise in analyzing bloodstains patterns. Frazier replied that no one had specifically investigated the vehicle with intent to study or examine the bloodstains, as that was not a technique the agency used at that time.

I then specifically asked, "Was more blood found on the hood as opposed to the blood found on the trunk?"

His unexpectedly abrupt answer was, "You mean 8,000 stains versus 10,000 stains?" His tone and clipped speech made it clear he was angry.

I didn't say a word, knowing I was broaching a subject he did not want to address. I just stayed on the line, hoping he would not hang up. After a short pause Frazier continued in a more congenial tone, speaking slowly and softly .

> *You know... the headshot came from the rear. If there was more blood on the rear of the limo, it was because it flowed out of his head as they drove down the road.*

I just let the comment go. We both knew the President's head was in Jackie's lap on the drive to Parkland and his explanation was impossible. However, I was not about to ask him to defend himself or the organization to which he had a lifelong commitment.

BEVERLY OLIVER MASSEGEE

It was 1997, and I had just arrived at the hotel for the JFK Lancer Annual International Conference on the Kennedy Assassination, frequently referred to as November in Dallas. As I walked past the restaurant toward the lecture hall, I happened to notice a small group of people sitting in a booth. The conversation was animated, but only one person really captured my attention. She was beautiful, had a lovely smile, and what they call Texas hair—a big, blond, bouffant. Her dress was flashy and she talked with hands laden with rings. It was no wonder she was the center of attention; she almost demanded it with her bubbly laugh and enthusiastic conversation. Wow, I thought, Dallas women are something!

This was going to be a great conference, and I was looking forward to meeting the speakers and witnesses who might attend. I was particularly interested in meeting Ed Hoffman and Beverly Oliver Massegee. Hoffman was the deaf mute who witnessed a shooter behind the picket fence and Oliver the famous *Babushka Lady*. Since the identity of the woman wearing the scarf in the Zapruder film was unknown, she had simply become known as the babushka lady. Oliver was discovered by a assassination researcher in the early 1970s after a suprising conversation about November 22 and where she was that day. She explained how she was in Dealey Plaza, where she was standing, and yes, she was wearing a scarf. She was the babushka lady, which meant she was very close to the President when he was killed.

I was approaching the lecture hall when Debra came up asking if I had seen Beverly Oliver Massegee in the restaurant as I passed by. As soon as Debra mentioned her name, I knew the woman in the restaurant who had garnered my attention was Beverly Oliver. I hurried back to the restaurant, and introduced myself. "Sit down, honey," she said in a voice as smooth as silk, "join us while we reminisce." Such began the story of one of the most interesting and engaging witnesses I would be privileged to meet. Beverly Oliver was only 17 when she went to Dealey Plaza to see the President she so admired; she stood only 20 feet away when he was killed. How she came to be in the Plaza is a story in itself.

In 1962, Oliver went to work as a singer at the family amusement park, Six Flags Over Texas. While there, she met and began dating Larry Ronco, an Eastman Kodak representative. In 1963, Oliver began working as a singer at Abe Weinstein's Colony Club. She also knew Jack Ruby and, despite being just seventeen, was a frequent visitor to his Carousel Club. In November 1963, Ronco went to New York, returning with a movie camera as gift for Oliver. Unquestionably, the most important mystery of the Babushka Lady's story is that she filmed the motorcade. The Zapruder film shows her position on the south side of Elm Street, which means that her film would be a mirror image of the Zapruder film. The most significant portion of her film would not necessarily be the Presidential limousine, but what could be seen behind it. The background to Oliver's film would unavoidably include the Texas School Book Depository and the Grassy Knoll.

Oliver chose a place near the curb on Elm Street next to a father and son, later identified as Charles Brehm and his son. As the motorcade came into view, Oliver began to film. She continued to film the President even after he was shot. Oliver went home and did not venture out until Monday night when she went to work at the Carousel Club. When she arrived at work, two men who she believed to be FBI Agents, asked for the film from her movie camera. She gave it to them, believing them when they said it would be returned to her in a few days. As she entered the club, reporters stopped her and asked if she knew Jack Ruby; and, although she had shared dinner with him at Campesi's Egyptian Lounge the night before the assassination, she denied knowing him.

Some people choose to deny Beverly Oliver Massegee is the famous Babushka Lady. She seems to take that graciously in stride. No other person has ever come forward claiming to be woman wearing a scarf and filming the assassination. More importantly, over the years, Oliver has proven she is an honest, God-fearing woman who has no reason to lie. I have heard her share her story many times, each time very similar to that first hearing when I was so captivated with her in Dallas. The last time she spoke to me concerning her personal experiences she was articulate and sincere.

> *I didn't realize I had heard a gunshot. The sound just wasn't familiar. I only knew it was a gunshot when I saw the President's head. I don't know how many shots were fired, but I know one came from the picket fence area. There was someone there and smoke there. I am convinced the man who shot the President was in that area. Somebody killed my President before my very eyes, and they got away with it. After the assassination, I always felt threatened. Lots of folks who testified are no longer around. After all, if they can kill the President of the United States, they can kill me.*

I have been many times to the JFK Lancer Remembrance Program in Dealey Plaza, the place Oliver describes as hallowed ground. She often performs *Amazing Grace* acapella during the November presentation. Her powerful voice rings out over Dealey Plaza with clarity of emotion that brings chills to the listeners. A few years ago, her rendition was especially captivating; the crowd was hushed for a moment while the last notes hung in the air. In the silence, she turned, looked at me, and said, "I love the Lord, and I loved my President."

AUBREY RIKE

I had met Aubrey Rike several times, but never really conversed with him on a personal level until he decided to write a book. Aubrey was born in 1937, in Dallas, Texas. He joined the U.S. Marine Corps in 1955 at age 17 and was discharged two years later. Back home in Dallas, he was employed as a driver for the Ambulance Service Company. Aubrey married Glenda in 1960, and in 1965, their son Larry was born. Aubrey went to work for the O'Neal Funeral Home & Ambulance Service in 1961. While employed with O'Neal's, he was at Parkland Memorial Hospital when President Kennedy was brought in.

Aubrey had a rough draft of his book, titled *At the Door of Memory*, which I agreed to edit. The book lacked a personal side of Aubrey he wanted people to know, but wasn't sure how to include. We decided to just sit and talk and record the conversations for reference. One of the first things he discussed was how he parked the ambulance on a side street behind the crowd anxiously anticipating the Presidential limousine to coming into view. His first time seeing the President and Mrs. Kennedy in the motorcade was from his position perched on top of the ambulance.

> *The President and Jacqueline Kennedy looked absolutely wonderful, both glowing with happiness. The President was stately, dressed in a suit, waving and smiling broadly at the crowd as they passed. Mrs. Kennedy was wearing a pretty pink suit with a matching hat, her gloved hand waving to the people pressed along the road. Suddenly, the President of the United States was looking directly at me. He was smiling and waving as though he had recognized me as an old friend.*

Later, in Trauma Room 1, Aubrey found himself at the center of an unequaled time in history as he assumed the impromptu undertaking of providing assistance to First Lady Jacqueline Kennedy and President Kennedy. We each cried as he told of the President's grieving widow trying to place her ring on her husband's finger. Aubrey gently assisted her by applying lubricant to her husband's finger. He also helped place the President's body into the casket and later aided Mrs. Kennedy into the hearse, despite being shoved away by a Secret Service agent.

Later, I laughed until my sides hurt hearing about him taking his pet spider monkey to visit with his boss. And I winced in sympathetic pain as I heard of his less than successful bull riding adventures. Aubrey was filled with stories of harrowing ambulance rides, and of once chasing a run-away gurney bouncing down the street with a thrashing, but strapped-in patient. He also talked about meeting the gregarious Jack Ruby, who he nicknamed "The Twenty Dollar Man."

Regardless of all the interesting things Aubrey could speak about, the most important for him was always his family. He and Glenda had been married 48 years when I was interviewing him. He still looked at her with a certain gleam, and, although he was a little frail, he seemed protective of her. He talked with pride of his son, and made it plain that nothing he had ever done was as important as his family. Aubrey left this world on Thursday, April 22, 2010 at the age of 72. He was a funny, intelligent, well spoken, man of integrity. He was my friend.

ACKNOWLEDGMENTS

Just saying thank you seems so mediocre when someone helps you achieve the milestone of writing a book. But, there seems to be no other way to express my gratitude for the support, assistance, and encouragement shown by others.

Jim Marrs, thank you for the thoughtful and kind foreword. Your comprehension of the subject matter and the ability to convey its significance to the Kennedy assassination is invaluable. I so appreciate your long-standing efforts to bring truth and clarity to the assassination; you have been fighting the myths of the assassination a long time. As such, you were the perfect person to have written the foreword of this book.

William "Billy" LeBlance, Certified Forensics Crime Scene Investigator, my thanks for your review of the forensic materials and for writing the Preface to *Enemy of the Truth*. Your support will never be forgotten.

Paul, thank you for the love and support you have always demonstrated. You were far more tolerant of my unconventional writing hours than I had any right to expect.

Debra, you were the initial incentive for writing *Enemy of the Truth*; thank you for the push. You continuously elevate my knowledge of events and persons surrounding the Kennedy assassination and will always have my admiration.

To my children, Darrell, Mesha, and Ashley, thank you for supporting my dream and for demonstrating in your lives that dedication to the truth matters.

An impartial eye looking over your work is so important. Thank you Bob Druwing for your keen eye and your thoughtful editing suggestions. Thank you Brian Edwards and Frank Beckendorf, Jr. for your perceptive comments and skillful editing. More than just my editors, you are my friends. I will always appreciate your quiet encouragement when my enthusiasm for the tedious job of writing waned.

There is a magnificent group of people that have helped me, most notably by continually inspiring me to reach beyond what I thought I could achieve. My sincere gratitude is extended to Barry Ernest, Barry Krusch, Dr. Cyril Wecht, Ian Griggs, Larry Hancock, Stuart Wexler, and Larmar Waldron for their expert comments. This would have been a much harder endevor without John Harris, Steven Berry, Holly Blackmon, Joe Hall, Denise Jimenez, Joey Granati, Deb Galentine, and Martin Shackelford. Special thanks for proof reading to Denise Tatum, Alan Dale and Ashley Sleaper.

It would be impossible to acknowledge adequately all the support and inspiration I have continuously received from my friends and colleagues in the Kennedy assassination research community. Your challenges, critiques, comments, and questions all helped shape the content of *Enemy of the Truth*. Please accept my thanks and know I appreciate each of you.

My gratitude and respect is extended to the Dealey Plaza witnesses and others personally touched by the assassination, who were willing to share that experience with me. Thank you Aubrey Rike (deceased), William Newman, Beverly Oliver, Marina Oswald, Ed Hoffman, Bobby Hargis, and Robert Frazier in particular

This book would not have been possible without the assassination researchers who earlier blazed a trail in the search for truth, who read the documents, and published books and articles so others could know the facts concerning the death of President Kennedy. My thanks and respect for your achievements cannot adequately be expressed.

A Note on Citations

References to the Report of the President's Commission on the Assassination of President Kennedy (Washington, D.C.: Government Printing Office, 1964) follow this form: WCR page number; WCR150, for example indicates page 150 of the Report.

References to the 26-volume Hearings Before the President's Commission on the Assassination of President Kennedy follow this form: volume number H page number; for example, 8H155 refers to volume 8, page 155.

Commission Exhibits introduced in evidence before the Warren Commission are designated CE and a number; CE399, for example, refers to the Commission's 399th exhibit.

Executive Sessions of the Warren Commission are cited as WCEX date: page; for example, WCEX 0127:193-194 refers to Warren Commission Executive Session on January 27. Page 193-194.

References to the House Select Committee are noted as HSCA volume: page; for example HSCA 7:81.

Reference to Assassination Record Review Board Medical Documents are AARB Medical Document Number: page. For example AARB MD 44:55-56 references Medical Document 44, pages 55-56.

BIBLIOGRAPHY

DALLAS POLICE FOLLOWED PROTOCOL

Aarts, Henk, & Dijksterhurs A. P. (2000). Habits as knowledge structures: automaticity in goal directed behavior. Journal of Personality and Social Psychology, 78(1), 53–63.

Alyea, Tom. Facts and Photos.
Retrieved from http://www.jfk-online.com/alyea.html

Becker, Ronald, & Dutelle, Aric W. (2012). Criminal Investigation (4th ed.). Massachusetts: Jones & Bartlett Learning.

Brown, B. G. (1963). 1963b; Hand drawn sketch of book arrangement southeast corner of the sixth floor, Texas School Book Depository: Box 9, folder 4, item 17. Dallas Municipal Archives.
Retrieved from http://jfk.ci.dallas.tx.us/box9.htm

Dienstein, William. (1952). Technics for the Crime Investigator. Illinois: Charles C. Thomas.

Eysenck, Michael. (2004). Psychology: An International Perspective. New York: Psychology Press, Ltd.

Fitzgerald, Maurice J. (1951). Handbook of Criminal Investigation. New York: Greenberg.

Gaensslen, R., & Lee, Henry. (2001). Advances in Fingerprint Technology (Second ed.). Florida: CRC Press.

Gemberling, Robert P. (1963). Commission Document 5 - FBI Gemberling Report of 30 Nov 1963 re: Oswald. Report of the President's Commission on the Assassination of President Kennedy (Vol. 26, pp. 131, 829). Washington, DC.
Retrieved from http://www.maryferrell.org/mffweb/archive/viewer/ showDoc.do?docId=10406&relPageId=134

Grossman, Dave, & Christensen, Loren W. (2004). On Combat: The Psychology and Physiology of Deadly Conflict in War and Peace. Illinois: PPCT Research Publications.

Hawthorne, Mark R. (2009). Fingerprints: Analysis and Understanding. Florida: CRC Press.

Heffron, Floyd N. (1958). Evidence for the Patrolman. Illinois: Charles C. Thomas.

Kirk, Paul L. (1953). Crime Investigation. Illinois: Charles C. Thomas.

Kirk, Paul L., & Bradford, L. (1965). Crime Laboratory: Organization and Operation. Illinois: Charles C. Thomas.

McAdams, John. (2011). JFK Assassination Logic: How to Think about Claims of Conspiracy. Washington, DC: Potomac Books.

Savage, Gary. (1993). JFK First Day Evidence. Louisiana: The Shoppe Press.

Sayers, Albert. (1963). FBI document 180-10115-10327: Weitzman Statement. Federal Bureau of Investigation.
Retrieved from http://jfkassassinationfiles.com/fbi_180-10115-10327

Schwabe, Lars, & Wolf, Oliver T. (2009). Stress prompts habit behavior in humans. The Journal of Neuroscience, 29(22), 7192–7198.

Scott, Walter. (1951). Fingerprint mechanics: a Handbook, Fingerprints from Crime Scene to Courtroom. Illinois: Charles C. Thomas.

Sneed, Larry A. (1998). No More Silence: an Oral History of the Assassination of President Kennedy. Texas: University of North Texas Press.

Studebaker, R. L. (1963). 1963c; Scale drawing, sixth floor Texas School Book Depository: Box 9, folder 7, item 3. Dallas Municipal Archives. Retrieved from http://jfk.ci.dallas.tx.us/box9.htm

Thorn, C. A., Atallah, H., & Graybiel, A. M. (2010). Differential dynamics of activity changes in dorsolateral and dorsomedial striatal loops during learning. Neuron, 6(5), 781–795.

Turvey, Brent E., & Petherick, Wayne. (2008). Forensic Victimology: Examining Violent Crime Victims in Investigative and Legal Context. California: Academic Press.

U. S. Census Bureau. (1963). United States Census of Population (Vol. Statistical Abstracts 1951–1994). U.S. Government Printing Office.

Unknown. (1963). 1963a; Hand drawn sketch, possible sixth floor box locations: Box 9, folder 4, item 17. Dallas Municipal Archives. Retrieved from http://jfk.ci.dallas.tx.us/box9.htm

Warren, Earl, Russell, Richard B., Cooper, Sherman, Boggs, Hale, Ford, Gerald R., Dulles, Allen W., McCloy, John J., et al. (1964). Report of the President's Commission on the Assassination of President Kennedy. Washington, DC: United States Government Print Office.

Westbrook, W. R. (1963). 1963d; Release of piece of wood: Box 7, folder 10, item 20. Dallas Municipal Archives. Retrieved from http://jfk.ci.dallas.tx.us/box7.htm

Yamashita, Brian, French, Mike, & Scientific Working Group on Friction Ridge Analysis, Study and Technology. (2011). The Fingerprint Sourcebook. Washington, DC: National Institute of Justice.

Yin, Henry H., & Knowlton, Barbara J. (2006). The Role of the Basal Ganglia and Habit Formation. Neuroscience, Nature Reviews, 7, 464–476.

EAR WITNESSES ARE RELIABLE

Beck, Steven D., Nakasone, Hirotaka, & Marr, Kenneth W. (2011). An Introduction to Forensic Gunshot Acoustics. Presented at the 162nd Acoustical Society of America Meeting, California. Retrieved from http://www.acoustics.org/press/162nd/Beck_4aSCa3.html

Blauert, Jens. (1997). Spatial Hearing: The Psychophysics of Human Sound Localization. Massachusetts: The MIT Press.

Clark, Brandon Louis. (2011). Effect of Barrel Length on the Muzzle Velocity and Report from a Mosin-Nagant 7.62x54R Rifle. Honors College University of South Florida, Florida. Retrieved from http://www.honors.usf.edu/documents/Thesis/U82488180.pdf

Dobreva, Marina S., O'Neill, William E., & Paige, Gary D. (2011). Influence of aging on human sound localization. Journal of Neurophysiology, 5, 2471–2486.

Galanor, Stewart. (2002). List of 178 Witnesses, compiled for the HSCA Surell Brady. Retrieved from http://www.jfklancer.com/pdf/ 178-Witnesses.pdf

Garrison, Jr., Dean H. (2003). Practical Shooting Scene Investigation: The Investigation and Reconstruction of Crime Scenes Involving Gunfire. Florida: Universal Publishers.

Ghazanfar, Asif, & Lemus, Luis. (2010). Multisensory integration: vision boosts information through suppression in auditory cortex. Current Biology, 20(1), R22–R23.

Goldstein, E. Bruce. (2001). Sensation and Perception (Sixth ed.). California: Wadsworth Publishing Company.

Goodridge, Steven George. Multimedia Sensor Fusion for Intelligent Camera Control and Human-Computer Interaction. North Carolina State University.

Green, D.M. (1979). Report No. 4034: Analysis of Earwitness Reports Relating to the Assassination of President John F. Kennedy. Report of the Select Committee on Assassinations of the U.S. House of Representatives. Washington, DC: U.S. Government Printing Office. Retrieved from http://mcadams.posc.mu.edu/russ/jfkinfo/jfk8/sound2.htm

Greveris, Leonard W., & Skochko, Harry A. (1968). Silencers: Principles and Evaluations. Pennsylvania: United States Department of Army.

Grossman, Dave, & Christensen, Loren W. (2008). On Combat: The Psychology and Physiology of Deadly Conflict in War and in Peace (Third.). Illinois: Warrior Science Publications.

Kang, Jian. (2010). Sound Environment: High - versus Low - Density Cities. In Ng, Edward (Ed.), Designing High-density Cities for Social and Environmental Sustainability. United Kingdom: Cromwell Press Group.

Maher, Robert C. (2007). Acoustical Characterization of Gunshots. Proceedings of IEEE Workshop on Signal Processing Applications for Public Security and Forensics (pp. 109–113). Washington, DC: SAFE Journal. Retrieved from http://www.coe.montana.edu/ee/rmaher/publications/maher_ieeesafe_0407_109-113.pdf

Maher, Robert C. Acoustical characterization of gunshots. Retrieved from http://www.coe.montana.edu/ee/rmaher/publications/maher_ieeesafe_0407_109-113.pdf

Maxim, Hiram Percy. (1909). The story of the noiseless gun. (Page, Walter H., Ed.)The World's Work, 18(11), 573–575.

McGurk, H., & MacDonald, J. (1976). Hearing lips and seeing voices. Nature, 264, 746–748.

Minnery, John. (1987). Firearm Silencers Volume II (Second ed.). Arizona: Desert Publications.

Popper, Arthur N., & Fay, Richard R. (Eds.). (2005). Sound Source Localization. Springer Handbook of Auditory Research. Germany: Springer -Verlage Publishing.

Santarelli, S, Kopčo, N, Shinn-Cunningham, B. G., & Brungart, D. S. (1999). Near-field localization in echoic rooms. Journal of the Acoustical Society of America, 105, 1024.

Schindler, Allen. (2007). Spatial Ambience and Sound Localization Programs. Eastmen Computer Music Center (ECENTIMETERC) Users' Guide. New York: Eastman School of Music. Retrieved from http://ecentimeterc.rochester.edu/ecentimeterc/docs/ USERSGUIDE/section7.pdf

Select Committee on Assassinations of the U.S. House of Representatives. (1979). Findings of the Select Committee on Assassinations in the Assassination of President John F. Kennedy. Washington, DC: U.S. Government Printing Office.

Truby David J. (1972). Silencers, Snipers and Assassins. Colorado: Paladin Press.

U. S. Department of Army. (1968a). Silencers: Principles and Evaluations (No. Report #R-1896). U. S. Department of Army.

U. S. Department of Army. (1968b). Ordnance Maintenance, The Springfield Rifle, M1903, M1903A1, M1903A3, M1903A4 (Second ed.). Washington, DC: United States War Department. Retrieved from http://www.milsurps.com/showthread.php?t=20877

U. S. Department of Army. (1968c). Ordnance Maintenance, U.S. Rifles, Caliber .30, M1. M1C (Sniper's), and M1D (Sniper's). Washington, DC: United States War Department.

Warren, Earl, Russell, Richard B., Cooper, Sherman, Boggs, Hale, Ford, Gerald R., Dulles, Allen W., McCloy, John J., et al. (1964). Report of the President's Commission on the Assassination of President Kennedy. Washington, DC: United States Government Print Office.

Yost, William A. (2004). Auditory, Localization and Scene Perception. In Goldstein, E. Bruce (Ed.), Blackwell Handbook of Sensation and Perception. United Kingdom: Blackwell Publishing.

BLOOD IN ZAPRUDER IS FAKED

Barach, E., Tomlanovich, M., & Nowak, R. (1986). Ballistics: a pathophysiologic examination of the wounding mechanism of firearms. Journal of Trauma, 26, 225–235.

Bor, Jonothan. (2006). Only 5% survive gunshot wounds to head. The Baltimore Sun. Maryland. Retrieved from http://www.baltimoresun.com/health/bal-te.brain05oct05,0,2310918.story?page=1

Bugliosi, Vincent. (2007). Reclaiming History: The Assassination of President John F. Kennedy. New York: W. W. Norton & Company, Inc.

Charters, A. C. (1976). Wounding mechanism of very high velocity projectiles. Journal of Trauma, 16, 464.

CliffsNotes.com. (2012). Skull: Cranium and Facial Bones. Retrieved from http://www.cliffsnotes.com/study_guide/topicArticleId-277792,articleId-277566.html

Conway, Debra. (2000). The Running Woman, Toni Foster. Kennedy Assassination Chronicles. Retrieved from http://www.jfklancer.com/pdf/toni.pdf.

Costella, John. JFK Assassination Film Hoax. Retrieved from http://assassinationscience.com/johncostella/jfk/intro/

DeMuth, W. E. Jr. (1974). Ballistic characteristics of "Magnum" sidearm bullet. Journal of Trauma, 14(3), 227–229.

DeSario, Jack P., & Mason, William D. (2003). Dr. Sam Sheppard on Trial: The Prosecutors and the Marilyn Sheppard Murder. Kent State University Press.

DiMaio, Vincent J. M. (1999). Gunshot Wounds: Practical Aspects of Firearms, Ballistics, and Forensic Techniques (Second ed.). Florida: CRC Press.

DiMaio, Vincent J. M., & Zumwalt, R. E. (1976). Rifle wounds from high velocity, center-fire hunting ammunition. Journal of Forensic Sciences, 22(1), 132–140.

Dziemain, A.J., Mendelson, J. A., & Lindsey, D. (1961). Comparison of the wounding characteristics of some commonly encountered bullets. Journal of Trauma, July(1), 341–353.

Fackler, M. L. (1987). What's Wrong With the Wound Ballistics Literature, And Why (No. Military Trauma Research Institute Report No. 239). California: Letterman Army Institute of Research. Retrieved from http://www.rkba.org/research/fackler/wrong.html

Federal Bureau of Investigations (Ed.). (2009). Scientific working group on bloodstain pattern analysis: recommended terminology. Forensic Science Communications, Forensic Science Communications, 11(2). Retrieved from http://www2.fbi.gov/hq/lab/fsc/backissu/april2009/standards/2009_04_standards01.htm

Fetzer, James H., Costella, John, & Healy, David. (2003). The Great Zapruder Film Hoax: Deceit and Deception in the Death of JFK. (Fetzer, James H., Ed.). Illinois: Catfeet Press.

Finck, Pierre A. State of Louisiana vs. Clay L. Shaw. , No. 198-159 (M703) (New Orleans District Court Section C 1969). Retrieved from http://www.history-matters.com/archive/jfk/garr/trial/Feb_24/html/Feb_24_0054a.htm

Freidrichsen, Joe, Lander, Denali, Zarske, Malinda Schaefer, & Yowell, Janet. 20/20 Vision. Integrated Teaching and Learning Program and Laboratory, University of Colorado at Boulder. Retrieved from http://www.teachengineering.org/view_activity.php?url=collection/cub_/activities/cub_human/cub_human_lesson06_activity1.xml

Goldstein, E. Bruce (Ed.). (2010). Encyclopedia of Perception. California: Sage Publications, Inc.,

Gutierrez, Sherry P. (1996). The JFK case: what does the blood tell us? (Evica, George Michael, Ed.) The Kennedy Assassination Chronicles, 2(4), 16–19.

Itek Corporation. (1976). John Kennedy Assassination Film Analysis. Retrieved from http://www.maryferrell.org/mffweb/archive/viewer/showDoc.do?docId=60448

James, Stuart H., Kish, Paul E., & Sutton, Paulette T. (2005a). Introduction to Bloodstain Pattern Analysis. Florida: CRC Press.

James, Stuart H., Kish, Paul E., & Sutton, Paulette T. (2005b). Principles of Bloodstain Pattern Analysis: Theory and Practice. CRC Press.

Karger, Bernd. (2008). Forensic Ballistics. In Tsokos, Michael (Ed.), Forensic Pathology Reviews (pp. 139–172). Germany: Humana Press.

Kirk, Paul L. (1952). Crime Investigation. California: University of California Press.

Lodge, John E. (1935). Camera wizards of the movies bring realism to the screen. Popular Science, 129(3), 22–24.

MacDonell, Herbert L. (1995). COPA Conference.

MacDonell, Herbert L. (1992). Segments of history: the literature of bloodstain pattern interpretation. International Association of Bloodstain Pattern Analyst News, 8(1), 3–12.

Marrs, Jim. (2002). Crossfire: the plot that killed Kennedy (Tenth ed.). New York: First Carroll & Gaf.

MFRC-Midwest Forensics Resource Center. (2008). Bloodstain Pattern Analysis Video Collection. Research & Development. Iowa. Retrieved from http://www.ameslab.gov/mfrc/rd

Newman, William. (1995). Blood Observed in Dealey Plaza.

Parker, N. Leroy, Bedore, Larry R., Cooper, Karen K., Fowler, Pamela, Miller, T. Allen, & Showalter, Janice. (1982). Summary Report of the Bloodstain Pattern Analysis Research Group. Florida: Sanford Regional Crime Laboratory, Tampa Regional Crime Laboratory, Tallahassee Regional Crime Laboratory, Jacksonville Regional Crime Laboratory, and Pensacola Regional Crime Laboratory.
Retrieved from http://www.bevelgardner.com/index.php?articles

Pearl, S., Peletier, P., Kim, E. S., Williams, P. X., Mcentimeterew, M. J. C., Perez, J. E., & Coates, P. (2012). How to Calculate Color Contrast from RGB Values. Had2Know - Technology.
Retrieved from http://www.had2know.com/technology/color-contrast-calculator-web-design.html

Pizzola, Peter. A., Roth, Steven, & De Forest, Peter R. (1986). Blood Droplet Dynamics—I. Journal of Forensic Sciences, 31(1), 36–49.

Rees, Robert R. Nellie Connally: That Day in Dallas. The Cyber Profile Journal.
Retrieved from http://web.lconn.com/mysterease/connally.htm

Sario, Jack P., & Mason, William D. (2003). Dr. Sam Sheppard on Trial: The Prosecutors and the Marilyn Sheppard Murder. Ohio: Kent State University Press.

Stephens, Boyd G, & Allen, Terence B. (1983). Back spatter of blood from gunshot wounds - observations and experimental simulation. Journal of Forensic Sciences, 28(2), 437–439.

Sweet, Michael J. (1993). Velocity measurements of projected bloodstains from a medium velocity impact source. Canadian Society of Forensic Science, 26(3), 103–110.

SWGSTAIN. (2012). Scientific Working Group on Bloodstain Pattern Analysis. Legal Resources.
Retrieved from http://www.swgstain.org/resources/ark/usblood

Tetcher, Brass. (2012). 9 millimeterPolice Hornady 90gr XTP impacting ballistic gelatin. Brass Fetcher Ballistic Testing. Retrieved from http://www.youtube.com/watch?v=jexyDDA3TBU

Victor, B. (1939). Medecine sociale et toxicologie. Annales De Medecine Legale De Criminologie Police Scientifique, 19, 265–323.

Warren, Earl, Cooper, Sherman, Boggs, Hale, Ford, Gerald R., Dulles, Allen W., & McCloy, John J. (1964). The President's Commission on the Assassination of President Kennedy. Washington, DC: U.S. Government Printing Office.

THE LIMO STOP

Alverez, Luis W. (1976). A physicist examines the Kennedy assassination film. American Journal of Physics, 44(9), 813–827.

Angrilli, Alessandro, Cherubini, Paolo, Pavese, Antonella, & Manfredini, Sara; (1997). The influence of affective factors on time perception. Perception & Psychophysics, 59(6), 972–982.

Artwohl, Alexis A. (2002). Perceptual and memory distortions in officer involved shootings. FBI Law Enforcement Bulletin, 158(10), 18–24.

Artwohl, Alexis A., & Christensen, L. W. (1997). Deadly Force Encounters. Colorado: Paladin Press.

Bar-Haim, Yair, Kerem, Aya, Lamy, Dominique, & Zakay, Dan. (2010). When time slows down: The influence of threat on time perception in anxiety. Cognition & Emotion Journal, 24(2), 255–263.

Cole, Jeffrey. (1995). UCLA Center for Communication: Television Violence Monitoring Project. National Commission on the Causes and Prevention of Violence. Retrieved from http://www.digitalcenter.org/webreport94/toc.htm

Droit-Volet, Sylvie, Fayolle, Sophie L., & Gil, Sandrine. (2011). Emotion and time perception: effects of film-induced mood. Frontiers in Integrated Neuroscience, 5(33). doi:10.3389/fnint.2011.00033

Garwin, Richard L. (1992). Memorial Tribute for Luis W. Alvarez. National Academy of Engineering, 5(Memorial Tributes). Retrieved from http://www.fas.org/rlg/alvarez.htm

Hasher, Lynn, Goldstein, David, & Toppino, Thomas. (1977). Frequency and the conference of referential validity. Journal of Verbal Learning and Verbal Behavior, (16), 107–112.

Hirsh, Ira J., & Sherrick Jr., Carl E. (1961). Perceived order in different sense modalities. Journal of Experimental Psychology, 62(5), 423–432.

Holloway-Erickson, Crystal M., McReynolds, Jayme R., & McIntyre, Christa K. (2012). Memory-enhancing intra-basolateral amygdala infusions of clenbuterol increase Arc and CaMKII-alpha protein expression in the rostral anterior cingulate cortex. Frontiers in Behavioral Neuroscience, 62(5). Retrieved from 10.3389/fnbeh.2012.00017 (url)

Klinger, David. (2002). The Law Enforcement Officer's Use of Deadly Force and Post-Shooting Reactions (Office of Justice Programs, National Institute of Justice, Department of Justice No. 192286) (p. 139). Office of Justice Programs, National Institute of Justice, Department of Justice. Retrieved from http://www.cops.usdoj.gov/CDROMs/UseofForce/pubs/PoliceResponsestoOfficerInvolvedShootings.pdf

Manis, Glykeria. (2011). My 9/11 Escape from the World Trade Center. Retrieved from http://www.my-911-escape-world-trade-center-110908.html

Marrs, Jim. (1992). Crossfire: The Plot That Killed Kennedy (Sixth ed.). New York: Carroll & Graf Publishing, Inc.

Warren, Earl, Boggs, Hale, Cooper, Sherman, Dulles, Allen W., Ford,
Gerald R., Russell, Richard B., McCloy, John J., et al. (1964). Report of
the President's Commission on the Assassination of President Kennedy.
Washington, DC: United States Government Print Office.

Wise, Jeff. (2009). Extreme Fear: The Science of Your Mind in Danger. New
York: Palgrave Macentimeterillan Publishing.

Wise, Jeff. (2010). The Moment that Last Forever. Writing About
Science, Technology and Adventure. Retrieved from http://jeffwise.
net/2010/09/18/the-moment-that-lasts-forever/

BALLISTICS PROVE ONE SHOOTER
AFTE, Criteria for Identification Committee. (1998). Theory of
identification as it relates to toolmarks. Association of Firearm and Tool
Mark Examiners Journal, 30(1), p. 86.

Baker, Mary T., & Kelly, Margaret Ann T. (2000). Scientific Examination
of JFK Assassination Evidence. National Archives Press Release.
Washington, DC.
Retrieved from http://www.archives.gov/press/press-releases/2000/
nr00-25.html#report3

Committee on Scientific Assessment of Bullet Lead Elemental Composition
Comparison, N. R. C. (2004). Forensic Analysis Weighing Bullet Lead
Evidence. Washington, DC: The National Academies Press.
Retrieved from http://www.nap.edu/openbook.php?record_id=10924

FBI, (2005) Retrieved from http://www.fbi.gov/news/pressrel/press-
releases/fbi-laboratory-announces-discontinuation-of-bullet-lead-
examinations

Frazier, Robert A. State of Louisiana vs. Clay L. Shaw. , No. 198-159
(M703) (New Orleans District Court Section C 1969).
Retrieved from http://historymatters.com/archive/jfk/garr/trial/
Feb_21c/html/Feb_21c_0011a.htm

Goho, Alexandra. (2004). Forensics on trial. Science News, 165(13), p. 202–204.

Guinn, Vincent P. (1979). JFK assassination: bullet analyses. Analytical Chemistry, 51(4), p. 484–493.

Hamby, James. (1999). Identification of projectiles. Association of Firearm and Tool Mark Examiners Journal, 6(5/6), p. 22.

Miller, George E., Miller, David E., & Rowland, F. Sherwood. (2002). In Memoriam of Vincent Perrie Guinn.
Retrieved from http://www.universityofcalifornia.edu/senate/inmemoriam/VincentPerrieGuinn.htm

Peters, Charles A. (2002). The basis for compositional bullet lead comparisons. Forensic Science Communications, 4(3).
Retrieved from http://www.fbi.gov/about-us/lab/forensic-science-communications/fsc/july2002/peters.htm

Randich, E., & Grant, P. M. (2006). Proper Assessment of the JFK Assassination Bullet Lead Evidence from Metallurgical and Statistical Perspectives (p. 52). U.S. Department of Energy by University of California, Lawrence Livermore National Laboratory.
Retrieved from https://e-reports-ext.llnl.gov/pdf/337848.pdf

Randich, Erik, Duerfeldt, Wayne, McLendon, Wade, & Tobin, William. (2002). A metallurgical review of the interpretation of bullet lead compositional analysis. Forensic Science International, 127(3), p. 174–191.

Randich, Erik, & Grant, P. M. (2006). Proper assessment of the JFK assassination bullet lead evidence from metallurgical and statistical perspectives. Journal of Forensic Sciences, 51, 717–728.

Schlesinger, H. L., Lukens, H. R., Guinn, V. P., Hackleman, R. P., & Korts, R. F. (1970). Special Report on Gunshot Residues Measured by Neutron Activation Analysis (No. USAEC Report GA-9829). Virginia: U.S. Atomic Energy Commission, National Science and Technology Information Service, U.S. Department of Commerce.

Select Committee on Assassinations of the U.S. House of Representatives. (1979). Findings of the Select Committee on Assassinations in the Assassination of President John F. Kennedy. Washington, DC: U.S. Government Printing Office.

Spiegelman, Cliff, James, William A., Tobin William D., Sheather Simon J., Wexler, Stuart, & Roundhill, Max D. (2007). Chemical and forensic analysis of JFK assassination bullet lots: Is a second shooter possible. Annals of Applied Statistics, 1(2), p. 287–301.

Stupian, Gary W. (1975). Lead isotope ratio measurements: a potential method for bullet identification. Journal of the Forensic Science Society, 15(2), p. 161–164.

Warren, Earl, Russell, Richard B., Cooper, Sherman, Boggs, Hale, Ford, Gerald R., Dulles, Allen W., McCloy, John J., et al. (1964). Report of the President's Commission on the Assassination of President Kennedy. Washington, DC: United States Government Print Office.

Wexler, Stuart. (2012, August 12). Compositional Analysis of Bullet Lead in The Kennedy Assassination Evidence.

AFTE, Criteria for Identification Committee. (1998). Theory of identification as it relates to toolmarks. Association of Firearm and Tool Mark Examiners Journal, 30(1), p. 86.

Baker, Mary T., & Kelly, Margaret Ann T. (2000). Scientific Examination of JFK Assassination Evidence. National Archives Press Release. Washington, DC.
Retrieved from http://www.archives.gov/press/press-releases/2000/nr00-25.html#report3

Committee on Scientific Assessment of Bullet Lead Elemental Composition Comparison, N. R. C. (2004). Forensic Analysis Weighing Bullet Lead Evidence. Washington, DC: The National Academies Press. Retrieved from http://www.nap.edu/openbook.php?record_id=10924

Frazier, Robert A. State of Louisiana vs. Clay L. Shaw. , No. 198-159 (M703) (New Orleans District Court Section C 1969). Retrieved from http://historymatters.com/archive/jfk/garr/trial/Feb_21c/html/Feb_21c_0011a.htm

Goho, Alexandra. (2004). Forensics on trial. Science News, 165(13), p. 202–204.

Guinn, Vincent P. (1979). JFK assassination: bullet analyses. Analytical Chemistry, 51(4), p. 484–493.

Hamby, James. (1999). Identification of projectiles. Association of Firearm and Tool Mark Examiners Journal, 6(5/6), p. 22.

Miller, George E., Miller, David E., & Rowland, F. Sherwood. (2002). In Memoriam of Vincent Perrie Guinn. Retrieved from http://www.universityofcalifornia.edu/senate/inmemoriam/VincentPerrieGuinn.htm

Peters, Charles A. (2002). The basis for compositional bullet lead comparisons. Forensic Science Communications, 4(3). Retrieved from http://www.fbi.gov/about-us/lab/forensic-science-communications/fsc/july2002/peters.htm

Randich, E., & Grant, P. M. (2006). Proper Assessment of the JFK Assassination Bullet Lead Evidence from Metallurgical and Statistical Perspectives (p. 52). U.S. Department of Energy by University of California, Lawrence Livermore National Laboratory. Retrieved from https://e-reports-ext.llnl.gov/pdf/337848.pdf

Randich, Erik, Duerfeldt, Wayne, McLendon, Wade, & Tobin, William. (2002). A metallurgical review of the interpretation of bullet lead compositional analysis. Forensic Science International, 127(3), p. 174–191.

Randich, Erik, & Grant, P. M. (2006). Proper assessment of the JFK assassination bullet lead evidence from metallurgical and statistical perspectives. Journal of Forensic Sciences, 51, 717–728.

Schlesinger, H. L., Lukens, H. R., Guinn, V. P., Hackleman, R. P., & Korts, R. F.,. (1970). Special Report on Gunshot Residues Measured by Neutron Activation Analysis (No. USAEC Report GA-9829). Virginia: U.S. Atomic Energy Commission, National Science and Technology Information Service, U.S. Department of Commerce.

Select Committee on Assassinations of the U.S. House of Representatives. (1979). Findings of the Select Committee on Assassinations in the Assassination of President John F. Kennedy. Washington, DC: U.S. Government Printing Office.

Spiegelman, Cliff, James, William A., Tobin William D., Sheather Simon J., Wexler, Stuart, & Roundhill, Max D. (2007). Chemical and forensic analysis of JFK assassination bullet lots: Is a second shooter possible. Annals of Applied Statistics, 1(2), p. 287–301.

Stupian, Gary W. (1975). Lead isotope ratio measurements: a potential method for bullet identification. Journal of the Forensic Science Society, 15(2), p. 161–164.

Warren, Earl, Russell, Richard B., Cooper, Sherman, Boggs, Hale, Ford, Gerald R., Dulles, Allen W., McCloy, John J., et al. (1964). Report of the President's Commission on the Assassination of President Kennedy. Washington, DC: United States Government Print Office.

Wexler, Stuart. (2012, August 12). Compositional Analysis of Bullet Lead in The Kennedy Assassination Evidence.

THE GRASSY KNOLL HEADSHOT

(ICRC) International Committee of the Red Cross. (2007). Customary International Humanitarian Law. Retrieved from http://www.icrc.org/customary-ihl/eng/docs/home

Adams, Bradley J. (2006). Forensic Anthropology. New York: Infobase Publishing.

Anderson, Robert William Gerard, & McLean, Jack. (2005). Biomechanics of Closed Head Injury. In Reilly, Peter L. & Bullock, Ross (Eds.), Head

Injury: Pathophysiology and Management (Second ed., pp. pp. 26–40). United Kingdom: Hodder Arnold Publishers.

Buikstra, Jane, & Prevedorou, Eleanna. (2012). John Lawrence Angel. The Global History of Paleopathology: Pioneers and Prospects. New York: Oxford University Press.

Carnes, William H., Fisher, Russell S., Morgan, Russell H., & Moritz, Alan R. (1968). Clark Panel Report. Retrieved from http://www.history-matters.com/archive/jfk/arrb/master_med_set/md59/html/Image00.htm

Coe, Joe I. (1982). External beveling of entrance wounds by handguns. The American Journal of Forensic Medicine and Pathology, 3(3), 215–219.

Coupland, Robin M., Rothschild, Markus A., & Thali, Michale J. (2011). Wound Ballistics: Basics and Applications. (Kneubuehl, Beat, P., Ed.) (Translation of the revised third German ed.). New York: Springer -Verlage Publishing.

Dankbaar, Wim. (2003). Interview with Robert "Tosh" Plumlee; 6/4/1992. JFK Murder Solved. Retrieved from http://www.jfkmurdersolved.com/TOSHTRANS1.htm

DiMaio, Vincent J. M. (1998). Gunshot Wounds: Practical Aspects of Firearms, Ballistics, and Forensic Techniques (Second ed.). Florida: CRC Press.

Dodd, Malcolm J. (2005). Terminal Ballistics: A Text and Atlas of Gunshot Wounds. Florida: CRC Press.

Edgerton, Harold E. (1936). Death of a Light Bulb. Arts Connected: Tools for Teaching the Arts. Retrieved from http://www.artsconnected.org/resource/10447/death-of-a-lightbulb-30-caliber-bullet

Eisenberg, Melvin A. (1964a). MEMORANDUM FOR THE RECORD: Conference of April 14, 1964, to determine which frames in the Zapruder movies show the impact of the first and second bullets. Retrieved from http://mcadams.posc.mu.edu/wcsbt.htm

Eisenberg, Melvin A. (1964b). MEMORANDUM: Determination of the Trajectories of the Three Shots.
Retrieved from http://mcadams.posc.mu.edu/wcsbt.htm

Erickson, Robert. (2008). JFK: Inside the Target Car. JFK: Inside the Target Car. Discovery Channel.

Ervin, John. (2011). 308 Winchester Federal 150gr Fusion JSP fired from a HK91 Impacting Ballistic Gelatin.
Retrieved from http://www.youtube.com/watch?v=jE9xjUVcszs&feature=fvwrel

Finck, Pierre A. State of Louisiana vs. Clay L. Shaw. , No. 198-159 (M703) (New Orleans District Court Section C 1969).
Retrieved from http://www.history-matters.com/archive/jfk/garr/trial/Feb_24/html/Feb_24_0054a.htm

Fung, H. S., Lau, S., Wai, A. M. W., Lai, A. K. H., Chan, M. K., Wong, W. K., & Chan, S. C. H. (2008). Gunshot Injury in Hong Kong: Report of 2 Cases. Journal of Hong Kong College of Radiologists, 11, 85–88.

Haag, Michael G., & Haag, Lucien C. (2011). Shooting Incident Reconstruction (Second ed.). California: Elsevier ink.

Hawks, Chuck. Rifle Ballistics Summary. Rifle Ballistics Summary.
Retrieved from http://www.chuckhawks.com/rifle_ballistics_table.htm

Helmenstine, Anne Marie. (2012). Newton's Laws of Motion.
Retrieved from http://chemistry.about.com/od/mathsciencefundamentals/a/newtons-laws-of-motion.htm

Hornady, Steve. (2012a). Ballistics Calculator. Hornady Manufacturing Ballistics Calculator. Web Page.
Retrieved from http://www.hornady.com/ballistics-resource/ballistics-calculator

Hornady, Steve. (2012b). 222 Rem 50 gr V-MAX™ Superformance. Hornady Manufacturing, 222 Rem 50 gr V-MAX™ Superformance.

Retrieved from http://www.hornady.com/store/222-Rem-50-gr-V-MAX-Superformance/

Humes, James H. (1964). Autopsy Report and Supplemental Report. Report of the President's Commission on the Assassination of President Kennedy (Vol. Appendix IX, pp. 536–546). Washington, DC: U.S. Government Printing Office.
Retrieved from http://www.history-matters.com/archive/jfk/wc/wr/html/WCReport_0281b.htm

Itek Corporation. (1976). John Kennedy Assassination Film Analysis.
Retrieved from http://www.maryferrell.org/mffweb/archive/viewer/showDoc.do?docId=60448

Karger, Bernd. (2008). Forensic Ballistics. In Tsokos, Michael (Ed.), Forensic Pathology Reviews (Vol. 5). New Jersey: Humana Press.

Lantz, Patrick E. (1994). An atypical, indeterminate-range, cranial gunshot wound of entrance resembling an exit wound. Journal of Forensic Medicine and Pathology, 15(1), 5–9.

Leestma Jan E.,, & Kirkpatrick, Joel B. (2008). Gunshot and Penetrating Wounds of the Nervous System. Forensic Neuropathology (Second ed.). Florida: CRC Press.

Levy, Angela D., & Harcke, H. Theodore. (2008). Essentials of Forensic Imaging: A Text-Atlas. Florida: CRC Press.

Mahinda, H. A. M., & Murty, O. P. (2009). Variability in thickness of Human Skull Bones & Sternum – An Autopsy experience. Journal of Forensic Medicine and Toxicology, 26(2), 26–31.

MFRC-Midwest Forensics Resource Center. (2008). Bloodstain Pattern Analysis Video Collection. Research & Development. Iowa.
Retrieved from http://www.ameslab.gov/mfrc/rd

Minnery, John A. (1981). Firearm Silencers, Volume Two. Arizona: Desert Publications.

Myers, Dale K. (1995). Secrets of a Homicide: JFK Assassination. Secrets of a Homicide: JFK Assassination. Retrieved from http://www.jfkfiles.com/index.html

Nonte George C. Jr. (1978). Firearms Encyclopedia. Harper & Row.

Oehmichen, Manfred, Auer Roland N., & König, Hans Günter. (2006). Forensic Neuropathology and Associated Neurology. Germany: Springer -Verlage Publishing.

Prahalow, Joseph. (2010). Forensic Pathology for Police, Death Investigators, Attorneys and Forensic Scientist. New York: Humana Press.

Quatrehommea, Gérald, & Iscan, M. Yasar. (1998). Analysis of beveling in gunshot entrance wounds. Forensic Science International, 93(1), 45–60.

Rushing, Gregory D., & Britt, L. D. (2008). Patterns of Penetrating Injury. In Peitzman, Andrew B. (Ed.), The Trauma Manual: Trauma and Acute Care Surgery (Third ed.). Pennsylvania: Lippincott Williams & Wilkins.

Smith, O. C.,, Berryman, H. E, & Lahren, C. H. (1987). Cranial fracture patterns and estimate of direction from low velocity gunshot wounds. Journal of Forensic Sciences, 32(5), 1416–1421.

Stokes, Louis, Downing, Thomas N., Preyer, L. Richardson, Fauntroy, Walter E., Burke, Yvonne Brathwaite, Dodd, Christopher, Ford, Sr., Harold, et al. (1978). Investigation of the Assassination of President John F. Kennedy. Washington, DC: U.S. Government Printing Office.

Treibitz, Alan, & Freed, Gary L. (2003). Evaluation of the Animation of the Kennedy Assassinatiuon Created by Dale Myers. Retrieved from http://www.jfkfiles.com/jfk/html/zaxis.htm

Tunheim, John R., Graff, Henry F., Joyce, William L., Hall, Kermit L., Joyce, William L., & Nelson, Anna Kasten. (1998). Final Report of the Assassination Records Review Board. U.S. Government Printing Office.

Viel, Guido, Gehl, Alex, & Sperhake, Jan P. (2009). Intersecting fractures of the skull and gunshot wounds. Forensic Science, Medicine, and Pathology, 5(1), 22–27.

Warren, Earl, Boggs, Hale, Cooper, Sherman, Dulles, Allen W., Ford, Gerald R., Russell, Richard B., McCloy, John J., et al. (1964). Report of the President's Commission on the Assassination of President Kennedy. Washington, DC: United States Government Print Office.

William Robert "Tosh" Plumlee. (2004). Robert "Tosh" Plumlee Declaration, 11/21/2004. JFK Murder Solved. Retrieved from http://www.jfkmurdersolved.com/toshfiles.htm

Wilson, Anthony J. (1999). Gunshot Injuries: What Does a Radiologist Need to Know? RadioGraphics, 19(September), 1358–1368.

Two Headshots

AANS - American Association of Neurological Surgeons. (2011). Gunshot Wound Head Trauma. American Association of Neurological Surgeons. Retrieved from http://www.aans.org/en/Patient%20Information/ Conditions%20and%20Treatments/Gunshot%20Wound%20Head%20 Trauma.aspx

Alverez, Luis W. (1976). A physicist examines the Kennedy assassination film. American Journal of Physics, 44(9), 813–827.

Costella, John. (2011). Josiah Thompson Changes his Mind on z313. JFK Assassination Forum. Retrieved from http://www.jfkassassinationforum.com/index. php?topic=4892.0;wap2

Coupland, Robin M., Rothschild, Markus A., & Thali, Michale J. (2011). Wound Ballistics: Basics and Applications. (Kneubuehl, Beat, P., Ed.) (Translation of the revised third German ed.). New York: Springer -Verlage Publishing.

Cronin, Duane S. (2010). Material properties for numerical simulations for human, ballistic soap and gelatin (No. W7701-061933/001/QCL). Defence Research and Development Canada. Retrieved from pubs.drdc.gc.ca/PDFS/unc94/p533085_a1b.pdf

DiMaio, Vincent M. J. (1993). Gunshot Wounds: Practical Aspects of Firearms, Ballistics, and Forensic Techniques. Florida: CRC Press.

Fackler, M. L. (1987). What's Wrong With the Wound Ballistics Literature, And Why (No. Military Trauma Research Institute Report No. 239). California: Letterman Army Institute of Research. Retrieved from http://www.rkba.org/research/fackler/wrong.html

Greenberg, Michael I., Hendrickson, Robert G., & Silverberg, Mark (Eds.). (2004). Greenberg's Text-Atlas of Emergency Medicine. Pennsylvania: Lippincott Williams & Wilkins.

Hornady, Steve. (2012). Ballistics Resource. Hornady Manufacturing Ballistics Resources. Retrieved from http://www.hornady.com/ballistics-resource

Itek Corporation. (1976). John Kennedy Assassination Film Analysis. Retrieved from http://www.maryferrell.org/mffweb/archive/viewer/showDoc.do?docId=60448

Karger, Bernd. (2008). Forensic Ballistics. In Tsokos, Michael (Ed.), Forensic Pathology Reviews (Vol. 5). New Jersey: Humana Press.

Lieberman, Daniel E. (2002). The Evolution of the Human Head. Massachusetts: Harvard College.

Lifton, David. (1982). Best Evidence. New York: Signet.

MFRC-Midwest Forensics Resource Center. (2008). Bloodstain Pattern Analysis Video Collection. Research & Development. Iowa. Retrieved from http://www.ameslab.gov/mfrc/rd

Piersol, Allan, & Paez, Thomas. (1987). Harris' Shock and Vibration Handbook (Third ed.). McGraw-Hill Professional.

Radford, Gemma Elizabeth. (2009). Modelling Cranial Gunshot Wounds and Back spatter. University of Otago, New Zealand. Retrieved from http://otago.ourarchive.ac.nz/handle/10523/393

Rohkamm, Reinhard. (2004). Color Atlas Of Neurology. New York: Georg Thieme Verlag.

Szamboti, Toni. (2012). A critical look at Luis Alvarez's jet effect explanation for the head movement of John Kennedy when he was assassinated on November 22, 1963. JFK Lancer Jet Efect Rebutal. Retrieved from jfklancer.com/pdf/Jet_Effect_Rebuttal_II_(4-17-2012).pdf

Thompson, John T., & LaGarde, Louis Anatole. (1904). The Thompson-LaGarde Report. Unblinkingeye.com. Retrieved from http://unblinkingeye.com/Guns/TLGR/tlgr.html

Thompson, Josiah. (2005). Bedrock Evidence in the Kennedy Assassination. Mary Ferrell Organization. Retrieved from http://www.maryferrell.org/wiki/index.php/Essay_-_Bedrock_Evidence_in_the_Kennedy_Assassination

Tunheim, John R., Graff, Henry F., Hall, Kermit L., Joyce, William L., & Nelson, Anna Kasten. (1998). Final Report of the Assassination Records Review Board. Washington, DC. Retrieved from www.archives.gov/research/jfk/.../report/arrb-final-report.pdf

Vinas, Federico C., & Pilitas, Julie. (2011). Penetrating Head Trauma. Medscape. Retrieved from http://emedicine.medscape.com/article/247664-overview

Walilko, T. J., Viano, David C., & Bir, C. A. (2005). Biomechanics of the head for Olympic boxer punches to the face. British Journal of Sports Medicine, 39(10), 710–721.

Warren, Earl, Boggs, Hale, Cooper, Sherman, Dulles, Allen W., Ford, Gerald R., Russell, Richard B., McCloy, John J., et al. (1964). Report of the President's Commission on the Assassination of President Kennedy. Washington, DC: United States Government Print Office.

THE SINGLE BULLET THEORY

Burkley, George Gregory. (1963). White House Death Certificate. Washington, DC.
Retrieved from http://history-matters.com/archive/jfk/arrb/master_med_set/md6/html/Image0.htm

Carnes, William H., Fisher, Russell S., Morgan, Russell H., & Moritz, Alan R. (1968). Clark Panel Report.
Retrieved from http://www.history-matters.com/archive/jfk/arrb/master_med_set/md59/html/Image00.htm

Cramer, Gregory D., & Darby, Susan A. (2005). Basic and Clinical Anatomy of the Spine, Spinal Cord, and ANS (Second ed.). Missouri: Elsevier Mosby.

Crenshaw, Charles A., & Shaw, J. Gary. (2001). Trauma Room One: The JFK Medical Coverup Exposed. New York: Paraview Press.

Custer, Jerrol Francis Assassinations Records Review Board Assassination of President John F. Kennedy Deposition of Jerrol Francis Custer (1997). Retrieved from http://history-matters.com/archive/jfk/arrb/medical_testimony/Custer_10-28-97/html/Custer_0001a.htm

Eisenberg, Melvin A. (1964a). MEMORANDUM FOR THE RECORD: Conference of April 14, 1964, to determine which frames in the Zapruder movies show the impact of the first and second bullets. Retrieved from http://mcadams.posc.mu.edu/wcsbt.htm

Eisenberg, Melvin A. (1964b). MEMORANDUM: Determination of the Trajectories of the Three Shots. Retrieved from http://mcadams.posc.mu.edu/wcsbt.htm

Erickson, Robert. (2004). JFK: Beyond the Magic Bullet. Australia: Discovery Communications, Inc. Retrieved from http://www.youtube.com/watch?v=dGW-u_6pDN8

FBI. (1963). FBI Summary Report. Retrieved from http://www.maryferrell.org/mffweb/archive/viewer/showDoc.do?absPageId=327202

Finck, Pierre A. (1965). Report to Brigadier General J. M. Blumberg from Lieutenant Colonel P. A. Finck: Autopsy of President Kennedy. Retrieved from http://archive.org/stream/KennedyAutopsyReportWarrenCommissionReport/AutopsyOfPresidentKennedy_IncludesWarrenCommissionReport#page/n0/mode/2up

Finck, Pierre A. State of Louisiana vs. Clay L. Shaw. , No. 198-159 (M703) (New Orleans District Court Section C 1969). Retrieved from http://www.history-matters.com/archive/jfk/garr/trial/Feb_24/html/Feb_24_0054a.htm

Haag, Michael G., & Haag, Lucien C. (2006). Shooting Incident Reconstruction (Second ed.). Academic Press.

Hewlett, A. B., & Ranger, D. (1961). Tracheostomy. Post Grad Medical Journal, (37), 18–21.

Holzner, Steven. (2011). Physics 1 for Dummies (Second ed.). Indiana: Wiley Publishers.

Hoover, J. Edgar. (1964). Commission Document 1383 - FBI Letter from Director of 12 Aug 1964 re: Main Street Mark on Curb. Retrieved from http://www.maryferrell.org/mffweb/archive/viewer/showDoc.do?docId=11778

Humes, James H. (1963a). The Assassination of John F. Kennedy Autopsy Report and Supplemental Report (No. Autopsy No. A63-272). Retrieved from http://www.jfklancer.com/autopsyrpt.html

Humes, James H., Boswell, J. Thornton, & Finck, Pierre A. (1967). Review of Autopsy Materials by Humes, Boswell and Finck (1/26/67) Assassination Records Review Board (ARRB) Medical Exhibits. Washington, DC: U.S. Government Printing Office. Retrieved from http://www.maryferrell.org/mffweb/archive/viewer/showDoc.do?docId=595&relPageId=1

Itek Corporation. (1976). John Kennedy Assassination Film Analysis. Retrieved from http://www.maryferrell.org/mffweb/archive/viewer/showDoc.do?docId=60448

Jefferies, George. (1963). George Jefferies JFK Film. Retrieved from http://www.youtube.com/watch?v=JY384ITlbTw

Livingston, Robert B. Crenshaw, et al v. Sutherland. , No. 73-93 (18th Judicial District, Johnson County, Texas 1993). Retrieved from http://www.maryferrell.org/mffweb/archive/viewer/showDoc.do?docId=605

McClelland, Robert. (2012). Robert McClelland: Interview Concerning Shored Throat Wound.

McKnight, Jerry. (2001). Tracking CE 399: The "Stretcher Bullet" and the Case for a Dallas Conspiracy. Kennedy Assassination Chronicles, 7(3), 22–26.

Perry, Malcolm, & Clark, Kemp. (1963). Dallas Doctors First Statements. Retrieved from http://mcadams.posc.mu.edu/press.htm

Rankin, J. Lee. (1964). Rankin Letter to Hoover.
Retrieved from http://mcadams.posc.mu.edu/wcsbt.htm

Select Committee on Assassinations of the U.S. House of Representatives.
(1979). Findings of the Select Committee on Assassinations in the
Assassination of President John F. Kennedy. Washington, DC: U.S.
Government Printing Office.

Thompson, Josiah, & Aguilar, Gary. The Magic Bullet: Even More Magical
Than We Knew? History Matters.
Retrieved from http://www.history-matters.com/essays/frameup/
EvenMoreMagical/EvenMoreMagical.htm#_ednref9

Tunheim, John R., Graff, Henry F., Hall, Kermit L., Joyce, William L., &
Nelson, Anna Kasten. (1998). The Final Report of the Assassination
Records Review Board. U.S. Government Printing Office.
Retrieved from http://www.maryferrell.org/mffweb/archive/docset/
getList.do?docSetId=1004

Walls, Ron, & Murphy, Michael. (2012). Manual of Emergency Airway
Management (4th ed.). Pennsylvania: Lippincott Williams & Wilkins.

Warren, Earl, Boggs, Hale, Cooper, Sherman, Dulles, Allen W., Ford,
Gerald R., Russell, Richard B., McCloy, John J., et al. (1964). Report of
the President's Commission on the Assassination of President Kennedy.
Washington, DC: United States Government Print Office.

Name Index

About the Author

Author Sherry P. Fiester

Sherry P. Fiester, a Certified Senior Crime Scene Investigator and Court recognized expert begin to apply her professional expertise to the Kennedy assassination in 1995. Fiester is a court certified expert in Crime Scene Reconstruction and Blood Spatter Analysis Louisiana, Mississippi and Florida, totaling in over 30 Judicial Districts and Louisiana State Federal Court. She is an instructor in Crime Scene Investigation and Blood Spatter Analysis at state and national levels and is published in both fields.

Fiester presented her findings at the 1995 Coalition on Political Assassinations (COPA) Conference in Washington, DC; at the Dealey Plaza Echo Kennedy Assassination Conference in the UK in 1996; and at JFK Lancer's November in Dallas Conferences since 1996. Fiester is a recipient of the JFK Lancer-Mary Ferrell 2003 New Frontier Award, given in recognition of research that furthers the investigation of the assassination of President Kennedy.

Now retired from police work, Fiester is a prominent author, lecturer, and educator. *Enemy of Truth: Myths, Forensics, and the JFK Assassination.* is her first in a series of upcoming publications utilizing various forensic diciplines to address important subjects of interest to Americans in the 21st century.

Printed in the USA
CPSIA information can be obtained
at www.ICGtesting.com
LVHW090723060124
768273LV00003B/10